A History of Norwegian Literature

THE GOTHAM LIBRARY
OF THE NEW YORK UNIVERSITY PRESS

The Gotham Library is a series of original works and critical studies, published in paperback primarily for student use. The Gotham hardcover edition is primarily for use by libraries and the general reader. Devoted to significant works and major authors and to literary topics of enduring importance, Gotham Library texts offer the best in literature and criticism.

Comparative and Foreign Language Literature:
Robert J. Clements, Editor
Comparative and English Language Literature:
James W. Tuttleton, Editor

A HISTORY

OF

NORWEGIAN LITERATURE

BY

Harald Beyer

Translated and Edited by EINAR HAUGEN

NEW YORK UNIVERSITY PRESS
for The American-Scandinavian Foundation

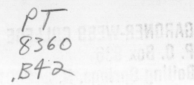
Copyright 1956 by The American-Scandinavian Foundation

Library of Congress catalogue card number: 56-6801

ISBN: 0-8147-1023-9(paperback)

Fourth Printing, September 1979

First published in Norway, 1952,
as *Norsk Litteraturhistorie*

Printed in the United States of America

To

JOHAN FALKBERGET

Torchbearer
and
Mountain Poet

Translator's Preface

THE AUTHOR OF THIS HISTORY, to whom we owe in addition a number of distinguished articles and monographs, is a professor of Norwegian literature at the University of Bergen. His work as surveyor of all Norwegian literature began with a school text published in 1933, which was expanded and entirely rewritten in the present work published in Oslo in 1952. When The American-Scandinavian Foundation chose this volume to represent Norway in its contemplated series of Scandinavian histories of literature, it gave the translator carte blanche to adapt, rearrange, or even rewrite the book in order to produce a volume that might be most useful for introducing Norwegian letters to an American public. This sensitive task was undertaken by the translator with the full consent of the author and a feeling of responsibility to the author as well as the public.

A guide to the literature of a nation is charged with many tasks. In so far as it is historically arranged, it must parallel the course of social, political, and intellectual development of the nation. But it cannot become identical with any of these, since it deals primarily with creative literature, which consists of the unique products of artistic genius. It must therefore evaluate its materials according to their literary quality, both in selecting and in discussing them. It must also give the reader some idea of the topics and situations dealt with by the authors selected, which requires an understanding of the world in which these authors lived. This brings with it a need for biographical data about the principal authors, data that explain their choice of themes if not their success as literary artists. To combine all this into a single volume of manageable size and readable style is no mean feat, as reviewers of Professor Beyer's original have pointed out.

But it seems evident that the choice of authors and works to be discussed, of the judgments to be handed down, of the biographical, cultural, and historical material to be included, will reflect not only the personal outlook and literary skill of the author, but also the purposes for which he wrote the book. A history of literature written for the guidance of one's fellow citizens must have an emphasis different from one written for foreigners. One of its major purposes is that of teaching a people to respect and admire its own traditions, and of bringing to its attention writers and values that run the risk of being forgotten by the current generation. In turning to a different audience, which is equally unfamiliar with the old and the new, the writer would almost certainly wish to add a good deal of explanatory material which his countrymen had already acquired through other sources. He would also wish to drop some minor authors, whose work could not be expected to attract foreigners, and the discussion of some topics of primary interest to Norwegians. He might even modify some of his judgments in the conviction that an international point of view requires a re-evaluation of the contributions of some, if not all, writers.

I have proceeded on the assumption that changes in the author's text should be made only when the above considerations applied. I have supplied information, omitted some minor works and writers, rearranged some sections to secure greater clarity, and rewritten a very few sections (I assume special responsibility for the Introduction and the biographies of Bojer, Wildenvey, Bull, Øverland, Hoel, Rølvaag, and Grieg). For students of the subject who cannot read the original language I have provided references to further readings in English and footnotes to all the translations of literary works mentioned in the text. The list of translations should be as nearly complete as possible. This will bring out the spotty nature of the translations available and show which major works have not yet been published in English. All titles have been translated as literally as possible in the text (within the bounds of readable English). If the titles of the published English translations are different, these are given in the footnotes.

All translations of literary quotations have been made by the undersigned, unless otherwise marked. Permission to use translations is hereby gratefully acknowledged: Henry A. Bellows, *The Poetic Edda* (The American-Scandinavian Foundation); Olive Bray, *The Elder or Poetic Edda* (Viking Society, London); L. M. Hollander, *The Skalds* (Princeton University Press for The American-Scandinavian Foundation); Illit Gröndahl, tr., *Draumkvæde* in *Studia Norvegica I* (Oslo); Illit Gröndahl, G. M. Gathorne-Hardy, and J. Bithell, trs., "Poems by Wergeland," in *Poems by Henrik Wergeland* (Gyldendal and Hodder and Stoughton);

Charles Wharton Stork, tr., *Anthology of Norwegian Lyrics* (Princeton University Press for The American-Scandinavian Foundation); C. H. Herford, tr., *Comedy of Love* (Scribner's); F. E. Garrett, tr., *Lyrics and Poems from Ibsen* (Dutton); K. G. Chapman, translations from *Haugtussa;* W. M. Payne, tr., *Arnljot Gelline* by B. Björnson.

With these words I commend Professor Beyer's book to its new audience, in the hope that it may provide a stimulating guide to the treasure house of Norwegian literature.

EINAR HAUGEN

Madison, Wisconsin

Contents

Norway and Her Literature

THE HISTORY OF NORWEGIAN LITERATURE begins with the history of Norway and encompasses a thousand years of her national growth. To the ancient Romans Norway was scarcely a name, merely a part of that vaguely defined Ultima Thule which lay at the uttermost ends of the earth. Even to our own day Norway has remained a marginal country, the last outpost of West European culture to the north. Thanks to the Gulf Stream the climate relaxes sufficiently to provide a decent and comfortable livelihood. But living in Norway has always meant a tussle with nature for the daily bread and a nearly hopeless attempt to annihilate the realities of distance. Other nations are compact, like Denmark; or rich in natural resources, like England. But in Norway men have always had to travel far to meet their fellows, and the habitable spots have been pin points in an endless expanse of forest, mountain, glacier, and plateau. Here is a country as large as the United Kingdom and Ireland, but with only one sixteenth as many people. The slightly over three million Norwegians are separated by fjords, forests, and mountains which in former days could only be traversed by means of boat or toilsome roads.

New ideas from abroad often had to reach Norway by devious routes, and were often outmoded in the great centers of culture when they were just being accepted in Norway. Yet nothing is more inspiring than the persistent eagerness with which Norwegians have followed and assimilated the ideas current in western civilization. The time lag has been cut down as means of communication have improved, and today Oslo's cultural life is distinguishable only in details from that of Paris, London, Copenhagen, or Nashville, Tennessee. This is not necessarily an improvement, for ideas were often the better for having had time to simmer down and mature before they reached Norway. They were less undigested and could grow into something genuinely original by being mated with the

[1]

stock of experience which this large, rugged, and altogether incredible country had stored in its inhabitants.

One of the many paradoxes about Norway is that it is at once a young and an old nation. In point of fact Norway has been a modern nation with all organs of government only since 1905. But there are dates behind this one which represent stages in the long progress of a people. There is a constitution that has been in force since 1814, inspired in form and content by the American and French which preceded it. The present King Haakon bears the number VII to emphasize that he belongs to a line of kings which had been interrupted since 1387. The most famous of his preceding namesakes claimed dominion in the thirteenth century over parts of present-day Sweden, over several island groups off the coast of Scotland, over Iceland and Greenland. There were suggestions of an imperial air about Norway of those days, and even earlier, when viking chieftains had hopped from island to island and even reached the American coast. For three centuries Norwegian vikings maintained a solid dominion in Ireland, and a slender but flourishing Christian colony in Greenland, with a bishop and a dozen churches. The kings of Norway tried to follow the fashions of the French court since King Olaf, their first Christian saint, named his son Magnus after the great Charlemagne. They had just sworn off a paganism which had remained in these parts long after the Anglo-Saxons and the Franks had forgotten that they had ever bent knees to Odin and Thor. In the colony of Iceland a peculiarly tough breed of Norwegians preserved these traditions until the world was ready to rediscover them once more.

Modern literature in Norway is deeply marked by this combination of the old and the new. There is a freshness and vigor which only youth can give, but also the mature perspective of a thousand years of background. If one compared the literature of modern times to a tree whose roots are to be explored, one would find that like the Yggdrasil of ancient Norse myth it has three principal roots. There is that oldest one which reaches back into the pagan and early Christian past. This has meant much to Norwegian writers even though they perforce must share it with Iceland. The poems of the *Edda* and the prose of the sagas are the threshold of Norwegian literature, though one cannot say that they are everyday reading among the people of today. But one of the books from this period is so important, though it was written in Iceland, that a modern Norwegian nation is almost unthinkable without it—Snorri

Sturluson's *History of the Kings of Norway,* written some seven centuries ago.

The second root arose in a friendlier but less lofty soil than that of the first; this is the world of the ballad and the folk tale. From the thirteenth to the seventeenth century folk literature was almost the only form of literary composition open to the Norwegians. The international themes and forms of folk literature were here elaborated into a world of fantasy full of grotesque shapes and bizarre adventures. Somehow these came to mean far more in the modern literature of Norway than the sagas and the Eddas, for they came closer home to men's bosoms and liberated the forces of fancy. There was a special warmth in these plaintive songs and homely tales which endeared them to lay and learned.

But throughout all the rejoicing over the treasures of folk and faerie, the third root provided the hard core of day-to-day support in Norwegian cultural life. This was the root that extended from Norwegian urban culture back into the centuries of union with Denmark. The transition from medieval to early modern life took place under the ægis of Denmark, with all the revolutionary changes suggested by such words as Reformation, Renaissance, and Rationalism, three R's which are as fundamental in Norway as in most other western nations. The Danish root has been much neglected in recent years, but it has not withered away, even though some Norwegians would ignore it, or even amputate it. At least from 1660 to 1814 the capital of Norway was Copenhagen, where her citizens went to complain of mistreatment, her sons to gain their higher learning, and her ambitious men to win preferment. Here they could find the institutions of a typical West European capital, libraries, museums, a university, a theater. Here they met the latest ideas and the latest books, and if they had anything to communicate, Copenhagen gave them the chance through its newspapers, its publishers, and its booksellers. The Norwegian writers of this period were Danish as well, in the sense that they wrote the same language and partook of the same culture as their Danish contemporaries. In the case of some it is even difficult to say for sure whether they were more Norwegian than Danish; even when they insisted on their Norwegian nationality they did not feel this a violation of their loyalty to the "Twin Kingdoms." Even after the forcible separation of 1814, it was long before Norway could manage without the Danish channel to European culture. When she was finally weaned, she could still never wipe out the gains these centuries had given her. The tradition that led from Ludvig Holberg through Johan Herman Wessel to Wergeland, Welhaven, Bjørnson, and Ibsen is inextricably bound up with Danish names like Ewald, Oehlenschläger, Heiberg, Grundtvig, and Kierkegaard.

Impulses to writing have thus come from many sources, but the themes were those that rose from the experiences of the writers with the country itself. An ever fertile source of inspiration for the artists of Norwegian writing have been the mountains, the sea, and the forests. This triad provides perhaps the basic harmony of Norwegian literature. A literature that has grown up among mountains may lack luxuriance and light-hearted gaiety, but it has the advantage of seriousness and greater perspective. Thus Ibsen's use of the mountains to symbolize artistic freedom reminds us of the practice of the Hebrew prophets who climbed their Sinai to talk with God. But the mountains may also be confining, giving the literature a pent-up, narrow-chested quality reflecting the many secluded communities amid the fjords and mountains. It may turn into a horizonless literature, circling about the problems of a locality until it loses touch with the current of the age and the universally human. But within these same valleys the longing may be awakened to surmount the enclosing ranges, to make one's way out into those distant places where freedom and beauty beckon.

Such a longing may bubble away in the aimless backwash of the eddying fjord, but more often it finds its way to the open sea. The ocean has probably had an even greater impact on Norwegian literature than the mountains. The poets have experienced it in very different ways; as Kielland put it, "The sea has a special word for each one who stands face to face with it." Some have seen it as a liberator and purifier, others as a frightening demon, the mystical and destructive spirit of nature, which nevertheless attracts and fascinates. Most often it symbolizes, in Kinck's words, "yon high road to wine and the sun and the South." Bjørnson put into it all his longing for the infinite, while Ibsen made it represent such diverse things as a life of freedom and adventure or the utter hopelessness of the "depths of the sea." In Olav Duun's picture of the tempest we feel through his description that the sea is fate itself.

The contrast of sea and mountain was apparent already in pagan times and forms the subject of a strikingly human dialogue between the god Njord and his wife Skadi. She was the ski goddess from Jotunheim, and found that life by the sea was not to her taste. She could not sleep for the crying of the sea gulls, and longed to be back in the mountains. But her husband was equally upset by the howling of the wolves among the mountains, so that after nine nights he abandoned his wife and returned to his ships by the sea. But the poets show that it is not always one's birthplace that makes one a lover of sea or mountain. Garborg, who was born by the sea in southwestern Norway, wrote brilliant descriptions of the barren but beautiful highlands. Bjørnson, on the other hand, born amid mountains, had little taste for the heights. He liked his mountains seen from below, and was most strongly attracted by the sea. Whether by contrast or by association, these two natural features have the deepest possible significance for Norwegian writing not purely urban or intellectual.

But to these we may add a third feature, the forest. While the mountains often represent something sterile or unemotional, the forest generally calls upon the mystical. In the woods the poet can dream of hidden and secret forces. This is the world of the fairy tale, where every crackling twig may suggest the creatures that inhabit the forest, real or unreal. Here the wanderer can spend his time in the company of an old huntsman, tracking down the capercailzie and the grouse, with their strange love songs. He can bring to the forest his bleeding heart, and he may find comfort in the echoing bird song which Welhaven immortalized in his line "Tirilil Tove, langt, langt bort i skove." Or he may instead be seized by the terror of nature which stimulated so many tales of the underground folk, the elves and the pixies who misled the wanderer and never let him go again with his wits.

In no European country are the contrasts of nature so overwhelming as in Norway. It rises steeply from the sea, surrounded only by naked reefs and skerries, is cracked into narrow fjords and channels, which lead gradually into the "dark, church-still valleys," the desolate mountain wastes, the endless forests, and the open, smiling country. It is a country, in Bjørnson's words, "toward the eternal snows," lacking often in surface warmth, with a sharp wind blowing over it. Rarely have the poets been able to cultivate the blue flower of beauty, the art for art's sake. There is a more insistent note than in the writings of their neighbors and kinsmen, the Danes and the Swedes. The contrasts of nature have helped to sharpen the Norwegian eye for drama, so that even their novels and their poems are dramatic. They are less gracious than the Danes, less lofty than the Swedes, and more inclined to satire than either. Even in the lyric they are rarely idyllic or restful, but rather unquiet and persistent. Their writings, like the fruits that ripen under the midnight sun, have a marked and savory taste which is all their own.

From *Antiquity* to the *Vikings*

THE BEGINNINGS OF NORWEGIAN LITERATURE are veiled in the mists of time. Although we know that people were living in Norway in the Paleolithic age, at least 10,000 years before the birth of Christ, we have no recorded word from them until about 200 A.D. From the centuries that followed down to the beginning of the Viking Age nearly 600 years later we have a handful of inscriptions which throw a precious but flickering light on their early life and letters. The alphabet used was different from those of the Greeks or Romans, though it was clearly based on them, and had been invented in central Europe by the Germanic tribes most nearly in contact with classical culture. The letters were twenty-four in number and were called *runes* ("secrets") because they were thought to have magic power and belonged only to the initiated. The few words inscribed in this oldest alphabet are enough to tell us that the people who then inhabited Norway were Germanic tribes who spoke a language not very different from that mother tongue which became the ancestor of English, Dutch, German, and Scandinavian.

Runic inscriptions were most frequently carved on gravestones, no doubt to protect the dead by their power. There is often a rhythmic quality in them, sometimes embellished by alliteration, with now and then even a personal note, as in the Opedal inscription at Ullensvang: "Birgingu, be thou at rest, sister mine, dear to me, Vagar." They sometimes foreshadow the magic chants of the *Edda,* where we read that runes were inscribed on the bear's paw, on the eagle's beak, on the wolf's claw, on gold and glass and many other potent things, on the teeth of Sleipnir, Odin's horse—in all twenty-four different places or the number of the runes in the *futhark,* as the runic alphabet is called. Odin was the master of runic lore: "Victory runes must thou know, if thou wouldst have victory, and carve them on your sword hilt." There were other runes that

[6]

might be helpful in healing sickness, in assisting at childbirth, for making beer ferment. Behind these versified chants we glimpse the figure of a gray-haired priest or seer—why not also a poet?

Community of language made it easy for stories and poems to travel from Germany to the north, and we can be sure that the runic alphabet was not the only cultural novelty that was passed along. The Germanic tribes were on the march during these early centuries of our era. They were living along the rim of the Roman Empire, which had recently been extended to their borders. They were looking in on the greatest civilization of their day, fascinated by its pomp and glitter. Roman coins and ornaments have been found in Norwegian soil, and we may be sure that along with the material refinements came stories of gods and heroes which excited wonder and interest among the natives. Traces of classical and Christian conceptions are found in Scandinavian myths of a much later date: the figure of the "white" god Balder, the world tree of Yggdrasil, the self-sacrifice of Odin, the end of the world, and the rise of a new heaven and a new earth. But they have been adapted to pagan thinking in their long journey from Rome across the entire Germanic world to Norway.

Around 100 A.D. the Roman writer Tacitus wrote about the Germans that in their songs of battle "the chief aim is to produce a raucous tone and a rattling noise." But they must have had a more pleasing form of poetry also, if we can judge by the heroic poems of the English, the Germans, and the Scandinavians from a few centuries later. These all show a direct descent from an older type of verse which must once have been common to them all. This verse was composed in an epic line of four beats, with an irregular number of unstressed syllables, held together by alliteration of at least two stressed syllables, one in each half of the line. Not only was the verse form common, but many of the themes as well. Memories of the great events that followed the Germanic migrations and the invasion of the Huns were preserved in heroic poems that were not written down until more than seven hundred years after the events. The tragic death of King Ermanaric of the Ostrogoths in 375 A.D., the fall of Gundiharius and the other Burgundian kings in 436, the supposed murder of Attila the Hun on his bridal night in 453—all of these were woven together with a fairy tale about the fabulous hero Sigfrid who killed the dragon and rescued the sleeping maiden, but who lost both gold and maiden and was himself killed by his best friend.

In ancient Norway and Iceland these themes were favorites for many centuries. We do not know when they were transmitted into Scandinavia, but they were certainly known before the beginning of the Viking Age. The oldest poet whose name we know, Bragi the son of Boddi, refers to Ermanaric's death in a poem composed soon after 800. The Oseberg ship, found in Norway and built about the same time, contained a wagon which may be a copy of an even older wagon; on its sides there is a carving which represents Gunnar playing the harp in the snake pit. This Gunnar is none other than the Burgundian king Gundiharius. By 1200 the scattered poems were gathered into a prose narrative, called the *Volsunga Saga,* by an Icelandic saga teller, about the same time as an Austrian bard composed the *Nibelungenlied* over the same theme.

In an unlettered culture rhythmic form serves as a support for memory, thus keeping much traditional lore alive. In *Hervor's Saga* we find poems of a strangely antique cast, and it was common to turn lists of ancestors or divinities into doggerel form. A lyric hand may even be perceived in the law texts, which nowadays pass as a most prosaic form of letters. In the Icelandic *Tryggðamál*—no doubt of Norwegian origin—a man who breaks his sworn word is threatened with dire punishment: he will be hunted down, "as far as men chase wolves, Christians go to church and pagans to their temples; as far as fire burns and earth is green, ships sail and shields glitter, sun shines and snow falls." Then comes an image that is given poetic form:

> Falcon flies   in the long spring day,
> With a friendly wind   under both his wings.

We can thus be assured that there were poets in Norway before the Viking Age, but we have no certain evidences of their work. The life of the Norwegians was still but dimly lighted at a period when the other Germanic tribes were making European history. The period of the great migrations after the fall of Rome in 310 A.D. did not at first involve the Norwegians. The Franks set up their government in the Roman province of Gaul and founded the French nation. The Saxons in the north and the Alemanni in the south became the ancestors of Germans, Dutch, and Swiss. Angles from southern Denmark and Saxons from the west of Germany crossed the North Sea and won England from the Celts. In time all of them were Christianized, gave up their piratical, turbulent ways, and settled into a relatively peaceful existence. But when the kettle had stopped boiling in southern and central Europe, it began anew in the north. In the eighth century the vikings poured forth from the bays and harbors of Scandinavia to repeat the exploits of their Germanic kinsmen in the centuries that preceded. They were eager to acquire some of the wealth and luxury of the nations to the south of them. They looted or they traded, as the occasion might demand, and won for themselves a reputation as the fearful scourge of their times.

They stamped their name on a period of Scandinavian history, these vikings, but their piratical, commercial, and colonizing activity was only a part of their story. A rich body of poetry and prose has descended from their time, reflecting more fully the ethics and the emotions of these people than any other body of literature from a Germanic tribe in the Middle Ages. Their poetry was of two clearly distinct types, one more popular, known in our day as the Eddic, and one more sophisticated, known as the Skaldic. These run parallel throughout the period, but the Eddic gives the impression of greater antiquity as the one that most nearly carries on the tradition of the old Germanic verse. Its authors are all anonymous, while the Skaldic verse is the product of named poets, or skalds, as they were called, craftsmen in verse whose names usually remained attached to their products.

The poetry of the Viking Age reflects the many passions of a restless and exciting era. In its often rugged lines we can relive the viking's victories and defeats, his taste for adventurous voyaging abroad, his fear of witchcraft and the powers of darkness, his proud and overbearing spirit, his concern with building a good reputation, and his curious but human mixture of fatalism and faith in his gods.

Very often we find ourselves on the sea, especially in the Skaldic poems. The sea was the viking's path to "fee and fame." More than once we hear of hardships at sea, of hands that are stiff with cold or bloody from rowing. The foaming waves sprinkle the prow, the breakers roar against the rocks, and the billows tower up before the ship like beetling cliffs. The skald Kormák sees "the prow making rents in the clouds" and "the ocean jostling the moon." The skalds enjoy themselves at sea, ón the "ship's road." They like, in Hallfred's words, to hear the spreading sails "chatting with the ropes." They are not without feeling for the play of colors on the ocean.

Now and then we get a glimpse of Norway's nature, her flora and fauna. There is mention of the bear, the stag, and the reindeer. We see wolves chasing the goats down the mountainside, and eagles perched in the ash trees of an evening. We see a lonely knotted pine withering away on the mountain heights, and the cow herder with his hazel stick in hand. We hear of memorial stones that are raised by the wayside, and get in one famous poem, *The Lay of Rig,* a direct reflection of Norwegian social structure.

The mountains were felt as little more than an obstacle to the meeting of men. We read of the horse which wearied of its pack on the mountain paths, and of the man who came close to losing his life when he waded the mountain streams. We understand what it meant to get back to one's house and home, as it is expressed in these lines from the Eddic book of proverbs, the poem *Hávamál*:

> Fire he needs   who with frozen knees
> Has come from the cold without;
> Food and clothes   must the farer have
> The man from the mountains come.

Translated by H. A. Bellows

There could be something sinister about the mountains, their "frost-cold" sides and their "wolf valleys," their "flood-wet fells and dismal slopes." Their mystery is reflected in references to sacred waters that fall from Heaven's Mountain, from the Peaks of Love, from the Tops of Snow and Sun. We see the mountains gleam, hear the waterfalls cascading, and see the eagles winging away above them. We glimpse a ski track left by Lapps. But only once does the mountain have a personal meaning for a skald; this is in a stanza by Sigvat in memory of King Olaf and their happy voyages together:

> So long as Olaf lived,
> And boats bore me about the land,
> The peaks and precipices steep
> Smiled the whole length of Norway.

But now that the king is dead, the glitter has left the mountains, and now "all the leas of the land are unbright."

We meet the viking king on his headland fastness, and we go with him to war and battle, more in the Skaldic than in the Eddic poems. We see very little of the day-to-day existence, and very seldom do we meet the humble folk—only in the *Hávamál, The Lay of Rig,* and some of the individual Skaldic stanzas. We do not so much meet the actual viking life as the viking dream. The farmer is not tragic, and therefore there is little place for him in this poetry. Its heroes live on the tragic plane, to borrow a modern term.

But even here we can meet two contrasting types, the man of good fortune and the man of shadows. The first is often embodied in the skald, who is brave and openhearted, boldly seeking the joys of life; but the latter is the medicine man, the mystic who feels himself to be in the grasp of evil powers. The contrast reappears in later times, in such an opposition as that between Bjørnson's faith in life and need of social contact on the one hand and Ibsen's gloomy individualism in works like *The Warriors of Helgeland* and *Brand*.

The Poetic Edda

STORIES OF GODS

MOST OF THE EDDIC POEMS we know have been preserved in an Icelandic parchment manuscript dating from about 1270.[1] Bishop Brynjolfur Sveinsson laid hands on it in 1643 and sent it to King Frederik III in Copenhagen in the year 1662. The learned of that time found here many of the poems that Snorri had quoted or retold in his *Edda*, and believing that Sæmund the Learned had composed the poems, they called it *Sæmund's Edda* (*Sæmundar Edda*) to distinguish it from Snorri's. More generally it came to be called the "elder" as against the "younger" *Edda*, although the name properly belongs to the younger work. In English the "elder" *Edda* is perhaps best known as the *Poetic Edda*. There are a few poems of the same kind in other sources, most of them fragmentary, which suggests that we have only a small part of the Eddic poetry that once existed.

Their Icelandic preservation tells us nothing about their origin. Scholars were long of the opinion that no Eddic poem could be older than 800 A.D. because the change from Early to Old Scandinavian would have destroyed their rhythm. It is true that such a change as that from *harabanaz* to *hrafn* ("raven") is unthinkable in some poems, but there are others whose versification is so loose that early Scandinavian forms are not excluded.

[1] The following translations of the mythological poems of the *Edda* have been made: Henry Adams Bellows, *The Poetic Edda* (New York, 1923); Olive Bray, *The Elder or Poetic Edda* (London, 1908); Lee M. Hollander, *The Poetic Edda* (Austin, Texas, 1928); Benjamin Thorpe, *The Elder Edda* (London, 1866); A. S. Cottle, *Icelandic Poetry or the Edda of Sæmund* (Bristol, 1797); Vigfússon and Powell, in *Corpus Poeticum Boreale*, (2 vols. Oxford, 1883).

More recently discovered inscriptions, such as that of Eggjum in Sogn, appear to show that the Old Norse forms go back earlier than previously thought. On the other hand, Norwegian ornamentation like that of certain stave churches from the thirteenth century, as well as literary sources, show that the subject matter lived for a long time in both Norwegian and Icelandic tradition. Not only did the old skalds know *Hávamál* and the lays of Sigurd the Dragon-Slayer, but King Sverre (d. 1202) must have known some of the old poetry, for he turned words quoted from the *Lay of Fafnir* against his son Sigurd Lavard who had shown his cowardice in battle.

During these centuries when the Eddic poems were being composed and cited, many must have been lost and reshaped. Influences no doubt played upon them from various cultures and periods, from Irish poetry and Greek conceptions as well as from European feudalism. The Eddic poems interacted on one another and may even have picked up elements from the poems of the skalds.

The problem of their date is closely interwoven with the problem of their place of origin. There were certainly poems of this type in Denmark and Sweden also, but most of these are preserved only in Latin paraphrases by Saxo Grammaticus. Those that give the greatest impression of antiquity must go back to Norway, before the settlement of Iceland. The allusions to landscape, flora, fauna, and social customs appear to corroborate this conclusion, although Icelanders might of course have seen these things in Norway and one poet might have borrowed from another. But it seems wisest to conclude that poems describing a clearly Norwegian background are of Norwegian origin, even though it is strange that none of the poems generally assumed to be Icelandic have any peculiarly Icelandic allusions. This is so much the more curious as the only Eddic poem supposed to have originated in Greenland does to some extent reflect a Greenland environment.

The versification of the Eddic poems is based on the old epic line of Germanic verse. Its most common form is that which may be called Old Lore Meter (*fornyrðislag*), with four lines in each stanza and four stressed syllables in each line. The startling innovation from Germanic meter here is the organization into stanzas, with clearly divided halves:

> Hearing I ask   from the holy races,
> From Heimdall's sons,   both high and low;

> Thou wilt, Valfather,   that well I relate
> Old tales I remember   of men long ago.

Translated by H. A. Bellows

The alliteration is a general Germanic characteristic, found in Old English and German verse as well, and takes the place of the rhyme in modern poetry by marking rhythm and tying lines together. Alliteration applies only to stressed syllables, and means that at least one such syllable in each half-line has the same initial consonant (or a different initial vowel) as one syllable in the other half-line. The alliterating syllable can be either or both of the two stresses in the first half; but in the second it must always be the first stress, which is called the chief stress of the line (e.g., *holy* in line 1 above, or *high* in line 2). A different meter, known as the "Speech Meter" (*málaháttr*), arose by increasing the number of unstressed syllables and is found in only three poems, *The Lay of Hamdir, The Song of Atli,* and *The Lay of Atli.* It is actually the meter most like that of the old Germanic line.

Another, and peculiarly Scandinavian meter, is the "Chant Meter" (*ljóðaháttr*), used in twelve of the Eddic poems, chiefly monologues and dialogue poems, often containing proverbial or mythological lore. Here the second and fourth lines have been shortened so that the two halves have become one, with only two or three stressed syllables; most of the *Hávamál* is composed in this meter:

> Less good there lies   than most believe
>   In ale for mortal men;
> For the more he drinks   the less does man
>   Of his mind the mastery hold.

Translated by H. A. Bellows

The mythological lore contained in these poems was hardly the possession of the entire people, but rather of a chieftain class. Nor do they tell us much about worship and prayer. The gods are conceived as magnified human beings, with human virtues and vices.

Some Eddic poems are securely pagan in their thinking, e.g. *Hávamál* and the lays about Grimnir and Vafthrudnir, possibly also *The Lay of Skirnir.* Others give the impression of having originated under the spiritual pressure of Christianity. The victorious advance of the new religion from the south made the pagan Norsemen wish to bolster their faith. Just as the grave mounds from the last pagan period show a greater magnificence than the earlier ones, so some of the mythological poems (especially *The Sibyl's Prophecy*) look like a protest against the new doctrine, a last spasmodic defense. But there are also poems that seem more like learned reconstructions from the Norse Renaissance of the twelfth century.

One should be cautious, however, about interpreting the jesting tone of some poems as a deliberate ridicule of the gods. Thor in *The Lay of Thrym* cuts a funny figure dressed up as a bride and gorging himself at the bridal feast; but in the end he wins, and kills or mutilates the evil giants. In *Loki's Mocking* the gods are derided, but only by Loki, the liar and enemy of the gods, and in the end he is driven away by Thor with his hammer. If the poem was really composed during the period of conflict between paganism and Christianity, it must be understood as a reply to criticism of the pagan gods: "Just wait till Thor comes and puts a stop to this kind of lying talk!"

The first poem in the *Edda* manuscript is called *The Sibyl's Prophecy* (*Vǫluspá*), which may not be its original name, since only its conclusion concerns the coming events. But its location at the head of the collection is probably due to the panorama it gives of Old Norse cosmology. Dated by scholars at the end of the tenth century, it gives the impression of having been composed by a poet who was stirred by his topic and succeeded in giving the poem a more personal tone than the other Eddic poets.

The poem consists of visions recounted before the people at their sacred meeting. The speaker is an old wise woman, educated among the giants from the early ages. She tells at Odin's behest of how the universe came into being in the days of the giant Ymir, when there was neither heaven above nor earth below, no sand nor sea nor soothing waves, no green grass, but only a yawning abyss. Then came the sons of Bur who created Midgard, the earth. But still there was neither order nor law: "The sun knew not what place she owned, the moon knew not what power he had, the stars knew not which places they possessed." Then the sacred gods sat down on their council seats and decreed the names of night and day, of morning, noon, and evening, and of the numbering of the years. This was the golden age of the gods, their time of peace, when they played at tables in the courtyard. But a warning of strife was sounded: three troll maidens from the Giants' Land were coming, and the gods created the dwarfs to forge weapons. One day Odin and his brothers found the first pair of human beings, Ask and Embla, still without life and color. Odin blew into them the spirit of life, Hønir gave them thoughts, and Lodur blood and color. But under the roots of Yggdrasil, the world ash, live the goddesses of fate, the Norns, whose names are Past, Present and Future. "Law they make, life they give to the children of man, and fate they utter."

The warrior mentality which fills so many of the old poems is absent in *The Sibyl's Prophecy*. War brings nothing but unhappiness in its train. Gullveig, who perhaps symbolizes the hunger for gold, is the cause of a war among the gods themselves, between the Æsir and the Wanes. Odin throws his spear, and the first world-embracing war breaks out; "broken was the board wall in the fortress of the gods, and the Wanes leaped out on the open field." After this has been composed, a war between gods and giants breaks out because Thor and the gods have broken their word. Evil grows apace. Odin seeks wisdom in the well of Mimir where he has to give up one of his two eyes. Through Loki's schemes Odin's beloved son Balder is killed, and is not saved even by his mother's tears; and Loki himself is punished.

Now the Sibyl turns to the days to come, when sacred bonds of kinship will be broken among men, and the times will be "an axe age, a sword age, a wind age, a wolf age." But out of the distress of the times (perhaps the days of Eirik Blood-Axe) comes the prophecy of a new world and a new age. Out of the sea rises a new earth, once more greenclad: "waterfalls roar, eagles fly above, hunting their fish in the mountains." Then the gods will meet again on the Fields of Ida and find golden tables in the grass. Fields will grow unsown, and Balder will come back. At the end comes "the Mighty One" from above, meeting the evil dragon Nidhogg who flies with corpses in his feathers and drawing blood from the dead. Perhaps they are going to the great Day of Judgment.

None of the other Eddic poems has the nobility of *The Sibyl's Prophecy,* the poem of the "ruling powers" which no one can wholly penetrate. But the one called *Balder's Dreams* (*Baldrs draumar*) has a certain kinship with it. Here, too, we meet an elderly sibyl. Odin, calling himself the Wayfarer, awakens her from a long, deep sleep beneath the earth and asks for news from Hel, the kingdom of death. He wants to know who is going to be the slayer and the avenger of Balder. Close to *The Sibil's Prophecy* is also *Hyndla's Lay* (*Hyndluljóð*), which Snorri quotes in his *Edda* and calls the "short Sibyl's Prophecy." Here, too, there is a survey of the world of gods and a prophecy about a greater god who will come and whose name the sibyl dares not utter.

Most of the poems about gods give mythological information, often in dialogue form, and are therefore also didactic. But the didactic poem above all is the *Hávamál,* or *Sayings of the High One.* As we have it now, it consists of at least five different poems, composed during the ninth and tenth centuries. The common element is that Odin is supposed to be the narrator of these poems. But the Odin we meet is strangely composite, being the highest god, the god of poetry and runes, and also a down-to-earth man of the world.

There is a great difference between the exalted quality of *The Sybil's Prophecy* and the everyday, practical morality of the *Hávamál.* Nevertheless the rules of life in this "Book of Proverbs" (the first eighty stanzas) are formulated in such a monumental way that one must call it great art. First comes a passage about the welcome owed a guest who has sought the refuge of one's home, tired and hungry. But the guest also has his responsibilities. He must not talk too much, not drink too much; he must not be greedy, or laugh stupidly at all that is said, and not believe that all who smile at him are his friends. If he is ignorant, he had better keep silent. He shall not forever remain as a guest at one place. Then comes a praise of home: he is lucky who has a place to dwell, for "bloody is the heart in the breast of him who must beg for every meal."

Then comes a section on friendship. A man shall be cautious in his choice of friends and never be a friend of his enemy's friend. But when he has a good friend, he should give him all his heart and visit him often. For it is hard to be without friends:

> The pine tree wastes   which is perched on the hill,
>   Nor bark nor needles shelter it;
> Such is the man   whom none doth love;
>   For what should he longer live?

Translated by Olive Bray

Even though the stupid man is scorned, there are also warnings against being too wise. The wise man is seldom happy, but the medium-wise man is the one who gets along best in life. This means that he must be hardworking, get up early in the morning, keep his wits about him, and ride to the *thing* well dressed and well fed. Fire on the hearth and sun in the fields make a man happy, if his health is good. But it is better to be crippled than dead. A lame man can ride, a maimed man can herd cattle, and a deaf man can fight. It is better to be blind than burned; for the dead man is of little value. Yet he may live on even after death, if he has a son who can keep his memory green. This section reaches a climax in its teaching about fame, the word that lives on when a man is gone:

> Cattle die,   and kinsmen die,
>   And so one dies one's self;
> One thing I know   that never dies,
>   The fame of a dead man's deeds.

The other sections of *Hávamál* are less unified. The most interesting passages in them tell about Odin's relation to women. He made love to Billing's maid, and was badly fooled. One should have no faith in woman's word, for "on whirling wheels their hearts are made." But Odin himself was perhaps getting only what he deserved, for he admits to having deceived Gunnlod, the girl who helped him win the gift of poetry. Of merely documentary interest are the sections called *Runatal,* where Odin tells of winning knowledge of the runes by sacrificing himself, and *Ljóðatal,* where he enumerates eighteen magic songs he has learned.

In *The Lay of Vafthrudnir* (*Vafþrúðnismál*) we meet Odin again as the god of wisdom. The poem tells the story of a contest in words between Odin, disguised as Gangrad, the Wanderer, and a giant whom Odin goes to visit in Giantland in spite of warnings by his wife Frigg. The poet has pictured the two opponents vividly, Odin who taunts his host, and Vafthrudnir who threatens the stranger that he will not leave the hall alive if he cannot answer aright. When Odin is able to answer all his questions, he gains the giant's respect, and is invited to take a seat in the hall. Then it is Odin's turn, and Vafthrudnir stakes his head on the answers. Vafthrudnir gets along well until he is asked what Odin whispered in Balder's ear when he lay on the funeral pyre. Then the giant realizes that he is contending with Odin and admits his defeat: only Odin himself could know that! Even though Odin wins, the giant is no mean opponent.

In *The Lay of Grimnir* (*Grimnismál*) we meet Odin in relation to mankind. Here the god is visiting his foster son, King Geirrød, but in disguise because he wants to find out the truth of the rumor that he is too stingy to feed his own retainers. The rumor appears to be confirmed when the king lets Odin sit without food for eight days between two hot fires. Only the king's son Agnar gives him drink from a horn. This strange situation is in reality only a framework for a long recital by Odin of mythological information on the dwellings of the gods, on Valhalla and life there, on the ash Yggdrasil, and on all his own names. At last he reveals himself as the dreadful one: "Now you see Odin himself." In a prose postcript it is told that Geirrød stumbled onto his own sword and was followed as king by his son Agnar, who ruled the land for many years.

The gods are portrayed in more human guise in other mythological poems. This is particularly true of *The Lay of Skirnir* (*Skírnismál*), a lyrically tinged poem of the sungod Frey's love for the giant maiden Gerd. The basis of this story is a fertility myth which is reminiscent of the Greek story of Persephone. Frey was the god of fertility, and the name of Gerd is connected with the word for an enclosed field, while Barri, the grove where they are to meet, means "barley." Sixteen gold plates found in southwestern Norway show the meeting of the two; the plates had been buried in the ground to make it fruitful. But the story told in the poem is human in its portrayal of Frey's parents, who are puzzled by their son's moping, and of Frey himself whose helpless longing is expressed in the words: "Long is one night, longer are two, how can I wait for three? Often a month seemed shorter to me than half a night now." The dramatic dialogue and the action of this poem suggest the possibility that it was originally the text of a fertility ritual, and in this case it would be unique in Germanic literature.

Odin and Thor were often thought of as rivals; this appears most clearly in *The Song of Graybeard* (*Hárbarðsljóð*). Thor has been busy as usual finishing off giants with his powerful hammer, and is on his way home when he gets to a fjord too wide to cross. There is a ferryman on the other side, who turns out to be Odin in disguise, now calling himself Graybeard. Instead of ferrying Thor across, he abuses him. Thor is roused by this description of himself as a vagabond and glutton to respond in kind. Thor's honest but simple boasting is here placed in comic relief to Odin's slyer thrusts. Thor is clearly the farmer's, the common man's god, rough and ready, but easy to fool, while Odin's power is rooted in subtler wisdom, characteristic of a more sophisticated chieftain and warrior class.

Thor's adventures were numerous, and one of them is told in *The Song of Hymir* (*Hýmiskviða*). Thor is to bring back a beer vat for the gods from the giant Hymir who lives at the end of the heavens. One day he and the giant go out fishing to replenish the larder after Thor's fantastic eating. Thor uses the head of an ox as bait, and gets none other than the Midgard Serpent on his hook. He manages to haul it out of the sea as far as the boat's edge, but Hymir is terrified at the sight of this world-encircling monster and cuts the line so that the serpent sinks back into the sea. This fish story is followed by other exploits of Thor, ending with his taking the beer vat, which is seven miles deep! The vat is used in the feast described in *Loki's Mocking* (*Lokasenna*). In this poem the trickster Loki abuses all the gods in turn, accusing them of the most vicious crimes. At length they turn him out, and Thor comes to punish him. Then Loki gives up:

> Spoke I to the gods,   spoke I to the sons of gods,
>   All that my wishes whetted;
> But for you alone   I shall leave the hall,
>   For you I know will strike.

The poem of Thor above all others is *The Lay of Thrym* (*Þrymskviða*), which is also the one that lived the longest in folk tradition throughout Scandinavia, and the best known in our own time. It surpasses the rest in its clearly constructed plot and its comic overtones. The characters are sharply portrayed: Thor angry because he is afraid of being called effeminate, Loki sly and inventive, Freya delighted to lend her magic feather dress, but furious at the implication that she might be overly eager to get married. Her anger bursts all bounds so that her brooch flies off and lands on the ground. The gods meet in council, while the goddesses chatter about the latest scandal: Have you heard that Freya is going to be married to one of those dried-up old giants? The giant king Thrym is proud and lustful as the "bride" approaches, and all his awakening suspicions of her are stilled by the wise attendant. The comedy grows as he tries to kiss the bride, but starts back the length of the hall as he meets "her" fiery eyes. Finally there is the poor giant sister who had begged him for bridal gifts, but gets blows instead as Thor breaks up the whole party and carries back the hammer he had lost.

The poems about Thor are obviously for entertainment only. Their ambiguous attitude to one of the leading gods has made it difficult to date them. But there can be little doubt that *The Lay of Alvis* (*Alvíssmál*) is a late poem, for the Thor we meet here is quite another person. He has promised his daughter to the dwarf Alvis as the prize in a mythological quiz program, but cheats him of the reward by keeping him until the sun rises and turning him into stone. As in *The Lay of Vafthrudnir*, the story is only a frame for mythological instruction.

In a class by itself among the Eddic poems stands *The Lay of Rig*

(*Rígspula*). A mythological framework is here used to describe the social classes of ancient Norway, possibly *ca.* 800 A.D. The god Heimdall, calling himself Rig, visits three homes: the slave's, the farmer's, and the chief's. Each of these is vividly and amusingly portrayed. The slaves eat coarse bread and broth; they are dressed in simple, old-fashioned clothing; their business it was to bear the burdens: "Home bore he faggots the whole day long." Their children bear names of abuse, such as "The Stinking," "The Sluggard," "The Noisy," "The Fat-legged," and "The Horse-fly." Even physically they are distinguished from the finer breeds of man:

> The skin was wrinkled   and rough on his hands,
> Knotted his knuckles, ...
> Thick his fingers, and ugly his face,
> Twisted his back, and big his heels.

Translated by H. A. Bellows

With this is contrasted the life of the yeoman farmer. Here the food is "calf's flesh boiled, the best of dainties"; the man's "beard was trimmed, o'er his brow a curl," while the woman had a band on her head, a smock on her breast, "on her shoulders a kerchief with clasps." They work at wood carving and weaving. Their son is "ruddy of face, and flashing his eyes," and his work is one of dignity:

> Oxen he ruled,   and plows made ready,
> Houses he built, and barns he fashioned,
> Carts he made,   and the plow he managed.

Translated by H. A. Bellows

But in the earl's house is the greatest magnificence: the portal is wide, the floor is strewn, the table is covered with embroidered linen, and the food is "loaves so thin, white from the wheat," "meat all browned, and well-cooked birds," while "in the pitcher was wine, of plate were the cups." Here the master of the house had warlike tasks—"wound strings for the bow, shafts he fashioned, and bows he shaped." The lady was an ornament:

> Gay was her cap,   on her breast were clasps,
> Broad was her train,   of blue was her gown,

Her brows were bright,   her breast was shining,
Whiter her neck   than new-fallen snow.

Translated by H. A. Bellows

The poem ends with a description of Kon the Young, a son of the earl, who clearly represents the king himself, the highest in the land. He learns to use the mysterious runes, "runes everlasting, the runes of life," as well as the speech of birds, the use of the sword, and the ability to "quiet minds and sorrows calm." The end of the poem, where he is about to start forth on a warlike expedition against the enemy, is lost. This reference to the king, in whose honor the poem probably was composed, shows that it can hardly have come into being before the end of the ninth century.

The poems of the gods are varied and colorful, comprising as they do high tragedy as well as the broadest humor. Several of them have a dramatic form which suggests that they may have been performed on ceremonial or festive occasions. This has been mentioned above in connection with *The Lay of Skirnir;* but it could also have been true of *Loki's Mocking, The Lay of Vafthrudnir,* and *The Lay of Thrym.* We can almost hear the roar of viking laughter in the hall at a performance of *The Lay of Thrym.*

STORIES OF HEROES

The life nerve of heroic poetry is a faith in the immortality of fame, the halo of heroism of which the *Hávamál* speaks.[2] The step from mythological to heroic poetry is not great; the gods intervene in the lives of the heroes, and many of the heroes have divine origin. Popular memory inflated and romanticized the old kings and heroes and turned them into supermen. They are actually more idealized and less human than the gods themselves, with fewer personal traits. All the heroes are unwavering, their followers bold, the slaves cowardly; love is pure but unhappy, the bonds of kinship unbreakable, and the duty of vengeance inescapable. In spite of this tendency to clichés, many of the characters are vividly seen and portrayed. The style of narration is the same as in the mythological poems, with an epic-dramatic emphasis on the high spots only. The dialogue is usually more effective in the heroic poems: the words fall like

[2] Translations of the heroic poems will be found in the versions of the *Poetic Edda* by Bellows, Hollander, and Thorpe listed in the preceding chapter. Additional poems of Eddic type are translated by L. M. Hollander in his *Old Norse Poems* (New York, 1936), including several not mentioned in the text above.

axe blows, keen-edged and fateful, inciting or derisive, but also uncompromisingly honest.

In the thirteenth century, when the *Edda* collection and *The Saga of the Volsungs* were made, the poems were arranged in groups according to their subject matter. But the groups did not originally constitute units; the individual poems were made at vastly different periods, with each poet taking up the hero or heroine that interested him, and often with quite different sympathies.

Two of the poems, *Gro's Chant* (*Grógaldr*) and *The Lay of Fjolsvinn* (*Fjǫlsvinnsmál*), have so much mythology in them that they might as well have been included in the preceding section. They are stories of love and magic, related to *The Lay of Skirnir* and *Balder's Dreams*. But it is quite possible that they are relatively young, made up in the Christian era about 1200 A.D. on the basis of learned tradition and Celtic fairy tales.

The Song of Grotti (*Grottasǫngr*) is also a mixture of myth and folk tale; it is the story of the mill that made the ocean salt. The folk tale is Danish, but the poem appears to have been composed in Norway. King Frodi at Leire in Denmark has bought two powerful slave women, the giant maidens Fenja and Menja, to turn his magic mill and grind out gold and happiness for him. All goes well, and the mill turns out peace and happy days as the slave women sing at their work, until the king is seized by gold hunger. He drives them to their work, gives them no rest, longer than "between each time the cuckoo sings." The sisters are angered, the timbers tremble, and the millstone cracks. They grind away more and more madly, and their songs grow ever wilder; for now they are grinding out weapons and flames, death and destruction. Here the poem ends, but Snorri, who included it in his *Edda*, adds that King Frodi was killed that night by King Mysing who took the sisters with him. The ship sank, however, and now the mill grinds salt at the bottom of the sea.

The Lay of Volund (*Vǫlundarkviða*) is the well-known story of the smith Wayland, a myth that opens a perspective back to the time when the first weapons of iron were being forged. The elemental passions of love, hate, vengefulness, and grief are here portrayed with a force not exceeded in any of the other poems. It opens in sunshine and fairy tale mood as three maidens disguised as swans come flying from the south and alight beside a lake. They put aside their swan dresses, and three brothers, sons of the Lappish king, gain power over them. "Egil won All-rune, Slagfinn won Swanwhite, and Volund, All-wit." But after seven years they long for their homes and fly away. Egil and Slagfinn set off on skis to find them, but Volund waits for All-wit to return while he forges rings for her. While he is asleep, King Nidad from Närike in Sweden seizes his treasures, cuts the tendons of his knees, and puts him off on an island to forge gold for the king's treasury. The small sons of the king trustfully visit Volund to watch him work, but he kills them and makes drinking bowls from their skulls for the king and queen. When Bodvild, the king's daughter, comes to get a ring repaired, he rapes her. After his vengeance is complete, he laughingly takes to the air on wings he has made for himself, as he mocks the king and his daughter. In this poem, as in the *Song of Grotti,* there is a moral: the use of force leads to retribution. Volund and his brothers have to suffer because they used force against the Swan maidens, just as King Nidad and his queen suffer for their crime against Volund.

The only poem in the *Edda* that mentions Norway is *The Lay of Helgi Hjorvardson (Helgakviða Hjǫrvarðssonar).* Helgi's father Hjorvard is described as a king of western Norway, but his historicity is doubtful. The poem as we have it is fragmentary and the pieces are joined by prose passages. There is a vigorous dialogue (often called *The Speech of Hrimgerd)* between Atli, Helgi's watchman, and Hrimgerd, the daughter of a giant whom Helgi had killed. She then speaks to Helgi and demands as her reparation that he shall spend a night with her. But he refuses because he is bound to Svava. There is also a motif about a witch who caused his brother Hedin to swear that he would marry Helgi's betrothed Svava. But the inevitable tragic conflict between the brothers is turned aside by letting Helgi die in a duel with someone else. He then asks his brother to marry the girl and assume the duty of vengeance. There is a more humane and conciliatory spirit in this poem than in the other heroic poems.

The two *Lays About Helgi the Slayer of Hunding (Helgakviða Hundingsbana)* are of vastly different age and value. The so-called "first" poem is actually younger and smacks of the age of chivalry with its emphasis on outer glamor and grand words, but it lacks depth. Only in the second, older poem do we find a treatment that is worthy of the theme of heroic love. Helgi is placed in the unhappy position of having to kill the father and brothers of the woman Sigrun, whom he loves. In the end the youngest of her brothers, Dag, becomes the avenger who kills Helgi. Even though Sigrun is portrayed as a valkyrie, she is more the loving woman, and her images in praise of Helgi are moving: "As high above other chiefs stood Helgi as the nobly-shaped ash amid the miserable brambles, or as a young deer dripping of dew raises his head over low-legged beasts." Touching is also the encounter of Helgi and Sigrun when she goes to visit him in the grave mound.

The great bulk of the heroic poems, however, fifteen in all, deal with the famous Germanic epic material of the Nibelungs, or Gjukungs, and the Volsungs. Most of this refers to historic events that took place in central Europe during the period of the great migrations from the fourth to the sixth centuries. The myths and legends clustered about these events are contained also in the *Nibelungenlied,* but the form in which they were preserved in the *Poetic Edda* is far more primitive and represents an older stage in their history.

The chief figure in the story, Sigurd the Dragon-slayer, is represented as a king of the Franks on the lower Rhine, but there is no historic basis for this statement. Many have supposed that he is identical with the Merovingian king Sigibert, who was married to a Brunihildis, the Brynhild of the poems, and was killed at the instigation of Fredegunde in 575 A.D.

In a prose introduction to *The Lay of Regin* (*Reginsmál*), it is told that Sigurd, the son of Sigmund, the son of Volsung, has grown up at the court of King Hjálprek in Denmark. Here he acquires also his horse Grani. At this court there is a matchless smith named Regin, skilled in magic, but cruel. He is Sigurd's foster father and tells him of ancient happenings: Once Odin, Hønir, and Loki came to a rapids where Otter, son of Hreidmar and brother of Regin and Fafnir, had hidden himself in the shape of an otter. Loki killed the otter with a stone, the gods skinned it and took the hide with them. But Hreidmar recognized his son and demanded satisfaction. The gods were to fill the hide with gold and cover it outside as well. They forced the dwarf Andvari to give them the gold. But when he had to give them a ring which he wanted to keep, he laid a curse on the gold: it should bring misfortune on whoever owned it.

The misfortune that goes with the gold becomes the theme that joins several of the poems about Sigurd and the Gjukungs. First Fafnir and Regin demand a share of the treasure, and when Hreidmar refuses, Fafnir thrusts his sword through him. Then Fafnir takes all the gold and transforms himself into a dragon brooding on the treasure at Gnita Heath. Regin now forges a sword named Gram for Sigurd. Together they travel to Gnita Heath and find the track of the serpent Fafnir.

The Lay of Fafnir (*Fáfnismál*) tells the story of how Fafnir was killed. Sigurd digs a ditch across his path to the water hole and pierces him with his sword. The dying Fafnir realizes that Regin is the instigator and gives Sigurd good advice. Regin drinks Fafnir's blood to gain strength for a battle with Sigurd. But when Sigurd is roasting the serpent's heart, he burns his finger, puts it in his mouth, and suddenly understands the speech of birds. Three titmice are singing in a nearby tree about Regin's deceitful intentions and advise the hero to kill him. These are voices he is forced to obey; he kills Regin and carries off the gold on Grani's back.

The Lay of Sigrdrifa (*Sigrdrífumál*) recounts the next episode in his life, the meeting with the sleeping valkyrie in a hall on Hindar Mountain. He rides up the mountain on his way to the land of the Franks and there makes his way unharmed through a fire that reaches up to the skies. In an enclosure of shields he finds someone asleep in a coat of mail. But when he takes off the helmet, he sees it is a woman. She awakes and tells him that Odin had put her to sleep with a sleeping thorn because she had not chosen the fallen warriors for Valhall according to his wishes. She calls herself Sigrdrifa and teaches him runic wisdom.

In the *Edda* manuscript eight leaves are missing, on which three poems about Sigurd must have been written. The latter part of a fourth poem is saved, and is usually called *Fragment of the Sigurd Lay* (*Brot af Sigurðarkviðu*). Much of the lost part can be reconstructed from the *Volsunga Saga*.[3] Sigurd reaches the court of the Gjukungs, i.e. the sons of King Gjuki, Gunnar and Hogni, who live on the Rhine. He becomes their foster brother and marries their sister Gudrun. Gunnar has learned about Brynhild, daughter of King Budli and sister of King Atli. He wants to court her, but she will only marry the bravest of all men, the one who dares to ride through the magic fire that burns around her castle. Sigurd then takes Gunnar's shape, rides through the fire on Grani, and engages himself to Brynhild. They sleep together three nights; but Sigurd places his naked sword between them. Then Sigurd and Gunnar trade shapes again, so that Gudrun thinks Gunnar was the one who performed the great feat.

At this point *Fragment of the Sigurd Lay* starts; this may be the oldest of the Sigurd poems we have. Gunnar and Hogni, egged on by Brynhild's slanderous assertion that Sigurd had broken his oath of fosterbrotherhood, get their younger brother Guthorm to join them in killing Sigurd. Gudrun is crushed by her grief. But Brynhild laughs:

[3] The Icelandic prose version of the Sigurd story, based on poems like those in the *Edda*, is available in a modern translation by Margaret Schlauch, *The Saga of the Volsungs* (New York, 1930), and in an archaic idiom by Eirikr Magnússon and William Morris, *Völsunga Saga* (London, 1870).

Then Brynhild laughed—   the building echoed—
One time only   with all her heart.

Yet such is the mystery of the female heart that Brynhild, who is said
to be the same person as Sigrdrifa, also loved the hero Sigurd whom she
plotted to kill. She awakens at night and cries out her grief. But "all fell
silent at this speech; few could understand this woman's heart who cried
over that which she laughingly had egged them to do." Only now does
she tell about the sword which lay between her and Sigurd.

The whole story of Sigurd's life and death is summed up in a poem
called *The Prophecy of Gripir* (*Grípisspá*), but this is a late poem from
the thirteenth century and quite confused.

The First Lay of Gudrun (*Guðrúnarkviða I*) pictures the wife's grief
at Gunnar's death. She does not cry like other women, nor does she speak.
Not until she sees Sigurd's wounds does she sink down on her bed, her
hair falling down and her tears rolling; now she weeps so that the geese
begin cackling in the yard. At last she finds words to express what Sigurd
had been to her:

So was my Sigurd   o'er Gjuki's sons
As the spear-leek grown   above the grass,
Or the jewel bright   borne on the band,
The precious stone   that princes wear.

Translated by H. A. Bellows

But Brynhild, too, is broken by her sorrow. She turns the bright steel
against her heart and begs to be burned on the pyre with Sigurd. The
story is told in a poem called *The Short Sigurd Lay* (*Sigurðarkviða in
skamma*), though it is the longest of them all; the "long" one must
be lost. In this poem Brynhild is less of the valkyrie; she admits that she
"was worst toward him whom she loved the most." In a short poem called
The Hell Ride of Brynhild (*Helreið Brynhildar*) she defends her actions
to a giant woman who tries to block her path to the kingdom of the dead.

In *The Short Sigurd Lay,* which is not one of the oldest poems, the
chief motive for the killing of Sigurd is a desire to possess the golden
treasure of Andvari, which Sigurd took away from Fafnir. In *The First
Gudrun Lay* the curse goes with the gold also, but now it passes on to
Gunnar. King Atli, Brynhild's brother, wants to avenge his sister's death,
but they are reconciled and Atli gets Gudrun for a wife. In a poem en-

titled *The Second Gudrun Lay* (*Guðrúnarkviða II*), containing many culture traits of the tenth century, Gudrun tells King Theodoric about her fate. A moving passage is the one in which she tells of the horse Grani coming into the yard after Sigurd's death, with empty saddle and drooping head.

The Lay of Atli (*Atlakviða*) is more forceful in tone and builds on Gothic traditions. King Atli invites Gunnar, the Burgundian king, to visit his court, but his wife Gudrun has woven a wolf's hair into a ring and they realize that she is warning her brother not to come. Nevertheless he decides to go, in order to show that he is not afraid; with him go two brothers, including the faithful Hogni. The close of this poem achieves a fine dramatic quality in the scene where Atli tries to get from the brothers the secret of the treasure. Gunnar refuses to say where it is buried as long as there are others who know. They then cut out the heart of a slave named Hjalli. But Gunnar sees it trembling on the platter and knows that this cannot be Hogni's heart. They then carve out Hogni's heart, who laughs while they do it. "This trembles but little on the platter," says Gunnar, "still less did it tremble when it lay in the breast." Now Gunnar is safe and he laughs out loud: "Now I am the only one who knows where the treasure is. Let the Rhine keep its gold!" Gunnar is thrown into the snake pit, where he plays the harp before he is finally put to death. But Gudrun wreaks fearful vengeance on her husband for the death of her brothers. First she kills his sons, roasts their hearts and serves them to him. Then she burns the hall over Atli and his men, after she first has let the little dogs escape.

The same story is told in *The Ballad of Atli* (*Atlamál*), but here less skillfully and more verbosely. It is interesting that here, as in the wood carving on the Hylestad church portal, Gunnar plays with his toes in the snake pit because his arms are tied.

The Third Gudrun Lay (*Guðrúnarkviða III*) falls somewhat outside the main thread of the epic. Here we learn that Herkja, a maid at Atli's court, has spread a rumor about Gudrun and King Theodoric, from which Gudrun frees herself by a trial by ordeal. In *The Weeping of Oddrun* (*Oddrúnargrátr*), a relatively late poem, Oddrun, sister of Atli, tells about her love for Gunnar. She is the object of his playing in the snake pit. But she gets there too late to save him, for Atli's mother had already gnawed her way into his heart in the shape of a serpent.

But in *Gudrun's Egging* (*Guðrúnarhvǫt*) we are right in the epic stream once more. After Atli's death, Gudrun wanted to drown herself;

but she could not sink and drifted across the sea to King Jonakr's land. She was then married to him and had the sons Hamdir and Sorli. Her daughter by Sigurd, Svanhild, is brought up here and married to King Jormunrek the Mighty, who is none other than the Ermanaric reported in Roman sources as a king of the East Goths in the fourth century. But the king thinks his wife is unfaithful and has her trampled to death by wild horses. Gudrun then eggs her sons on to avenge their sister. But the most stirring part of the poem is Gudrun's loving retrospect on her life. She recalls her children, those she killed and those who are now riding to their death; she remembers Svanhild with the shining hair being dragged in the dust by wild horses, and she thinks about Sigurd, her "beloved friend," and the dying Gunnar.

The Lay of Hamdir (*Hamðismál*) tells the final story of her sons and closes the epic; this may be the very oldest of all the poems. Here is described the parting of the sons from their mother, their journey, and their battle with Jormunrek. On the way they meet their half brother Erp, a strangely twisted and provoking kind of boy. They get into a dispute with him and kill him; but this leads to their own destruction, for the brother would have been able to help them. Nevertheless they succeed in carrying out their vengeance, even at odds of two against a thousand, and can therefore die happy. They stand on piles of fallen Goths like eagles on a branch. The heroes' renown will live long after them. This powerful poem ends in a stylized picture, ornamental and realistic in the spirit of the Viking Age:

> Then Sorli beside   the gable sank,
> And Hamther fell   behind the house.

The remaining poems of Eddic type are found in other manuscripts, often only in fragments. This is the case with *The Lay of Hlod* (*Hlǫðskviða*), which tells of the battle with the Huns, apparently on the basis of Gothic traditions. King Hlod leads an army of Huns against his half brother, the Gothic king Angantyr, in order to gain his father's inheritance. Such place names as Danparstadir—city on the Dnjepr—and the Harfada Mountains, or the Carpathians, occur in the poem. Some have thought that it builds on reminiscences of the battle of the Catalaunian fields (451); but it is more likely that it refers to a battle between Goths and Huns in the forests by the Vistula after the death of Attila (453).

Hjalmar's Death Song, which occurs in a manuscript of *The Heidrek*

Saga and in *The Saga of Orvar-Odd,* is probably Swedish in origin. Angantyr the son of Arngrimr wants to force the Uppsala king to give him his daughter. But she is defended by Hjalmar the Proud and the Norwegian Orvar-Odd. Although the poem deals with old events, it was scarcely composed before the twelfth century.

The poem *Bjarki's Lay* (*Bjarkamál*) must have been a mighty one, since it was quoted by Thormod Kolbrunarskald before the battle of Stiklestad and in part preserved by Snorri Sturluson. This Danish heroic poem was perhaps the best known of all the poems in Scandinavia. It tells of Bodvar Bjarki and his men and of the death of Hrolf Kraki. But the Danish hero who was most widely celebrated was Starkad. He was the ideal viking, the man who stirred up the softhearted youth who were "more interested in spearing tidbits of chicken than in doing manly deeds." There must have been Norwegian poems also in the cycle dealing with Starkad, including one poem which told of his youthful deeds and another about his death. Their contents are known only from the Latin paraphrases by the Danish historian Saxo Grammaticus.

The only hero of certain Norwegian origin in the heroic poems is King Half who appears in the saga of *Half and His Heroes.* In a poem called *The Lay of Innstein* (*Innsteinskviða*) one of the heroes advises Half not to visit his stepfather; but Half does not care, and so loses his life. In another poem, *The Lay of Hrok* (*Hrokskviða*), we get a description of viking life at King Half's court. This king probably lived in the seventh century.

From the western isles came the theme of *The Spear Song* (*Darraðarljóð*), preserved in *Njál's Saga,* which tells of the battle at Clontarf in Ireland in 1014. On the day of the battle a man saw twelve valkyries sitting in a shed and singing as they wove. Their weaving guided the course of battle, for they used human heads as loom stones, entrails of men as their web and woof, and their weaving implements were swords and arrows. *The Spear Song* is reminiscent of the best in the *Poetic Edda,* but the other fragments approach more closely to medieval balladry.

Even though there is little history to be derived from the heroic poems, they constitute a precious reflection of life in the North before the Viking Age. This poetry gave to their lives some glamor of heroism and permitted their warriors to bask in the light of the great Germanic heroes. Nothing less than a deep-seated kinship of spirit could have driven them to retain so tenaciously and over so many centuries the memories of Sigurd, Gunnar, Brynhild, and Volund.

Poetry of the Skalds

IN A SURVEY OF OLD NORSE POETRY we are practically compelled to sub-
divide by poetic types. But a division into Eddic and Skaldic poetry does
not mean that the former necessarily precedes the latter; on the whole
these two types run parallel to each other.[1]

They cannot always be sharply distinguished. Some of the Eddic poems,
for instance *The Sibyl's Prophecy,* have Skaldic elements, and it sometimes happens that skalds make use of Eddic meters or even sing of Eddic
heroes. Bragi, son of Boddi, made poems about Hamdir and Sorli, Hogni
and Hedin. But his poem is no Eddic poem; it is a shield poem. Like
several of the older skalds he praises men and deeds pictured on a shield
and thereby praises the owner of the shield. The emphasis here, in contrast to the Eddic poems, is not on the theme, but on the poetic style and
on the praise.

The skalds who created the Eddic poems probably did not think of
themselves as original poets, but rather as adapters of traditional material.
Therefore they are anonymous, much like the authors of the later ballads.
The Eddic poems, again like the ballads, take an objective position with
regard to the material; the poet never speaks on his own behalf. In the
Skaldic poetry this is different. It is subjective; the skald steps into the
picture—this is *his* poem. He describes, praises, incites, scorns. His poem
is contemporary, while the Eddic poem tells of ancient days. Most often
he even sings of that which he has seen himself, particularly battles, which
play a much larger role in the Skaldic than in the Eddic poetry. All this

[1] The only account of the skalds in English is Lee M. Hollander's *The Skalds* (Princeton
and New York, 1945), which includes a generous selection of their poems, excellently
translated, with illuminating introductions and notes. Some Skaldic poems are also
included in his earlier *Old Norse Poems* (New York, 1936). For references to the sagas
dealing with skalds see the next chapter.

does not exclude the likelihood that some of the known skalds may also have composed Eddic poems.

The skald usually composed his verse in honor of a prince. His poem required an elevated mode of expression to give the prince his due meed of praise and glory. The prince's enemies were to be flouted, while *his* deeds were held up in festive regard. In return for his effort the skald usually expected a reward, fame and gold rings, a sword with gilded hilt, a loaded ship. For such purposes the Eddic language and the Eddic versification were much too plain and trivial.

All Old Norse poetry made use of art words with a special ring of solemnity instead of the everyday terms, known from Snorri's *Edda* as *heiti* or "names": "all-powerful" for king, "brand" for sword, and the like. But there were also the *kennings,* or metaphorical paraphrases which may have originated as taboo words, but were used with great art. They resemble in principle such modern expressions as "steed of the desert" for camel, or "white coals" for electricity. Some kennings are mere statements of fact, as when Thor is called "Sif's husband," or a generous man (usually the prince) is called "breaker of rings." All such expressions are common enough in the Eddic poems also. But the characteristic form for skaldic kennings is the metaphorical type, in which a whole simile is condensed into one expression. The skald does not say that "the warrior stood there as erect as a tree, with a sword in his hand"; he says, "There stands the sword-tree." Not satisfied with this, he can substitute new kennings for each of the members of this kenning. He can call the sword "the fire of the wound," and he can call the tree "Odin's gallows," since Odin once hung on a tree for nine nights. The warrior may then be referred to as "Odin's gallows of the wound-fire"! In this way the kennings may become regular riddles, with as many as seven links. The spontaneity of the images often disappears, and we feel it as more of an exercise in ingenuity than as genuinely poetic expression.

While even the oldest Skaldic poems have forms so complex that they suggest a long preceding development, there is no tendency in the period we know toward a development from simple to more complex. On the contrary, from the end of the tenth century there is a tendency toward greater simplicity, fewer and simpler kennings. But in the twelfth century the kennings grow in number, perhaps in connection with the antiquarian interest in the period of historical writing and mythical sagas.

No less intricate than the language is the versification. The stateliest and most intricate form is the *dróttkvætt,* or Royal Meter. The stanzas

have four lines as in the Old Lore Meter, but the two halves of each line
have been expanded from two to three beats, so that they are usually
printed as full lines of six syllables each. An example is the following
stanza from Einar Helgason's *Lack of Gold* (*Vellekla*):

Rignði (hjǫrs) á hersa
(hríðremmir) fjǫr víða
(þrimhyndr of jók þundi
þegns gnótt) méilregni,
ok haldviðurr hǫlda
haffaxa lét vaxa
laufa veðr at lífum
lífkold Hǫars drífu.

Darts rained death on hersar[2]
down, sent from the hands of
him-who-hastens-sword-fray:[3]
Herian's host[4] he increaseth;
strengthens he-who-steereth-
steeds-of-sea[5] the shower-of-
ice-cold-arrows[6] falling
on the throngs of warriors.

Translated by L. M. Hollander

We see that the poet counts syllables, and in addition to the usual
alliteration uses a form of rhyme. In the odd-numbered half-lines two
syllables have identical following consonants (hjǫrs—hers), while in the
even-numbered half-lines two syllables have identical vowels and consonants (hrið—við). These rhymes, or assonances, were called respectively
skothending and *aðalhending;* but they are different from the rhymes
of modern verse in being within the verse line, not at the end.

This kind of complex versification, with its mushrooming kennings
and elaborate meters, makes severe demands on word order. The relatively free word order that a highly inflected language can employ is here
driven to its extreme. Sentences are so intricately intertwined that it must
have required a good deal of training to comprehend such a poem
immediately. The skald had a chance to make it more understandable
by his oral recitation. But even though such a poem glitters with brilliant,
even witty figures of speech, it has over it something distorted, overloaded,
and static. The intertwined sentences are not unlike the wood carving of
the period, with the elaborate and endless windings we see on the Oseberg
ship and elsewhere.

A proper poem in honor of a prince was supposed to have a refrain
(*stef*) and was then called a *drápa*. A *flokkr* was regarded as less dignified;

2 Chiefs.
3 Prince.
4 Dead warriors.
5 Prince.
6 Battle.

here the stanzas were not separated by refrains. But the skald was not confined to princely occasions. He could make poems in honor of the dead, or of a family. He could make scurrilous verses about his enemies, or love songs to a woman. The two latter kinds were forbidden in Iceland, but thrived no less lustily for that. Even occasional improvisations and lyrics could be tossed off with great virtuosity; they were called *lausarvisur* and were made wherever Norsemen traveled, from Vinland and Greenland to Palestine.

We know the names of about 250 skalds from 800 to 1300 A.D., but most of their poems have been lost. They have been preserved to us solely through the activity of Snorri and other saga writers, so that we usually get only isolated quotations. In some cases the poems quoted can be identified as spurious, i.e. as having been made up later than they claim to be.

An Icelandic list from the twelfth century, *Skáldatal,* mentions a few skalds from the period before 800. But Bragi Boddason the Old is the earliest skald whose poetry has been preserved. He must have lived in southwestern Norway in the early 800's. He is said to have visited the court of the Swedish king Björn at Birka and the Norwegian king Hjor in Hordaland. Ragnar Sigurdsson, with the surname Lodbrok, presented him with a shield containing engraved images from mythology and legendary history. The grateful Bragi then composed his shield poem, *The Drápa of Ragnar (Ragnarsdrápa).*

Harald Fairhair, who first united Norway in the latter half of the ninth century, also adorned his court with an abundance of skalds. Here, as in his political activities, Charlemagne may have been his model. On his "skaldic bench," reports the saga, sat the oldest one Audun Ildskjelda, and beside him Olve Hnuva, Guttorm Sindri, Thjodolf from Hvinisdalr, and Thorbjorn Hornklofi. "By their clothing and by their golden rings one sees that they are the king's beloved friends; scarlet cloaks they carry with fair borders, silver-chased swords . . ."

Thjodolf from Vest-Agder is best known for his *Ynglingatal* in honor of King Ragnvald, a cousin of Harald's. Snorri's *Ynglinga Saga* in the *Heimskringla* is built on this poem. A shield poem, like *Ragnar's Drápa,* is the *Autumn-long (Haustlǫng),* so-called perhaps because it was composed in the autumn. Only twenty stanzas are now extant; they tell of the goddess Idun who was carried off by the giant Thjassi, and of the battle between Thor and the giant Hrungnir. Its descriptions are colorful, but they do not approach the Eddic poems which deal with the same themes.

Thorbjorn Hornklofi was the poet of the great battle of Hafrsfjord where Harald finally destroyed the opposition to his rule over Norway. His *The Lay of Harald* (*Haraldskvæði*) is constructed in the form of a conversation between a valkyrie and a raven. The valkyrie asks and the raven answers, for the raven is on its way from the battle with bloody beak and raw flesh in its claws. The poem praises Harald as the great king of the Northmen, he who commands warships

> With reddish ribs and   with reddened war-shields,
> With tarred oar-blades   and with tents foam-besprinkled.

> *Translated by L. M. Hollander*

He is the king who "wants to drink his Yule ale away from home" and since boyhood has been "weary of the warm cottage and down-filled mittens." Harald's victory is celebrated in triumphant words:

> Then hid under benches,   and let their buttocks stick up,
> They who were wounded,   but thrust their heads keelward.

> Home from Hafrs-firth   hastened they eastward,
> Fled o'er the Jadar,   of ale-cups thinking.

> *Translated by L. M. Hollander*

While *The Lay of Harald* is in an Eddic meter, *The Din Poem* (*Glymdrápa*) is in the Royal Meter. We have only a few fragments of this poem; it was composed in honor of Harald's youthful expeditions and battles, but also to commemorate his defense of the country against pirates and lawbreakers. There were other poems about the king, including some by a woman skald called Jorunn, but little is preserved of these.

When Eirik Blood-Axe died, a poet whose name we do not know composed a memorial ode at the request of his queen Gunnhild. Only a part of this *Eirik Poem* (*Eiríksmál*) is preserved, but what we do have is grandly conceived, in Eddic meters. The poet carries us to Valhall, where great preparations are being made, so great that the god Bragi thinks Balder must be returning from Hel. But Odin informs him that King Eirik is coming, and he send the Volsungs Sigmund and Sinfjotli to greet him. Odin himself had summoned Eirik, for he needs his help against the coming end of the world, Ragnarok: "The gray wolf is aiming at the seat of gods." Then Eirik arrives with five kings in his train, but here the poem ends and we are not allowed to witness the meeting of Eirik and Odin.

This poem was good enough to be imitated by another and better-known poet, Eyvind Finnsson, in a memorial ode (*Hákonarmál*) to King Haakon the Good (*ca.* 946-961). Haakon was a half brother of Eirik who followed him on the throne of Norway. Eyvind bore the scornful nickname of "Skald-destroyer," perhaps because of his imitative inclinations. Said to have been a great-grandson of King Harald, he must have been born around 915, but was not heard of until just before the battle of Fitjar in 961. In his poem Odin sends out the valkyries Gondul and Skogul to watch over the battle and pick Haakon as one of those who will die. After the battle Odin sends out Hermod, the warrior god, and Bragi, the god of poetry, to receive him with honor. The high quality of this poem lies in its matchless descriptions of battle:

> Burned the wound-fires[7]   in bloody gashes,
> The long-beards[8] were lifted   against the life of warriors—
> The sea-of-wounds[9] surged high   around the swords' edges,
> The stream-of-arrows[10] ran   on the strand of Storth-isle.

> *Translated by L. M. Hollander, slightly modified*

A striking characteristic of this poem, as well as of the *Eirik Poem,* is their partisan favoring of the pagan gods. Both Eirik and Haakon had been baptized, but gave up their Christianity against the fervent opposition of their pagan countrymen. The skalds are determined to keep their memory alive as pagan kings. Eyvind even goes so far as to praise Haakon for his orthodoxy, though the truth was that he did not dare to tear down the temples:

> Then was it seen how that sea-king had
>   Upheld the holy altars,
> When Haakon all did hail with welcome,
>   Both gods and heavenly hosts.

> *Translated by L. M. Hollander*

In the last stanza the skald reminds the people of some lines from the

7 Swords.
8 Battle-axes.
9 Blood.
10 Blood.

Hávamál and turns them against Haakon's successors, who plundered the temples and subjugated the people:

> Cattle die   and kinsmen die,
>   Land and lieges are whelmed;
> Since Haakon to   the heathen gods fared
>   Many a host is harried.

Translated by L. M. Hollander

Eyvind was not only a court poet. He also made shorter poems, and an ode which he composed in honor of "all Icelanders" brought him a gift of honor from the Icelandic Althing. But from the end of the tenth century the tables were turned: Icelandic skalds were being paid by Norwegian kings to sing their praises. The Icelanders went still farther abroad, to Danish, Swedish, even to Anglo-Saxon kings who had Norsemen in their pay. A few of the Icelandic skalds were born in Norway, but nearly all of the court poets were born in Iceland. After the time of Eyvind, the poems by Norwegian skalds that have been preserved consist exclusively of single stanzas. Several of the Norwegian kings, however, were skalds, just as Harald Fairhair and Haakon the Good had been. The sagas report this accomplishment for Olaf Tryggvason, Olaf Haraldsson, Magnus the Good, Harald the Hard, Magnus Bareleg, and Sigurd the Crusader.

The greatest of all Icelandic skalds, indeed the most complex and characteristic of all the viking skalds, was Eyvind's contemporary, Egil Skalla-Grimsson. His grandfather Kveldulf and his father Skalla-Grim had both been skalds, and were perpetually at odds with the kings of Norway. Skalla-Grim settled at Borg in western Iceland and became the progenitor of a gifted family. The saga describes the boy Egil as self-willed and vengeful. As an adult he became skilled in magic, quarrelsome, and greedy for gold, but also a good father and husband, with a strong family pride. He was still a young man when he fell out with Eirik Blood-Axe and killed one of the king's sons. Before he left Norway, he set up a pole inscribed with magic runes intended to lay a curse upon the king and queen. He then capped the pole with a horse's head. Some time later he was shipwrecked on the coast of Northumbria and fell into the power of the very king he had cursed, who in the meanwhile had been driven out of Norway, perhaps as the result (understood) of Egil's curse. The saga tells dramatically of how he saved his life by composing the poem

called *Head Ransom* (*Hǫfuðlausn*), an ode in honor of Eirik in a unique
end-rhymed meter which Egil seems to have created. The poem praises
Eirik for his exploits in war, but does so in a dignified and manly way,
without servility.

Far more personal in its flavor is Egil's ode of grief on the loss of his
sons, *Loss of Sons* (*Sonatorrek*). In the year 975 Egil's favorite son Bodvar
was lost at sea. The saga describes how Egil then locked himself into
his enclosed bed and refused to eat. But his daughter Thorgerd tricked
him into drinking milk, and then talked him into making a poem in
honor of his sons, for he had lost another son, Gunnar, a short time
earlier. This poem became a whole family portrait, a valid expression
of the yeoman and the viking in Egil, deeply human and at the same
time characteristic of his age.

The poem is not schematic; one stanza leads on to the next, forces itself
out as the mood rises and falls. The skald recalls his father's and his
mother's death, and now his sons':

> For my kin   hath come to an end,
> Like a tree   o'erturned by the storm.
> Unblithe he   who bears the corpse
> Of dear kin   from his dwelling place.
>
> *Translated by L. M. Hollander*

But his defiance and desire for vengeance take the upper hand. He
will break with the gods, avenge himself on the gods of the sea Ægir and
Ran; it would be all over with them, "if my suit with sword I could press."

> But strength to cope   I could not muster,
> So meseemed,   with my son's slayer:
> Soon will it   be seen by all
> How helpless   the hoary warrior.
>
> *Translated by L. M. Hollander*

But little by little the poet is able to come to terms with the gods. Even
though he bows unwillingly to them, he does not forget that Odin gave
him the art of poetry and the kind of temper that made his enemies come
out in the open where he could recognize them. The poem ends in a
resigned and peaceful spirit. "When he finished with the poem," says the
saga, "he got out of his bed and sat down in the high seat." Egil composed

many other poems besides these two, but only a few of them are preserved; he died around 980.

The coming of Christianity in the generation from 1000 to 1030 must have meant a crisis in the making of Skaldic poetry. We have seen how the author of the *Eirik Poem* and Eyvind Finnsson championed paganism against the new faith. Earl Haakon, the last pagan ruler of Norway, gathered the skalds around him and gave their art its last pagan renascence. His best-known skald, the Icelander Einar Helgason (Skálaglam), was a pupil of Egil's. In a poem in honor of Haakon he praises him for having raised again the "holy altars" so the "gracious godheads" could receive their "olden sacrifices."

> Increase gives the earth as
> Erstwhile, since the generous
> Lord lets flock the folk, all
> Fearless, to their worship.

In Iceland several of the skalds made poems about Thor; Úlf Uggason composed an ode about the pictures in Olaf Peacock's hall, where were depicted Thor's battle with the Midgard Serpent, Balder's burning, and the battle between Loki and Heimdall. And when Olaf Tryggvason's missionary Thangbrand came to Iceland, he was met by spiteful poems from the skalds.

But the advance of the new faith came whether the skalds willed it or no, and gradually its influence began to be felt among them also. It was difficult to adapt the Skaldic form, which had its roots and much of its imagery from the pagan mythology. The gift of poetry came straight from Odin. The difficulty of uniting old and new is most evident in a skald like Hallfred "the troublous skald," as the king called him. Hallfred's father came from Norway, but he was born in Iceland of an Icelandic mother. He went to Norway and was one of the pagan Earl Haakon's skalds; later he was baptized by King Olaf Tryggvason. Once when Olaf refused to listen to a poem of his, he threatened to give up Christianity again for paganism: "For those teachings are not [a whit] better matter for poetry than the poem I have made about you." The saga says that "Hallfred did not abuse the gods, when others spoke ill of them. He said it was not necessary to disparage them even though one did not believe in them." He accepted the king's faith, but his poems show his vigorous independence of mind. In his memorial ode to the king he uses no kennings involving the pagan faith and he praises the Christian king. But in his love poems he does use a good many pagan kennings.

The theme of love was one that occupied the poets much less than in later times, but it was far from absent in spite of the strict limits that were placed on such poetry. A girl's reputation could be ruined by a love poem, and the poet risked the vengeance of her family. Nevertheless there were love poets, and whole sagas that tell their story. Kormák was one of these, perhaps the most complex and lyrical of them all. He is best known for his poems to Steingerd, whom he was never quite able to win. Gisli Sursson became most famous as one of the great outlaws, but he composed many love poems to his faithful wife Aud. Typical for the times was also Thormod Kolbrunarskald, the "Skald of Coal-Brow," whose poetry is preserved in the saga that tells his tragic tale. He was a Christian, but there is little evidence in his poetry of a forgiving or humble spirit. He spent three years of his life pursuing the slayer of his foster brother to Greenland; and he ended his days beside King Olaf at the battle of Stiklestad.

The sainted King Olaf was probably the one who saved the skalds from giving up the art. Himself a poet, Olaf had composed beautiful deeply felt verses about Steinvor, whom he never won, and about Ingigerd, who became a queen of Russia. He loved the art of the skalds, and he appreciated their value as historians and propagandists. Snorri tells us that before Olaf's last battle at Stiklestad he told the skalds to enter the inner phalanx for their protection: "For you shall be here and see the events that occur, so that you can tell about them and make poems about them later on."

The king's nearest friend among the poets was Sigvat Thórdarson, his counselor, envoy, and royal marshal. Sigvat came to Norway from Iceland in 1015 and was the same age as the king. In many of his verses there is a greater love for the king and a more Christian spirit than in the rest of Olaf's skalds. He was the improviser and the humorist among the skalds. He tells of traveling on strenuous journeys in the king's behalf, where he met troublesome heathens who were annoyed when he disturbed them at their sacrifices. On a journey to Sweden, he composed these stanzas:

> On the long road hastens, hungry,
> My horse at twilight, coursing—

Stars stream out—forward,
The straw scenting, to our quarters.

Readily will look the ladies
And lasses, as we are passing
By the road, on the dust of our riding
Fast, up to Rognvald's castle.
Let us spur to speed our horses,
Sprightly, so that maidens high-born
And fair from the hall may hear us
Whisk by as we gallop briskly.

Translated by L. M. Hollander

Sigvat had taken part in some of Olaf's battles, and made excellent poems about them. But in the fatal year of 1030 he was gone, on a pilgrimage to Rome, something which Thormod pointed out to the king during the battle: "It would be sparse around your banner, O king, if we were all away on pilgrimages!" Sigvat heard about the king's death when he had returned as far as the Alps, and composed a poem in his honor. When Olaf's son Magnus became king, some of his followers urged that vengeance be taken for the death of his father. But in a poem called *The Outspoken Verses* (*Bersǫglisvísur*) Sigvat reminded the young king of the promises he had made when he became king: "Weary of sack are thy warriors, ween I, and wrathful the farmers." Magnus changed his policy on Sigvat's advice and came to be known in later years as "the Good."

The art of skaldcraft flourished throughout the eleventh and twelfth centuries. But the relationship of king to skald was no longer as personal as it had been between Haakon and Eyvind, Olaf and Sigvat. Harald the Hard (1042-1066), to be sure, gathered skalds about him, and was a good skald himself. He had made some jolly love poems in Constantinople. But there was more distance now between the king and his skalds. Christian themes began to creep into the poems, some of them even taking up the legendary exploits of King Olaf. Arnor the Earls' Skald showed genuine religious feeling by creating kennings to describe God and the angels and making up a meter called *hrynjandi* which was influenced by Latin hymns. The high point in this development came with Einar Skulason, who composed the poem called *The Ray of Light* (*Geisli*). The ray of light is Olaf, and the poem was recited in the Christ

Church at Nidaros in the year 1152 in the presence of three kings, Eystein, Sigurd, and Inge. "The whole church was filled with a sweet fragrance," reports the legend.

The only significant Norwegian-born skald in this period was Ragnvald Kolsson, the earl of the Orkney Islands. He was an all-around personality, adventurous and humorous, with a great gift for improvising verse. He made poems about a woman who had fallen into a well and frozen so she could say nothing but "ata-tata" and "hutu-tutu"; he made verses also about his own skills and exploits. In 1151 he started off on a pilgrimage to Jerusalem. On the way he fell in love with the viscountess Irmengard of Narbonne, whom he celebrated in true troubadour manner. In the Orkney Islands he gathered skalds about him, and together with the Icelander Hall Thorarinsson he composed the *Key of Meters, (Háttalykill)*, which illustrated the various Skaldic meters by means of poems celebrating such well-known heroic figures as Sigurd the Dragon-slayer and Ragnar Shaggy-breeches.

Toward the end of the twelfth century skaldcraft gradually fell into disuse. The skalds no longer composed; they wrote, so that one can smell the writing desk. Interest in their art was weakening; King Sverri had twelve skalds at his court, but nearly all of their production is lost. It is characteristic that now when paganism no longer was dangerous, the kennings based on pagan allusions grew more numerous again. The poems were mostly imitative, or they began to tend in the direction of the troubadours and the ballads. Snorri's attempt to infuse new life in the art by his *Edda* was in vain. The skalds could not compete with the saga writers. Nevertheless, the custom of having court poets was strangely persistent; as late as the time of Eirik Magnússon (1280-1299) there were five skalds at court.

The Sagas

IN ENGLISH the word "saga" has been borrowed from Old Norse to mean a heroic epic in prose. But in Old Norse it was a word of larger meaning, related to English "say." It could refer to any tale of some length, and there could be sagas of bishops, saints, trolls, outlaws, and common farmers just as well as of kings and heroes. The sagas were indeed the prose counterpart of viking poetry, and many of them were recited by the same men and at the same places. They must have flourished as far back as traditions of family and tribe had been kept alive, but they did not receive their final shape as art until they were first written down.[1]

This could not occur until the Latin alphabet had been brought to Scandinavia by the Christian missionaries and adapted to the Norse tongue. The runic alphabet was not used for the writing of longer texts; its purpose was primarily magic. But the masters of the Latin alphabet were the clerics, and they did not at first interest themselves in the writing of secular traditions. Their first task was to make their religion known among the people by producing sermons and saint's legends. The laws that established the order of church and state were also crucial; it appears that work on the Norwegian laws began during the first century of Christianity, before 1100. In the summer of 1117 the Icelandic Althing voted to have the laws of the country "written in book."

But the Icelanders very soon took the further step of writing down historical traditions of life at home and in the mother country. Sæmund

---

[1] Collections of saga translations are *The Saga Library* by William Morris and Eirikr Magnússon (6 vols., London, 1891-1905), in which the sagas are rendered into an archaic and unreadable English; *The Northern Library* (4 vols., London, 1895-1899); *Norroena*, ed. R. B. Anderson (15 vols., New York, 1906); *Origines Islandicae*, tr. G. Vigfússon and F. Y. Powell (2 vols., Oxford, 1905). Numerous individual saga translations have appeared; a bibliography will be found in Halldór Harmannsson, *Catalogue of the Icelandic Collection* (Ithaca, N.Y., 1914), and supplements (1927, 1943).

the Learned, who died in 1133, had studied in Paris and wrote in Latin a chronological account of the Norwegian kings from Harald Fairhair (or Halfdan the Black) to Magnus the Good. Others contributed to a learned literature on grammatical, astronomical, and theological subjects, as well as translations of Latin historical writings.[2] The first to write history in the native tongue was Ari the Learned (1067-1148), who was both cleric and chief. His *Book of the Icelanders (Islendingabók)*[3] contained in its first edition an account of the kings of Norway and established a chronology that became the base of the later sagas of kings and clans. Ari was concerned with the accuracy of his sources and well versed in the history of other countries. Another monument of Icelandic learning was *The Book of the Land-taking (Landnámabók)*[4] written later and by an unknown author. This was a list of about 400 Icelandic pioneers, with information on their places of origin, their settling in Iceland, and their family connections.

The rise of the written saga must be seen against this background of learned antiquarianism in the pioneer society of Iceland. Alongside the learned men who made it their business to note the basic facts there were storytellers who could elaborate the facts and give them flesh and blood. In Iceland historical research and narrative skill entered into an unusually happy combination.

This was connected with the fact that the emigrated Norwegians in Iceland were organized into great families or clans on a definitely aristocratic pattern. In Norway the royal family arose as a rival to the noble families and succeeded in reducing their power. But in Iceland a man's social status was dependent in some measure on his kinship. If he wished to be somebody, he had to know his ancestry right back to the first settler and even beyond, in Norway. The emigrants carried their social organization with them, and it was a great help to the returning Icelander if he could establish his kinship with the royal family of Norway.

Most of the sagas that relate to Icelandic families deal with events from 874, when Iceland was settled, and down to 1030, shortly after the coming of Christianity. The years from 1030 to 1150 were a relatively peaceful period, when the oral traditions of the early years had a chance to acquire epic form. When the new struggles of the late twelfth and early thirteenth centuries began, the old themes acquired renewed interest.

[2] See *First Grammatical Treatise,* tr. and ed. Einar Haugen (Baltimore, Md., 1950).
[3] Tr. H. Hermannsson (Ithaca, N.Y., 1930).
[4] Tr. as *The Book of the Settlement of Iceland* by T. Ellwood (Kendal, 1908).

But in Norway the events were continuous, so that tradition never got its chance to become fixed, and the stories existed only in the form of short tales and anecdotes.

The favorite forum of saga telling in Iceland was the Althing, where the free men of the country met every summer to make the laws and hear the news. It even happened that the deliberations of the assembly were interrupted when a ship arrived from Norway with news of the outside world. Still more enlightening is the story told in a saga of Harald the Hard. An Icelandic saga teller had entertained the Norwegian king and his men every evening during the autumn. But when Christmas approached, the Icelander was distressed because he started running out of material. He then asked the king for permission to tell the story of the king's own travels abroad, and spent the Christmas on this saga. When he was done, the king asked: "Where did you learn about all this?" The Icelander answered: "It was my custom every year to ride to the Althing, and there I learned a piece of the saga each year from Halldór Snorrason." This Halldór had himself accompanied Harald on his voyage to Constantinople.

But we must not fall into the error of older scholars who regarded the sagas as purely historical. They were meant primarily as entertainment, and even the written texts were sometimes intended more as a support of memory than as books to be read. The saga teller sought to make his story dramatic and his situations effective. Like all medieval authors, he constructed conversations that were more or less imaginary, though some of their characteristic turns of phrase may have a historical basis. Now and then the sagas report alternate versions: "Some say this, others say that; but I think it happened in this way . . ." The sagas are often embroidered with fairy tale motifs, as in the story of King Harald Fairhair and the Lapp girl Snæfrid. Dreams are also frequent, as in so many medieval writings. The farther away from Iceland the events occur, the more fantastic they become, and some of the tales that tell of early viking days include battles with berserks, the robbing of burial mounds, and the rescue of fair women from the power of the trolls.

Even so the basis of the sagas is one of real experience, and many of them are first-rate historical sources. Their geographical data are usually correct, even concerning foreign countries, and testify to a remarkable feeling for detail. The events they report can often be checked against foreign sources. The story told in *Egil's Saga* concerning Ottar's journey to Bjarmeland agrees with the story as told by Alfred the Great, and the story of Harald the Hard and his voyage to Constantinople checks with Greek sources. But the story of Sigurd the Crusader's entry into Constantinople is pure legend.

The most conspicuous stylistic characteristic of the saga is its objectivity. Whether the events are probable or not, the saga proceeds in the same unruffled course and preserves its outer calm. There is no lyrical description of landscape or feeling for nature. Gunnar of Hlíðarendi's famous words in *Njál's Saga* stand isolated: "Fair is the hillside; never has it seemed fairer, with its pale fields and newly mown meadows." These words are not expressive of the author's feeling, but contribute to his portrait of Gunnar's character. What the saga lacks in interest in outer nature, it makes up in its study of human nature. Character revealed through action and speech is its chief triumph, even though one notes at times a tendency to create types rather than individuals. The Gudrun of *Laxdøla Saga* shows reminiscences of the Brynhild of heroic poetry, as when she says near the end of her life: "I was worst toward him whom I loved the most." But the woman in the saga is much more comprehensible than the one in the heroic poem.

There are many such notable instances of vivid characterization in the sagas. King Eystein noticed that his skald Ivar Ingemundsson was silent and unhappy. When he asked him for the reason, Ivar obstinately refused to tell. The king finally wormed his secret out of him: he grieved for a woman he could not have. That will be a simple matter, said the king. His word could mean a good deal in such a case. But Ivar would not accept his help: "My brother is married to her." Then the king promised to take him along to fine feasts where he would meet many "courteous" women. But the skald answered that whenever he met other lovely women, he felt his loss the more deeply. The king then offered him property, money, ships, but Ivar repeated his refusal. Then Eystein knew only one more thing he could offer, of little value compared to the others. If the skald wished, he could come to him every day, and "then we shall talk about this woman, as you wish it and we best can think it." In this way the king helped the skald get over his sorrow.

Depending on their theme, the sagas can be divided into royal, family, and fiction. Except for some of the royal sagas, practically all of them were written by Icelanders. But in all groups there are many that throw light on Norwegian conditions, that have absorbed great quantities of specially Norwegian tradition, and that even take place in Norway. This is especially true of the royal sagas, which nearly all deal with the royal family of Norway. Meager indeed would have been our knowledge of medieval Norway if it had not been for the loving labors of Icelandic saga writers.

THE ROYAL SAGAS

"To his master and father, the reverend Eystein, archbishop of Nidaros, the humble sinner Theodricus presents his respectful prayer in the dutiful obedience which he owes him."

These are the self-effacing words with which the first known historian of Norway, Theodricus the Monk, began his Latin chronicle of the kings of Norway from Harald Fairhair to about 1130. He wrote his *Historia de antiquitate regum Norvagiensium* shortly before 1180, basing it in part on a collection of legends about St. Olaf which Archbishop Eystein had made around 1170. He refers also to foreign sources, but must have used oral narrative, for he appeals to the Icelanders "who remember all these things because they have old poems that tell about them." But Theodricus was no saga teller; his book is pure chronicle and smacks of the cloister. He adorns his narrative with learned digressions and pious meditations. Indeed, his piety is such that he breaks off his narrative when the civil wars begin, for, he declares, "it is a shame to tell posterity about the crimes and murders, the perjuries and patricides which now took place, of how warriors despoiled the holy places, scorned God, plundered churches and houses, raped women and committed other misdeeds which it would take too long to recount."

Theodricus's preface suggests that he thought of himself as the first historian. But it is quite possible that he was preceded by an anonymous writer who produced the *Historia Norvegiae* which was found in Scotland by P. A. Munch in 1849. Written for foreigners, this chronicle includes a description of Norway, the Orkneys, the Faroes, and Iceland, and an account of the Norwegian kings down to St. Olaf's arrival in Norway (1015); the rest is lost. This may have been written by one Master Arnulf at Munkelif Monastery in the 1170's for an English friend, Master Thomas Agnellus. It is a poor piece of work, written in bad and affected Latin. But it contains some data that may be more accurate than those known to the Icelanders.

The earliest effort along this line by an Icelander after Ari the Learned was written by Eirik Oddsson around 1160, an account of the kings of his time. The work, which bore the curious name of *Hryggjarstykki*

("Back Piece") is lost, but was used and partially incorporated by Snorri and the *Morkinskinna* writer. There are also from this time some anonymous fragments of an old saga about St. Olaf. Some time between 1170 and 1190 two Icelandic monks at Thingeyrar Monastery, Odd Snorrason and Gunnlaug Leifsson, wrote works on Olaf Tryggvason in Latin, which were soon translated into Norse. They wrote to glorify Olaf, who after all had christianized Iceland; Odd Snorrason's work, the only one preserved, is well told, but seems extremely credulous.

The abbot at Thingeyrar monastery was Karl Jónsson. He became the official historiographer of King Sverri, who wrote while "the king sat over him and told him what should be written." The saga writer has here taken over the role of the skald, perhaps after the model of foreign courts. Abbot Suger in France had written for Louis VI and Louis VII; in England Henry II was just getting his history written, and Otto of Freising had written for Frederic Barbarossa on the basis of material furnished by the emperor himself.

Abbot Karl came to Sverri in 1185, the year after the defeat of Magnus Erlingsson, and it is easy to understand that the king wanted his history written. This would secure his power and frighten his opponents. Even though *Sverri's Saga*[5] is thus a partisan document, it speaks of Sverri's opponent Magnus with respect. As a work of literature the saga is not one of the best. Its loose construction and excessive detail shows that the material had not had a chance to mature in oral narration. But Sverri's speeches are splendidly reported, and we can hear Sverri's own words as he "sat over" the writer. One of his speeches appears as a separate document, written by a learned man who may have studied in Bologna, his so-called *Speech Against the Bishops* (*Varnarræða*). This was Sverri's reply to the bishops who had excommunicated him for his struggle on behalf of the royal power against the church.

Around 1190 appeared the first of the surveys of Norwegian history, the so-called *Extract* (*Ágrip*). The unknown author, possibly a Norwegian, covered the period from Halfdan the Black to 1177, but he was not a good storyteller and the composition is clumsy. Far better was the *Morkinskinna* ("Rotten-skin") so named from the condition of the parchment, which was written by an Icelander around 1220. This work is notable for its Skaldic poems and numerous anecdotes, some of which belong to the best in Norse storytelling, including the above-mentioned tale of Ivar Ingemundson and the story of the Greenlander Audun and

[5] Tr. as *Sverrissaga, The Saga of King Sverri of Norway* by J. Sephton (London, 1899).

his polar bear. A third survey, the *Fagrskinna* ("Fair-skin"), was written in Norway by an Icelander around 1230. This was the saga that King Haakon Haakonsson asked to have read aloud on his deathbed; when this was done, he asked for the saga of his grandfather Sverri. It is characteristic that all three of these surveys end in the year 1177, where Sverri's saga begins; the same is true of *Heimskringla,* as we shall see.

There were other historical sagas dealing with Norsemen in the old Norwegian colonies, and related to the history of Norway. One of these was *The Saga of the Jomsvikings (Jómsvíkinga saga),* another *The Saga of the Men of Orkney (Orkneyinga saga),*[6] and a third, *The Saga of Sigmund Brestison (Færeyinga saga),*[7] which deals with the chief of the Faroes. In many passages these reach the same high quality of narrative as do the best of the royal and the family sagas.

SNORRI STURLUSON (1179-1241)

There is no other figure in Old Norse literature with a stature comparable to that of Snorri Sturluson. He was skald and critic, saga writer and politician, ambitious for fame and power, but at heart a true artist. He united in his personality all the currents of the Norse renaissance, the learning of Ari, the narrative skill of the saga, and the enthusiasm for old traditions.

He was born in 1179 at Hvamm in northwestern Iceland. His father, Sturla, had fought his way to power from a humble beginning. His mother, Gudny Bodvar's daughter, was related to the skalds Egil Skalla-Grimsson and Markus Skeggjason. He himself was brought up as the foster son of Jón Loptsson, the wealthiest and most powerful chief in Iceland. Jón had grown up in Norway; his grandfathers were King Magnus Bareleg and Sæmund the Learned, so that he united in his person the royal and learned traditions that came to be the characteristic interest of his foster son Snorri. Jón had established a school for clerics on his estate Oddi at his own expense and thereby made it a center of Icelandic learning and culture. Snorri's interests must have been directed at a very early age toward skaldcraft, reading, and Norwegian history.

During most of his life, however, he was embroiled in Icelandic political

[6] *The Saga of the Jómsvikings* has been translated by Lee M. Hollander (Austin, Tex. 1955); *Orkneyinga Saga* has been translated by A. B. Taylor (Edinburgh and London, 1938), also by J. H. Hjaltalin and Gilbert Goudie (Edinburgh, 1873).
[7] Tr. as *The Tale of Thrond of Gate commonly called Færeyinga Saga* by F. York Powell (London, 1896); as *The Saga of the Faroe Islanders* by Muriel A. C. Press (London, 1934).

life. He married into wealth when he married Herdis Bersi's daughter, who made him the owner of Borg, the family estate of Skalla-Grim. Later on he gave up his first wife and married Hallveig Orm's daughter, said to have been the richest woman in Iceland. He acquired the estate Reykjaholt and was elected Law-speaker, the highest position in the gift of his countrymen, in 1215. Such success could not but arouse controversy, and among his bitterest enemies were some of his own kin, his brother Sigvat and his nephew Sturla. In 1218 he extended his sphere of influence by leaving Iceland for Norway, where he was received with the honor due a leading Icelandic chieftain and skald.

In Norway the new king, Haakon Haakonsson, was only fourteen years old and the real power was held by Earl Skuli, who became a good friend of Snorri's. When a controversy arose between Icelanders and Norwegians, Snorri succeeded in persuading Skuli not to send a punitive expedition to Iceland. In return he promised to do what he could to extend the power of the Norwegian king in Iceland and was given the title of nobleman. He spent two years in Norway, traveling around to many places, and undoubtedly added greatly to his store of historical and geographic lore. When he returned to Iceland, he made a great show of power, held his feasts "in the Norwegian manner," and drew up his troops as he had seen the king of Norway do it. But he did little to carry out his promise. Instead he sent the rulers of Norway the most elaborate of Skaldic poems ever made, the 99-stanza *Háttatal,* in 1223. This was composed in honor of Skuli and Haakon, and every stanza was in a different meter.

The *List of Meters* (*Háttatal*) is preserved to us as a part of Snorri's handbook in poetics for young skalds, the so-called *Prose Edda.*[8] He may have begun this in Norway, but completed it at any rate after his return to Iceland. His hope seems to have been that it would lead to a revival of interest in skaldcraft. The first part of his book is of the greatest interest for modern readers, however, because of its systematic account of the old Norse pagan myths. Called "The Beguiling of Gylfi," it is composed in the form of a dialogue between two fictitious characters, Gylfi, a Swedish king, and Odin himself, split into a kind of trinity. The second part, "The Poesy of Skalds," starts out as the same kind of fictitious conversation about the diction of Skaldic poetry, but after a time Snorri drops the fiction and speaks in his own person. The third part, the

[8] Tr. as *The Prose Edda* by A. G. Brodeur (New York, 1929), also by George Webbe Dasent (London, 1842), and Rasmus B. Anderson (Chicago, 1880).

Háttatal, uses Snorri's poem to illustrate a running commentary on the various meters of Skaldic poetry. While this idea was not original with Snorri, his poem shows greater virtuosity than its predecessor, the *Key of Meters* (*Háttalykill*) of Ragnvald Kolsson and Hall Thorarinsson. But even so it is a mere tour de force without genuine poetic value.

It was a logical step for Snorri to proceed from skaldcraft to the writing of Norwegian history. In the poetry of the skalds he had the very best evidence concerning this history, for their poems were so intricately constructed that it was not easy to distort them. He had a treasury of poems by more than two hundred named skalds covering some four centuries of Norwegian history. The earlier historians had used Skaldic poems also, but Snorri was the first to state explicitly their value as historical sources. In his preface to the *Heimskringla* ("Circle of the Earth") he wrote: "It was the practice of skalds to praise most highly the person for whom they made their poem. But no one would have dared to tell a man about deeds which everyone present knew to be lies and loose talk. That would have been mockery and not praise."

The idea of writing a complete history of Norway does not seem to have occurred to Snorri, however, until after he had completed a separate saga of St. Olaf. He combined various sources, both secular and clerical, in his account, and showed good judgment in avoiding much of the purely legendary material current in his day. The picture we get of Olaf is that of a determined and ruthless ruler who used every means to advance the cause of his religion, but who did not really absorb the spirit of that religion until after his flight to Russia and his attempted comeback in 1030.

The rest of the *Heimskringla,*[9] or *History of the Norwegian Kings,* as Snorri himself called it, consists of an introductory series of sagas which describe Olaf's ancestors and predecessors all the way back to Odin, and a following series that brings the story down to the beginning of Sverri's saga in 1177. Snorri dictated his text to copyists, and did not hesitate to make use of older sources *in extenso.* But he winnowed the material carefully and put his own personal stamp on it. Snorri alone lets rain and fog rest upon the coast when Olaf suddenly realizes that he has lost

[9] Tr. as *The Heimskringla* by Samuel Laing (London, 1844); his version is available in Everyman's Library, vols. 717 (*Heimskringla: The Olaf Sagas*) and 847 (*Heimskringla: The Norse King Sagas*); as *The Stories of the Kings of Norway* by William Morris and E. Magnússon (London, 1893-1905); and as *Heimskringla* by Erling Monsen (London, 1932). (The title *Heimskringla* is derived from the opening words of the book, in the *Ynglinga Saga,* which mean "The Circle of the Earth.")

Norway. Snorri as artist gives his story life and visual reality. As a historian he works in the tradition of Ari, to whom he devotes more than half of his preface. As a storyteller his model was Abbot Karl Jónsson. But Snorri surpassed both.

Some have been of the opinion that he was also the author of *Egil's Saga*.[10] His nephew Sturla Thordarson wrote in the biography of Snorri that Snorri had "written saga books," so it is not impossible. But in the the absence of positive evidence, it is dangerous to assert it purely on the basis of stylistic similarity. Snorri did not get a chance to work undisturbed at his literary endeavors for very many years. In 1237 he had to flee to Norway for a renewed two-year stay. But now open enmity had broken out between Haakon and Skuli, and Snorri was Skuli's friend. When the king forbade him to return to Iceland, Snorri defied his order. The king's vengeance pursued Snorri into his very home, where an agent of the king found him and killed him on the night of September 22-23, 1241.

Snorri was a man ambitious for power and honor, but no fighter. The accounts we have of him seem to suggest that he was too much inclined to see both sides of a question, too reasonable and humane for his age. The local rivalries in Iceland did not interest him, and he preferred to avenge himself with mocking poems rather than with weapons. Although he was an Icelander, he was more interested in Norway than in the traditions of his own country. His great history was not only the best history of Norway, but many centuries later it came to play a fundamental role in the history of the country itself.

THE FAMILY SAGAS

In contrast with the royal sagas, but more like the Eddic poems, the family sagas of Iceland are of anonymous authorship. One reason may be that when they were first written down around 1200, the writers felt themselves to be merely noting down oral tradition and not composing anything original. The earliest sagas show this quality of purely traditional narration, e.g. *Heiðarvíga Saga, Reykdøla Saga, Vápnfirðinga Saga*,[11] *Droplaugarsona Saga*.[12] They are episodic and relatively brief.

[10] Tr. as *The Story of Egil Skallagrimsson* by W. C. Green (London, 1893), and as *Egil's Saga* by E. R. Eddison (Cambridge, England, 1930).
[11] Tr. in *Four Icelandic Sagas*, 75-102, by Gwyn Jones (Princeton and New York, 1935).
[12] Tr. in *Three Icelandic Sagas*, 95-136, by Margaret Schlauch (New York and Princeton, 1950).

Later it became the practice to join together several such tales into a narrative relating to longer periods and larger areas, as in the *Ljósvetninga Saga* and *The Eyrbyggja Saga*.[13] Toward the end of the century there came into being long historical novels based on real events, but with elements of chivalric and heroic adventure, such as *Laxdøla Saga*,[14] *Njáls Saga*[15] and *Grettir's Saga*.[16] These show a much more definite authorship than do the rest. But all of them are marked by a consciously artistic intention of psychologically characterizing the personalities described.

Here as in the heroic poetry the interest is centered on individual figures. But the sagas do not always deal with bold warriors; just as often the heroes are sharp-tongued skalds, wily chieftains at the Althing, extraordinary men and women about whom stories have been shaped. Only occasionally, as in *Chicken-Thori's Saga* (*Hænsna-þóris saga*) are the protagonists merely cantankerous and self-seeking. Psychological realism is the strength of the family saga. The characters are more complex and subtle than could be accommodated in the viking morality of the Eddic poems. The wise, beardless Njál tries to avoid conflict as long as possible; but when strife has broken out, he is inflexible. Njál's son Skarphedin is pale and serious, always unruffled; but he smiles when he is provoked, a frightening smile. Other characters are presented humorously, like the boaster Björn or the scoundrel Mord. The sagas show an understanding of female characters as well. Hallgerd in *Njál's Saga* is beautiful and vengeful, and she is the evil fate of her three husbands. The women in the *Laxdøla Saga* are faithful and keen-witted, but also quarrelsome and sometimes petty. Aud, the wife of Gisli Sursson,[17] is a deeply felt portrait of the faithful wife, while Helga in *Gunnlaug's Saga*[18] is more of a stereotype.

The style of narrative is usually sober and given to understatement.

[13] Tr. as *The Story of the Ere-dwellers* by William Morris and E. Magnússon (London, 1892), also in abstract form by Sir Walter Scott in his *Illustrations of Northern Antiquities* (Edinburgh, 1814).

[14] Tr. as *Laxdæla Saga* by Thorstein Veblen (New York, 1925), as *Laxdæla Saga* by Muriel A. C. Press (2d ed.; London, 1906), and as *The Story of the Laxdalers* by Robert Proctor (London, 1903).

[15] Tr. as *The Story of Burnt Njal* by G. W. Dasent (Edinburgh, 1861), also in abbreviated form as *Heroes of Iceland* by Allen French (Boston, 1905); tr. as *Njál's Saga* by Carl F. Bayerschmidt and Lee M. Hollander (New York, 1955).

[16] Tr. as *The Saga of Grettir the Strong* by George Ainslie Hight (Everyman's Library, 1913); as *The Story of Grettir the Strong* by Allen French (New York, 1908), adapted and abridged from the version by Morris and Magnússon (London, 1869).

[17] In *The Saga of Gisli, Son of Sour*, tr. R. B. Allen (New York, 1936); also tr. as *The Story of Gisli the Outlaw* (Edinburgh, 1866).

[18] Tr. in *Three Icelandic Sagas*, 1-46, by M. H. Scargill (New York and Princeton, 1950).

Very occasionally do we get graphic images, drastic and somewhat tortured, as when Egil is described sorrowing over his brother's death: "One eyebrow was drawn up to the hairline, the other hung down on his cheek." Expressions like this are more reminiscent of Irish style and may suggest a connection.

A saga normally begins by enumerating the hero's ancestors, usually from the first settler of Iceland and down. Occasionally, as in *Gunnlaug's Saga,* the coming events are foreshadowed by a dream; this was a common medieval device, found also in the royal sagas. Then the action gradually unfolds until the catastrophe is reached, and after that the story is soon brought to a close. The characters are made known by what they say and do, though the storyteller will often summarize their qualities in a short descriptive passage. But he does not usually pass judgment on them or express his personal views. Conversations are a major device in the narrative, being used to prepare the action and illuminate the characters. Rafn the Skald says to Gunnlaug in a poem that there are other women just as lovely as his lamented Helga. "That may be," says Gunnlaug, "but it seems not so to me." When Grettir was declared an outlaw, the general attitude to him is well expressed in the words: "Many wished him a happy journey, but no one said welcome back." Just as in the royal sagas, Skaldic poems are interspersed; but here many of them are purely for adornment and are made up by the writer of the saga.

The chief theme of the family sagas is the feuding life of the Icelandic clans in the tenth and early eleventh centuries. Every part of Iceland is represented, and the stories take us back and forth across its surface. The stories of the noble outlaws make up a group all its own. Gisli Sursson is a brave and fine fellow who is outlawed because he performed the vengeance that was his duty. The hero of *Grettir's Saga* is also innocently convicted, a staunch and kindly man. All the rest of his life he has to wander about in the mountainous wasteland battling trolls and ghosts. However unreal this part of his story may seem to us, it was real enough to his own times. Nor does it entirely lose touch with reality, for Grettir the Strong was the man whose death was avenged farthest away from Iceland: his slayer was killed in Constantinople.

The family sagas enlighten us about Norse mentality both before and after the coming of Christianity. Many of them must have been penned by clerics, but they are usually free from clerical moralizing. A saga like that of Hrafnkel gives us a fine picture of pagan sacrificial practices. We also get many glimpses of daily life, whether at the Althing or among shepherds, at salmon-fishing or whaling. We are present at horsefights and at the ball games of the young. Such everyday events can be used to start an action. In *Vatnsdøla Saga*[19] Ingolf's ball rolls over to Valgerd's feet, so that she draws her cloak about her; in this way they get to talking and become acquainted.

In all there are about thirty family sagas, which build on a myriad of traditions. But around 1300 A.D. the traditions were exhausted, and saga writing came to an end.

THE FICTION SAGAS

The third group of sagas are those that Scandinavian scholars have called the "sagas of ancient times," but which the Old Norsemen them-selves called "lying sagas." While the family sagas, even at their most improbable, claim to be history, these "fiction sagas" were frankly intended as entertainment. They usually deal with the centuries preceding the historical period which for Norway began with Harald Fairhair. They often contain a historical kernel or deal with a historical figure, but the stories they tell are largely drawn from fairy tales or chivalric romances. Their scene is usually Norway or countries to the east, Gothland, Sweden, Russia, and they love to tell about fantastic journeys to the land of the trolls, or to the White Sea region, Greece, and other remote or improbable places.

Like the other sagas, these were preserved in Iceland, and many of them must have been written as early as 1250, possibly stimulated by Snorri's *Edda* and parts of the *Heimskringla,* where he made use of just this kind of tradition. A number of them were included by the Danish Saxo in his *Gesta Danorum* around the year 1200.[20] Saxo retold them in Latin, and in his patriotic zeal, he located many of them in Denmark. But a good many of them have their scene of action on the western coast of Norway, so that it is generally assumed that they are of Norwegian origin. But Saxo expressly stated that he had them from Icelanders, including the sagas of Hadding, of Gram, of Hother, of Starkad's youth, and others.

Much of this material must have accompanied the Icelanders on their departure from Norway, but references to the telling of such sagas in the historical accounts show that they could also be made up and that some people disapproved of them. In the year 1119 a wedding was held at

---

[19] Tr. as *The Vatnsdalers' Saga* by Gwyn Jones (Princeton and New York, 1944).
[20] *The First Nine Books of the Danish History of Saxo Grammaticus,* tr. by Oliver Elton (London, 1894).

Reykjaholar in western Iceland. Here the farmer Hrolf from Skalmarnes told "the saga of Rongvid the Viking and Olaf Lidmannsking, and how the grave mound of Thráin the berserk was broken open, and of Hromund Greipsson, with many poems in it. This saga Hrolf had made up himself." Hromund is mentioned in the *Book of the Land-taking* as the ancestor of an Icelandic family; he had lived in Telemark in the eighth century. This saga was later told to King Sverri, who said that such "lying sagas" were the most entertaining ones. In the same way, Snorri's nephew Sturla managed to ingratiate himself with Magnus the Law-Mender's queen in 1263 by telling the saga of Huld, a troll woman. Odd the Monk was one of those who objected, however, for he stated that he wrote his saga of Olaf Tryggvason in order to replace "stepmother sagas," as he called them, "in which the king gets the worst of it."

But such opposition did not help too much, for the stories corresponded to the wish of the people for pleasant, escapist entertainment. Their popularity in Norway is reflected by the great number of medieval ballads which drew their themes from the fiction sagas. While the heroic poems and the family sagas often were of a tragic cast, the fiction sagas generally ended happily. Double, or even triple weddings were a not uncommon form of ending. All difficulties were solved by the judicious application of magic and witchcraft.

Some of the fiction sagas have the same structure as the family sagas, with genealogies and a realistic manner of narration even when the events themselves are quite fantastic. Odin is a favorite character, appearing in disguise to help the hero. The hero has often been raised among the giants, and has clothes to which no sword can do injury, or even weapons that are irresistible. There is nowhere any attempt at character analysis, though the stories are not without humor.

The Volsunga Saga deals with this period, but is not like the other fiction sagas, since it is based chiefly on the heroic poetry of the *Edda,* possibly also on a lost *Saga of Sigurd.* Some of the oldest motifs can be found in *Norna-Gest's Saga*[21] which is intimately connected with the story of the Volsungs. The ancient Norna Gest had been in the service of Sigurd the Dragon-slayer, and he tells King Olaf Tryggvason of this hero and others he has known. He carries with him a small candle; the Norns have promised him that he will not die so long as this is not burnt. At the persuasion of Olaf he lets himself be baptized, lights the candle, and dies. The life candle motif is of Greek origin. Another saga from the age of

21 Tr. in *Stories and Ballads of the Far Past*, 11-37, by N. Kershaw (Cambridge, 1921).

Germanic migrations is that of *Hervor and King Heidrek*,[22] from which is derived in turn *Ormar's Saga*. *The Saga of Hrolf Kraki* builds on episodes of Danish history from around 500 A.D. *The Saga of Ásmund the Hero-slayer* is identical with that of the eighth-century German *Hildebrandslied*. In berserk madness Hildebrand kills his own son and brother.

Many of the fiction sagas find their favorite themes in an idealized picture of the vikings. The viking marauders had by this time retreated far enough into the past to form the subject of imaginative embroidery. Many of these were Norwegian in origin, e.g. *The Saga of Half and his Heroes*, which tells of King Alrek at Alrekstead in Hordaland. The hero in *The Saga of Arrow-Odd* (*Ǫrvar-Odds saga*) is from Jæren in southwestern Norway. He has three arrows that hit everything they are aimed at and return to the archer by themselves. He makes many fantastic journeys to the northern region of the trolls, but also to Aquitania, Russia, Greece, Antiochia, and Sweden. It is a peculiarity of his that "he had to stay sometimes with pagan men and sometimes with Christians." A copy of this saga was owned by Bishop Arne in Bergen around 1300. There are Norwegian heroes also in the saga of Ketil Salmon and his son Grim Shaggy-cheek.

The most artfully constructed of the viking sagas is *The Saga of Fridtjof the Bold* (*Friðþjófs saga*).[23] Written around 1300, this tale takes place in Sogn and is a story of romantic love in the spirit of chivalric poetry. It is well told, with feeling and character portrayal, but it has not been possible to find any historic basis for the story. There is probably a good deal more history in the saga of the Danish king Ragnar Shaggy-breeches. He was a historical figure who sacked Paris in 845 and fell in England or Scotland in 866. The saga has him killing a serpent who had encircled the maiden's bower of the beautiful Thora Borgarhjort. In the end he is caught and thrown into the snake pit. Here he composes *The Lay of Kraka* (*Krákumál*), a poem of the twelfth century, ending: "Laughing I shall die."

The saga tradition thus ends on a note that connects it with the fairy tales and legends of earlier and later centuries. A saga unbound by the critical sense of historians is nothing more than a fairy tale. It is the peculiar glory of the emigrants to Iceland from Norway that they created and developed a form of narrative that wedded history with fantasy in an age when the two were normally kept severely apart.

[22] Tr. in *Stories and Ballads of the Far Past*, 79-143, by N. Kershaw (Cambridge, 1921).
[23] Tr. in *Viking Tales of the North*, 75-111, by R. B. Anderson (Chicago, 1877), and in *Three Northern Love Stories*, 69-122, by E. Magnússon and William Morris (London, 1901).

Foreign Culture and Norse Tradition

IT WAS NOT SURPRISING that Snorri made friends with Skuli rather than Haakon when he was at the Norwegian court. Skuli with his interest in skaldcraft represented the Norse tradition, while Haakon was oriented more toward the courtly, medieval literature from abroad. To be sure, the *Fagrskinna* ("Fairskin") manuscript of the royal sagas may have been prepared at his request, but he was far more zealous in promoting the translation of foreign romances. This was in keeping with the whole movement toward the feudal practices of other European courts in the reigns of Haakon (1217-1263) and Magnus the Law-Mender (1263-1280). New titles were introduced at court: the royal attendants (*skutillsveinn*) were promoted to knights, the taper bearers (*kertisveinn*) were made into squires, and Earl Skuli was made a duke. In the last years of the twelfth century the Gothic style of architecture had been introduced, and a new sculpture began to flourish. This was the period of the chivalric romance.

Even so, the Norse tradition did not at once die out. The verse romances were translated into sagas, as were the saints' legends, while in Iceland the Latin hymns were made over into Skaldic odes. In 1264-1265 Snorri's nephew Sturla Thordarson wrote *The Saga of Haakon Haakonsson* at the request of Haakon's son Magnus. This saga was contemporary in the same way as *Sverri's Saga,* but without the passionate one-sidedness of the latter. Sturla had to pick his way cautiously among conflicting ideas. In relating the story of Skuli's attempted rebellion against Haakon, he had to consider that while Haakon was the king's father, Skuli was his grandfather, and that Magnus's mother Margaret, Skuli's daughter, was still alive. Many of those who had fought against Skuli were now cool to Magnus. Sturla adorned his narrative with Skaldic poems, including some of his own, but not for the same reason as Snorri. He also wrote a saga about Magnus, after the king's death, but this is nearly all lost.

COURTLY LITERATURE

A new and more glamorous atmosphere meets us as we cross the threshold to the knightly sagas.[1] These heroes have other ideals, different concepts of honor, new modes of being. The rough and ready life of the old Norse literature gives way to one in which "courtesy," or courtliness, becomes the main goal. These ideals are reflected even in the style, which becomes more subjective, more artful and melodious. The sentences are often adorned by alliteration, with a splendor of phrase which can rise to heights of virtuosity. But we miss the concise, oral, realistic style of the old sagas. The new literature takes us out of the viking hall, with its armed and shaggy warriors, into the medieval castle, populated by well-groomed footboys and by willowy maidens with pious glances and "hair fairer than gold."

A great proportion of the medieval romances can be traced back to the world of Celtic imagination. This was a fantastic world of misty contours, changing and colorful, filled with the creatures of popular belief, and sensitively embodying impressions of nature. There was little of reality, but a great deal that was mystical and seductive—shadows and sudden glimpses of the sun, the lapping of the waves and moonlight through sundered clouds. The Celtic legends had been taken up by poets in northern France as early as 1150, later by English and German poets, and made into lyric poems and longer epics. Of these the most popular in Scandinavia were those that dealt with King Arthur and the knights of the Round Table.

The historical King Arthur lived in the sixth century and was a leader of British armies resisting the invasion of the Angles and Saxons. But the French poets turned him and his knights into the noblest heroes of the age. They had them setting out to find the Holy Grail, the cup in which Joseph of Arimathea collected the blood of Christ, and which was thought of as identical with the chalice of communion. These knights came to represent the Christian ideal of knighthood, the crusading spirit.

One of the three knights who was found worthy to see the Holy Grail was Percival, or Parsifal. The saga about him, which was written in the time of Haakon Haakonsson, is a prose paraphrase of the verse epic by the French Chrestien de Troyes. But the French poem was incomplete, and for this reason the saga lacks the dramatic tension of the German

[1] Selections of the translated literature of the period can be found in *Survivals in Old Norwegian,* tr. H. M. Smyser and F. P. Magoun, Jr. (New London, Conn., 1941).

Wolfram von Eschenbach's magnificent poem on the same theme. The author of the saga made an anticlimactic conclusion to his story by letting Percival get married to Blanchefleur and live on as a happy and famous knight.

Another of the knights of the Round Table was Iven, or Ywain. His story is told in *The Saga of Iven,* based on Chrestien de Troyes's *Ywain.* The hero Ywain journeys from Arthur's court and finds a miraculous spring and a chapel nearby overgrown with vines. He fights with a mysterious knight, marries his widow, saves a lion from a serpent, and is called the Knight of the Lion because the lion always accompanies him. The main theme is the struggle between love and knightly honor. Nearly related to this saga is the one about Erec, based on Chrestien's poem *Erec et Enide.* Erec is the noble knight who goes out to fight for his lady and to help all who are in need.

The most popular of all these sagas was the one about Tristram and Isolde (here called Isond). Its preface informs us that it was written as early as 1226 by Brother Robert at King Haakon's command, and like the others it was based on a French original. As a boy Tristram is kidnapped by Northmen who take him to England. Here he goes to the court of his uncle, King Mark, who sends him to Ireland to bring him the beautiful princess Isond. But by mistake he and Isond drink a love potion, which binds them mystically together even after she is married to King Mark. They continue to love each other throughout life, and defy human as well as divine laws in doing so. Nevertheless they save their souls, and God even allows two trees to grow from their graves, which are placed on opposite sides of the church. The trees join their crowns above the church roof, showing that the power of love endures even after death.

Other stories of love were translated from the French, one of them *The Saga of Elis and Rosamund* by the same Brother Robert at Haakon's request. The collection called *Songs with Strings (Strengleikar)* contains a number of gallant episodes, based on lost poems by a French lady, Marie de France, at the English court of Henry II.

While the preceding were of Celtic origin, there were some from other legendary cycles as well. *The Saga of Flores and Blanchefleur* is of oriental origin. *The Karlamagnus Saga* is based on the French *Song of Roland* of about 1100 and was probably written around 1250. Its main theme is the battle between Roland and the Moors at Roncesvalles. Even the old Germanic themes were revived, this time in an extensive compilation called *The Saga of Didrik of Bern (Þiðriks saga af Bern)* and written about 1250 by a man in Bergen. This saga was based on Low German poems and stories brought to Bergen by the Hanseatic merchants. The hero, Didrik, is the Ostrogothic king Theodoric, and Bern is the city of Verona. But the saga also tells about many other heroes of the Eddic world—Sigurd the Dragon-slayer, Attila, Volund the Smith, Ermanaric, and others. Many episodes agree with those of the *Nibelungenlied,* but the saga also builds on lost poems. It is therefore of great value for the study of the legends, but does not impress one with its artistry.

THE KING'S MIRROR

The only monumental work from the Norwegian Middle Ages is *The King's Mirror* (*Konungs skuggsjá*), also known as *Speculum Regale.*[2] In this book the cultural ideals of medieval Europe found their expression on Norwegian soil. While there are models for it in other literatures, it is nevertheless original and personal in its mode of expression. It tells us much about cultural conditions and ideals of education in Norway.

In his preface the author says that he will not state his own name in order that no one may "reject the useful teachings that might be found in the book, either because of scorn or any kind of enmity toward the one who wrote it." From this and other remarks we may judge that he must have been a prominent man. He was a good theologian, well versed in foreign and native letters, as well as in astronomy. His observations of sunrise and sunset indicate that he must have lived for a time in northern Trøndelag. But he had traveled and seen a good bit of the world. There is reason to believe that the work was made for one who was to become a king, as the title suggests. But the author still declares that it is "written for all and may be used by all just like the public commons." A number of guesses have been made concerning its authorship, one theory being that it was Einar Gunnarsson, nicknamed "Butterback," who was archbishop from 1255-1263. If this is correct, it would have been written for Haakon the Young, who died in 1257, or his brother Magnus. It had a significant influence on the law code of Magnus the Law-Mender.

Just like the first section of Snorri's *Prose Edda,* and like many foreign works, *The King's Mirror* is written in dialogue form. A son asks, and his father answers. First the son wants to know all about the practices of merchants. His father gives him much and good advice on how to behave in foreign countries so that one may not be laughed at. He tells about the

2 Tr. Laurence M. Larson (New York, 1917)

weather and times of sailing, about animal life in the Greenland seas, about strange things in Iceland and marvels in Ireland, about the heavenly bodies and the northern lights. But he actually says very little about the trader's life.

Then the son asks about the king and customs at the court. The father gives him a vivid description of the duties and tasks of the courtiers in war and peace. But his chief stress is on law and justice, which he explains with many learned interpretations of the Bible. It is a man's duty to be thoughtful, considerate, and just. He must be modest and moral, but also merry and courteous. The king's rights and duties are a major theme in the book. Although the author is pious, he does not advocate any clerical supremacy. God has given both the king and the bishop a sword for the chastisement of mankind. The king's sword always bites, and very harmfully when it is used unrighteously. But the bishop's sword bites only when it is righteously used. It is of the highest importance that the king make wise and moderate judgments.

The book reflects vividly the best culture of its day, and shows us an author who combined a national with an international outlook. He advises his readers to learn the customs and languages of other people, above all Latin and French, "the two languages that reach the farthest," but "still you should not neglect your own tongue." He writes about crop failures and the distress of the civil wars. But the worst is when "failures occur among the people themselves, or in the customs and wits of those who rule the country; for one cannot buy from abroad either good customs or wits if those are destroyed which one had before in the land." The author is advanced in many of his views. Not only is he aware that the earth is round, as were all the learned in his age, but he also mentions that people may possibly live on the opposite side of the earth, the antipodes, an idea that men were being burned for some hundreds of years later.

The style of *The King's Mirror* reflects many influences, not least that of the Norwegian Bible translation, *Stjórn,* written around 1220 or earlier. But we also find alliterations and proverbs that remind us of *Hávamál,* and a lyric quality that surpasses the best knights' sagas. "When Winter Day is come, the East Wind takes to sorrowing because he has lost his headpiece, the golden crown, and puts on his head a hat of clouds as he groans miserably."

In the preface the author says that the work will consist of four parts. He intends to write first about the trade and customs of the merchants, then of those that the king and the nobles should have; but he will also write of the work and habits of learned men, and about the labor of the farmer and those who build the country. Unhappily the last two sections, telling of the clergy and the farmers, are missing, and were probably never completed.

CLERICAL LITERATURE AND RELIGIOUS POETRY

Many scholars have pondered the question of how deeply Christian ideals penetrated among the people of medieval Norway.

We may take it for granted that in many parts of the country the change of religion was quite superficial. Paganism lived on in new forms, as it did in all parts of Europe. Earlier Thor had been the hero who fought against the giants for the protection of man, and his weapon had been the hammer: St. Olaf now took over the role of fighting the trolls, but with the power of the cross. The belief in spirits persisted, only that the old gods had now joined the forces of evil and were among the spirits that had to be conjured away. But there is reason to believe that the leaders of culture, both in Norway and Iceland, were fully on a level with European Catholicism. There are many accounts of pilgrimages to Rome and the Holy Land, and the sacred writings of the period reflect the deep impression of Christian thought.

Since the art of writing had been brought to Scandinavia by the Church, it was natural that most of the earliest writing was done by clerics and on religious themes. The priests needed books for reading aloud in the churches, saint's legends and sermons. Some of the oldest of these were the legends of the sainted king Olaf. A short account of his life was sent to England as early as 1050. Around 1070 a larger collection of stories was prepared, possibly by Archbishop Eystein. The book was written in Latin and was known throughout the Roman Catholic parts of Europe.

This collection was included in one of the oldest Norwegian-language manuscripts found in Norway, Norwegian Book of Homilies (Norsk homiliebok, ca. 1200). The name would lead one to think it was only a book of sermons. But the first part is a translation of the Anglo-Saxon Alcuin's On the Virtues and Vices (De virtutibus et vitiis). Most of the sermons were also translated, but some must have originated in Norway. This is true of the remarkable "Stave Church Sermon," in which the parts of the church are used as symbols of the religious life. "The Doomsday Sermon" may also be Norwegian, as indicated by its contents and popular style.

The religious prose literature of Norway and Iceland was abundant, but usually derivative and unimaginative. We have sagas of the Apostles, and sagas of the Holy Men, a saga of the miracles of the Virgin Mary, even a saga about the Archangel Michael. Closest to the old sagas are the Icelandic Bishops' sagas. One of the most interesting Norwegian texts is the fragment of *Brandanus saga*. Brandanus was an Irish saint who set off to find "the country that was promised the saints." He had many strange adventures, including an encounter with the sea serpent, on which he landed under the mistaken impression that it was an island. On a somewhat more real island he found a marvelously tall tree near a spring. Every branch on the tree was covered with snow-white birds. When Brandanus asked a bird who they were, it answered, "We fell down from heaven." In the story we find also the ancient dream of a blessed land, known from the writings of Hesiod and other classics.

Another saint's saga which points far back is that of *Barlaam and Josafat*, translated from the Latin either by or for Haakon the Young. In this saga the story of Buddha's life is told, though in Christian revision. Typical of the visionary and apocalyptical literature of the times is the story of the Irish knight Tundalus or Tyndall, who saw heaven and hell in 1149. An Irish monk in southern Germany wrote about these visions in Latin, and Haakon Haakonsson had the book translated around 1250. In the Norwegian version, called *Duggals Leizla,* Tundal is transported into the hereafter from a Wednesday to a Saturday noon. He gets to see the sufferings of the damned, but also the reward of the blessed. This saga was influential in shaping the later Norwegian *Dream Ballad*.

Another poem that should be mentioned as entering into the background of the *Dream Ballad* is the Icelandic *Song of the Sun*.[3] This is one of several Icelandic poems that reflect a genuinely personal experience of the Christian religion. But the poet used the chant-meter form of the Eddic poems, and its vision is a kind of Christian counterpart to that of *The Sibyl's Prophecy*. The poem reports a dream in which a young man's dead father appears to him and tells him about life in the present and its rewards in the hereafter. He tells of the robber who once had shown kindness to a wayfarer, who had been betrayed and murdered, but saved by God. He tells of lovers who were sundered by death, of close friends who met in combat for the sake of a blond woman. He describes death in crass and moving images, finally going on to the life of the blessed: "Men I saw

[3] Tr. as *The Sun Song* in *Old Norse Poems*, 101-15, by L. M. Hollander (New York, 1936).

then, who had given help to the poor with generous hearts; angels read over them the sacred books and the writings of heaven." He asks his son to pass his poem on to the living:

> This song of mine   which from me thou hast learned
>   Shalt thou to the living teach,
> The Song of the Sun   which some day will prove,
>   To be the least of lies.

The adaptation of this visionary material to the forms of a new age came with the composition of *The Dream Ballad (Draumkvæde)*[4] by an unknown Norwegian master around the year 1300. This miniature *"Divine Comedy"* tells the story of one Olav Åsteson who may be none other than Saint Olaf, son of Åsta. As in Tyndall's vision, the life of the dead is portrayed in powerful images:

> I have been up to the clouds above
> and down to the dyke full dark.
> Both have I seen the flames of hell
> and of heaven likewise a part.

> *Translated by I. Grøndahl*

There is an oppressive silence in the kingdom of the dead which is effectively described:

> Neither did my good horse neigh,
> Nor barked my dog aloud;
> None of the early birds did sing,
> They all to me seemed cowed.

> *Translated by I. Grøndahl*

From the north come the evil powers, led by Odin, who appears under the name of Grim the Graybeard "upon a jet-black horse." From the south come the hosts of heaven: "In front rode Michael, lord of souls, with Jesus Christ beside." Now Michael blows the "long horn," the trump of doom, and the souls of men tremble as they must appear for judgment. Each one is given his punishment to fit the crime: the murderer has to carry his victim, the stingy one must bear a cope of lead as narrow as his

---

[4] Tr. in *Studia Norvegica*, by Illit Grøndahl (Oslo 1946); also tr. as *The Dream Vision* by Theodore Jorgenson in *The Trumpet of Nordland by Petter Dass* (Northfield, Minn., 1954).

own soul. Those who have moved the boundary markers to cheat their neighbors are threatened with this punishment:

> The men I next came up with,
> They carried burning clay:
> God's mercy be with those poor souls
> That carried bournes away!
>   In the trial-porch
>   Shall stand the seat of doom!

Translated by I. Grøndahl

At the end is described the reward that will go to the kind and the helpful: "Blessed is he who in this life gave shoes to the needy poor." There are several different refrains, which bring out the poetic quality of the poem: "The moon it shines, and the roads do stretch so wide."

In Norway all poetry went over to the ballad form shortly before 1300. In Iceland the Skaldic strophe lived on, though in a new shape. The creator of the new meter, called the Lily Meter (*liljulag*), was Eystein Ásgrimsson. He was a monk, but was impelled by his stubborn spirit to break the monastery rules and was banned by the bishop. Twice he went to Norway, and he died as a monk in Elgeseter Monastery near Trondheim in 1361. His magnificent poem *The Lily* (*Lilja*)[5] is a tribute to the Virgin Mary. It has a splendid artistic composition, and a more deep-felt religious sincerity than anything else we have from the Old Norse period.

[5] Tr. Eirik Magnússon (London, 1870).

Ballads and Folk Tales

THE URGE TO SEEK renewal of one's national tradition by burrowing into the treasures of the past is not of equal strength at all times. In Norway the search for organic continuity between the medieval and the modern cultures reached a special intensity during the Romantic Era in the early nineteenth century. The men of that period were eager to heal the break that had taken place when Norway lost her standing as an independent country in the fourteenth century. It became a matter of national pride to find the link that joined the broken halves of Norwegian history. The unions of the Scandinavian royal houses which brought with them the peaceful incorporation of Norway into the United Kingdom of Denmark-Norway also led to the growth of organs for cultural life in Copenhagen and a corresponding dearth of written expression in Norway.

The link was found in the *ballads* and the *folk tales* which were current among the common people throughout the great gap in official literature.

Old Norse poems and sagas were still being recited in the twelfth century when the earliest ballads came into being. There are a few ballads that draw directly upon poems of the *Edda*. The story from the *Lay of Thrym* is retold in the ballad of *Torekall*, which tells of how Thor got his hammer back. The chief motif of the *Lay of Helgi Hundingsbani* reappears in the ballad of *Sir Hjelmen (Herr Hjelmen)*. Sigurd the Dragon-slayer is the hero of a ballad called *Sigurd Svein,* drawing its materials from such sources as *Gripir's Prophecy* and *Didrik's Saga.*

The Norwegian ballads are part of a common stock of ballads that were known also in Sweden and Denmark, some even in England, and many of them are preserved to us only in the Faroe Islands. It is not easy to be sure of the homeland in such cases, but scholars have concluded that the most characteristically Norwegian ballads were those that dealt with witchcraft, the so-called "troll ballads."

Troll ballads were often drawn from the stories told in the "lying sagas," which in turn go back to folk tales and popular legends. A favorite theme in these ballads as well as in the folk tales was the story of a troll who comes to the royal palace and demands the princess as his mate. In this ticklish situation the knights are cowed and helpless, but who other arises to save the day than the young page whom no one had noticed. The motif of boy-wins-princess sometimes requires him to do battle with the ugly trolls in their own country after a long and arduous expedition. There are other grisly creatures in this magic world, including a sea monster called the *draug* and a dangerous but handsome water sprite called the *nøkk*, or nixie. Mermaids provide a pleasant but no less risky diversion.

The search for sources of these materials leads us far afield in the realm of European folklore. The ballad of *Heming and King Harald* (*Heming og Harald kungjen*) combines themes from the saga about King Olaf Tryggvason and the legend of the matchless bowman which was later associated with the name of William Tell. The Sagas of Romance were pillaged for ballad motifs, so that we have the story of Roland in the ballad of *Roland and King Magnus* (*Roland og Magnus kungjen*), that of Tristram and Iseult in *Bendik og Årolilja,* that of Ywain the Arthurian knight in the ballads of *Kvikjesprakk* and *Iven Erningsson*. But there are also ballads with specifically Scandinavian material, as in the story of Young Ormålen who calls on his dead father in the grave mound to give him the magic sword. While this comes from the *Saga of Hervor,* other ballads reflect stories found in such sagas as those of *Hromund Greipsson* and *Orvar Odd. Åsmund the Bold* (*Åsmund Frægdegjæva*) builds on an Icelandic short story of the same name. Ballads like this must have been composed in Old Norse, but they lived on for centuries into the period of the modern Norwegian dialects.

In general, however, the ballads represented a sharp break with the Old Norse past, particularly in their poetic form. They came with a new kind of social amusement, the dance, and were made to be sung. The ultimate source of this entertainment appears to be France, probably by way of England, and it had reached Iceland as early as 1119. In that year a wedding is reported in *The Saga of the Sturlungs* as having provided "many kinds of entertainment, including dancing, wrestling, and the telling of sagas." The priests frowned upon the new amusement and thundered against it, but their caveats could not deter the people from gamboling on the green. We have the priests' word for it that people even forgot themselves on vigil nights in the church yards or at the sacred springs on Midsummer Eve, and passed their time dancing rather than watching.

The earliest words sung to the dancing were single stanzas, lyrical or satirical in content, no more than four lines in length. In their soft measures we can often glimpse the life of the times:

> Away I was by the icy crags,
> Where the snow did twirl about me;
> Many, alas, are the weary steps,
> We tread in the world so stoutly.

The strophe often referred to the dancing itself and could remain with the dance even after the entry of the narrative ballad, which came to Scandinavia either from England and Scotland or Germany some time after 1200. Each ballad had its refrain, which was repeated for every stanza. It did not always follow the stanza, but could be interpolated if the ballad stanza had only two lines. An example is the ballad of *Olav and Kari*:

> Olav was home for years full eight,
> —Tread me not too near!
> Before he would see his mother's face.
> —In the meadow my sweetheart is dancing.

The divided refrain here alludes directly to the dance. The noble ladies sang the second line, the knights the fourth, while one member of the dancing circle directed the singing of the ballad itself. Refrains were not necessarily associated with the theme of the ballad, and could be borrowed from one ballad for another. But often they did fit the story or part of it: "Where shall the young knight find his beloved?" "In the garden of roses there runs our steed." "Young Heming could steer his skis so well."

The number of different ballads preserved in Norway runs to something over 150, nearly all of them having been rescued from extinction by scholars who wrote them down from the lips of the people in the early nineteenth century. They are much fewer in number and in range of themes than the Danish ballads, but include some of the same ballads.[1] Compared to the Danish, the Norwegian tradition is conspicuously lack-

---

[1] Tr. E. M. Smith Dampier in Axel Olrik, *A Book of Danish Ballads* (Princeton, 1939). The ballads *Bendix and Olrun, Olav and Kari, Villemand and Magnhild, Margit Hjukse,* and *Steinfinn Fefinsson* are translated by Theodore Jorgenson in his *The Trumpet of Nordland* (Northfield, Minn., 1954).

ing in historical ballads, possibly because nothing much happened in Norway in the fourteenth century, when most of the ballads were being composed. The few that do tell us about kings and nobles are from about 1200, but they show more interest in private than in public affairs.

Taken as a whole, the ballads give us many fetching glimpses of life and thought in the Middle Ages. They tell us of the struggle between Christianity and witchcraft, of the duty of vengeance and courtly life, of unearthly piety and barbaric cruelty. *Ivar Elison* is like a family saga, concentrated and dramatic:

> The shirt has hung on the stony wall,
> No one has donned it again.
> The shirt has hung all soaked in blood,
> Since your blessed father was slain.

Others are like the "lying sagas" in their eagerness to exaggerate, as in *Roland and King Magnus*:

> The sun was darkened on its course
> By the reek of human blood.

Even though the characters of the ballads are types rather than individuals, they do reveal a new spiritual climate, especially in their attitude toward love. No hero of the *Edda* would have expressed himself in the words Bendik used to Årolilja:

> I think as well of thy golden hair,
> As of apples that bend the tree—
> Happy is he who makes thee his bride,
> God save him from loss of thee.

The mountains play a considerable role in the ballads, especially in the ballads of witchcraft. The mountains were the home of the demons, where the princesses were magically transported, and the heroes rescued them from a fate more cruel than death. Only one ballad hero mounts to the top; this is Young Heming who shows his skiing skill by slaloming down the mountainside. The descriptions of Olav Åsteson's journey in the *Dream Ballad* sound like a reminiscence of painful mountain crossings. But as a rule the nature we meet is a gentle one, quite different from the

ominous one of the Eddic poems. In the ballads we are more likely to find
spring and summer, with flowers in bloom, birds singing, and the squirrels
frisking in the linden tree. A great role is played by the noble game, the
hart and the hind:

> There grows so many a noble tree,
> The birch and also the lind;
> There play so many noble deer,
> The hart and also the hind.

The new gentleness is most apparent in the religious ballads, as we
already have seen it in the conclusion of the *Dream Ballad*. An even more
profound picture of Catholic Christianity is found in *Olav and Kari*, ulti-
mately drawn from an old Frankish legend, but here transplanted and
transformed in the spirit of a later age. The conclusion is matchless, with
its combination of homeliness and dignity:

> Kari came unto heaven's door,
> The Virgin Mary opened for her.
>
> The Virgin Mary brought her a seat,
> "Sit, little Kari, and rest your feet!"
>
> "You need not place a seat for me,
> I'm not too good to stand for thee."

Whereupon she intercedes with Mary on behalf of her worst enemy.

The structure of the ballads is episodic and dramatic, with much use of
dialogue, leaping from peak to peak without reference to the intervening
valleys. There is extensive use of repetitive stanzas, with only slight variation, to serve the use of the dance, but also to build up suspense, just as in
the folk tales. They are not sentimental, but take an objective attitude,
with short, vigorous characterizations, and frequently show an earthy
humor.

The ballads of the thirteenth and fourteenth centuries were composed
by or for the nobility and reflect its ideals of life. The scene is usually a
castle or a manor house, and there is much reference to silver and gold,
to silks and velvet. The characters are busy hunting with falcons or hawks,
or they joust in the gaming field either on horse or foot. But the ballads
were gradually taken up by the common people also, and from the fifteenth
to the seventeenth century these were the makers of ballads. A new kind

of stanza, the *nystev,* arose in connection with a form of entertainment that was much used at parties. This was a duel of wits where the contestants tried to outdo each other in verse making. The narrative ballads from this later period were usually jocular, sometimes even making fun of the knightly ideals, as in the one called *The Raggedy Boy (Fanteguten)*:

> The raggedy boy came riding his horse,
> The maiden combed her hair on the porch.
>
> "You needn't display your hair for me,
> I don't intend to make love to thee."
>
> "No matter if you court or no,
> I well am able to bid you go."

While the country folk went on making ballads in this newer style down to the nineteenth century, their efforts were rarely noticed by the learned. In the sixteenth century Master Absalon mentioned a ballad about Count Alv Erlingson and the false Margaret who was burned in Bergen. The oldest manuscript version of a ballad is from 1612 and the first to be printed is from 1647. Norwegian ballads are sometimes included in Danish collections from this period. But their real discovery had to await the nineteenth century and its search for the life line of Norwegian literature.

The prose folk-say that accompanied the ballads among the country people of Norway may be even less precisely dated and localized than the ballads. Folk tales were of many kinds, from wholly fantastic entertainment to the sober tales of local history. It is customary in Norwegian folklore scholarship to divide the tales into two groups according to whether they were believed or not. Those that are consciously imaginative and have no attachment to the real world are called *eventyr,* which might be rendered as "fairy tales," though they include many stories that are not about fairies or other supernatural creatures. Those that appear to have laid claim to credence are called *sagn* (German *Sage*), for which there is no adequate English word; some have used "legends" to translate it. The *sagn* is often localized to a particular person or place, appeals to the testimony of real people, and includes realistic details. The *eventyr,* on the other hand, takes place "once upon a time" and involves characters that are obviously types and have no local habitation. The distinction is often hard to draw, for we cannot always be sure of what people really believed. The *sagn* are obviously full of fairy tale motifs, while the *eventyr* may sometimes be localized.

The *eventyr* are even more cosmopolitan in their contents than the ballads. However Norwegian they may have become in their stylistic details through centuries of telling, nearly all of them can be traced to the stock of folk tale types that are common to all of Europe and large parts of Asia.[2] One of the stories that is considered to be purely Norwegian has won wide popularity in American storybooks for children, *The Three Billygoats Gruff*. Others that may be less authentically Norwegian but have found many readers in America are *The Gingerbread Boy* and *East of the Sun and West of the Moon*. The folk tales of Norway have become the best known of all foreign tales, next to Grimm's (and Andersen's, which are not folk tales at all), thanks largely to the translation by George Webb Dasent of Asbjørnsen and Moe's collections in 1858.[3]

These stories reached Norway at the most varied times. The Norse myths about Loki and the gods contained many fairy tale motifs, as did the sagas, both historical and unhistorical. The Normans in Sicily learned many stories from the Arabs and passed them on to Europe. They were carried further by pilgrims, crusaders, and merchants. The mendicant monks were among the most diligent spreaders of folk tales, for like modern revivalist preachers they loved to salt their sermons with stories that would hold the attention of their audiences. They would then reinterpret the stories in moralistic or symbolic terms.

In spite of their foreign origin, the tales have acquired a strong Norwegian coloration. This is especially noteworthy in their treatment of nature. When the Ashlad travels from horizon to horizon, he is making his way across Norwegian mountains, and the trolls he downs are in keeping with this nature. Its features are so much a matter of course to the narrator that he stops to describe them only when there is something supernatural about it. But there is also a strong infusion of daily country life behind the forests of gold and silver. We see the man cutting hay and his wife gathering sticks. We take part in the baking of *flatbrød* and the brewing of beer. Even the king, who dominates so many of the tales, has·acquired the shape of the local bigwig. There is little of the aristocracy left when he is pictured as standing on the doorstep to his palace, smoking

[2] For a discussion of these types and the role of the Norwegian folk tales see Stith Thompson, *The Folktale* (New York, 1946), esp. 17-18, 399, 467.

[3] *Popular Tales from the Norse* (Edinburgh, 1858); *Tales from the Fjeld* (London, 1874). These have frequently been reprinted under various titles. Later collections by other translators are: H. L. Brækstad, *Fairy Tales from the Far North* (London, 1897); H. and J. Gade, *Norwegian Fairy Tales* (New York, 1924); Sigrid Undset, *True and Untrue* (New York, 1945); Abel Heywood, *Norwegian Fairy Tales* (London, 1895); F. H. Martens, *The Norwegian Fairy Book* (New York, 1922).

a long pipe and amiably watching the passersby. He wears his crown like a hat and his ermine like a dressing gown that only barely covers his portly form.

Old materials and new have been molded together into a form agreeing with Norwegian traditions and environment. Jesus is pursued by wolves, exactly as if he were Odin himself. Greek and Norse giants are turned into trolls. The hero of the folk tale is the Ashlad, a character who has often been held to be the most Norwegian of all, though he is just a variation on the Horatio Alger theme of the successful boy. He seems lazy and indifferent at first, being called the Ashlad because he likes to spend his time stirring up the fire and loafing around the house. He is laughed at by his brothers, but his stupidity is only apparent. It is a mask he uses to cover up his basic qualities. He has genuine curiosity where the others are dull, and he is strong, kind, and quick-witted. One day he lets the mask fall, and asks for a chance to test his mettle. In a trice he outdistances the rest, and particularly shames his elder brothers, the teasing Per and Pål who have become synonyms for stupid mediocrity in Norway.

The style associated with Asbjørnsen and Moe's retelling of the folk tales is not one that is found in all parts of the country. Their stories are strongly marked by the jovial, often grotesque humor of the East Norwegian folk. Other parts of the country have other qualities. In Setesdal and western Telemark we find more of the old saga style, with a conscious verbal art extending even to the rhythm of the sentence. But a common trait of all Norwegian *eventyr* is their objective, superficially realistic manner. Even the most unlikely events are told with a straight face. This style is a means of making the fantastic seem real and reasonable. When the boy is on his way to Soria Moria castle, he does not hang on to the North Wind, but to its cloak. When animals and trees talk like human beings, this will scarcely appear credible to grownups. But it brings the situation to life when the fox talks with the dragon and uses the vocabulary of a pompous judge: "My dear dragon, I am afraid this will require us to conduct a local inquest." Such touches of realism help to make the characters at once real and distant, seen and imagined, whether we think of the good daughter and the bad stepdaughter, the trolls and the fairies, the devil and St. Peter, the Virgin Mary and the village tailor, or the Lord and the blacksmith.

The purpose of the *eventyr* is to entertain, but it may also contain an obvious moral. The good and the helpful are always rewarded. Now and then the moral is of rather doubtful value, as in *The Master Thief,* and occasionally there are glimpses of satiric intent, in the pictures drawn of the local authorities, the sheriffs, the judges, and the pastors.

The *sagn* or local legends are hardly to be reckoned as a separate literary form. They are often mixed with the *eventyr*, as in the story of the *Mill that Grinds on the Bottom of the Sea*, where a folk tale about the rich and the poor brother contains a legend explaining how the sea came to be salt. Each community and every period has had its *sagn*, some of which may have arisen locally but most of which are wandering tales that have been diffused from distant points. Nevertheless research has shown that folk memory can be amazingly tenacious, as when local tradition in Strinda claimed that an armed horseman was buried under a large rock in that community. Excavation showed that the horseman was there all right, bearing armor over a thousand years old.[4]

The *sagn* represent the interests of the people over many hundreds of years, and they include stories of the most varied kind: from encounters with all kinds of supernatural creatures by the local citizens to tales of the Black Death and other historical events of national significance. The only old king who remained alive in folk tradition down to the present was St. Olaf, concerning whose Christianizing of Norway the most fantastic tales have abounded in all parts of the country. Only in the mountain valleys of Setesdal, Telemark, and Hallingdal did traditions remain alive that were in any way comparable to the sagas of Icelandic families. But they lack the artistic quality of these, though they have many interesting details and dialogues. They bear witness to the human desire to fill one's everyday existence with elements that appeal to the imagination, without being in any way comparable to either the *eventyr* or the ballads.

[4] Some Norwegian *sagn* are included in William A. Craigie, *Scandinavian Folk-Lore* (London, 1896) and in H. L. Brækstad, *Round the Yule Log* (London, 1881), reprinted as P. C. Asbjörnsen, *Christmas Fireside Stories* since 1919.

Reformation and Humanism

"THE SPIRITS ARE AWAKENING! It is a joy to be alive!" wrote Ulrich von Hutten, the German humanist, knight, Lutheran, and poet.

Many others felt the same in the years after 1500. It was a period of spiritual fermentation, with new ideas in the air. The great explorers had widened the geographical horizon and men like Copernicus had opened up a new universe. The old globe was no longer the center of the world with the stars marching solemnly around it. Instead, the earth itself had been flung out into the firmament and took part in a circle dance around the sun. Men's ideas were also being disturbed in their courses. Scholastic philosophy, which was the logic of Aristotle applied to religion, no longer ruled undisputed. Through the study of Greek classics the humanists circumvented the theologians. From the Italian Renaissance a new conception of art spread westward and northward. Nor was learning as exclusive as it once had been, for printing was beginning to spread it to more and more people.

The sixteenth century has been called Europe's springtime. But spring is not merely a time of renewed light. It is also the period when the ice breaks up and April storms begin. Many stereotyped cultural forms began to dissolve, but so did that security of mind which the Catholic church had given. In those countries where the Reformation won, the insecurity was strongest. Belief in the devil grew, a more dangerous and menacing devil than the stupid one in the folk tales. He had many helpers. A professor in Basel calculated that there were 2,665,886,746,664 little devils in the world. With devil worship came the witch hunt.

Denmark took an active part in the awakening spiritual life of the times. Tycho Brahe made a European name for himself by his observations of the stars. Hans Tavsen, Jørgen Sadolin, and many others were early protagonists of the Reformation. Hans Mikkelsen translated the New

Testament as early as 1524, followed by Christjern Pedersen in 1529, while the humanist Povel Helgesen attacked the Lutherans and wanted to reform the Roman church from within. Niels Hemmingsen became the great theologian of the new movement, who made the University of Copenhagen a center of Lutheranism, even though he was later deposed as a "Crypto-Calvinist." Peder Palladius became the great agitator. Everywhere there was activity, from satiric writing to hymnology. In Sweden it was much the same. The New Testament appeared in Swedish in 1526 and the whole Bible in 1541. The early introduction of the Reformation led to a long and bitter struggle. The brothers Olaus and Laurentius Petri joined with Laurentius Andreæ in the battle against Catholicism. The tradition is old and venerable, said their opponents. "The devil is old and yet no better for that," replied Olaus.

In Norway there was no such spiritual springtide in the Reformation. The change of religion was introduced by compulsion, in most places completely without preparation. A few Lutheran preachers came to Bergen in the 1520's, but their efforts to remove some saints' images led to no spiritual controversies. Many of the priests were irritated because now they had to be Lutherans, and some of the country people carried their resistance to the point of killing a couple of new ministers. But there was no controversy that led to the creation of literary monuments.

The typical expression of the attitudes of the time is *The Hamar Chronicle (Hamarkrøniken)* of about 1550, probably written by an old choirmaster named Trugels. The author looks back sadly at the old days and touchingly describes the last Catholic bishop, Mogens, who was captured by Sir Truid Ulfstand: "As Sir Truid and the Bishop were walking together, and as the bishop came to the shore, he fell to his knees and thanked God in heaven for every day he had had. Thereafter he bade the canons and priests good night; then he bade Hamar Cathedral and cloister good night; then he bade the courtiers, the common people, the citizens and farmers good night, and begged them all to pray well for him, and said that he thought he soon would come back to them, but saying also: 'Oh God Father in heaven, if we do not meet before, then God grant we do so in heaven.' This prayer he uttered as he wept and said 'Vale, vale, vale.'"

The feeling that runs through *The Hamar Chronicle* was undoubtedly shared by many of the best men of the times. In the sixteenth century, Norway was at her lowest point, not only politically and economically, but also culturally. The last archbishop of Norway, Olav Engelbrektsson, who was also chairman of the Norwegian royal council, made the last attempt to assert Norwegian independence. When he had to flee, all was over. A short time later churches and monasteries were pillaged of their art treasures or torn down, the stones were used for fortifications or taken to Denmark, the church silver was melted down, and the old manuscripts, no doubt including sagas also, were burned as "papist" or used as covers of account books.

While Luther's doctrines thus led to national renaissance and consolidation in other countries, the Reformation in Norway became the beginning of a lengthy slumber. In this period also Danish became the written language of Norway. In our day this is often felt as the greatest loss, the great break in continuity. But it is a far too modern notion to think that it was so felt at that time. There was no conscious Danish policy behind this, as we can see from the fact than the Dane Erik Valkendorf had the non-Latin part of Brevarium Nidrosiense printed in Norwegian in 1519 (in Paris). His successor as archbishop, the patriotic Norwegian Olav Engelbrektsson, however, used a mixture of Scandinavian forms in his correspondence. That the Danes were not deliberately carrying on a linguistic Danification is evident also from the story of the Icelandic version of the New Testament which was printed and authorized in Copenhagen. It was translated by an Icelander who had a Norwegian father, had grown up in Norway and been educated at Bergen Cathedral School. That the Norwegians had to be satisfied with Christian III's Danish Bible (translated by Christjern Pedersen around 1550) was due to the fact that there was no longer any distinct written language in Norway.

The traditional forms of writing in Norway in the thirteenth century had been developed in Bergen and Trondheim. When the royal chancery moved to Oslo in 1229, a few characteristics of East Norwegian speech began to appear in writing. But the development toward a new Norwegian norm was interrupted by the union with Sweden and later Denmark. Mixtures of the three languages were common, and even encouraged by the monastic order of St. Birgitta.

In the meanwhile spoken Norwegian was developing rapidly in the same direction as other West European languages. The Old Norwegian structure with four cases of the noun and three persons in the verb was disappearing. Many old words were going out of use and new words were being borrowed from the nearest language of prestige, Low German. The Old Norwegian that was still being written, particularly in legal documents, was so old-fashioned and difficult that only the lawyers found it easy to understand. The new Danish written language was more modern in form, and easier to understand for people who lived in the Norwegian coastal cities or in some East Norwegian communities. Even Norwegian authors refer to Danish as "the language we now speak in Norway," and they describe their own written language as "the Danish or seacoast Norwegian which everyone can understand."

Another factor in the development was the absence of printers in Norway, which required Norwegians to have their books printed abroad, usually in Denmark. Not until 1643 was a book printed in Norway.

The mileposts in the change from Norwegian to Danish are as follows: Royal documents were written in Danish from 1450 on. Around 1553 the first Danish Bibles came to Norway. The church law was in Danish, as was the catechism and the hymnbooks. The old Norwegian law codes and many legal documents in the country communities were still in Norwegian in the sixteenth century, but by 1600 the Danish language had won a firm position in all spheres of life. In Norwegian pronunciation it had become the spoken language of the cultivated class, while the old dialects lived on as the daily speech of the country people and the less privileged classes in the cities.

From the middle of the sixteenth century faint reverberations of humanistic ideas begin to be heard in Norway. They do not lead to any loosening of religious orthodoxy or liberation from superstition, but they do encourage the founding of a historical-topographic literature which remained an important aspect of Norwegian cultural life down to the eighteenth century and later. Men like Master Absalon and Peder Claussøn are not impressive for their learning in Greek and Latin, but should be remembered for their warmhearted interest in Norwegian nature and history.

Like some of the Italian humanists, these Norwegians were fascinated by the ruins of ancient greatness in their own country, and the deplorable fact of present-day impotence under foreign rule. They were less interested in the geniuses of the Renaissance than in such pedestrian antiquarians as the papal secretary, Blondus Flavius, a man who wrote the history of Rome from the fifth to the fifteenth century, and books about the antiquities of Rome and the topography of Italy. The weakness of Norway led to a search for knowledge about its past and hopes for its future.

The center of this movement was Bergen, Norway's largest city, which was also the home of Norway's most important seat of learning, such as it was, the Cathedral School. In Bergen there was a constant source of conflict between the Norwegians and the merchants of the Hanseatic League.

In the sixteenth century Norwegians were beginning to assert themselves against the commercial dominance of the Hansa in their own country. The humanists sympathized with this spirit and felt it both a moral and national issue to oppose the Hanseatic merchants, "a flock of rude, impertinent blackguards, who come into this kingdom, scorn Norway, and say that there have never been either kings or noblemen here," to quote the words of Master Absalon.

Absalon Pederssøn Beyer was born in 1528 on the farm Skirdal by the Aurland Fjord in Sogn. He lost his parents early and was sent to school in Bergen by an uncle. Here he was adopted by the Bishop (or Superintendent, as he was then called) Geble Pederssøn, "for which he has his everlasting reward and shines more brightly than the sun," as his stepson later wrote. In 1544 Geble sent the boy to Copenhagen, where he lived in the house of another bishop, the above-mentioned Peder Palladius. From here he proceeded to the best known of all Lutheran universities, Wittenberg, where he studied with Palladius's friend Philipp Melanchthon for two years. He then took his Master's degree in Copenhagen and became a lecturer in theology at the Bergen Cathedral School. Later he was notary of the cathedral chapter and chaplain at the castle of Bergenhus. He died in 1575.

Absalon was far from the only Norwegian who studied abroad in this period. German universities were often visited by Norwegian students. But Absalon must have had a more thorough education than most of his contemporaries. The men who trained him were all humanists, from his foster father Geble to the famous Melanchthon. He even followed the example of his teachers at Wittenberg in organizing dramatic performances among his pupils, the first known performances in Norway. Absalon mentions one of these in his diary, a play called *Adam's Fall* (*Adams fald*), which "I, master Absalon, caused to be acted here in the churchyard with great trouble and expense." The acting was so successful that one of his pupils kept as a nickname a term used about him in the play and, because of this, he later got into a quarrel which led to his death. The custom of school plays was a favorite diversion in many countries, recommended by men like Luther and Melanchthon.

Absalon's keen interest in the life about him is attested by the notations in his diary, which is preserved to us under the name of *Bergen's Chapter Book* (*Bergens Kapitelsbog*). He began his diary in Latin, but shifted to Norwegian in 1561. His intimate description of life in Bergen includes with equal impartiality news of the Seven Years' War and town gossip concerning street fights, drinking, and whoring, the persistent rainfall of Bergen and strange signs in the heavens. But we also get a vivid picture of the author himself. In the midst of his sermon of December 30, 1565, "large rocks fell down from the steep mountain above the school." He departed at once from his text and held a thunderous sermon about "the neglect which parents in this city show in the upbringing of their children." He attacks the morality of his times in vigorous terms and calls Bergen "thou ugly sister of Sodom and Gomorrha." But we also get pleasant glimpses of his family life: "On the same day my daughter finished learning her ABC-book, after she had gone to school for 12 weeks." His descriptions of dramatic events are sometimes as graphic as that of the old sagas: "Then Lasse thrust his dagger into Christopher's breast, and Christopher his dagger into Lasse's heart. Christopher at once sat down in a chair and died. But as Lasse turned and was going to leave by the door, he fell, and neither of them ever spoke again."

Absalon had a deep veneration for the Danish governor of Bergen, Erik Rosenkrantz, whom he always thought of as a Norwegian because of his Norwegian mother and close connection with Bergen. Rosenkrantz was actively trying to break the stranglehold of the German merchants on Norwegian trade, and one of the weapons in his struggle was the historical support that men like Absalon could give him. The judge Mattis Størsson (d. 1569), who was one of this circle of Bergen humanists, wrote the story of how the Hansa first had established itself in Norway. As he presented it, this was one unrelieved tale of violence, deceit, and encroachment. He also produced *Chronicle of Norway* (*Den norske Krønicke*), chiefly based on Snorri, which served as an inspiration for the others who worked with the subject in this period. When it was printed in 1594, it was the first printed account of Norwegian history. Another judge, Laurents Hanssøn, who lived in Bergen for a short time in the 1550's, also tried his hand at translating the sagas about early Norwegian kings.

The chief product of the Bergen circle, however, was Absalon's own *Concerning the Kingdom of Norway* (*Om Norgis Rige*), written in 1567 and easily the most learned book written in Norway till then. But its chief interest derives from the national feeling that illuminates it. Absalon tells the history of Norway in the light of the contemporary situation. He finds a useful analogy in the life of a human being: Norway has had its childhood, its adolescence, its vigorous youth, and even its full manhood. "Then Norway was honored and respected; then she had a golden crown on her head and a gilded lion with a blue axe." But it is a law of history, which Absalon had learned from Melanchthon, that kingdoms flourish for only 500 years. Like certain modern historians, he believed that kingdoms have their life cycles, with "fatal periods." "From the day that Norway fell under Denmark and lost its own kings and masters, it has also lost its manhood strength and power, and is now growing old and gray-haired and so heavy that it can no longer carry its own wool." In this "raving old age, in which she is becoming a child once more," Norway has permitted the Germans to plant themselves firmly on the cliffs of Norway, and when they once "have the Norwegian sand in their shoes," it is not easy to get them out again. But suddenly the author turns on his readers: Norway still has some "strength, wisdom, and power," and he describes the gifts God had given to the country. The patriot takes the upper hand in him, and bold ideas rear their heads: "Yet might Norway still awaken from her sleep some day, if she got a good regent over her. . . ." No wonder that the Danish scholar Ole Worm in the seventeenth century accused Absalon of "tribuere affectibus" (giving in to his feelings).

Peder Claussøn Friis (1545-1614) was neither so learned nor so far-sighted or sensitive as Master Absalon. He was the vigorous Lutheran pastor, who worked among the people and did not draw back even from a fist fight at a Christmas party. His attitude to the Norwegians involved no dreams, but a highly realistic awareness of their qualities in the present. His experiences with his own parishioners has taught him that the Norwegians "have always been a hard, contrary, disobedient, self-willed, restless, rebellious, and bloodthirsty people, as I cannot deny that they still are." In particular he declared that the people of Telemark were "shameless devils who carry on adultery, murder, manslaughter, heresy, prostitution, fighting, and other vices that go with these."

His attitude may be colored by the fact that he never went abroad where he could compare other nationalities with his own. He lived his entire life on the peaceful southwest coast of Norway. Born in Egersund and educated in Stavanger, he held a pastorate in Audnedal where he succeeded his father. Although he lived in this remote region, he quickly won a reputation for learning, particularly in matters relating to the history and customs of Norway. None of his many writings were printed during his lifetime, but they were widely known through handwritten copies. They were written in a simple, but informative style, and were diligently used by later writers.

In spite of his pastoral condemnation of the Norwegians, he showed good patriotic fervor in his choice of themes. One of his books was a description of *Animals, Fish, Birds, and Trees in Norway*. He also wrote of the history of Norway's old colonies, Iceland and Greenland. He compiled a topographic description of the Stavanger diocese which he later expanded to a work entitled *Description of Norway* (*Norriges Bescriffuelse*). But the most famous of his works was a translation of Snorri's *Heimskringla* and other royal sagas, which first appeared in print in 1633 under the title of *Chronicle of the Kings of Norway* (*Norske Kongers Chronica*). In a revised edition of 1757 it came to be the favorite reading of the Norwegian people. More than any other single work it prepared Norway for the resumption of national existence which was thrust upon it in 1814.

Peder Claussøn, as he is usually called, was thus a true son of the Renaissance in his zeal for learning and his keen eye for nature. He does not often go out of his way to express personal feelings, but in a passage that was struck out by his Danish publisher he significantly pointed out that "there was always in former ages an inborn hate and bad agreement between Danes and Norwegians, which remained in the Norwegian people's hearts and nature down to this day." For a loyal subject of Denmark-Norway this was going a bit too far. In spite of his sober style, we can often perceive his pleasure in Norwegian nature, and his love of the bear hunts and the daily pursuits of the country folk which he describes in great and concrete detail. Even his severity can be tempered by a glint of humor, as when he writes about the twigs of the birch tree: "They are used chiefly for switches to be applied to children in schools and homes, for which reason the birch must be reckoned a blessed tree among all others."

In spite of the work of these and other learned men, the sixteenth century was not a period of great spiritual advances. Lutheranism became a state orthodoxy, while superstition was rampant among the common people. In 1590 Master Absalon's widow, Anne Pedersdotter, was burned as a witch, although the clergy of Bergen tried to save her.[1] Even Peder Claussøn and the author of *The Hamar Chronicle* had no doubts about the existence of the sea serpent. The so-called Oslo humanists contributed little to general enlightenment, since most of their work was in Latin. Best known in his time was the theological lecturer at the Cathedral School in Oslo, Master Halvard Gunnarssøn, who composed a history of Norway in Latin verse, as well as some bucolic poetry. His writings

---

[1] A play by H. Wiers-Jensen, *Anne Pedersdotter*, tr. by John Masefield (Boston, 1917), was written about this episode.

were all printed in Rostock in Germany between 1596-1606. He reached the people only with his translation from the German of *Spiritual Question Book* (*Aandelig Spørgsmaalsbog*, 1602). This was intended to provide entertainment at parties to replace the excessive drinking which he felt was characteristic of the younger generation. This predecessor of the modern quiz program gained extraordinary popularity and was reprinted in innumerable editions. An example of its spiritual level is the question: "Where is it written that God watches over our hair? Answer: In Matthew 10 Christ says: But the very hairs of your head are all numbered." The book was popularly called "The Pastor's Torment," which one can well understand. The general interest in this book is indicative of the cultural horizon in the sixteenth and seventeenth centuries.

Petter Dass and the Baroque Age

THE SEVENTEENTH CENTURY has been called the Age of Learning, but also The Prosy Century. The whole era is characterized by dry-as-dust learning. Only one Norwegian writer of the period has needed no dusting off, namely the pastor at Alstahaug, Petter Dass. On his best works the dust has never had time to settle.

But in general the dust lies thicker on the yellowed folios of this period than on anything written by Norwegians either before or since. There was more literary activity than in the centuries preceding, but much of it consisted of learned interpretations and commentaries, dogmatic hair-splitting and philological speculations, endless adulatory verse and verbose sermons. We get some impression of its spirit when we read Holberg's *Erasmus Montanus,* where he lashed the Latin disputations of his own later day, which were carried on more for the sake of seeming learned than for advancing knowledge. Yet one can sometimes blow the dust off the old writings and gain a picture of the people behind them, feel the personal anxieties behind the theological polemics, the vitality in the baroque and bucolic verse, the local patriotism in the topographic descriptions, the humor in the travel accounts, the religious sincerity in the contorted hymns.

In many ways Norway won for herself a more satisfactory position within the union with Denmark during these years. We find no more of the anti-Danish outbursts that characterized some of the earlier writers. Economic progress and participation in common wars led to the growth of a Dano-Norwegian patriotism which was not incompatible with a feeling of pride in the traditions and accomplishments of Norwegians.

It is an expression of this local nationalism when Christen Jenssøn, a pastor in Sunnfjord, gathered Norwegian dialect words into his *Norwegian Dictionary or Glossary (Den Norske Dictionarium eller Glosebog,*

1646). For the most part, however, it appeared in the many topographic descriptions which ministers and teachers published during these years. There were historians, too, like the Icelandic-born Tormod Torfæus, who was royal historiographer and called attention to the Norwegian claims on Canada through the Norse discoveries of America in the eleventh century. A less critical spirit was the pastor Jonas Ramus, who tried to prove that Odin and Odysseus were one and the same and that his Charybdis in reality was the great maelstrom in northern Norway.

In general, however, the writings of this period were more cosmopolitan than national. The learned wrote for one another, chiefly in Latin. This was the period when the imitations of classical bucolic poetry flourished in all Europe. Shepherds and shepherdesses with Latin names were considered far more interesting than the everyday farmhands of Norway. The program was to create an art poetry in the taste of the times, to dignify the Danish language by using it in forms hallowed by the models of antiquity. Versifying was even a favorite method of social advancement, for an applicant for a position could count on greater favor if his application was in verse. Classical verse schemes were adopted bodily without regard to their suitability for Danish. The main concern was that the verse form be absolutely regular. The great teacher for the Scandinavians on this point was the German Martin Opitz, who created a school with his *Buch von der deutschen Poeterey* (1624).

Around the middle of the century the baroque style appeared in Dano-Norwegian literature, religious and secular, in the style of writing as well as in the adornment of the books themselves. We need only look at the title of a pastoral treatise by one Knud Sevaldssøn Bang published in 1651: "The Sweet and Fine-tasting Breast-Milk of the Catechism, Extracted from the two Breasts of God's Love, the Old and the New Testament." Poetry was cluttered up with elaborate imagery, and showed a special fondness for allegories and plays on words. The writers were free in their use of contrastive and drastic expressions, a mixture of dread and faith, a need for describing darkness, storm, and fire, or mankind in a battle against the elements which would have been hopeless but for the intervention of God. In spite of all that to our taste seems artificial and hollow, we can occasionally feel the dramatic tension between ecstatic joy and crushing sorrow in the poets' hearts.

A typical representative of the Dano-Norwegian literary world was Anders Arrebo, born in Denmark, but Bishop in Trondheim for a time. He was a disciple of his age and used the whole classical apparatus of deities to describe the forces of nature. His poetry is full of learned digressions, artificial word combinations, quaint comparisons, all in the spirit of late humanism and the baroque. His poem *Hexaëmeron* (written about 1630, printed 1661) was built on a French poem and described "The World's First Week's Six Days' Splendid and Mighty Deeds." The valuable parts are the description of North Norwegian nature, the sea, the maelstrom, the Norwegian rivers, the whales, and the bird life. He describes the magic methods used by the Lapps in hunting the great auk, and specially praises the hardy and useful reindeer. Even if his poetry has some charm, one feels that he was writing as a stranger and for strange readers. But even though he lacked Norwegian home-feeling, he was one of the men from whom the pastor Petter Dass could learn.

There are others who may be reckoned as the predecessors of Dass, even though their products have little value. Dass did have one contemporary who was personally known to him and with whom he exchanged rhymed letters, Dorothe Engelbretsdatter (1634-1716), whom even Holberg called "the greatest poetess the Northern kingdoms have had." There were not many to choose from, so he may have been right, but her poems on religious themes were favorites for a long time. She was even granted full remission of taxes by the king, the first poet's stipend in Norway. Her collection entitled *Song Offering of the Soul* (*Sjælens Sangoffer,* printed in Christiania in 1678) finds little interest today, though it was a favorite in Norwegian valleys for centuries. We enjoy better her exchanges of poetic coquetry with the Reverend Petter. The great hymnologists of the period were not Norwegian but Danish, above all Thomas Kingo.

The special position of Petter Dass (1647-1707) in his times was due to the qualities that still keep his work alive: the stamp of reality which his best writing evinces, and the heartfelt generosity, the lively imagination, the spontaneous love of nature, and the playful earnestness that infuse it. His luxuriant verse may seem verbose at times, but charms us again and again. His popularity through three centuries is also due to his identification with his own people, his harmony with the essential resonance in its character. He became an educator of his people who succeeded in combining theological learning with everyday common sense.

He was born at North Herøy in Alstahaug parish, not far from the church which he served most of his life. He was sent to the Cathedral School in Bergen, where he read the comedies of Terence and learned to write Latin verse. After this he studied in Copenhagen for three years, and he tells amusingly in his verse of the poverty with which he had to contend: "A penny then was as welcome as a dollar now." "In the shop I found some handsome books; the owner told me: 'Produce the money, and you shall have them.' But I had neither goods nor inheritance from my blessed father." His pockets were empty, his clothing was ragged, but nevertheless he won his way into the learned world and could dispute on theological matters in Latin verse. The difference between him and the others of his age lay in the contact which he maintained with the common people. Learning did not swallow him up and separate him from his own background. He became the poet of everyday life among a hardy people. In spite of the baroque touches in his titles and his style, there is breadth and vigor in his writings, which harmonizes well with the fantastic contrasts of nature in northern Norway.

The masterpiece that carried his name far and wide among the people, though it was never printed in his lifetime, was his *Trumpet of Nordland (Nordlands Trompet)*.[1] This description in verse of Nordland, or the three northern provinces of Norway, was begun in 1678 and not completed until around 1700. By this time he had learned to know the life of the people in the north in all its phases, for he had lived among them as teacher, chaplain, and at length as parish pastor. His long, descriptive poem begins with a greeting to the people themselves, and it is obviously not written for the learned world, but for the laity:

> Be greeted, ye men who inhabit the North,
> The master who guides and the servant at work,
> Be greeted all men who wear homespun!

The vigorous meter which runs through the entire poem matches well with the active spirit of his description. The nature he portrays is the sea in storm, dotted with shipwrecks, floating oars and rudders, corpses in their fish-stained jackets. But he also knows the beauty of the glassy sea on a summer evening, when the hundreds of boats rock in the midnight sun and the fish dart around like streaks of silver.

> Thou lively cod! how I near had forgotten
> Thy leaping and jumping and jolly cavorting
> To note in my writings at all.
> How handsome thy dance around Midsummer tide
> When the sun is aloft and the weather is fine!
> 'Tis enough to quicken one's heart.

Throughout the *Trumpet of Nordland* there is a lively air of energy

[1] Tr. as *The Trumpet of Nordland* by Theodore Jorgenson (Northfield, Minn., 1955).

and good humor, whether the poet is describing the life of the people, the minister's activity, the relations of the fishermen to the merchants in Bergen, or a misfortune at sea. His unshakable faith in God makes him look confidently at dangers that would blanch a weaker man. His pastoral duties led to constant journeys at sea in all kinds of weather, and he was familiar with the thought that the sea might become his grave. There was no sentimentality in him, and his orthodoxy was so deeply rooted that he took little interest in the theological controversies of his day. But he was deeply concerned that the people should learn their religion and morality in a pleasant form, and he spent much of his time turning the religious texts of the church into verse.

The most important of his efforts in this direction were his *Catechism Songs* (*Katechismus-Sange*). While one of his colleagues published an eight-volume commentary on the Catechism, the Reverend Petter made the whole thing clear to those who were supposed to learn it by writing songs which were sung by fishermen at sea and shepherd boys on the mountains, even as far as the Faroe Islands. In these songs he is the representative of the state and the church, the Confession of Augsburg and the law of King Christian V. But his authoritarian purpose does not prevent him from showing the most realistic understanding of pedagogy. Under the Fifth Commandment ("thou shalt not kill") he gives his readers a description of anger personified as a woman, which could hardly help having its effect:

> She causes wrinkles in your forehead,
>   She twists your mouth in fearful ways,
> Transforms you to a devil horrid,
>   Fills your lips with raging foam.
> Your eyes she spreads so very wide
>   As if in each there dwelt a fiend,
> And to your face she drives the blood,
>   Till you're suffused with ruddy mien.

His religious poetry reflects a deeply personal piety which sometimes reaches the monumental. Usually it is earthbound, however, and brings us personally close to the man himself. He is severe, to be sure, but also willing to forgive when people do their duty and are obedient. The examples are homely ones, taken from daily life in Norway rather than from exotic countries. It must have been a blow to this active personality when his health failed around 1700. Even his vision gave way and others had to copy out his poems. He tells it in his own vivid way:

Before the letters were thin as threads,
But *now* they stand like cables.

Other afflictions are reflected in his later poems, the pains of a gallstone infection, the burning of Bergen in 1702. But always the emphasis was a positive, constructive one, reflecting his courage and unquenchable optimism.

His books were read in handwritten copies during his lifetime, printed and reprinted in many editions after his death. His *Spiritual Pastime* appeared in 1711, the *Catechism Songs* in 1714, the *Trumpet of Nordland* in 1739. Around 1800 it was said by Sivert Aarflot, who knew the country folk of Norway: "Petter Dass's songs have had the greatest share in the education and morality of our people."

Ludvig Holberg

IN NORWEGIAN LITERATURE the eighteenth century and Ludvig Holberg are synonymous terms. All that this century represented in the shape of wit and common sense, of awakening cultural life, of widening intellectual horizons, is concentrated in this one man. There was no form of letters practiced by the men of his century in which he did not also try his hand. In some of them he achieved a distinction which has kept his name alive as the one true genius in the joint literature of Denmark and Norway. In both countries he is affectionately referred to as "Father Holberg." His statue stands by the Royal Theater of Copenhagen as it does by the National Theater of Oslo, and his plays regularly come back to their stages. He is claimed by both countries, and he will bulk equally large in the literary histories of both. The fierce exclusiveness of modern nationalism has made it hard for Norwegians to accept Holberg as the citizen of both kingdoms that he was. Norway was the country of his birth, which he always cherished; but Denmark was the country of his achievement.

In this, as in other matters, Holberg was not pedantic. For there was no type of personality he abhorred more than the pedant. This may have been due to the ease with which a man in his occupation of professor could fall into just that weakness. He was, indeed, compelled to associate with obvious pedants in the University of Copenhagen. But his definition of pedantry was much wider than the usual one. He found pedants everywhere, not just in university life. In his comedies, which only occasionally deal with academic people, there are nevertheless many who are called pedants and there is much ridicule of pedantry.

He once wrote an essay in which he explained what he meant. Pedants, he wrote, are "the kind of people who treat bagatelles with respect and who immerse themselves so much in useless subtleties that they forget their chief duties and most urgent concerns, who busy themselves with the husk and neglect the kernel, and fall in love with their own follies."

First of all, he says, there is the *learned* pedant: "He searches with such zeal for the origin and etymology of Latin and Greek expressions that he can produce no etymology for his own children, but has to say: 'Ask my substitute!'" But there is also the *court* pedant: his classical authors are the tailors and wigmakers. Then there is the *state* pedant: his passion is state secrets, and he carries it to such absurd lengths that he resembles the secretary who did not dare tell anyone that the burgomaster had gotten ink on his handkerchief, "since police affairs must be kept secret." There are pedants in the *law* who employ as "many useless subtleties and unimportant distinctions in the law as in philosophy." Even Mars has his pedants just like Apollo, for the military show theirs in absurdities of military drill and in their purely perfunctory duels. "You can wrap a pedant in a lion's skin and arm him with the club of Hercules: he still remains a pedant." Even the orthodox theologians come in for some of his sharp comments on pedantry.

Only in one social class did he find very little pedantry, namely among the peasants: "One can say that of all classes no one is freer of pedantry than the peasant class." But they were in turn badly ridden by superstition, which Holberg ridiculed with almost equal vehemence. "Needles, pins, and shavings are your gods," declares the saucy Pernille to the superstitious Roland in the play *Without Head or Tail.*

Holberg's critique of pedantry on the one hand and superstition on the other is an expression of the rationalistic philosophy which led him to take the "middle course" in all things. He poked fun at extremities of all kinds, whether they were extremities of orthodoxy or of radicalism.

There was occasion enough for this in his own country. Toward the end of the seventeenth century Denmark-Norway had lost contact with the great currents of intellectual life in Europe. The passion for humanity which had been the criterion of the true humanists and awakened their interest in historical and philological study had turned into pure formalism. Orthodox religion and Latin grammar had combined to change a love of learning into a method without content, a subtle sophistry of knowledge.

This was peculiarly true of metaphysics, the teachings concerning the supernatural, which had largely been inherited from medieval scholasticism. This gothic structure was sublime in its consistency, at least as elaborated by Thomas Aquinas, magnificent in its harmony. Even before the Reformation it had been hollowed out by the newer scientific views, but many of the Protestant men of learning at Copenhagen were still wrapped up in this structure and unable to raise their sights beyond it. Metaphysics was to them the supreme test of formalistic learning, because it gave the speculative method, the "philosophia instrumentalis," free rein, unchecked by observable facts. Sublimity was replaced by subtlety, spirit by learned cant, consistency by pedantic methodology.

The superstitions of the common people flourished in part precisely because of the indifference to their problems shown by the learned. Every unusual event was popularly interpreted as an omen of something else. If a peculiar herring was caught in the Kattegat, it was a sign of impending catastrophes. If a little girl was born with some odd-looking formations on the top of her head, it was thought to be a warning of the Lord's displeasure with the new fashions in women's hats. Books were published around 1700 in which such ideas were advanced in all seriousness, making even the Lord into a kind of super-pedant.

Holberg's task became that of clearing the air in Denmark-Norway of the trend toward pedantry. This was one of the contributions of eighteenth-century thinking in general, and Holberg here brought the Twin Kingdoms into harmony with the best thought of his times. He asked that orthodoxy give way to common sense, that Latin be replaced by the native tongue, and that purely learned studies yield to practical inquiries into the nature of man and his world. These were ideas he advanced in all his writings, seriously in his essays and histories, more lightheartedly and effectively in his comedies and poems.

Of course he did not succeed in uprooting pedantry, for every age has its pedants. But he delivered a vigorous blow at the pedantries of his age, and the hearty laughter with which he cleaned house in the stuffy Denmark-Norway of his day has continued to resound ever since. The wind he raised began by blowing the powder off the wigs, and ended many years later by blowing the wigs clear off.

Ludvig Holberg was born in Bergen on December 3, 1684, as the youngest of twelve. His father, Lieutenant Colonel Christen Nilssøn Holberg, was a farm lad from Trøndelag who had worked his way up from a private's rank, an unusual accomplishment in those days. He had been in the service of Malta and Venice, had wandered on foot through all of Italy just to satisfy his curiosity, had taken part in the Norwegian wars with Sweden, and had been sent as a truce negotiator to the English during the battle of Bergen in 1665. The author's mother, Karen Lem, must have been a thoughtful and energetic woman. She was descended from a distinguished and widely ramified Bergen family of merchants and government officials. Ludvig lost his father when he was just a year old and his mother when he was eleven. He was sent to his mother's cousin, the pastor Munthe in Fron in Gudbrandsdalen, bearing the nominal title of corporal. He may have been intended for the army, but, if so, the plan was dropped and he was soon sent to the Latin school in his native city.

There are a number of traces in his works of the association with Norwegian farmers, but the years in Bergen meant much more to him. He must have spent much time strolling about and observing the lively traffic of Norway's greatest seaport and center of commerce. He was small and delicately built, so that he took no part in the fist fights of his school companions. He merely "attended" them, as he puts it. He used his eyes and reported on many comical episodes of his youth. There was the time when the citizens' guard was having drill, and the commander could not remember in a hurry the (German) expression for "right about face." Instead he said: "Now turn your rumps back to the City Hall!" When people laughed at him for this, he answered: "It is all the same, just so the thing gets done." This Holberg uses as an illustration of a man who was not a pedant and of whom he therefore approved. Like the disrespectful servant Henrik in his comedies, he must have had a keen sense for comical situations, a ready laughter at all pomposities, and a strong sympathy for practical solutions.

Holberg was here expressing a view which must have been widely held by the citizens of his native Bergen. They were solid, practical merchants who felt a distaste for the useless ostentation of the nobility. He tells with admiration of the merchants at the Bergen dock that they were so busy they hardly had time to reply to a greeting. They did not hesitate to take a hand in the work, and would roll the barrels of fish themselves if it was necessary. They were hard-working, economical, and orderly, qualities which he later came to value very highly. There is none of the aversion of later romantic writers here for the "bourgeois"! The highest ideals of the bourgeoisie were also Holberg's.

He carried this spirit into the Latin school where he entered upon a career of learning. The principal, Søren Lintrup, was a great lover of Latin disputations, the ancestor of our modern school debating. He was so proud of the work of his pupils that he even had some of the best disputations printed in a learned journal. But Holberg never learned, he wrote later, "how many predicaments and predicables Logic could put into the field in case of war." He was a diligent enough pupil, but was clearly more interested in the life of the city round about him, which reminded him of a veritable Noah's ark because of the many strange creatures in it, as he later wrote.

Holberg was graduated in 1702 and spent a year or so in the nearby district of Voss as a tutor in the house of the local pastor, occasionally even substituting in the pulpit. The country folk liked his sermons, he tells us, but the pastor was less pleased, for they lasted only a quarter of an hour. Holberg's impertinent reply was that "if tautologies and unnecessary repetitions were removed from the pastor's sermon, we would have spoken at equal length." This activity was merely a digression in Holberg's life, as were his theological studies at the University of Copenhagen. He matriculated there in 1702 immediately after his graduation, and returned after his school teaching to take a degree in theology in 1704. No sooner was he back in Bergen than his wanderlust got the better of him. He disregarded the well-meant advice of his elders, sold the little he had for sixty dollars in cash, and embarked on a ship to the Netherlands. Perhaps he wanted to see the scenes of the War of the Spanish Succession; perhaps his father's example lured him; perhaps he just wanted to see the world. In any case he never returned to Bergen.

This first foreign journey of Holberg's turned out to be a failure. His age, his health, his finances were all inadequate for the trip. It ended in a retreat to his native land, but this time to the town of Kristiansand on the south coast. Here he eked out a living by giving lessons in French. He must have been something like the Erasmus Montanus whom he made fun of in his famous play. He had people saying about him: "This is the learned chap who knows so many languages: he can talk French, Italian, Polish, Muscovite, and Turkish." He shocked the good citizens by first maintaining and then retracting a thesis he had read in a Dutch book, attempting to prove that "women are not human beings," much as Erasmus Montanus proves that his mother is a stone. He had a rival in a Hollander who happened to be in Kristiansand and also professed to teach French. They agreed to hold a public debate to show whose knowledge of French was the greater: "I fenced with him in Norwegian-French, and he parried with his French-Dutch so that I do not believe the French language has ever been worse mistreated. Both of us spoke badly and incomprehensibly enough when we were by ourselves, but it must have been manifold worse in the state of anger which then possessed us." At length, he says, they made a compact to divide the business.

While the Dutch adventure must have meant something to Holberg in spite of his difficulties, it was the later journeys that gave him his perspective and enabled him to inaugurate a new age. In 1706 he went to England and stayed there for two years, studying history at Oxford while he made his living by teaching French and flute playing. England was highly congenial to Holberg, and the practical nature of English scholarship and literature must have reinforced his own bent in this direction. His own views were closely akin to those of the English essayists of Queen Anne's reign, such as Addison and Steele, and he wrote works later in the vein of Swift. But there is no direct reference to his reading of English literature during these years, and we can only assume that he spent most of his time working in the Bodleian Library on the first of his numerous works concerning modern European history, his *Introduction to the History of the Leading European Nations* (*Introduction til de fornemste Europæiske Rigers Historier*). It was not published, however, until 1711, after he also had spent the winter of 1708-1709 traveling in Germany. His home when he was not traveling came to be Copenhagen, and he was now aiming at a professorship in the university. He gave a series of four lectures which reflect admirably his experiences and interests at this time: on travels abroad, on the value of history, on the pleasures of music, and on the knowledge of languages.

Holberg's interests were broad and stimulating, and his publications showed an attraction for contemporary events and recent history which was quite unusual in his time. His historical works were in a modern key, written to be read and not for the sake of increasing learning.[1] But his greatest task was still ahead of him, and the stimulus to this work came on his journey to France and Italy in 1714-1716. He was again in Paris in 1725-1726, but the decisive influence came in his youth.

Two names that come back again and again in Holberg's writings are those of Pierre Bayle and Molière. His plays are written under the aegis of Molière and his critical spirit was shaped in the school of Bayle. These were the two greatest contributions of France to Holberg's development, though there were many others, including the essayist Montaigne and the historian Montesquieu. The critical spirit of the age was expressed by writers in other countries also, but all of them could be read in the

---

[1] One of his historical works is translated into English: *An Introduction to Universal History*, tr. Gregory Sharpe (London, 1755).

libraries of Paris. There was the radical philosophy of Spinoza in Holland, the ideas of Leibnitz in Germany who tried to unite philosophy and Christianity, the experiential philosophy of John Locke in England which found expression in his *Essay concerning Human Understanding*. Philosophy and history emerge as disciplines independent of theology and biblical chronology. But of all these Bayle was Holberg's chief stimulus, and he tells how he stood in line outside the French Bibliothèque Mazarine with other students eager to get in first so they could read Bayle's *Dictionnaire historique et critique* (1697). This arsenal of eighteenth-century rationalism was not a dictionary at all, but a philosophical encyclopedia, in which Bayle used the footnotes to express his doubts about the soundness of orthodox thinking.

But Holberg did not use his time primarily to learn from books. He traveled on foot from Rome to Paris and got thoroughly acquainted with life in all parts of southern Europe. When he returned to Denmark, he was made professor; the chair he was offered was that of metaphysics, his most detested subject. He showed his distaste by first delivering an inaugural lecture, which he said himself was more like a funeral oration than an encomium of his subject, and then by proceeding to turn away from all serious writing to flirt for a time with the poetic muses.

This change surprised everyone, including himself. He later called it a "poetic fit, or seizure." It began when he wrote a poem in the manner of the Roman satirist Juvenal entitled *The Poet Advises his old Friend Jens Larsen Not to Get Married* (1719). This was a vital question for himself at this time, now that he had reached the age of thirty-five and had a position. In one of his later autobiographical writings he says that until he was forty he could not support a wife and after that he could not make her happy. But the main poem in the satiric vein is his comic epic *Peder Paars* (1719-1720).

It has been suggested that this poem is Holberg's contribution to the controversy that was then raging in Europe between the ancients and the moderns, or in other words, between those who thought that the Greek and Roman classics were better than the modern writers and those who defended the latter. This fits well enough with one aspect of the poem, its external form as a parody of the classic epics, particularly the *Æneid*. He makes fun of their ponderous gravity by telling the story of a most unheroic hero, a Danish tailor's apprentice, who undertakes a short trip from one Danish town to another in order to see his sweetheart Dorothea. The adventures that attend his voyage are greatly mag-

nified by having the Olympian gods interfere for and against him, but
in the end he never gets to his destination because the author lost interest
in finishing the work. Holberg was getting in a lick at the traditionally
accepted superiority of the ancients over the moderns, as we see from
the mock-heroic opening in classic style:

> I tell about a man, whose fate and gallant actions
> Should be in full recorded in every land's transactions;
> I sing about a hero, the mighty Peder Paars,
> Who undertook a journey from Kallundborg to Aars.
>
> ———
>
> He did not, like Don Quixote, leave his native town
> For mere adventure's sake, to win himself renown.
> Nor like Ulysses or Æneas did he strain
> To conquer men; he only wished to see again
> His darling Dorothea. A journey of some miles,
> Could it be worth such trouble, strife, and many wiles?
>
> ———
>
> But Envy! Though a long time thou didst rage and foam,
> At length thou hadst to see him safely home
> With people's admiration, with honor, fame return.
> See to it, that from such examples thou dost learn
> That him you hate the most, for him you clear a path
> To honor, make him strong and brave, though marked for death,—
> That hate like thine most frequently its purpose misses,
> And persecution turns a Peder Paars into a great Ulysses.

But the main burden of the poem is its satire on Holberg's own contemporaries. He has a whole gallery of comic figures, of whom his
unheroic hero Peder and his sly, plebeian squire, also named Peder, are
the best. He ridicules pedants, exposes the greed and ignorance of the
people, lashes the pettifoggery and stupidity of the bureaucracy. His
portraits stirred up anger in some quarters, but Holberg was in high
favor and could afford to laugh at his detractors. Criticism did not abate
his "seizure," rather the contrary.

In 1722 Copenhagen got its first Danish theater. Since 1720 Holberg
had been professor of Eloquence, which meant that he had been refreshing his knowledge of classical literature. The theater was directed by a
Frenchman who wanted Danish comedies for his repertoire. Holberg
became the man who supplied his wants. It was as if a dam broke within
him, and the comedies flowed from his pen. In fifteen months or less

he wrote fifteen plays! He had his motifs already in *Peder Paars* and the satires. Now it was just a matter of giving his types dramatic life, of shaping them in the round, and sending them forth on the stage.

The models for Holberg's plays were the best possible ones, the comedies of Plautus and Terence, and above all Molière. The intrigues in his plays are often traditional, and so are some of his characters, e.g. the braggart officer (Miles Gloriosus). But he always transplants them to native soil and builds on his own experience. His relation to Molière is not that of a pupil, but of a rival. He lacks completely the undertone of pain and passion behind the comedy of Molière. But he is a better portrayer of social manners and has more skill in comic situations. Molière's fools are ridden by their passions and are quite incurable, while Holberg's are the victims of objectionable habits and can sometimes be cured by a sound beating.

Holberg's comedies are marked by his experiences in Bergen, his travels abroad, and his meeting with Copenhagen. He kept his eyes open wherever he went for the "ridiculous in humankind." But he was also aware that he himself possessed some of the qualities that could serve as materials for a comedy. There is reason to believe that *The Weathercock* (*Den Vægelsindede*) was his first comedy. The main character, in comical female disguise, is a self-portrait, and from this play it is not far to *The Restless One* (*Den Stundesløse*). But Holberg also had some of the argumentative Erasmus Montanus in him, or the foppish Jean de France, or even the Political Tinker.

The Political Tinker (*Den Politiske Kandestøber*) appears to be the play that suited Holberg best.[2] He found expression here for his annoyance at all kinds of irresponsible prattle. It is a caricature on political life and as such retains its freshness. Here we meet the windbag Herman von Bremen, who knows everything better than everyone else. Among the other characters we find the political romanticist in Sivert the baggage inspector, who raves about the vikings, the cocksure Gert the furrier, who would like to whisper something in the ear of the Elector of Mainz, the phrasemaker Franz the cutler, who has no opinion of his own and always opposes the others with his "but—," and the perpetually dissatisfied Richard the brushmaker, who complains about the authorities but casts his vote on the same side as Niels the clerk—who is absent. Their Political College is a mock city council, in which the discussions as usual are a mixture of brazen self-interest, hypocritical phrases, intoler-

---

[2] Tr. O. J. Campbell and F. Schenck, in *Comedies by Holberg* (New York, 1914).

ance, and stupidity. When it is proposed that "certain families might be excluded from the highest positions of authority," the mentality is precisely that of our modern totalitarians.

Still more realistic in its psychology and its comic effects, if not in its plot, is the comedy of the peasant in the baron's bed, *Jeppe of the Hill* (*Jeppe paa Bierget*).[3] This is the portrait of the oppressed Danish peasant, his daily life and inmost thoughts, fleeced as he was by the bailiff, beaten and cuckolded by his wife, a sot who is at once kindly and brutish, but who is also full of gentle wisdom, a weak but witty man, without pride or character, but great in the simplicity of his heart. The plot is a well-known European motif which Shakespeare had also used in the prologue to the *Taming of the Shrew*. But the character that Holberg created in Jeppe was his own, a dramatic picture of human degradation which is said to have had its effect in liberating the Danish peasant. Holberg elsewhere refers to the Norwegian peasants as "noblemen in miniature," so that he could hardly have drawn his portrait from experiences in Norway. But the main theme is Holberg's fear of the tendencies to brutality and dictatorship which the too rapid release of the common man from his bondage might bring with it. In spite of his sympathy with the people, he was not a democrat in the sense of a Thomas Paine or a Thomas Jefferson.

Perhaps the most universally valid of Holberg's plays is *Erasmus Montanus*.[4] This raises the question: what is the real goal and purpose of education? Does learning have any value in itself, or is the important thing the relationship of man to his knowledge? Erasmus is a figure who borders on the tragic, but it only makes the comedy more poignant that he is right in his assertion of the earth's roundness. Rasmus Berg, alias Erasmus Montanus, might for a moment lead our thoughts to the great martyrs of science like Galileo and Giordano Bruno. But only for a moment! For the ex-peasant boy of Zealand is not being impelled by love of truth, but by love of self, his reputation as a man of learning, the ridicule of his learned friends in Copenhagen. His concern is not to find the truth, but to win the argument: "If anyone says this table is a candlestick, I will defend the statement. If anyone says that meat or bread is straw, I will defend that too. I have done so many a good time." The theme that gives this comedy its enduring value is its satire on half-digested learning, on the tendency of the semieducated to bluff others

[3] Tr. in *Comedies by Holberg* (New York, 1914).
[4] Tr. in *Comedies by Holberg* (New York, 1914).

with their fragments of knowledge. In our time Erasmus might have held forth on vitamins, relativity, or atomic fission. Among the other unforgettable types of this comedy is Peer the deacon, a village oracle, ignorant but sly, and always ready to make an extra penny: "I have arranged things so that I can say to a peasant . . . when it comes to scattering earth on the casket, 'Will you have fine sand or just common, garden dirt?'" Common sense also has its spokesman in Erasmus's unspoiled peasant brother Jacob. He is a true philosopher of the English school when he comments on Erasmus's argument proving that Peer the deacon is a rooster: "I should like to know whether, when Monsieur wins the dispute, will Peer thereupon be turned into a rooster?" When Erasmus admits that he will not, Jacob replies: "Well, then you lose the argument."

The most rollicking of Holberg's comedies is *Ulysses von Ithacia,* which combines the satire on pomposity with a parody of the popular German plays of his time, in which no attention was paid to the rules of classic drama concerning unity of time, place, or action. Heroic phrases and banal talk are mixed in the most comical way, and we are continually reminded that the ridiculous antics of gods, heroes, and clowns are mere reflections of human behavior: "Likewise with us!"

In many of his comedies Holberg made use of stock characters. All his Jeronimuses are akin, being conservative, opinionated, and often superstitious or mean and stupid. All his Henriks and Pernilles are rogues and plotters, with an impish repartee and a masterful grasp of every situation. The lovers, who often are named Leander and Leonora, are Holberg's least successful characters. They are mere cogs in the machinery of plot, and lack all individuality. Holberg is at his best when he can make up odd characters with some obvious failing, the braggart, the pedant, the society lady, the drunk, the witch, the chatterer.[5]

When Holberg returned from his last journey abroad in 1726, he published *Metamorphoses,* a Latin travesty of Ovid; and he wrote the first of his three autobiographical epistles in Latin. But he felt as if his poetic seizure were passing: "My blood is getting quite phlegmatic, according to my barber . . . so that I have resolved to conclude an everlasting peace with the world." There were outer factors as well, such as the fire of Copenhagen, the bankruptcy of the theater, and the victory

---

[5] Other plays of Holberg's are available in *Four Plays by Holberg,* tr. Henry Alexander (New York, 1946), *Seven One-Act Plays by Holberg,* tr. Henry Alexander (New York, 1950), and *Three Comedies,* tr. H. W. L. Hime (New York, 1912).

of pietism when Christian VI came to the throne and frowned on light amusements. Holberg wrote a piece called *The Funeral Service of the Danish Comedy*. Some years later, in 1748, the Danish theater was again opened under King Frederik V. Holberg wrote six comedies for the new theater, but they somehow lack the festive spirit of his early production.

Instead, Holberg turned to other forms of writing in which he also won renown. Perhaps this resulted from his achievement in 1730 of the professorship in history which he had always wanted. He wrote work after work concerning the history and topography of Norway and Denmark, as well as the history of the Christian Church and the Jews, and biographies of famous men and women. He published altogether something over 3,000 octavo and 6,000 quarto pages. He was not a research man, in the sense of one who makes small conquests in the field, but he was a keen critic of general theories who judged the events of the past from his knowledge of human nature and his logical views. He did not write for the learned, but for a new, cultivated public. He had the optimistic faith that one could learn from history, and he believed in moralizing. He discussed the great problems of history, the causes of advancement and failure on the part of whole peoples and cultures, and the causes of conditions in his own period. His clear and elegant style, his sense of humor which constantly finds expression in anecdotes, and his aversion for phrases and solemn nonsense made people read his historical works. In the Norway of his day they were probably more read than the comedies.

Holberg was not a good teacher, and in his later years he withdrew more and more into other kinds of work, particularly the financial administration of the university.

But he was not yet through with literature. His moralizing urge found expression in two popular forms of eighteenth-century writing, the imaginary voyage and the moral essay.

His imaginary voyage was intended to carry his ideas out beyond Denmark-Norway and was therefore written in Latin. *Niels Klim's Underground Journey* (*Niels Klims Underjordiske Reise*) was a satire on mankind which Holberg printed in Leipzig in 1741.[6] A Danish version by his fellow townsman Hans Hagerup appeared the year after. Holberg used the name of an old character he had known in Bergen, a precentor and book dealer who was distantly related to him. He lets this man

[6] Tr. as *Journey to the World Underground . . . from the Latin of Lewis Holberg* (London, 1755) and *Niels Klim's Journey under the Ground*, by John Gierlow (Boston, 1845).

examine a cave near Bergen and fall through the earth's crust into another world. Niels Klim then enters a series of countries that are caricatures of European states. There is a country where monkeys are in charge, and he wins great renown by introducing wigs. In this country everyone is concerned with ceremony, useless learning, hairsplitting legal decisions, disputations on abstract and impossible themes. But he also gets to a country called Potu, whose name is an inversion of Utopia. Here the peasants are at the top of the social scale. Women have the same rights as men, a favorite idea of Holberg's. The Potuans are highly amused by Niels Klim's report of the laurels he won in Copenhagen by doing research on the slippers of the ancient Greeks and Romans.

The story reminds us of other satiric travel accounts of the period, above all of Swift's *Gulliver's Travels,* but is less bitter in its tone. Nor does it approach Holberg's own comedies in creative power. The humor is no longer as vigorous, and the poet shows his age by his allegorical and symbolic mode of expression. But it is his most courageous work and was vigorously attacked, particularly by the clergy whom Holberg had not dared to attack in his comedies.

It was Holberg's ambitious plan to "recast the Dano-Norwegian public in another form." To carry this out, satire was not sufficient; he also had to state his ideas affirmatively and stimulate his readers to think for themselves. This he did in his *Moral Thoughts (Moralske Tanker,* 1744) and five volumes of *Epistles (Epistler,* 1748-1754)[7] which were in effect moral essays as we know them from Montaigne to Addison. We meet him here as the mature and thoughtful philosopher: "I consider that it is the philosopher's primary duty to examine accepted opinions and inquire whether or not they are well founded." But we also perceive the contrasts in his own nature more clearly, the struggle between his temperament and his ideals. On the one hand his temperament was nervous and choleric, impatient with stupidity, eager to exaggerate and fall into extremes, something he often held to be Norwegian qualities. On the other hand there was the classic ideal which he sought to attain, self-control, harmony, the need of following the "middle way," all that he praised the Danes for but which perhaps irritated him a bit also. In these essays Holberg is more personally present than in his other works, witty and incisive, truth-seeking and skeptical, unsnobbish and without superiority of caste feeling. He is both social and individualistic in his views. He

[7] Forty-nine of Holberg's epistles have been translated by Phillip M. Mitchell in *Selected Essays of Ludvig Holberg* (Lawrence, Kans., 1955).

abhors nothing more than "to live in a brutish unanimity like the dumb beasts." He encourages intelligent discussion: "For by disagreement the truth comes to light." But the highest of all requirements is Socrates' dictum, which he used in *Erasmus Montanus* and kept repeating in his essays: "Know thyself!"[8]

His religious views were tolerant, but in no way radical. He emphasized that faith is a personal matter: "I know that I shall gain salvation by my own faith and not by that of the parish pastor." Faith must be based on doubt, he maintains, and he extols the value of reason as the basis of a humane Christianity. He is not without a feeling for the mystical, but he does not wish to believe anything that is opposed to the evidence of the senses or that would reduce the majesty of God. He opposes orthodoxy on the one hand, sectarian fanaticism on the other, and he distinctly rejects Voltaire and the atheists.

Holberg was a faithful adherent of the enlightened despotism and a loyal citizen of Denmark-Norway. But he also had an interest in demonstrating the independent and equal status of his homeland Norway within the union. His cosmopolitanism kept him from being a patriot in the modern sense, but his interests pointed in the same direction as the Norwegian historical-topographic authors who preceded him. Without intending it, he even created occasional slogans for later agitators, as when he wrote that the Norwegians are one of the bravest people on earth because of the cold "which drives courage and boldness into the marrow and the heart." He also wrote about the twin kingdoms: "Denmark could be regarded as a lake which forever pours its waters into the great sea from which they never return, while Norway is like a river that runs into the same lake and thereby prevents it from being so quickly dried out." More important for Norwegian national feeling than this fallacious image was the simple fact that he was born in Norway.

Personally Holberg was a lonely man, a somewhat fussy bachelor, a bit of a hypochondriac. He was particular in money matters, even after he had become a baron and a wealthy proprietor. In his later years he found his best company among simple people, peasants and old ladies, or in playing his flute. Study became for him a substitute for an active life. When he heard from the doctor that he would not live long, he said: "It is enough for me that in all my life I have tried to be a useful citizen of my country, and I will gladly die since I feel that the powers of my soul are weakening."

He died on January 28, 1754.

---

[8] Cf. *Memoirs of Ludvig Holberg* (London, 1826).

Holberg's Successors

In the second half of the eighteenth century the poets of Denmark-Norway expressed two different and partially conflicting views of nature. The predominant enthusiasm of the times was for the orderly and productive landscapes which sustained life and increased prosperity. This had also been Holberg's view, who in spite of his fondness for Norway could not but regard her mountains as "aspera et horrida" (difficult and fearful). At the same time and often in the same authors there was a growing sense of the beauty and grandeur of nature in its virgin state. Rousseau's slogan of "back to nature" was heard in Denmark-Norway also, and writers were familiar with the works of such English poets as Pope and Thomson, *Die Alpen* by the Swiss Haller, or the German Klopstock's "seraphic odes." Since Norway had much more of "nature" in this sense than Denmark, the influence of this current in European poetry was to awaken a new interest in Norway and her wild mountain fastnesses. Norway's torrents and snow-capped peaks, her freedom-loving yeomen and their simple ways became fashionable themes for poetic apostrophizing.

The first Norwegian poet who clearly reflected this combination of rationalism and preromantic nature enthusiasm was Christian Braunman Tullin (1728-1765). His elegant and musical poem *The May Day* (*Maidagen*, 1758) won great acclaim, even from a critic and poet like Lessing. Although Tullin's father was a country lad from Gudbrandsdalen, he himself was an urban type, a merchant and city councilor. Using ideas drawn from Haller and the English poet Young's *Night Thoughts,* he became the first Norwegian poet to describe nature for its own sake. His poem is elegant and charming, but highly artificial in its fashionable nostalgia for the simple life: "Come, my Muse, and let us flee this melancholy prison." He did not succeed in giving a personal or national stamp to the foreign form. His Norwegian scenes are essentially murals in Swiss or English water colors or French rococo: "the sapphire-blue firmament," the "crystal mirrors" of the waves. The same is true of his other poems, in which we often find a combination of this stylish enthusiasm for nature with a keen eye for the practical values of life. They deal with such themes as "The Origin and Effects of Navigation" (1760) and "The Excellence of Creation with Respect to the Order and Connection of Things Created" (1763).

The period was one in which Norway made tremendous strides forward both materially and culturally. The growth of commerce and industry altered the balance of power between Denmark and Norway so that Norway could no longer be thought of as a mere province. Culturally Norway formed something of a counterweight to the overpowering German influence in Copenhagen, particularly Klopstock. A Royal Norwegian Scientific Society was established in Trondheim in 1760 on the initiative of Bishop Johan Ernst Gunnerus, who also tried to persuade the Danish government to establish a Norwegian university. Historians and men of learning like Gerhard Schøning arose who made it their chief task to study the history of Norway and lay the foundation of a special Norwegian school of history. Norwegian dramatists like Niels Krog Bredal and Johan Nordahl Brun won acclaim on the Danish stage.

The hearth of Norwegian national culture during these years was the so-called Norwegian Society (*Det norske Selskab*) which came into being among Norwegian academicians at the University of Copenhagen in 1772. This was not a political club, but a purely literary one with regular and irregular meetings at Madame Juel's coffeehouse. The emphasis was on good fellowship, encouraged by the punch bowl which formed a central feature of every get-together. The members wrote verse or prose and read it aloud to their fellows, discussed the literary problems of their times, and enjoyed each other's wit. They even gave prizes for the best verse and published a couple of anthologies. The general spirit of the group was one of aversion to the preromantic bombast of Klopstock and his Danish pupils, such as Johannes Ewald. They chose as their motto a passage from Horace: Vos exemplaria Græca (Let the Greeks be your models). The opposition between them and the Danes was therefore an aesthetic one which gradually developed into being also national. The Norwegian students were more conservative in their adherence to a rationalistic view akin to that of Holberg at a time when their Danish friends were accepting the new romanticism.

In its best years, around 1780, the society had as many as 120 members, of whom about a dozen were writers. But only one was a really notable talent, Johan Herman Wessel. He was not a poet of deep feelings or ideas, or a prophet with philosophic or patriotic passions. But he was a genius in a miniature field, that of the epigram and the parody. His special talent was that of the biting wit, whose happy improvisations in the circle of friends have become enduring parts of Dano-Norwegian literature.

Wessel was a pastor's son born near Oslo on October 6, 1742. He studied at Christiania Cathedral School, graduated with a high record in 1761 and then went on to Copenhagen for his higher education. That was the end of his career, however, for he became a so-called perpetual student, who never took the trouble to complete his work or find himself a permanent position. He gathered a great fund of knowledge, being accomplished in English and French, and knowing German, Spanish, and Italian. But his life was spent between the cafés and badly paid hours of tutoring or translating, with poor health and creditors as the unending torments of his life. There are points of contact between his experience and that of such poets as the Swedish Bellman or the French Villon.

If one were to find a basic idea in his poetry, it would be this: why bother? This is the burden of his jesting verse to be placed on his own gravestone:

> He drank with zeal, was seldom happy,
> His shoes were leaky as a sieve.
> He couldn't be bothered to do any work,
> At last he didn't bother to live.

He expresses the same idea in many ways. He makes a comparison with his brother, the mathematician Caspar Wessel: "He traces maps and reads the law. He is as diligent as I am lazy." But he also says it indirectly in one of his comic tales: "Listen," said Jupiter, "I can't be bothered. . . ." It was said in Copenhagen that no one could pronounce the words "why bother" with such energy as Wessel. The only good serious poem we have from his hand is a passionate defense of sleep.

Like his great Scandinavian contemporaries, Bellman and Ewald, Wessel was no success as a citizen, being intemperate, slovenly, and irresponsible, a bohemian who burned out at an early age. His great and overpowering passion was his love of good poetry. However kindly and tolerant he might be in private life, he was contemptuous of writing that seemed to him stilted, obscure, or false. He was influenced by English and French literature, and while he admired the classical French tragedy, he can scarcely have been fond of its pseudoclassical imitations, like Voltaire's *Zaïre*. His major work is a parody on just this kind of writing, the unforgettable *Love Without Stockings* (*Kierlighed uden Strømper*, 1772). This carries on the tradition of Holberg's *Peder Paars*, but like that poem it has a wider significance than that of the purely literary parody.

It is a satire on all poetic artificiality, all false solemnity, on big words that cover small actions, and on bourgeois vulgarization of the fate motif. His hero Johan is in a real quandary; on his wedding day he finds himself without them. He cannot marry without them, and fate has announced that unless he is married that very day, he will never be married. Johan is a most unheroic hero, being only a tailor's apprentice, but his sweetheart's confidante Mette says to him that it doesn't matter how cowardly he really is, just so he says the words that heroes say. Then everyone will think he is a hero. Nor does it matter if he steals himself a pair of stockings, if only he first goes through the motions of a debate between virtue and temptation, like every other hero on the stage. It does not even matter that he happens to steal while virtue has the upper hand. Johan is typed as the tailor of humorous tradition, with skinny legs and bad complexion from his unhealthy occupation. He is cowardly and fussy, more concerned with outward than inward qualities, and his fine customers have taught him to speak in elaborate turns of phrase.

All the characters are desperately attempting to live up to the requirements of classical tragedy, but fail at every turn. Johan's rival Mads is a rougher character than he. His difficulty is that he cannot add, he confuses furies and graces, and worries about living up to the role of tragic hero. Grete, the heroine, is a natural enough girl, but contorts herself trying to play the part of a heroine. Her plebeian taste for peas, herring, and pork, and her habit of immoderate swearing give the lie to all her social pretenses. There are also two confidantes, one female and one male, who frequently discuss how they are to manage things so that they will have the properly heroic touch. The characters all take themselves with inordinate seriousness, which makes them irresistibly comic. Their speeches are a charming mixture of high-flown rhetoric and everyday banalities. They sing parodic arias, with lines like these: "In my heart's fireplace there burns a resined brand of love which is lighted at both ends."

The plot is pure mechanics and conspicuous at all times, while the characters are marionettes marched around by fate. The action is restricted to a single day and place: Grete has her fatal dream, the lovers and the confidantes meet, Mads's trunk is examined and the theft discovered, the peas are eaten, and they all die—in the same room. This does not necessarily mean that Wessel rejected the classical unities of time and place, but he did show how artificial and unreal they could become.

The rest of his writing consists of epigrams and comic tales, all in verse. These are pure wit, without pretension to serious ideas. They point a finger of scorn at stupidity, or jest with a friend's qualities, including his own, as in the verse quoted above. His model in the tales was the Frenchman La Fontaine. His verse has a coquettish air, quick and elegant, with an unexpected twist at the end which is underscored by a surprising rhyme.

Wessel married in 1780 and had a son of whom he was very fond. But the marriage was not a success, for Wessel was unable to assume the duties of the family father. He was too much of an ironist, a melancholy man who wanted to laugh and be merry among his boon companions, a man who lived in the moment in order to forget. He died of typhoid, poor and miserable, only forty-three years old, on December 29, 1785. The tragedy he had thought of writing was completed only in his own life.

Nearly all the other members of the Norwegian Society returned to Norway after their student days or served Norway in other ways. But one can hardly conceive Wessel outside the atmosphere of Copenhagen, and certainly nowhere in the countryside. Like a character from Max Beerbohm he satirically wrote in one verse: "—but good Lord, everyone knows what a field looks like when it is green!"

Of the other members one of the most broad-minded and critical was Claus Fasting (1746-1791). From 1777 to 1782 he published in Bergen, the city of his birth, a newspaper called *Provincial Papers* (*Provinsialblade*). This early journal discussed the problems of the times somewhat in the spirit of Holberg, but from an even more rationalistic point of view. He was an admirer of Voltaire and advocated his ideas, so it is no wonder that he felt lonely and misunderstood in a bourgeois society like that of the trading city of Bergen. Though he had a quick, journalistic pen, he never managed to create any works of lasting artistic merit.

A much deeper impression was made by the writings of Johan Nordahl Brun (1745-1816), who had none of the intellectual qualities of Wessel or Fasting. He was a born leader, ambitious and self-possessed, assured that "all good Norwegians think as I do." His personality was the most powerful among the poets of his age, and he displayed it in many different forms, including lyrics, dramas, hymns, and sermons. He was at once pious, jolly, and argumentative; he could be charming and gracious, but also grasping for power.

Brun's early career in school was most unpromising, but in Copenhagen he unexpectedly blossomed out with a tragedy *Zarine* (1772), which may have been the stimulus to Wessel's parody *Love Without Stockings*. The same bombastic air filled his next work, the patriotic tragedy *Einer Tambeskielver* (1772), which was drawn from Snorri's *Heimskringla* and became the first Norwegian saga play. Brun's nationalistic purpose was made clear in an introduction in which he declared his desire to raise monuments to the ancient heroes of his country. He himself was born near the scene of his hero's life in Trøndelag, and felt a pious duty toward this part of Norwegian history. It was in the same year that he wrote the first Norwegian national hymn, one which came to mean a good deal more than he had probably intended. This was the song *For Norway, Land of Heroes* (*For Norge, Kjæmpers Fødeland,* 1771), which contained the surprisingly bold words:

> When once we get our dander up,
> We sweetly dream of freedom,
> But some day we may wake once more
> And break our chains and serfdom.

The song was later called a "Norwegian Marseillaise" by Henrik Wergeland, but he also noted that Brun's own life did not live up to it, and felt that it was not really Brun who spoke these words, but the "innermost of Norway's heart." The song, he said, was "spattered with wine, rather than blood." The Dano-Norwegian government showed its displeasure by confiscating it, and it was not published in any of Brun's collections of verse until after 1814. But it was widely known and sung, even when its father ignored it.

Brun was one of the leading figures in the founding of The Norwegian Society, but he never felt at home in Copenhagen. He was a red-blooded, outdoor man who wrote: "For my part I feel most at home when it is so cold that a journalist would freeze to death." Many of his best poems reflect his experiences in the Norwegian mountains, where he had climbed and skied from his early days: "We who are born among the cliffs find a special delight in climbing up on the steepest heights even when we could plod along in all comfort on the plain and in the valleys." As a bishop and leading citizen of Bergen he played an important role, but did not always feel that the environment gave sufficient nourishment for his literary ambitions: "Here we see nothing but business, hear of nothing but currency rates, shipping freights, codfish, and herring." Yet he felt very much at home, and became the spiritual authority of the city. He was himself thoroughly loyal to the existing institutions of his country, and he deprecated the spirit of the French Revolution and such radicals as Fasting, though he could show occasional glimpses of liberalism on such topics as lay preaching or women's rights. When the Dano-Norwegian union was dissolved, he agitated for complete Norwegian independence, but once the union with Sweden had been established in 1814, he accepted it with the respect for the *fait accompli* which is characteristic of men of his type.

Another Copenhagen student who became a poet-preacher was Claus Frimann (1746-1829). He won his chief popularity through *Songs of the People* (*Almuens Sanger*, 1790) and *The Singing Sailor* (*Den Syngende Søemand*, 1793). These contain vivid pictures of the life of the people, but without notable inspiration. His patriotic poems could be vigorous, and some of them are still remembered. A much finer talent was that of Edvard Storm (1749-1794), who never returned to Norway, but who created the first really poetic dialect verse since the ballads. His poems in Gudbrandsdal dialect express his own longing for the life of his boyhood in the mountain parsonage, and a number of them are still sung. The most popular of his poems, however, was *The Ballad of Sinclair* (*Zinklarvisen*), written in Danish ballad style, but expressing patriotic sentiments.

The last of the student poets was Jens Zetlitz (1761-1821), born in Stavanger and educated in Bergen. His patriotic tone, with its emphasis on the rough vigor of the Norwegian, is common to these later writers of the eighteenth century. But above all he was the heir of Wessel, the poet of club life, who celebrated the pleasures of the grape. Even in his Stavanger pastorate he was not averse to lifting his glass and singing the jolly songs that he had composed in his youth. With wine and song came also women, and his poetry includes some very fine love lyrics, in which nature and love enter into a close harmony. Some of his poems to his wife Elise are among his best work. His religion was one of this world, and pietism was far from his thoughts. He was an enemy of all sentimentality, and in his gay, worldly outlook he was not unlike his great-grandson, the novelist Alexander Kielland.

By 1800 political and democratic interests had supplanted the purely aesthetic ones among most Norwegian poets. The practical tasks that faced Norwegian leaders were absorbing their attention in a period of strain and distress for Norway. Literature in Norway fell far behind in comparison with that of Denmark and Sweden. There was no genius in Norway comparable to the Swedes Esaias Tegnér or Erik Gustaf Geijer, or of the Dane Adam Oehlenschläger and his followers who were laying the foundation for the literary golden age in their country. While the Danes and Swedes were creating a poetic and modern literature, the Norwegians were laying instead the foundations of a modern constitution.

A Young State and an Old Kingdom

THE MOST CHARACTERISTIC DOCUMENT of its times and the most significant Norwegian work of letters between 1790 and 1820 was the Constitution of 1814. The fathers of the Constitution were men who not only had experience in public affairs, but were also bearers of a broad humanistic culture. The artistic writing of this period appears feebler than that which preceded or followed it, and forms an intermezzo in the history of Norwegian literature. One reason for this was the momentousness of the political events, which drew the interests of the leaders away from art. Most important of all was the fact that these years saw the change-over from Copenhagen to Oslo (or Christiania, as it was then called) as the literary capital of the country. The Norwegian contributions to literature in the preceding generation had been a part of the common literature of Denmark-Norway, stimulated by the active literary life of Copenhagen. Oslo had been a mere provincial city, which as late as 1820 had no more than 15,000 inhabitants. Previous to 1800 there was only a modest cultural or artistic life in this city. Bergen had the richer traditions, being both a larger and a more flourishing city, but here, too, the dominant interest of the citizens was in trade, not culture.

The problems that faced the new Norwegian state in 1814 were so great that many good men doubted that they could be solved. It was necessary to build a sound economy, and at the same time maintain political independence within the union with Sweden. This meant a vigilant eye on the new partner, who obviously had the upper hand, and a perpetual assertion of the rights guaranteed by the Constitution. National symbols, such as the separate flag and the celebration of May 17 as the national holiday, were needed to awaken the patriotic emotions of the people, and therefore became important subjects of controversy during the early years of the state.

More difficult still was the cultural task that lay ahead, that of turning a provincial culture into a national one in a people of scarcely one million. The problem was one of recovering a treasure that had been lost at the same time as a new treasure was being created: an independent culture based on the old traditions but also modern and European in its form. It was a problem of keeping up with the times, but not letting oneself be swallowed by the current. Only a few optimistic souls like Henrik Wergeland dared to dream that it might be possible to reach a level equal to the best in the larger countries of Europe.

Nine tenths of the Norwegians were rural people, yeoman-farmers or fishermen, who are not rightly described as peasants since most of them had a sense of pride in land ownership which was denied the peasants of central Europe. In many valleys there was a folk culture with a structure of its own, but this was little known among the cultural leaders of Norway, and the farmers themselves had too little enlightenment to play a role in the national life. The cultural leadership in the eighteenth century had been in the hands of a wealthy merchant patriciate, but their rococo and empire style was not one on which a modern culture could be built. Economic reverses removed the basis for their leadership, so that the men who came to direct Norway in the first generations of the new century were of the official or bureaucratic class. These men combined elements of the old patrician culture with the traditions of the Dano-Norwegian civil servants, and some of them had also a certain contact with the rural class. They were the makers of the Constitution, and the writers of whatever literature came into being during this intermezzo.

Among the social institutions that helped to promote the cultural growth of Norway during these years were the theater and the university. A permanent theater had been established in Oslo in 1827, but it was still a provincial theater at which the first director was Swedish and the actors were Danish until the 1860's. Welhaven called it "an institute for catching moral and physical colds," and Wergeland raised a vigorous agitation to make it an expression of Norwegian literature, instead of a stage where third-rate foreign pieces were played for the entertainment of an unenlightened public. The establishment of a university in Oslo in 1811 was a concession by the Danish king to the precarious loyalty of the Norwegians. While it was small and had few means, the men who joined its faculty played an important role in the years that followed in giving Norway a standing in the world of learning. Notable names were won by the philosopher Niels Treschow, the geologist M. B. Keilhau, the physicist and astronomer Christopher Hansteen, and the mathematician Niels Henrik

Abel. These men were keenly aware of the currents of thought in their times, particularly the new romantic theories of the universe. Treschow arrived at a kind of pre-Darwinian concept of evolution, while Hansteen was thinking of the world as an expression of energy, in which light, heat, magnetism, and other forces were all one, merely expressed in different forms.

The relation of the new Norway to her ancient past was a difficult problem, but one for which there was a lively interest from the very start. Writers like Johan Storm Munch and Jacob Aall published saga translations, and C. M. Falsen wrote popular accounts of Norwegian history. Periodicals were published bearing names like *Saga* and *Urda* which evoked memories of the great Norwegian past. Men like W. F. K. Christie and Simon Olaus Wolff gathered material for the study of archaeology, place names, folklore, and dialects.

One of the most ticklish aspects of this relationship was that of the language. In the Constitution it was specified that all laws should be written in "the Norwegian language," chiefly to prevent Swedish from creeping into the Norwegian administration. But the Danes quickly protested when Norwegians started calling their language Norwegian. Linguists like Molbech and Rask pointed out that the only truly Norwegian language was that which the country people spoke in their dialects. But it was embarrassing to some Norwegians that their written language should be identical with Danish. Ideas from German romantics like Herder were spread into Norway: language should be an expression of the national character, or soul. A people without a separate language had no national soul. The question of whether the common language of Denmark-Norway should be called Danish or Norwegian or perhaps Dano-Norwegian when it was used in Norway soon gave way to the more radical issue: should the language reflect the separation from Denmark by becoming more Norwegian in its vocabulary and orthography?

Most of the leaders of Norwegian opinion before 1830 were trained in Denmark and had no desire for a sudden rupture of the bonds that tied Norwegian culture to Danish. When saga translators like Jacob Aall interspersed their texts with Norwegian dialect words, these men were offended. They felt themselves as partners in a Dano-Norwegian cultural area, and regarded every splitting of this area as a cultural impoverishment. They were infuriated when one of their members, the pastor Nicolai Wergeland, in 1816 published a vicious and unhistorical attack on Denmark entitled *A Truthful Account of the Political Crimes of Denmark Against the Kingdom of Norway from the Year 955 to 1814*. But the issue that was thus raised was one of fundamental importance for Norwegian culture in the century that followed: could and should Norway cut the apron strings by which she was tied to Denmark and build a culture all her own on the basis of ancient traditions from before the four-century-old Union?

Up to 1830 there was no evidence that the problem was anything more than academic. The one Norwegian writer with any originality, Henrich Steffens, lived and wrote in Germany as a close friend of the German romantics and came to exert a great influence on Danish romanticism. The occasional verse that was written in Norway during these years was largely a fumbling attempt to find Norwegian symbols to replace the Danish ones of the earlier generation. Reams of verse in the newspapers concerning the Dovre mountains and their solidity or enumerating the virtues of this youngest of European nations did not make up in originality for what they lacked in poetic form. Those few, like Mauritz Hansen, who were aware of the new romantic literature in Europe, were unable to get beyond its outworks. They could imitate its ruined castles and hooting owls, its compacts with Satan and accounts of insanity, its bombastic stories of murder, arson, and rejected lovers, but not its essential spirit.

The names that can be mentioned from these years are few and pale. There is Simon Olaus Wolff (1796-1859), who wrote stories of rural life and some patriotic verse. He is interesting chiefly as an early romantic, who wove dialect words and personal observations of peasant life into his writing. Henrik Anker Bjerregaard (1792-1842) wrote the prize-winning national anthem "Sons of Norway" in 1820, a song of which a malicious contemporary commented that "the enthusiasm which here shines forth is precisely of the kind that one might imagine a prize would produce." He was more successful with his musical comedy *Mountain Adventures* (*Fjeldeventyret*, 1824), with some charming scenes and dialect lyrics. The best of the generation was Mauritz Hansen (1794-1842), who had imagination and narrative skill, but allowed his talent to be frittered away in mass production. His writing was influenced by the great romantic contemporaries in Denmark and Germany, and even by Sir Walter Scott. His stories and dramas were based on Norwegian materials, either contemporary rural life or the historical background from the sagas. In this respect he set the pattern for many later Norwegian writers and probably influenced them.

The Age of Wergeland

THE WRITERS MENTIONED in the preceding chapter form only a prelude to the dramatic outburst of literary activity that characterized the 1830's. This was primarily embodied in the life and writing of two men, who were vastly different in outlook and temperament, and who came to symbolize two opposing trends in Norwegian life. They were Henrik Wergeland (1808-1845) and Johan S. C. Welhaven (1807-1873). The primitive and immature conditions of Norwegian culture had a directly opposite effect on these two personalities.

Even Wergeland must have felt the constricted circumstances of Norway as an artistic hindrance. He had no spiritual peers even among his friends and admirers. He was exposed either to adulation or to contempt, and received no competent guidance. But to the prophet in him, the fighter and the man of action, the immaturity of cultural life was a challenge. He conceived himself as the sower who should go forth in full kinship with the springtide forces of a new and budding nation.

Welhaven, too, was hampered in his growth by outer conditions, which may have killed some of his best qualities. But at the same time they stirred the fighting critic in him. He felt ill at ease and lonely in the young capital and yearned for a richer and more varied cultural life. He had been convinced at an early age that Norway could not afford to break the cultural bond with Denmark. He had become familiar with Oehlenschläger's poetry, Ingemann's elegiac plays and poems, and the aesthetic writings of his second cousin J. L. Heiberg. In the great poetry of contemporary Denmark he found the classic harmony which best satisfied the yearning of his own heart. He had formed a one-sided and rather dogmatic conception of the nature and purpose of poetry. Poetry is "a kindly glow," whose purpose is beauty and harmony. The poet creates this harmony by a severely controlled form, which presumes a long process of maturation in the soul. "Poetic activity," asserted Welhaven, "is thinking elevated and conditioned by imaginative feelings." At the same time he felt himself the heir of The Norwegian Society in its emphasis on poetic form and its polemic tendencies.

With this conception of art, which was acquired but at the same time congenial enough to his temperament, he met the phenomenon Henrik Wergeland, an unbridled natural force. The measure Welhaven had made for himself he tried to apply to the youthful poetry of Henrik Wergeland, the luxuriant and unpruned work of a genius. While he nourished in his heart the dream of an artistic society of the spirit, he had to listen to Wergeland's and *his* friends' blatant declamations about freedom, Norwegian homespun, and Norwegian artistic independence. With his mind full of admiration for Danish poetry he read Wergeland's farce *Harlequin Virtuoso* which ridiculed Norwegian dependence on Danish culture. Personally fastidious, even ascetic, he had to witness the carousing and stormy lives of his fellow students. No wonder that after a time Henrik Wergeland began to get on his nerves.

Both Wergeland and Welhaven bore within them a dream of Norway's future. Wergeland's yea-saying nature took an affirmative stand toward the budding forces in the people. He wanted to sing them full of hope, point forward and show the way. Welhaven's patriotism was at first negative in its implications. He wanted to clear away the weeds, cut away the wild growths, so that the buds which he loved might blossom. Both were fond of the saga age and saw the connection between it and the rural culture. Wergeland wanted to apply history to the problems of the day, educate the farmer and bring him up to political maturity in the national parliament. Welhaven's relationship to history was more aesthetic and his view of the peasant more romantic. Both were liberals who supported and loved the Constitution. But Wergeland wanted to realize its spirit in democratic reforms, a dynamic and creative program. Welhaven regarded freedom as something individual, internal and personal. The Constitution to him was a fence, a "hedge" which gave protection to the inner growth of freedom. "We have the Constitution, after all, why talk about it? Perhaps it has become a mere phrase to us, for the real freedom is not political but personal." All of Wergeland's talk of freedom thus sounded to Welhaven as empty prattle and bravado.

Today it is not hard to see that the two poets might have met in mutual respect if conditions had not forced them to do battle. Both of them were contemptuous of the empty snobberies of social life. But it is not likely that they could ever have won a deeper understanding of each other, and perhaps they both preferred an honest enemy to an uncertain friend.

Wergeland's supporters were numerous, but relatively few of them won a name in Norwegian history. They were patriotic, politically interested young radicals, some of them characters and revelers. Welhaven's supporters included some of the most capable young men in the country, who became the leading men in Norwegian culture and politics in the 1840's and 1850's, and even later. The struggle between the "patriots," Wergeland's group, on the one hand, and the "intelligentsia" or the "Danophiles" on the other, concerned many different problems. They disagreed on the relationship to Danish culture, on the nature and purpose of poetry, on the political role of the farmers.

But we must not imagine that there was complete agreement within either group on all of these and other problems. Ludvig Kristensen Daa, a liberal politician and historian who supported Wergeland, disagreed with his party on Scandinavianism, which he supported. P. A. Munch, the famous historian who supported Welhaven, did not favor Scandinavianism like most of his group. A. M. Schweigaard, a great jurist and political leader, was far more liberal in philosophic and cultural problems than many of the "patriots." But the real touchstone between the parties was not these or other issues, but the question: are you for or against Henrik Wergeland.

This was the first struggle in the history of Norway in which poetry became a spiritual force in social life. A cultural controversy was raging concerning the basic values of the people and the future of the country. But the controversy itself sounded more like a fist fight than a discussion. Precisely because the capital was so small, the argument came to bear a stamp of personal enmity and irritation. The opponents looked coldly at one another as they met daily on the streets, stepping, so to speak, on one another's toes. They were standing, one feels, on opposite sides of a waterfall and the only words that got across were those that were shouted the loudest, the words of abuse.

The controversy was the first skirmish in the cultural struggle of the century in Norwegian history, a symptom of the underlying battle for power in the new Norway. On the whole, it was a beneficial thing for the country that this controversy broke out, for it made the people aware of their own powers and laid a basis for discussion. But if we examine the actual literary results of the controversy, they are not overwhelming. Both Wergeland and Welhaven made their best contributions in quite different fields. It may even be asserted that they were slowed up in their development by the time spent on this controversy.

Welhaven's polemics against Wergeland, in verse and prose, were not his most artistic contribution to the controversy. His opening salvo, the poem "To Henrik Wergeland," has a certain rhetorical swing to it. But on the whole it is immature and pompous, unworthy of its author, with more brutality than wit, e.g. in its opening line: "How long will you rave against all reason?" Nor were his epigrams in the further controversy masterpieces. Of far greater interest, particularly as a document of the times, is *The Dawn of Norway* (*Norges Dæmring*, 1834), a sonnet cycle designed to expose the vulgarity and immaturity of his contemporaries. Some of the sonnets are good, and the work as a whole is well done, though hardly the masterpiece some have maintained. Our day has a hard time understanding either the unbridled rage or the admiration it stirred. We do not feel that the satire is witty or the terms of abuse particularly apt: "a foggy mob," "the wild, thoughtless host," "the flock of sparrows," etc. We can grant that there is some truth in the charges he levels against the patriots of his time when he has them declaiming in favor of a national isolation from everything outside their own country. But words like these do not fit Wergeland, who the year before had delivered himself of an attack on such isolation in a speech at the unveiling of the monument in memory of the jurist Christian Krohg: "Like Krohg's column we would be Norwegian in our inmost character, and yet under the citizen's wreath look free and far out into the world."

Even if we cannot go into ecstasies over the well-turned sonnets, we do not wish to overlook the serious artistic, national, and ethical ideals which underlie this poem. There is an undertone in it of wounded aesthetic sensibilities, of spiritual loneliness, a tone it was difficult to catch in the uproar of the controversy. We understand the subjective truth of Welhaven's own words to Camilla Wergeland: "What I am fighting for is far more precious to me than my own welfare, and I know of no consideration that would keep me out of this struggle as long as I am convinced that it is good." These words mean the more when we realize that it meant choking off an incipient love affair between him and the girl to whom he wrote, Henrik's own sister.

The most valuable parts of Welhaven's polemics are to be found in his indirect attacks. The poem "The Republicans" ("Republikanerne") is a masterpiece because of the monumental picture it gives of the martyr of freedom in contrast with the phrasemakers. Several of his allegorical poems with classical or biblical motifs belong to this group, such as the psycho-logically incisive "Glaukos," the noble "Protesilaos," the witty "Goliath," the attack on the lukewarm fighter "Sisyphos," the poem of the man who is strengthened by fighting, "Nehemiah," and some others.

The opposition to Wergeland became something of a fate for Welhaven. He grew to maturity in the shadow of an overwhelming genius, "a monster in everything, even in genius," as he is reported to have said in his later days. To Wergeland, on the other hand, Welhaven was only one of his many opponents, though often the most dangerous. But the struggle with the Intelligentsia did not, like some of the later controversies with old friends, "beget pearls" in his heart.

Wergeland demanded of his critics that they should respect his individuality, because he was clear from the beginning that poetry was his nature. He was willing to learn from the "criticism which they rejoice at being able to pour out upon the self-taught man." He was not so deeply hurt by the criticism of formal faults or aesthetic sins, as by the feeling that his critics wanted to quell his originality. They demanded, he thought, that he should be and write like everybody else, become one with Tom, Dick, and Harry, write pretty verse that would be suitable for framing, turn the wild flower garden of his poetry into a well-arranged, impersonal turnip field. He knew from the start that he was a genius, and he was not going to have his opponents tell him how to make poetry, or let them trim him and groom him with their recipes for poetizing. For this reason he could consider himself as elevated above the critics. He could even enjoy the fight. As he wrote to a friend: "Splendid to live in battle, when you have a sharp beak. I take my tobacco and my coffee in peace. But for the rest, let the pens fly! Let the beakers foam, the horse gallop, satires gush forth, sails dip, the rigging fill, and the breakers roll!"

But he left the theoretical defense to his father. When Welhaven had published *Henrik Wergeland's Poetic Art and Polemics Exposed Through Documents* (1832), Henrik's father replied a year after with *A Just Judgment of Henrik Wergeland's Poetry and Character*. Nicolai Wergeland here demanded that one must respect the sovereignty of genius, a view that marked him as the only broad-minded and unprejudiced critic Norway had at the time. "In the world of his ideas, his home, the poet is sole master. No one has anything to say there except he; that is his indisputable right." He would not accept any graduated scale: "I listen to the song of the birds and find it delightful even though I know they are not singing from notes." Like the philosopher Kant he maintained that poetry was something that could not be learned. While he was well aware of the formal sins of his son's poems, he regarded them as unimportant in comparison with his originality: "Henrik Wergeland does not need to sign any of his products to be recognized as their author." He was here using the standard that the brothers Schlegel had applied to Shakespeare.

Much of the polemic content of Wergeland's poetry from this period is of purely historical interest today. But many of his views on more general problems of literature show high artistic ability. His comments on Danish and German romanticism in an article on a Swedish poet, Ridderstad, describe this movement as "sofa literature." These writers, he declares, glorify the past at the expense of the present, they are "bards of diversion," who flee from reality and betray freedom. "Real poets," he declares, "did not shut their souls into closets. World history was assigned them, and they found their place in the world, formerly as leaders of hosts and teachers of kings, now as leaders of ideas and teachers of peoples. . . . As glorious visions in the air before a sailing vessel, so their images shone before their times." In his poem "To a Young Poet" he rejected the "archaeological" poets and cried to the young:

> Bard! Look thou not behind thee,
> Not toward the rune-covered stones,
> Not toward the grave-mound, barbaric days hiding!
> Those shields, let them lie! Let them moulder, those bones!
> Archaeologist ants, let *them* creep about on that mound,
> Them a handful of dust will—like snuff an old woman—inspire
> To tell tales that incredible sound.
>
> *Translated by I. Grøndahl*

The bard shall praise a different hero than those who lie dead in the grave mounds, namely the hero of freedom in his own day. He, too, sails over a great ocean as did the vikings; the sky is his grave mound and the sun is "the resplendent shield on its corners." "Bard! That mound shalt thou praise: Dost thou not see its blue crest?" Mankind is still bound in slavery, religiously, politically, militarily. But the poet shall take up his position on the unopened grave mound of the future, foresee the victory. For the poet is not a historian, but a prophet and a visionary:

> The earth-ball behind rolls History's thunder—
> The song of the Seer is the Lightning hurl'd before.

The controversy stimulated Wergeland's vitality, his need for expression, his creative sense, and it gave him the feeling of having accomplished something. The polemics and the satire expressed also his pleasure in teasing people, a boyish love for aggression. But in reality he regarded his satirical writing as inferior, and therefore he called the farces his "illegitimate children" and left this part of his production to his "half brother" Siful Sifadda. By publishing the farces under the pseudonym Siful Sifadda he kept his vision of the world of poetry unobscured and avoided being wholly swallowed up by the struggles of the day. But even in his most burlesque satire and frolicsome capers, the lyric poet occasionally rears his head. In the best of the farces directed against the Intelligentsia, such as *The Parrot* (*Papegøien,* 1835) and *The Constitutional* (*Den Konstitutionelle,* 1839), there is boldness of imagination, a sense of life's tragedy, exuberance and self-irony, baroque humor and beautiful lyrics, all in a wonderful harmony.

The controversies of the 1830's raged in many fields. Welhaven's friends broke out of the Student Society in 1832 and founded their own short-lived Student League. They published a periodical bearing the name of *Vidar,* the ancient Norse god who killed the Fenris wolf. But Fenris wolf Wergeland thrived in spite of their efforts. The newspapers took part in the struggle, with *Morgenbladet, Folkebladet,* and *Statsborgeren* on Wergeland's side, while the Intelligentsia founded *Den Konstitutionelle.* The attack on Welhaven's *Dawn of Norway* raised a great excitement, even to the extent of Nicolai Wergeland's urging that the book be burned. Welhaven himself was received with shouts by a mob that greeted him on his return from a journey abroad.

The theater was also involved, when a play, *The Campbells* (*Campbellerne*), written by Wergeland was performed (1838). His enemies hissed and whistled, with the whole affair winding up as a free-for-all between the parties. An unbroken line leads from this battle to the next in Norwegian theater history, in 1856. At that time Bjørnstjerne Bjørnson picked up Wergeland's program and led an army of 600 noisemakers into the theater because its director had failed to keep his promise of appointing only Norwegian actors. Bjørnson was thinking of the earlier event, and in an article he wrote: "Our immortal Henrik Wergeland, who was ahead of his time in this as in so many things, was the first who seriously and energetically spoke and wrote on behalf of a Norwegian stage. . . . Our dear Henrik Wergeland should have looked in on an evening like last Tuesday. He would have amused himself heartily in the howling storm of whistles which shook up the old prejudices. He would have stood in the midst of it, seen and prophesied from the signs he perceived, and he would again have cried out to the public his old words: 'Out of my way, you aestheticians!' "

If anyone were to undertake the fearful task of collecting every expression of opinion about Wergeland from his death to the present time, it would be an entertaining publication, replete with the strangest contradictions. We would find that he has been appealed to in support of the most varied opinions—for national self-sufficiency and for economic liberalism, for monarchical and republican forms of government, for a strong national defense and for pacifistic disarmament, for socialism and individualism, for Christianity and nature worship, for temperance and for the right to take a drink. His name has been used in discussions of the public schools, the place of Latin in education, the establishment of public libraries, the language issue, subsidies to agriculture, scholarships for poor children, even city planning in Oslo.

This shows how very much alive Wergeland still is. Ever since the 1870's and 1880's it has practically been a necessity to have Wergeland on one's side if a cause was to succeed. There is still truth in Bjørnson's words from 1896: "His dreams are those of our own young freedom. All that is promising for the future in it was first given form by him, or was prophesied by him, or was blessed by him."

If we ask the historians of literature how he should be placed, we also get various answers. We will learn that he was a rationalist, but also a romanticist; that he was a son of the Enlightenment and patriotic spirit of the eighteenth century, its cosmopolitan humanitarianism, but also the prophet of the nineteenth and twentieth centuries, the poet politician, the national bard, an idolizer of the peasant yeoman of the eighteenth and an agrarian politician with the demands of the nineteenth century. If we examine the roots of his culture, we shall have to stop in many places. We must take a look at Rousseau to understand his individualism, his worship of nature, his union of religious and political ideas. We will find ideas drawn from Voltaire and the Encyclopedists, but also from German romantic philosophy, Schelling and Steffens. We note an influence from Shakespeare in his striking imagery and his practice of mixing tragic and comic elements, and we see something of Byron in his manner of life. There are Norse sources in Snorri and the other saga writers. We must examine also the activity and the ideals of the men who created the Norwegian constitution at Eidsvoll, above all his own father Nicolai. But if we follow many of these influences back to their source, we will get back to his deepest roots, the very soil of West European liberalism, Jewish-Christian morality, Greek humanism, platonic and neo-platonic religiosity.

Wergeland was anything but a harmonic personality; many contrary tendencies fought for the mastery of his soul. But he had the capacity of the genius for harmonizing contradictory opinions, and he gave to all of them the stamp of his own personality.

If we take up a position at a sufficient distance from all the uproar that filled most of Wergeland's short lifetime, and read those poems and fairy tales that reveal his genius in its purest ray, we may be able to experience him as the ecstatic he was. We meet the man who wrote in *Hazel Nuts*: "When my soul conceived a poem, meseemed that it was breathing a higher, even a frosty atmosphere, as when the lovely snow crystals are on the branches and one can look infinitely far up through these into the deep blue air." We understand what he means by expressions like these: "There is kinship between the soul and the stars. . . . Their rays gild my soul with a stillness as of alabaster." This is the deepest source of his poetry.

His ecstasy, which may find expression in the calm of a frosty night just as well as in a volcanic outburst, is connected with his basic religious experience. He is in a half visionary state, more passive than active. He feels as if the soul for a short time actually leaves his body when his imagination has him in its power. It is a primitive, animistic conception, and more than just a bold metaphor when he writes in "Europe Liberated" that his soul shines from Caucasus or some other mountain, while his heart stands still, or that his soul is left behind like an abandoned swan in the straits of Salamis while his body wanders pale as a sleepwalker under the moon of Norway—until it is awakened by the July revolution. It is more than a poetic fiction when he says in "Toast to a Good Year" that the soul is reading "halo-encircled legends," the sun's farewell poem to the budding spring day, on the windows of Our Savior's Church, while the body stays behind as a ghost in the arbor.

This ecstasy in the original sense of the word, the feeling of being outside oneself, also gives him his sympathy with nature and its divinity. Only by purifying the soul of all earthly dregs will it be possible to describe his vision of the universe. His view of existence is dualistic, and he feels himself as both "a cherub and a beast." But he does not scorn matter, for there is spirit to it:

> Concealed there is a spirit in the dimmest grain of dust,
>   just as the word
> Slumbers hidden in the idea.

This basic conception is found in everything he wrote that bears the stamp of genius. He saw "the great in the little," saw divine ideas lifted up "on the weak straws of the grass," heard "a thousand mouths in the chattering garden path," discovered the plan of the universe in his rabbit's eye: "From tiny gnat-sparks and mammoth flames to the conflagrations of suns."

He believed also that nature stood in a closer relation to God than human beings and was accordingly more divine. Nature, like the starry forehead of the white narcissus, is "the mirror of innocence." In nature's Gothic cathedral, the spruce tree, there is no need of an altar, because nature can speak directly to the Creator, and "even the tiny mossrose pure" is a "chapel of heaven." For this reason it is a lesser crime to sin "in the shadow of the sacred pulpit than under the branch where the chaffinch sits."

His ecstasy is most often brought on by the beauties of nature, which cause him to forget friends and enemies, little things like "the first straw that spring shot forth, or the scarlet on a fly's wings," but above all the flowers, "the inner flame of earth," as he put it in a poem to a botanist.

The most rebellious, undisciplined, and reckless of all Norwegian poets is also the one who loved flowers the most passionately. They teem everywhere in his poetry, in poems to his fiancée, to his friends, even to his enemies in a couple of farces. He directs his most passionate prayers to them. All the wildflowers of the fields live in his poetry, especially those of spring, but just as often he turns to the flowers in his garden. All of them are his allies in the battle with his enemies:

> Blow the lily's
> Silver trumpets!
> Beat the tulip's
> Golden drums!
> Wield the halberd
> Of iris blue!

Smash with clubs
Of the Provence rose!
Slash with the jagged
Stars of the cornflower!
Fire the long
Muzzles of angelicas!
Hurl your quick stones,
Ballista of the balsam!

His favorite flowers for symbolic purposes were the rose, the lily, the apple, the balsam, the dandelion, and the lily of the valley. With "the lily of the valley's silver bells" he wants to ring lies out of the world. The dandelion, the balsam, and the cabbage rose symbolize the will to life, stubbornness, and fertility. Lilies and apple flowers represent innocence. The red and white roses are life and death: "for my white roses extinguish the blood of the red ones."

Flowers never seen before also spring forth from his visionary imagination. He dreams of "palm trees a hundred ells high, where the blue passion flower and the camellia climb up together," but also heliotropes in the stars and mallows in the moon. He presents his friend George Frederik von Krogh violets for his goodheartedness, laurels for his genius, oak leaves for his patriotism and his work for the peasants; but the flower for his sorrows "is known only in heaven." In his poem to King Oscar he prays that from his own grave may spring forth a mystical and unknown flower, the "birch-leg flower," in allusion to the "birch-leg" warriors in Norwegian history, "red as the lion's field in Norway's coat-of-arms."

Wergeland was earthy and red-blooded as few other poets. But he saw life on earth in terms of eternity. His faith in freedom was part of his religion. The craving for freedom is the sacred unrest in each man's heart, akin to the artistic impulse and the creative urge. God is the eternal guarantor of the victory of freedom, all supporters of freedom belong to heaven's party. Wergeland was so confident of freedom as heaven's cause, that he added: "If the angels were not free, there would be revolution in Heaven."

Henrik Arnold Wergeland was born in Kristiansand on June 17, 1808. His father was of rural stock from Sogn. Although Wergeland as the humanist he was did not place much emphasis on race or descent, it meant something to him that his father had his root in Norwegian soil.

His mother, Alette Thaulow, came of an old family of officials. She was cheerful of temperament, warmhearted and illogical, artistic in her tastes. The poet may have his artistic abilities from his mother's side, but certainly got his courage, his combativeness, and his recklessness from the Wergelands.

The family moved to Eidsvoll in 1817. Here Henrik and the other children had a chance to frolic in luxuriant natural surroundings. Here, too, Henrik was filled with the spirit that made him call himself the "six years' older brother of the Constitution." His years of study at Oslo Cathedral School awakened his interest in Greek life and thinking, which played an important role in much of his writing. Here, too, he acquired his basic view of history. But the most significant years for his work as a poet were the years 1826-1829, when he studied theology at the University of Oslo and romped through student life.

His writings from these years give the impression of a brilliant youth, filled with self-confidence, jubilant and sensitive, concerned with the mysteries of life. He wrote mad farces, but also the tragedy *Sinclair's Death* (*Sinclairs Død*, 1828). Above all he strewed out lyrical poems, on nature, friendship, and love. He fell madly in love with four different girls, none of whom returned his passion. He was serious enough about it, though his recollections of these affairs in *Hazel Nuts* tell in a humorous vein of the calamities which an enthusiastic and unlucky lover can bring down upon himself. His letters and poems from this period reflect the seriousness of his intentions. They enable us to sympathize with the genuine despair that made him jump off the barn bridge with a dull roar after he had been thrice rejected. We can also understand that he thought of going to Greece and following Byron's example. But we also realize that even if these love affairs were not happy in the usual bourgeois sense, they may have been so in a poetic sense. They released the poet in him. He transformed the oppressive unhappiness of love into a heaven-storming enthusiasm for all that was good and great. His all-inclusive, mythmaking fantasy caused him to create his Stella, an ideal image of the loved one, she to whom he was closest when he was farthest away from all women. She may be a Norwegian girl who wears a woolsy dress by way of protest against the flimsy clothing of the fancy ladies, but at the same time she is a spirit and weighs less than a hair of the usual daughter of Eve.

The poetry of Wergeland's youth has a strangely magnetic power, as we meet it in his *Poems, First Cycle* (*Digte. Første Ring,* 1829).[1] It is adolescent and immature, with many offenses against logic and feeling, but at the same time it bears the mark of genius. The images sparkle, the ideas crackle, and the poems are rich in the pain and joy of life.

In the center stands Stella, the subject and the object of his poetry. She was at first a beautiful star, reflecting its image in the water as the beauty of the beloved in the poet's soul. It may be true that the terrestrial girl does not understand his celestial harp—her heart is "full of earth." But the poet cannot let her go. He transforms her into the feminine spirit who some day will meet him in eternity:

> Some day mid coursing years, thy
> Soul I waiting shall meet,
> Stella! Stella!

The poet has gotten a glimpse into the imagination of the Creator and has read the poem of the universe. Here there are shining worlds with seraphim and cherubim, but also earth and the blood of animals. On the wings of a smile he swings out over the earth together with Stella. Like a two-headed swan they glide through the ether. In heaven they are going to watch over the loving hearts of earth. In the last poem of the collection, which like the first bears the title "To Stella" ("Til Stella"), the spiritual and the physical meet in heaven, where he celebrates his wedding with Hulda who became Stella. It takes courage to join him on this venture, for he and she will fly off through the universe, with worlds flying past, along the Milky Way, broad and long, "the Nile of Heaven." They float through portals of suns, song and the glory of pearls, until they reach God's festival hall, "full of the Hosanna of worlds," the smiles of happy spirits, the manna of the stars which drips from sunny beakers. There are cherubim in the bridal chorus singing hymns, while Byron plays the trumpet and Petrarch the guitar. Here Stella can choose for her bridesmaids Laura, beloved of Petrarch, Tasso's Leonora, Camoëns's Maria, and the mistresses of Byron.

The luxuriant variety and imaginative surplus of these poems is expressed in the images which flash past his eye and are continually given up for others. Even sounds are turned into visual images. He sees the soul of the harp flash like "a resonant lightning." Laughter becomes "a

1 Poems from this and later collections are found in the selections included in Henrik Wergeland, *Poems,* tr. G. M. Gathorne-Hardy, Jethro Bithell, and I. Grøndahl (Oslo-London, 1929). Some poems also appear in C. W. Stork, *Anthology of Norwegian Lyrics* (New York, 1942).

storm from the south, skimming the ocean on white sandals." Tones
flutter like ravens "which are unable to control their broad wings in the
wind." Thunder is like a "yellow and black" Fenris wolf, while the clouds
are like "black-frocked priests with shining pates, or like our Christ with
a bloody wreath of thorns around his crown."

His imagination frolics most freely in the poem "Napoleon," an
attempt to explain the origin of genius. Here we find his doctrine of
spirits: "Higher and higher, through spirals,/Rises the army of spirits/
Up to God." But the most mature, in form and content, and the most
charming is "My Little Rabbit" ("Min lille Kanin"). From light, leaping
rhythms he passes over to the "Wergeland line" proper, with its long
breath and billowing rhythm:

> When with skip and jump around
> You in loops and rings did bound,
> And across the moonlight flew,
> Like a cloud when heaven is blue,
> Drifting on the merry breezes
> Wheresoe'er its spirit pleases,
> Through the zenith, past the sun,
> Dark and free and full of fun:
> Then life's source I seemed to see
> In my corner, like a brook
> Sprinkling all its drops on me,
> Clearer far than in my book.

Translated by G. Gathorne-Hardy

Many thoughts and emotions filled Wergeland in the late 1820's as
he contemplated the international events of his time. The Holy Alliance
had ruled Europe for many years, the period when the peoples stood
like a "frozen sentry" at Napoleon's grave. But now things looked
brighter. The idea of freedom was blooming like "a flaming rosebush."
Ideas of social progress were in the air. Wergeland felt the world conflict
as a personal concern, and conceived the idea for a world poem or drama,
in which he would portray the struggle and development of mankind
in a series of visions "with a brush dipped in the sun." He wished to
make it at one and the same time an allegory of the spiritual world and
a personal confession, a Stella poem and the Bible of republicanism, "the
epic of mankind." He dedicated it to the spokesmen of Truth, Freedom,
and Love, including Lafayette and his own father.

He called it *Creation, Man, and Messiah* (*Skabelsen, Mennesket og Messias*), and made of it one of the most extraordinary masterpieces of Norwegian literature. It is romantic in plan and outlook, rationalistic in its ideas, difficult as a jungle to penetrate, teeming with brilliant images and banal details.

In the first part, *Creation,* the poet's imagination is sovereign. Out in space somewhere two spirits float, the male Phun-Abiriel, a "doubting, courageous spirit," and the female Ohebiel, a gentle, loving spirit. They become witnesses to the creation of the earth, which is portrayed as a struggle between Cajahel, the spirit of growth and fertility, and Obaddon, the spirit of death and renunciation. At last Cajahel creates his masterpiece, man, the highest animal, a little wiser than the elephant and the horse. Phun-Abiriel, the thinking spirit, stares at the newly created world. But he sees no sense in feeling reverence for this piece of clod. He is filled by a melancholy bordering on insanity, and envies man his thoughtless joy of life. To forget his own distressing thoughts he descends into Adam's body and begins a new eternity. To the mild and loving Ohebiel, his beloved from an earlier existence, this seems like a spiritual suicide. She wishes to prevent man from being degraded by marrying a woman who is not his spiritual equal. So she sacrifices herself for love and takes up her dwelling in Eve. In this way two kinds of spirit have entered mankind, an earthly one which it shares with all nature, and a heavenly one which stems from the two spirits.

The second part, *Man,* is less sustained than the first. The details predominate, but the main theme is clear enough. Mankind spreads out over the earth. Domination of the weak by the strong comes into being, as one man calls himself king and subjugates those who protest. Priesthood arises, as the wiser ones frighten the weaker ones and fill them with fear of the devil and dread of the unknown. These two powers make a compact which keeps the peoples in physical and spiritual slavery. But there are points of light in the darkness, for the nobler spirit is not extinguished in man. Republics with law and justice are established, democracy grows forth in the Greek city states. Prophets and philosophers see through the doctrine of force and the frauds of the priests. Zeno, founder of Stoicism, speaks against matter, the Epicurean proclaims his noble philosophy of life, the Peripatetics point out man's complex nature, the interplay of spirit and body. But highest of all is Plato, through his doctrine of pre-existence and love, Eros.

In the last section, *Messiah,* the poet felt himself bound by his theology to give a rationalistic explanation of miracles and dogmas. But there are grand passages here also. The life of Jesus is narrated according to the gospels, but with some additions. Jesus, as the greatest of mankind, unites Phun-Abiriel's passion for truth with Ohebiel's faith and love. The teaching of Jesus is expressed in the words: "The indissoluble threefold unity of Truth, Freedom, Love." Jesus meets resistance from the rulers, but his doctrine has struck root in the hearts of the people. The time will come when there are no more bloody crowns, nobility, priestly tyranny, executioner's steel, torches of slavery, and altars of sacrifice. The time will come when there is truth in the words that are spoken by mankind:

> Each will have his royal canopy within his forehead,
> Each will have his altar and sacred vessels in his heart.
> King will each man be upon the earth.
> Priest will each man be before his God.

Creation, Man, and Messiah gives a monumental expression to the ideas that were nourished by the best people in the period between the French revolutions of 1789 and 1830. In spite of weak passages, poor rhymes, needless repetitions, and superficial history, it is truly world literature, though it is not usually so regarded.

Immediately after the appearance of this work, the July revolution broke out in France. It is not surprising that the poet trembled in suspense. "Every hour beats the feverish pulse of our times," he wrote in a poem "Europe Liberated." He expressed his contempt for the bootlicking poets, and wrote his political-philosophical treatise *Why Does Humanity Progress So Slowly?* He went to Paris in 1831 and basked in the echoes of the revolution.

But reaction won the day in Europe, and the poet was filled with grief and rage. He was often oppressed by doubts and discouragement. He fumed against the czar's suppression of Poland in "Cæsaris": "You have buried all the free men of Europe." Only in the final hymn did he regain his faith in better times:

> The sparks from the sacrifice—eyes, that ascend
>   to the skies, and behold
> How days that are brighter, and kingdoms and cities
>   more fair than of old
> Laugh out past the ashes and smoke.

Translated by G. Gathorne-Hardy

He wrote against English policies in Ireland in "The Dirge of the Harp of Erin." Comparing Ireland to a lotus leaf fettered under the sea to England, he wrote:

> O that thy stalk could be freed! Then thou shouldst
>   drift to the fortunate
> Realm of the new world beyond, where Liberty
>   mightily throning
> From thee the demon should drive and gently, herself,
>   on thee settle.

Translated by J. Bithell

He also published his splendid cycle of poems entitled *The Spaniard* (*Spaniolen*), directed against reaction in Spain.

Wergeland's interests during this period included both universal and national themes. These are reflected in the collection *Poems, Second Cycle* (*Digte. Anden Ring,* 1833), which tells of greater depths and heights in the poet's heart than the previous poems. This includes the previously cited "To a Young Poet" ("Til en ung Digter"), and the symbolic "To a Pine Tree" ("Til en Gran"). While this may be a Norwegian tree, the idea is a universal one:

> The house of God is Nature's fane;
> No moss so small, no weed so plain,
>   But builds a chapel there.

Translated by G. Gathorne-Hardy

The imagery is no less exuberant than in his earlier poetry, but the poet succeeds oftener than before in holding fast to his metaphors and carrying them through.

No less universal is the basic idea in a treatise from the same year, *Speech to the Human Qualities in Humanity by My Horse Brownie.* He wanted the animals to benefit from the July revolution as well. Men were tortured by princes and their executioners, and men in turn tortured their animals. But should they not rather learn from their own sufferings to be kind to animals?

More important than his writing was life itself. In a defense of *Creation, Man, and Messiah* he had said that his life would become as faithful a prose commentary on the poem as possible. He would turn "word-ful" poetry into a "deed-ful" patriot. This was the spirit of his tremendous work for popular education. "I want to work, and I feel my strength," he wrote to the Society for Norwegian Welfare in 1830. "Give, load work upon me. . . ." He organized public libraries, handed out educational pamphlets, wrote an informative periodical of his own entitled *For Almuen* (*For the People*), wrote textbooks in history and botany, a reader for young people, gave speeches, lectures, and sermons, took part in the political campaigns as editor of the papers *Folkebladet* and *Statsborgeren*, published pamphlets of his own containing political ballads and fables, carried on lawsuits against people he suspected of exploiting the peasants, and helped poor people in every possible way. His personal activities were borne by the same zeal as his poetry. He was often reckless when anger seized him, as when he called a lawyer named Praëm "an offender against state and humanity." He was often unwary and gullible.

Wergeland's attitude to the farmer-peasants was tinged by the eighteenth-century admiration for the free Norwegian yeoman. But at the same time he had enough realistic knowledge of the farmer to know his economic circumstances and his outlook, both his good and bad sides. He was therefore not a typical romantic in this respect. To be sure, there are clichés in his poems, especially when he talks about women: "Pride dwells in the clear, blue eyes beneath the national kerchief." But he calls attention to the clash between reality and the romantic-Rousseauan ideas. Wergeland did not look upon the peasant as a man of the past, but as one of the future. He wanted him to walk behind his plow as an educated man, not as an ignorant clod in his secluded farm home. Even if the farmer's body was bound to Norwegian soil, his spirit should be able to fly around heaven and earth. Freedom demands thinking citizens. The farmer shall test what the parson says from his pulpit and what the judge says from his bench.

In his literary and cultural battle against the Danophiles in Norway and the reaction in Europe, Wergeland often sought support in Swedish poetry and in liberal circles in Sweden. He always entertained a great admiration for Swedish history and language. No one has characterized the Swedish language more handsomely than he did in his poem in Swedish to the hymnist Bishop Wallin: "the beautiful, which rings like silver, the proud, which has words of steel." But he was always on guard against Swedish political aggression and a leader in the support of Norwegian views. In the critical period of 1836-1837 he wrote his oft-quoted lines: "It would be best to loose the bond between horses that badly pull together!"

Wergeland was a great hero-worshiper. No one in Norway has done homage to more of his contemporaries than he. His work for freedom in Norway led him to express his admiration for Lafayette, Bolivar, Kosciusko, O'Connell, and poets like Byron, Delavigne, and Rouget de l'Isle. He was generally effusive in his homage, and he praised as geniuses many to whom we might assign a humbler status. The Norwegians whom he praised are mostly forgotten, except for the fame he has given them by his poems. The main thing for him was that their hearts were on the right side, that they had suffered for justice and freedom. As he says in his poem to George Frederik von Krogh:

> Is it not to kind-heartedness, genius, and unhappiness
> That God gives his fairest wreaths of immortality?

His homage went chiefly to those with whom he felt himself akin. In one of his finest poems he asked the famous violinist Ole Bull, an enthusiast like himself, to work for the abolition of Negro slavery in America, as an expression of gratitude for what the Norwegian constitution owed to the American. But he could also praise old opponents, especially when misfortune or death had struck them down.

Wergeland had been a theological candidate for nine years, and it was his highest desire to become a pastor, or "teacher of the people" as he liked to call it, a guide for the people in spiritual and material affairs. But the king and the cabinet had not been willing to give a churchly office to so radical and reckless a person, particularly since he was also constantly involved in lawsuits. In 1834 he had turned to the study of medicine, but he gave it up in 1836. In 1838 his prospects brightened when he got a position as librarian at the University Library, earned $390 in royalties from his play *The Campbells,* and bought himself a little house in Grønlia. Besides, he was engaged!

The girl's name was Amalie Sofie Bekkevold, and she was a simple tradesman's daughter, not at all like the girls whom Henrik had worshiped in earlier years under the name of Stella. About her future sister-in-law Camilla wrote, "She has of course no culture, but she replaces it with natural, good understanding and liveliness and a completely unprepossessing manner." Her influence on Wergeland's life and poetry, however, was enormous. Several of the love poems he wrote to her and published in 1838 under the title *Poems* (*Poesier*) are among his most successful lyrics. There are tender but manly poems like "Nameless" ("Navnløs"), tremulously expectant ones like "Voyage of My Beloved" ("Den elskedes overfart"), deeply sincere ones like "The First Hand-clasp" ("Det første Haandtryk"), sublime ones like "The Loved One's Slumber" ("Den Elskedes Slummer"). The chaotic quality is gone, and the opposition between terrestrial and celestial love has been dissolved in a harmony: "Oh innocent bride, thou hast reconciled the soul with the world, the blood with God." There are fewer stars in *Poems* than in the Stella poems, but many more flowers and a deeper feeling for nature. The ecstasy and the intensity are the same. The new poems are closer to reality than the youthful poems, more varied, manlier in tone, often classically pure in form.

A short time later he fell into conflict with his own party and was looked upon as a renegade. The issue was his relationship to the king, Charles John, the former General Bernadotte of Napoleon who was made king of Sweden and Norway. On numerous occasions he had fought against the king's policies, and yet he loved Charles John "with the ever-fresh love of a child." He saw in him the son of the French revolution, and he was convinced that the king had been converted to the Norwegian Constitution; he blamed the king's advisers for his reactionary policies. Wergeland had just lost his chance to get a chaplaincy because of a spree in the officers' quarters at the palace. The king then offered him a personal pension of $200 a year, and Wergeland accepted the money on the condition that he might regard it as payment for his work on behalf of popular education. He started at once publishing his paper *For Arbeidsklassen* (*For the Working Class*). But his enemies began making spiteful remarks about the "court pensioner."

A short time later he applied for a position as archivist in the National Archives, and was given it by the king, who rejected an appointee recommended by his cabinet. From now on it was asserted that Wergeland had sold himself to the king. The patriot and zealot for freedom had betrayed his past. It was of little use that he publicly declared himself as still in favor of a republic. Nor did it help that he continued to praise freedom and to work for the people. Most newspapers refused to accept his articles.

Wergeland was so deeply hurt by this turn of events that he wrote half-appealing attacks on his old friends, asking them to join him in work for the fatherland. When they pointed out the contrast between his past and his present, he wrote satirical attacks on them, and they generally agreed that his poetic vein was spent. But each time his opponents prophesied this, they turned out to be mistaken. Wergeland had rightly chosen the dandelion as his symbol: "the more it is stepped upon, the more it grows."

Loneliness was Wergeland's fate during the years that remained. But right now he stood at the height of his development. He had not changed his character, but he had become a mature artist and a greater human being. His philosophy and his driving energy remained the same, but his opinions had been clarified. He had learned from Herder that the evolution of mankind must be slow, and that the millennium cannot be expected in the immediate future. His work with *History of the Norwegian Constitution* (*Norges Konstitusjons Historie*, 1841) had shown him that even the Danish period had its significance for Norwegian national growth. One could not just skip over it. Now he also looked in a more conciliatory way at the Danish romantics, and he praised the humanity of the Danes. Loneliness had given him greater peace of mind and elevated his thoughts. "Vincere canendo," I shall conquer by my song, had become his motto.

Wergeland's admiration of the Constitution did not make him blind to its defects. One of its provisions which he began attacking early was its exclusion of Jews from Norway. In 1839 he sent the Storting a motivated proposal to repeal this section. When the proposal was rejected in 1842, he was bitterly disappointed in the attitude of his admired peasants who voted almost unanimously against it. He supplemented his agitation in prose with verse which includes some of his best writing, particularly the collections *The Jew* (*Jøden*, 1842) and *The Jewess* (*Jødinden*, 1844). His victory in this cause did not come until after his death, but it did come, and led to the erection of a monument on his grave by Swedish Jews, which is still its only decoration.

Wergeland's isolation from his friends and disappointment with the peasants led him to turn the more eagerly to the working classes and their meager conditions of life. The kernel of the labor problem in his opinion was: education, self-knowledge, morality. He never appealed to the class feeling of the proletariat, even though he criticized the upper class viciously enough. He warned the workmen against drink and immorality, superstition, vandalism, and cruelty to animals. He took up the question of housing and agitated in articles and songs for cleanliness. But the greatest task was to awaken the laborer's pride in humanity and in his native country.

* * *

> Be thyself in part and whole,
> That is victory's art, my soul!
> Like Saint Stephen, all alone
> Must thou stand and face the stone.

Translated by G. Gathorne-Hardy

While the journalists hounded him, he got married and wrote great poems like "Myself" ("Mig Selv"), "My Wife" ("Min Hustru"), and "My Wife's Return" ("Min Vivs Hjemkomst"). He still wrote farces, epigrams, and contributions to the controversies of his day. But he preferred to write songs for children and working people, dialect verse, sailors' songs, and fairy tales. In the long poem *Jan van Huysum's Flower-Piece* (*Jan van Huysums Blomsterstykke,* 1840) his mythopoeic fancy won one of its greatest triumphs. It tells the story which Wergeland wove around the flowers in a favorite painting of his by the Dutch painter Jan van Huysum. The flowers are mystical reincarnations of a family that had died at the hands of a ravaging army. The artist, by painting them so that the imagination can feel the life in them, reconciles old Adrian, the father and sole survivor, to life. This is magnificent romantic poetry at its best, though his poem "The Swallow" approaches and may even surpass it.

Wergeland's productivity was enormous during these years. Dramas like *The Venetians* (*Venetianerne*) and *The Cadets* (*Søkadetterne iland*) were not suitable for the stage, but have many fine lyric passages. Among his other works were *The English Pilot* (*Den engelske Lods*), with its glorification of England, and his biographies of Christian Lofthus and Ole Bull. Poetry streamed from his pen; making poems was his normal being with every healthy moment bringing forth another.

Then it happened that on May 2, 1844, he came home ill from the National Archives. Tuberculosis had struck down the lover of life and set him face to face with death. But instead of losing his courage, he entered upon a race with death. He still had so much to say to his people that he was happy over the sleepless nights which gave him time to make poetry. He revised the entire opus of *Creation, Man, and Messiah* and called it *Man*. In an added vision of the future he looked into a coming age of happiness with world peace, social understanding, tolerance, and humanity. He completed *The English Pilot*, wrote *The Jewess*, published *The Jewish Question in the Norwegian Parliament*, issued a reader, began a musical play, *The Mountain Hut (Fjeldstuen)*,[2] directed against emigration, wrote his lively and amusing memoirs, *Hazel Nuts (Hasselnødder)*, and produced some of his most enduring verse. Nor did he forget his other activities. He continued to publish *For the Working Class*, sent packets of seed to the farmers at Eidsvoll, kept the journal of the National Archives, built himself a new house, Heartroom, after his former home, the Grotto, had been sold. In all things he was faithful to his program: "*First* a man whose strength ne'er quails, and *then* a poet whose cheer ne'er fails."

"He died in a spiritual liberation so gently smiling of understanding and love that no more beautiful sight has ever been seen on the spiritual heavens of Scandinavia than Henrik Wergeland on his deathbed," said Bjørnson in his speech at the unveiling of Wergeland's statue in Oslo in 1881. As late as March 1845, he still had the strength to send his spirit gathering flowers for his country's queen three nights in a row in the poem "Journey to Brazil." The poem combines the imaginative exuberance of youth with the mastery of the mature poet.

But above all, the stormy radical had become the poet of conscience and neighborly love. Again and again he took up the question: Is there any use in poetry? Does poetry benefit life? He was an unpopular poet in a small nation, and his words, which should be the "army of truth," reached no farther than "the breath of his lips." To preserve his optimism he cast an eye on the evolution of the world in the poem "Follow the Call":

> Ah, but we ourselves are still
> Savages in mind and will,
> Yea, and often in our actions:
> Not the Indians of the West
> By such rancor are possessed,
> Though their thirst with blood they sate,
> Tribes that forests separate,
> As our Europe, rent in factions

[2] An account of this play and some of its poems are contained in Theodore C. Blegen and Martin B. Ruud, *Norwegian Emigrant Songs and Ballads* (Minneapolis, Minn., 1936), 75-98.

> By the bitterest party hate.
> Young as yet the world must be;
> All our long, long history
> Still is but its cradle-song,
> And its childhood's fairy-tale.

Translated by G. Gathorne-Hardy

The age of creation is not yet over, and the poet will help the Creator. Therefore the answer comes to him again and again:

> Up! If God's own voice invest
> With a storm thy heaving breast:
> Cry aloud in desert ways,
> And the dawn of better days
> From the dark thy word shall raise.

The most beautiful of his poems are those that deal with death. He loves life and cries to the spring, to the anemone, to the swallow, to the old maple tree that they must save him. But he also greets his illness as the April of his salvation. He lies talking to the moon some nights when he is at the hospital, and sometimes he jests with death as with a friend. Death is in reality a dandy, a Don Juan, "but he is handsomer behind than in front; how many people are not like that?" After he took his farewell of his people in the last chapter of *Hazel Nuts* in the clear and courageous words of the chapter "I Die," he felt this was too sentimental and added a phrenological address by his own skull.

At the end he wrote only of death, and of the flowers which told him fairy tales of life after death and revealed to him the secrets of heaven. On the other side of the grave he would find again all things, the flowers, his mother, Brownie his horse. "In a valley of clouds you will see him munching carnations on the left and violets on the right." It will delight his mother when he "charges up one of the mountains of the thunder or over the streams of the lightning."

On his deathbed Wergeland was reconciled with his old friends. They had discovered the bloody forehead which he had sustained by following the principle of "straight ahead." All Norway listened to the voice from the deathbed, a voice with such a strange ring, now whispering of secret matters, now humorous, now prophetic, but always with a wonderful freshness. But the finest greeting was sent to him by the Dano-Jewish poet Meïr Goldschmidt in a letter that reached him a couple of days before he died: "When I think of you, Wergeland, I am proud of being human."

On June 12, 1845, Henrik Wergeland died.

Discovery of a National Culture

AROUND THE MIDDLE OF THE NINETEENTH CENTURY Norwegians were made more intensely conscious of the great possibilities inherent in their native culture. Ballads and folk tales were made known to the reading public and inspired the poets to a more authentic treatment of national themes. The nature of the country was deliberately exploited by writers in all its infinite variety from seashore to mountain top. A new style of writing which was closer to natural speech and therefore was felt to be more Norwegian crept into literature from many sides.

This newly awakened interest, even a love for folk literature, nature, folk life, and language was well prepared by the development previously sketched, but was also akin to similar movements in other European countries. The dominant impulse was the so-called National Romanticism which came to Norway from Denmark and Germany, though there were influences also from Walter Scott's novels and Tegnér's *Frithiof's Saga*. The expansion of interest in these topics was so overwhelming that it has become common to refer to the period as the national "debut" or "awakening."

The interest in national themes was not a purely romantic one, however, since it led also to a mild form of realism, a "poetic realism" which is best exemplified in some of the writings of Welhaven. Much of the writing, art, and humanistic scholarship of the period was inspired by the desire to fill the gaps in Norwegian cultural history, to cement the bond between the old and the new Norway. As soon as the political conflicts aroused by the Constitution had been resolved for the time being, it became possible to deepen and expand the understanding of national culture.

This program was made explicit by both Welhaven and Wergeland in the 1830's, but as late as 1840 there was still only one rather primitive collection of folklore, published by Andreas Faye in 1833. What the men of this generation knew about folk music was limited to the inspiration of Ole Bull, to whom they paid homage from their varying points of view. But in the 1840's a great campaign of collection and publication made available untold treasures to poets and public alike. The chief foreign stimulus to this work was the fairy tale collection of the brothers Grimm in Germany. But while Faye had been content merely to report or summarize the stories in a dry and somewhat schematic way, Asbjørnsen and Moe in their two volumes of *Norwegian Folk Tales* (*Norske Folkeeventyr,* 1841-1844)[1] sought to preserve and reproduce the artistic values of the stories by retelling them in a style that was as oral as possible. They looked on their task as a national and artistic duty, and believed that a part of the Norwegian "folk soul" was revealed in these stories.

Here came from the woods and mountains strange figures which stood close to the heart and the imagination of the common people, in spite of the fact that the books called them superstition and nursery tales. They were salted by proverbs which sometimes went beyond what the printed page would bear. They could not be written in dialect as they had been told, for then they would not be read and understood. But in translating them into the book language, they demanded a different style from that which had been in vogue in books, one that preserved their character of oral narrative. Asbjørnsen and Moe had to create a new folk tale style, in which the vocabulary admitted new and vivid expressions from the dialects while the sentences were reshaped according to the rules of living Norwegian speech. Wergeland had sometimes gone even further in the use of dialect words, but he cared little about simplifying his syntax. *Norwegian Folk Tales* laid the foundation of a new Norwegian prose style.

The folk tales, like so many other phenomena of the age, were at once realistic and romantic—realistic in their picture of folk life, but viewed romantically by those who collected them. From Grimm and others Jørgen Moe had learned to see in the folk tales "a hint concerning the ultimate kinship of peoples in a far distant past." He believed that these stories were reminiscences of the common past of mankind, which then had been translated into literary form and later modified "by the natural impressions received by each people and the history which they experienced." The later collections, Asbjørnsen's *Norwegian Fairy Tales and Folk Legends* (*Norske Huldreeventyr og Folkesagn,* 1845, 1848), con-

[1] For references see *supra,* note 3, p. 73.

tained folklore, accounts of supposed encounters with the supernatural. Some students interpreted these as nature symbols and as expressions of the poetry of the common people, though Asbjørnsen himself looked more realistically upon them as having grown from the landscape itself and the misinterpretation of natural phenomena.

In February 1840 Wergeland wrote to the Swedish author Fredrika Bremer: "I do not think that the folk songs are entirely dead. But one would have to go into the mountains to find them. . . . A poet would have to wander throughout Norway to discover them, but then he had better not spend his time in the parsonages." That same summer Jørgen Moe published his *Collection of Songs, Ballads, and Verse in Norwegian Country Dialects,* while Olea Crøger and the pastor M. B. Landstad began collecting ballads in Telemark.

Moe's collection was no masterpiece, being chiefly a reprint of dialect verse already known. His introduction, however, expressed the hope that these revelations from the "depths of the folk" would be like "the awakening and life-giving spring wind" to art poetry. He looked upon it as a mission to build a bridge between the literature of art and that of the folk. Not until 1852-1853 was the first collection available of the true ballads from the Middle Ages, *Norwegian Ballads (Norske Folkevisor)* of M. B. Landstad, a book of some 900 pages with a supplement of folk melodies collected by L. M. Lindeman. All kinds of ballads were included in this collection, dealing with such themes as trolls, heroes, knights, and gods; some were jesting tales, and occasional verse of the kind called "stev." While a later, more scientific collection was published by Sophus Bugge, Landstad's large book was the one that had the widest influence on the public as well as on the poets. It made a deep impression on the youthful Ibsen, who drew many themes in his earlier dramas from this collection.

Landstad's material did not permit of a translation into book language, but he did his best to give the dialects a dignified form by adopting elements from the orthography of Old Norse. Ivar Aasen, who was the first scholar to make a genuinely scientific study of the dialects, advised him to keep closer to the present-day forms. Aasen himself was close to the people, and his own studies were made with the deliberate ideal in mind of creating for Norway a language that would be truly national and might perhaps some day take the place of the Danish that was then written in Norway.

There are varied opinions on the motives that led Aasen to make this radical proposal. Some have thought it was the social, or class motive, to make it easier for country people to reach positions of social influence. While this may have had some significance for Aasen personally, the whole philosophic and cultural basis for his venture was identical with that of the nationalistic and romantic trends of his time. Others had gathered dialect words and had realized that they descended from Old Norse, but not until Aasen's *Grammar of the Norwegian Folk Language* (*Det norske Folkesprogs Grammatik,* 1848) and *Dictionary of the Norwegian Folk Language* (*Ordbog over det norske Folkesprog,* 1850) was the actual proof available. He demonstrated the connection between the Norwegian dialects, especially in western Norway, and the language of the sagas. The romantic nationalists of his time felt it as a restoration or resurrection of the old language. The historian P. A. Munch praised the grammar as "a national monument, in which the whole people can take pride."

The ideas underlying Aasen's creation of a new written language in Norway had been formulated before him by S. O. Wolff, P. A. Munch, and Henrik Wergeland, but Aasen was the genius who succeeded in crystallizing the ideas by means of his intimate knowledge of the dialects, his keen linguistic sense, and his unflagging perseverance. His first samples in the new language were published in 1853, and showed a combination of elements from the most conservative fjord and mountain dialects with an orthographic framework reminiscent of Old Norse. Not until 1858, after Vinje had joined his movement, did any controversy arise. New editions of his grammar and dictionary were not merely expanded and revised, but bore titles which proclaimed that this was no longer intended to be just a folk language or a dialect, but a truly national substitute for Danish: *Norwegian Grammar* (*Norsk Grammatik,* 1864) and *Norwegian Dictionary* (*Norsk Ordbog,* 1873).

At the same time the movement to make the Danish language over into Norwegian by gradual stages began to gather momentum. This, too, had its roots in ideas strewn out by Wergeland and practiced by him. The theoretician of this movement was the schoolmaster Knud Knudsen (1812-1895), who called the attention of Norwegians to the fact that while the written language might be Danish, the true language of the cultivated classes was not Danish. The informal speech of cultivated people was Norwegian, and he agitated tirelessly for the introduction of its forms into writing. This was the origin of the many changes that have since been made in Danish as written in Norway, a series of orthographic changes having been initiated in 1907, in addition to a general tendency to introduce Norwegian dialect and colloquial words into the written language. National impulses have thus led towara a distinctly Norwegian language along two paths: a revolutionary break with Dano-Norwegian in the form of a new norm established by Ivar Aasen, and a reformist movement in the accepted Dano-Norwegian as advocated by Knud Knudsen and others. In our time the two norms are both officially accepted, and are being brought closer and closer together in the hope that they may some day be amalgamated into a single Norwegian language.

The central figure in the scholarship of the times was P. A. Munch (1810-1863), a learned and zealous historian. He helped Asbjørnsen and Moe with their studies of the folk tales, and he inspired and supported Ivar Aasen. He determined the form in which Landstad presented his ballads. Together with C. R. Unger and Rudolf Keyser he published Old Norwegian manuscripts. He founded research in the place names of Norway, and published an analysis of the Old Norse mythology. His chief work was *The History of the Norwegian People* (*Det norske Folks Historie,* 1851-1863) in eight huge volumes. All of these solidly documented studies were infused with passion for the national values involved, a dream of the great ancestors and their significance for the present. Munch became the leader of the so-called "Norwegian school of history," which established the importance of the Norwegian share in the Old Norse literature, previously called "Old Scandinavian." Their theory about Norwegian immigration from the northeast was well calculated to assert the priority of Norwegians over Swedes and Danes.

An important aspect of the imaginative writing in this period is its changed conception of nature. Wergeland was the nature lover par excellence in Norwegian literature, but his images were seldom intimate or locally colored. His landscapes were too often symbolic of ideas and did not live in his poetry for their own sake. Yet he pointed the way for the conquest of Norwegian nature in the poetry of the following generation. The romantic poets were firmly convinced that nature was the source of their inspiration. A typical remark was the answer that the violinist Ole Bull made when the Danish king asked him who had taught him to play: "The Norwegian mountains, Your Majesty."

Western Norway had the most typically romantic landscape, with its majestic fjords, narrow valleys, wild waterfalls, and occasional idyllic contrasts between blossoming fruit trees and overhanging glaciers. Welhaven, himself a native of western Norway, was inspired by the solemnity and nobility of this landscape, but he was also fond of the hills and forests of eastern Norway. This was the proper domain of Jørgen Moe, who gave deep personal expression to his love of his native Ringerike, "where the distant ridges are blue." Moe emphasized the childhood memories and the nostalgic yearnings evoked by the forests and the mountains. He brought out many realistic details in his descriptions of nature, as seen through the eyes of his own boyhood. The nature described by these writers is that which we find also in the painters of the age, from J. C. Dahl to Adolph Tidemand and Hans Gude. It is nature seen through emotion, rearranged and prettied by retrospection.

The pleasant melancholy of nature was the theme also of Bernhard Herre in his sketches of Nordmarka, the wooded regions north of Oslo, from 1841 and later. Like most of the national romantics he was fondest of nature when there was little risk of meeting other people, unless they somehow contributed to the mood he wished to enjoy, as in the case of folk-costumed peasants or extraordinary characters. Asbjørnsen had a more intimate relationship with the people, and succeeded in winning their confidence. In his collections he imbedded his folklore in descriptions of the people who told it and the nature which surrounded them. He was not just a summer tourist, but was there the year round and described nature in all its aspects. The high mountains especially were vividly portrayed by him, together with the huntsmen who inhabit them. These themes were picked up by many less skillful writers in his time, but above all they were made fruitful by Ibsen, whose *Peer Gynt* builds squarely on Asbjørnsen's descriptions of the Rondane mountains and their population, natural and supernatural.

Johan Sebastian Welhaven was born in Bergen on December 22, 1807. His father had then just been made a chaplain at St. Jørgen's Hospital, an institution primarily for leprous patients. He was a warmhearted man, who took a personal interest in the fate of his charges, and even brought them into his home. His wife Else Margrete Cammermeyer was related to the Danish poet Johan Ludvig Heiberg and appears to have had a good head and a lively manner, with a critical sense which she passed on to her son. The young Johan Sebastian received a deep impression from the family life of his childhood, but early developed some of that attitude of protest which came to be one of his leading traits. In school he was chiefly influenced by Lyder Sagen, who inspired in him a love of the classics through his interpretation of Homer. In Sagen's literature classes he also acquired his taste for formal precision and his interest in the Danish poets of the "golden age" and in German neoclassicists.

He entered the university in 1825, the same year as Wergeland, and planned to study theology as his father desired. But he never completed his course. In spite of his upper-class origin, he lived in modest circumstances—as did most of the so-called Intelligentsia—and had to earn his way by tutoring and some drawing. His real interest was in the reading of literature and aesthetic theory.

Welhaven's poetic talents developed slowly, without the heaven-storming impetuosity of his younger rival. He was not a poet of spring, but of the more contemplative seasons of the year. His poems were not brilliant improvisations, but musical and plastic in form. He believed that it was the task of poetry to evoke moods arising from the interplay of form and content. He expressed this theory vividly in his poem "The Spirit of Poetry ("Digtets Aand"):

> Out of the verse-form's texture
> So rigorously wrought
> A free-born spirit rises,
> The poet's primal thought.
>
> It dwelt long, long within him
> In formless, vague desire
> And there the ore of language
> Was melted by its fire.

Translated by C. W. Stork

He usually had his inspiration a good while before the poem found its proper form. His experience had to settle within him, until it became a memory, a gentle heat which gradually smelted the ore of the language. Only then could the poem get its proper personal cast, its form. As the fragrance rises from the rosebud when it opens, so the mood would rise from the lines of the poem and awaken a corresponding mood in the reader, kindling in his spirit "that fire which lay in the poet's soul before the strophe was conceived."

A good many readers were surprised by the gentle tone of the lyrics which Welhaven published at Christmas time in 1839. There were only occasional reminiscences of controversy. Most of the poems were tinged by sadness, including the ones he wrote about his childhood and one called

"The Village Churchyard ("Byens Kirkegaard"). There were also poems with a wider historical perspective, excellent poems like "The Republicans" ("Republikanerne") and "The Obelisk of Luxor" ("Obelisken fra Luxor"). There were even a few love poems, reflecting his abortive and pain-filled affair with Camilla Wergeland. It is easy enough to recognize Welhaven himself in the poem of the water sprite who bears in his innermost self an image of the rose, but who drowns his sorrows in noise and stir. Camilla is also present in the poem entitled "Maria," and in "The Last September Day" ("Den sidste Septemberdag") : "Amata, glorious and pain-filled! In the autumn scene I viewed thy image."[2]

In the poems Welhaven published in 1845 and 1848 he was even more definitely the poet of reminiscence. His natural talents and his life experiences combined to make him so. He had become engaged to Ida Kjerulf in 1837, but her mother opposed the connection and did not yield until the girl fell seriously ill. When he came to her one day near the end of November 1840 to tell her that he had been made an instructor at the university, she could only smile. A few days later she died.

Welhaven's outer gaiety in the company of friends was soon restored. He was a witty conversationalist, who could strike off sparks in his epigrammatic remarks. Vinje compared him to an electric machine. But the grief at Ida's death and his memories of her never left him. He gave a picture of his own feelings in the ballad "The Overturned Beaker" ("Det omvendte Bæger"). A knight has lost his wife. The monks try to comfort him, while his boon companions invite him to go hunting. "But sorrow followed the tracks of the game." Silent and without tears is his sorrow; he broods upon his grief. When he meets up with the dancing elves in the forest glen, an elfin girl promises him forgetfulness if he will empty the beaker she hands him. But then a beloved name echoes through his mind, and he seizes the beaker and tosses it high above the linden trees into the river. Now he has "tested his faith" and realized that sorrow is a life value. Now his hardness melts and he can cry out his grief, so that he can return to his tasks "with new-lighted courage."

Welhaven's poetry became not only a reminiscence of his personal sorrows, but also of the past of his own people. He turned, like the other national romantics, to themes from the sagas, the folklore and folk life. Many of these have become classics, including his "Ballad of St. Olaf" ("En vise om Hellig Olaf"), "Harald from Reine" ("Harald fra Reine"),

---

[2] A dozen poems by Welhaven are translated in C. W. Stork, *Anthology of Norwegian Lyrics* (Princeton, 1942).

"The Trotting Course" ("Traverbanen"), and "The Ride of the Pagan Gods" ("Asgaardsreien"). He regarded the last-named as his best. It is drawn from the story of a court trial, but was given life when he heard a lively folk dance played by a country fiddler. Nowadays the poem seems a bit on the oratorical and hollow side. Far more genuine and Norwegian is the poem "Dyre Vaa," with its subtle refrain and folk humor.

Welhaven often gave his themes a symbolic turn, as in "Hope of Renewal" ("Fornyelsens Haab") and the profound poem "In Kivledal" ("I Kivledal"). Here his sympathies are not with "Sirrah Peder the learned priest," who had so "stammering a tongue," but with the people who keep the old fairy tune alive. He is impressed by the delicacy and the sensitivity of the creatures of folklore. The water sprites and the woods fairies share his melancholy, but also his joy in nature. He rejects the coarse and brutal aspects of folklore, and will not really believe in the cow tail and the hollow back of the woods fairy (*huldre*).

The powerful national sentiment that was infused into Welhaven's poetry during this time was not weakened, but rather strengthened by his Scandinavianism. He joined with his sympathy for the other Scandinavian nations a pride that Norway no longer needed to feel ashamed in their presence. Norwegian national feeling no longer seemed to him incompatible with Scandinavian co-operation, since Norway had preserved more of the old traditions than the other countries. In a speech of January 13, 1846, he declared that the cultural "quarantine" which he had feared, presumably from Wergeland and his companions, now was past. But he emphasized, as Wergeland too would have done, "that no activity in the Scandinavian spirit can be greater or more significant than Norway's unceasing striving to carry through and guard her independence."

He had by this time found himself a niche in Norwegian society, as professor of philosophy (1846) and as president of the Art Association. He was a popular speaker, a sovereign arbiter of taste, a feared and admired lion of society. His university lectures had no permanent significance, but they attracted a large audience by virtue of his excellent delivery. He preferred to lecture on the history of literature and published essays on Holberg and Petter Dass, as well as a study of Ewald and the Norwegian Poets.

Welhaven had always had a strong religious sentiment, even though he did not care to study theology. He opposed all dogmatic controversy and the entry of politics into religion. He saw in Christianity a religion of peace in which the Christian and the humane were to be united. In his later poems the religious tone becomes predominant, even to the extent of constituting a rejection of some of his earlier ideas. In "A Singer's Prayer" ("En Sangers Bøn") he throws away his "singer's wreath" in favor of the eternity to which he looks forward from his religious thoughts.

In November 1868, when the Storting was to take a stand on the question of how large his pension would be, he experienced the last controversy about his name. On the same day he was honored by the students, who paraded to his door with their banners and standards. They sang to him the beautiful poem which Bjørnson had written to a melody by Grieg:

> Do you not smile now at the goal,
> You, who cradled through the winter
> The text of our spring?

He died on October 21, 1873.

*   *   *

Jørgen Moe (1813-1882) demanded in his introduction to the ballad collection of 1840 that the literature of a nation "shall reflect the life of the people in pure, chastened images according to its physical and historical background." This program, with its combination of romantic and realistic doctrine, became his guide as folk tale narrator and poet. In both cases the problem was to give expression to the characteristics of the people, "to enter into and to reproduce the people's life of home and heart."

He and Asbjørnsen planned the great collection of folk tales as early as 1837. It is impossible to say who has the chief honor of having conceived it, but of the two writers Moe was the superior stylist. From childhood he had heard the narrative of the people, and he had added to this a study of aesthetics and literature, particularly German and Danish. He did not have his friend's festive good humor or his popular manner, and yet he succeeded in retelling such vigorous tales as "The Devil in the Nut" and "The Blacksmith They Didn't Dare Let into Hell."

Moe's poetry remained unoriginal for a long time, being strongly under the influence of Oehlenschläger, Chr. Winther, and Welhaven. His later success in finding a personal style owed much to his study of folk literature. To an even greater extent than Welhaven he was a reminiscing poet, and won his chief popularity through poems that recreated episodes from his childhood or the folklore he then had heard. He published his first collection of poems in 1849, containing several fine pictures of folk life. His story for children, *In the Well and the Pond (I Brønden og i*

Tjernet, 1851), has remained a classic for its charming and amusing picture of child life.

Moe had taken a degree in theology, but practically given up the idea of becoming a pastor. Instead he became Norway's first university research fellow in folklore. But a short time later he experienced a religious crisis and turned to the pastor's career. He gave his folk tale notations over to Asbjørnsen but continued to interest himself in the work of gathering folklore. Moe was a reflective personality, who also possessed a quiet sense of humor. Even in his later years, when he wrote mostly occasional verse, he composed a few classic poems like "The Old Master" ("Den gamle Mester") and "The Young Birch" ("Ungbirken"). These were simple, clear symbols for the view of life which he had achieved for himself.

To posterity Peter Christen Asbjørnsen (1812-1885) has become identified as the fairy tale king in person. His lively humor, his rough but kindly manner, and not the least his jovial and decorative figure have contributed to this result.

His father was a glazier and instrument-maker in Oslo, a capable and respected man. Of his mother the poet reports that she was highly superstitious and saw ghosts and underground creatures every once in a while. He also heard many strange stories of the faerie world from the apprentices. But the most important factor in his development was the habit he got into early of hiking about in the woods and fields around Oslo. Although he was supposed to prepare for the university, he was so inattentive to his studies that he was sent to school in the country district of Norderhov where he met Jørgen Moe. They became friends for life and even went through the old Norwegian ceremony of sealing their foster brotherhood by mixing blood.

After completing his university entrance examination, Asbjørnsen was a tutor at Romerike for a series of years and started his career of taking down folk tales. At the end of 1837 he published some tales in *Nor,* a periodical for young people. His style was still immature and bookish.

While Asbjørnsen was enough of a romantic to be fascinated by folklore and find in it an expression of the folk soul, he was not a dreamer. His field of study was zoology and botany, which gave his descriptions of nature a sober realism. But his "frame stories," or background sketches, in the *Fairy Tales* are also descriptions of folk life, the first in prose in Norway, for example "An Evening in the Proprietor's Kitchen." His characters are not profoundly portrayed, but their main characteristics are well described, occasionally even caricatured. He narrates amusingly and spontaneously, vividly and impressionistically, sometimes carelessly. He is not prudish and never hesitates to use the strong words of popular usage. A description like that in "The Teamsters" ("Plankekjørerne," 1848) shocked many nice people.

He continued to publish folk tales until his last years, but most of his writings were in other fields. He helped to lay the foundations of marine biological research and discovered a starfish which he named the Brisinga from Freya's brooch. He studied forestry in Germany, was forester and for a time "sod master," doing a useful work for the reforestation movement. He was something of a literary jack-of-all trades, writing popularizations of all kinds, a *Natural History for Youth* (*Naturhistorie for Ungdommen*), but also a travel account from Egypt. He was a gourmet all his life, wrote a cookbook and carried on a controversy with Eilert Sundt on the right way of utilizing flour in the household. It is characteristic that he was the first to make the Norwegian public acquainted with the theories of Charles Darwin, as early as 1860, the year after the appearance of *The Origin of Species*.

Asbjørnsen tried to keep his editions of the folk tales abreast of the linguistic development by having them revised in the direction of popular speech at various intervals, something he wished to have continued after his death.

Among those who helped him in this task was Ivar Aasen (1813-1896), who also was a man of many interests. In his youth he had worked with botany alongside his linguistic studies. He was interested in history, and collected folklore and proverbs. But he was also, though in a narrow sphere, a genuinely talented poet.

He was the son of a small farmer in Ørsta in Sunnmøre, a community with a certain cultural tradition. Here Sivert Aarflot had founded the first print shop in a Norwegian country district. Here such pastors as the naturalist Hans Strøm and the poet Claus Frimann had been located. From childhood Ivar Aasen had been an avid reader, and when he became a public school teacher at eighteen, he turned to books for good. In 1837 he began to investigate his own local dialect, and in 1841 he went to Bergen to show his herbarium and his dialect studies to the bishop, Jacob Neumann, who was a member of the Royal Society of Sciences in Trondheim. The bishop was strongly interested in his grammar, as were Lyder Sagen and Wergeland's friend Fredrik Bugge. The latter got support for him from the Royal Society so that he could travel around the country and gather materials for his scientific work.

It was a great advantage for the new written language which Aasen created that he was a poet himself. His "Landsmål," as he called it, meaning "national" or "country" language, thereby acquired a harmonious and aristocratic air. At the same time it was a crucial problem for him to prove how well suited it was for poetry. Both his prose and his poetry testify to a mastery of style, with a great feeling for euphony and artistic form, though without a luxuriant imagination.

In 1855 he published the play *The Heir* (*Ervingen*). It is a weak drama, but became popular because of the clearly delineated folk types and the inserted songs. His little collection of verse called *Symra* (*Anemone,* 1863) was intended as the harbinger of a springtime in "Landsmål" verse. There are many reflections of his youthful struggles, a certain resigned air of skepticism and a deep melancholy, but also a didactic and satirical vein. He distinguishes sharply between the two cultures of Norway, the native, inherited culture of the farmers, and the imported European urban and official culture. His sympathies are entirely with the former and he makes it his mission to advance its cause against the latter. Aasen avoids all boastful or bombastic expressions, and some of his poems are almost gnomic in form. They express the inherited wisdom of the man who is close to the soil. But they also reveal the sensitive and often lonely bachelor behind the poems, a gentle philosopher who has pondered the basic problems of life, an unsophisticated soul who is best pleased by simple emotions that are awakened by simple things, like the old mountains, the homeward path, a spring day, and life itself. He shows considerable suspiciousness toward things that are modern and urban, but his conservatism does not stop him from sympathizing with the forces of social growth.

Of the many minor authors in this period, the most typical was Andreas Munch (1811-1884), a writer of lyrics, epics, short stories, and plays. His ready pen gave expression to all the currents of his age. He was mild and elegiac of character, but in his youth he wrote flaming verses in behalf of freedom and was active in the movement to give Jews admission to Norway. His writings were much read in his day, but his themes and his style were imitations of Oehlenschläger, and his fame paled quickly in the bright new sun that rose with the generation of Bjørnson and Ibsen.[3]

[3] Several of Munch's works were translated: *Solomon de Caus,* tr. J. Chapman (London, 1855); *Lord William Russell,* tr. J. Chapman (London, 1858); *William and Rachel Russell* tr. J. H. Burt (London, 1862); *The Maid of Norway,* tr. Mrs. R. Birkbeck (London, 1878).

Dreams and Reality

ALL ROMANTICISM is to some extent a protest against workaday reality and its demands.

The romanticist may dream about new and better times, prophesy about them, even work for them, as did Wergeland. He may set up ideal demands beyond all reasonable limits, like Brand in Ibsen's play by that name. Or he may have his ideals in the past. He can dream of renewing past glories, as did the national romanticists. As a rule there is an element of escapism in all romantic poetry. The romanticist wishes to dream away the banal demands of everyday life, or seeks recompense in the world of imagination and dreams for all that reality has failed to give him. The romanticist is often what psychologists would call a daydreamer.

If we examine the special vocabulary of romanticism, we find again and again words like yearning, dream, melancholy, reverence, intuition, the folk spirit—suggestive words that appeal to the imagination. We will hear "harp tones" in "darkling groves," where the poet enjoys "the peace of solitude," reminiscing about "the innocent days of childhood" or letting his thoughts be cradled on "the stream of memory." He may be sitting in the "slumbering vale" near the "shore of memory," looking at "the moon behind mysterious woods," hearing the "elves whisper" and "the nixie sing," lifting himself on "wings of yearning" to the "land of longing."

The supposed contrast between the romanticist and the "philistine," or "bourgeois," is not always as great as is supposed. Most of the Norwegian national romanticists entered into a compromise with reality by gilding it and beautifying it in a so-called "poetic realism" and in the romantic tales of folk life. In his own life the romanticist may, like Andreas Munch in his later years, be a bourgeois in his view of the questions of the day, while his poetry becomes a kind of artistic game for idle hours. At other times the clash between dreams and reality leads to a "romantic irony," as in the case of Vinje. The poet takes a diabolic pleasure in destroying his own dream. When this happens, romanticism is about to be dissolved.

The period of greatest flowering for national romanticism was the years from 1845 to 1850. During these years the enthusiasm was fresh and genuine. No skepticism, no pressing demands, no irony had as yet been able to do its deed.

It was a favorite idea of the romantics that all branches of art are fundamentally one. The poet should paint in words and the painters make poems in color. But poetry and painting should also give musical effects, and of architecture it was said that it is "frozen music." In reality, all art ought to be science and all science art, while poetry and philosophy should be one and the same. The most extreme of the German romantics had dreamt of a "universal poetry," a "poetry of poetry," which in the end was identical with religion. But even if this universal poetry seemed an unattainable ideal for the Norwegian romantics, they agreed that the various arts should work together in harmony.

This ideal was closer to realization in the year 1848-1849 than at any other time in Norwegian history. It became a demonstration on a grand scale of what national romantic art had to show. This year was the chalet girl's Sunday in Norwegian history, as has been said, in allusion to Ole Bull's song by that name.

Ole Bull had been in America and played "Norway's Mountains" ("Norges Fjelde") at Niagara Falls. After that he went to France, and at the head of a procession of Norwegians he marched to the city hall of Paris in the year of the February revolution and handed the poet Lamartine a Norwegian flag with a greeting from Norway to the French republic. When he returned to Norway in November, he was honored by students and poets. A short time later he invited the best known of the country fiddlers, "The Miller's Boy" ("Myllarguten"), as he was called, who came to Oslo on skis and held a concert together with Ole Bull on January 15, 1849. There sat this mountain peasant in a concert hall together with smartly dressed ladies, and gentlemen with kid gloves and eyeglasses. He "entranced" the "elegant world" with his country dances while he stamped out the rhythm.

Ole Bull was not the only one who returned home in 1848, and was received with enthusiasm. The February revolution had also driven the painters home from Düsseldorf. An Art Association was founded in the capital, and Asbjørnsen proposed that a scholarship fund should be raised by arranging a series of evenings at Christiania Theater at which painting, music, and poetry could be combined into a great national festival. This was carried out on March 28, 29, and 30, 1849.

First an overture was played which was a potpourri of Norwegian folk melodies. Then an actor read a prologue by Welhaven which ended with these words:

> Norwegian art unites us here tonight
> About its images of fjords and mountains,
> To be illumined by a magic taper.
> Its witching staff will open up our scene,
> And point to us its goal and its demands,
> And ask our folk to take it all to heart.

Then a large male chorus of students, business people, and craftsmen sang a "Welcome" directed by J. D. Behrens, after which the curtain rose on a tableau which the painter Tidemand had set up, while his colleague Gude had painted the backdrop, assisted by others. The tableau represented a painting which Tidemand and Gude completed later, "Evening on the Lake Krøderen." It was accompanied by Jørgen Moe's poem by this title, sung to a Norwegian folk melody.

> Now sinks the evening gently down
> With golden blush on sea and slope,
> A soundless silence and delicious peace
> Have dedicated nature to a quiet slumber.
> The greenish shores
> Gently fuse with the water
> In the mirror of the gleaming lake,
> Which catches their reflection.

Then came some numbers which included a reading of Andreas Munch's poem "Ave Maria," and Norwegian folk songs arranged by Lindeman. Then Ole Bull stepped on the stage and played fantasias on folk melodies to tremendous applause.

As an introduction to the next tableau, an actor read Jørgen Moe's poem "Fanitullen," after which it was performed as a painting by Tidemand. Ole Bull then played a composition he had promised the students at a celebration and now called "Visit to the Mountain Chalet." This was enthusiastically received, but there was no end to the cheers and applause when the curtain rose for the final tableau, which presented Tidemand and Gude's famous painting "A Bridal Procession in Hardanger," with the prettiest ladies and the most elegant young men of the town in the boat, all in national costumes. Painting, music, and poetry here fused in "an immortal triad," as Lorentz Dietrichson put it, when Andreas Munch's pretty poem to Kjerulf's seductive melody rang out in the hall.

But the February revolution had other effects than that of driving the painters home and stimulating Ole Bull to enthusiastic speeches about the French republic. It also helped to bring the idyllic phase of romanticism to an end and prepare the way for a literature of social criticism.

A young assistant at the apothecary in Grimstad spent his nights writing flaming appeals to the Magyars and others, urging them to rise against the oppression of their tyrants. He also wrote a play about a Roman rebel, Catiline, and himself later became one of the great rebels in literature. A schoolboy in Molde edited a handwritten paper with the proud name *Freedom (Friheden)* in the year of the revolution. He later called his contemporaries "the generation of 1848." The February revolution came to mean somewhat the same to Ibsen and Bjørnson as the July revolution had meant to Wergeland.

But the revolution of 1848 had practical consequences also, through the agitation of Marcus Thrane. This young idealist advocated socialistic ideas which influenced men like Ibsen and Vinje in their earliest years. His socialism was not extreme. All he asked was universal suffrage and some social reforms which were to improve the position of the peasant cotters. But he also organized some workmen's societies and he spoke the dangerous word "revolution" which frightened the bourgeoisie.

At the same time there was a religious reaction in some quarters against the ideas of the revolution. A pietistically colored orthodoxy came into power in the church and at the university. Landstad, the pastor who was previously associated with the collection of ballads, was put in charge of making a new hymnal for the church, and about fifty of his own hymns were included. A number of them show the influence of his preoccupation with balladry, and all of them reflect a deep and genuine piety. But most of the religious leaders were antagonistic to secular literature. From church and school, even from the university, were sounded many warnings against the liberal currents of thought which were making headway in the country. Among the common people a rash of schismatic and revivalistic sects began spreading in the wake of popular education and the new literacy. Many of these impressed the young writers with their obvious sincerity, their idealistic demands, and the enthusiasm they seemed to evoke among their supporters. But they were anticultural in their trend, and they could not give the writers new ideas or nourish their artistic urge.

As the older rationalistic religion lost its hold on the educated public, many felt a gnawing skepticism and a sense of emptiness. Welhaven complained in 1854: "Doubt has entered into our blood like a fever that stimulates at the same time as it exhausts us." Doubt was one of the leading motifs in Ibsen's youthful poetry also, from the same years. The poet who was beloved by young people in these years after 1850 was Heinrich Heine. While he had been known earlier, he was now appreciated for his irony, the alternation between romanticism and brutal reality, between dreams and awakening. The skepticism of the young people led in many cases to an aesthetic view of life, which was nourished by trends in Danish literary life. Danish writers like J. L. Heiberg, Meïr Goldschmidt, and Paludan-Müller were models of the young Norwegian writers Botten Hansen, Vinje, and Ibsen.

But the deepest impression of all was made by the poet-philosopher Søren Kierkegaard (1813-1855). His profound works, *Either-Or, Stages on Life's Way, Philosophical Fragments*,[1] and others probed the fundamental problem of his time. They not only encouraged the trend toward realism, but also took up the very basis of existence for discussion and revision. They faced their readers with the serious consequences of an aesthetic view of life, and they attacked the tendency of the Hegelians to reconcile or compromise the opposites. This thinker, who has won a world reputation, most recently in America also, set up the three possible views of life as a sharp contrast: the aesthetic, the ethical, and the religious. He said to his reader: Such and such are the consequences of such and such a philosophy of life. Think it over for yourself and choose one or the other. But choose! For himself he chose the religious view and raised a furious controversy by his brilliantly phrased attack on Christendom. He even maintained that Christianity did not exist, had never been put into effect. When he died in the midst of the controversy, it was a shock to the whole Scandinavian literate public. In Norway his influence encouraged a characteristic tendency toward absolute idealism. Kierkegaard's paradoxes appealed to a Norwegian trait of "either-or," an urge to carry ideas to their logical con-

[1] Translations are available of these and many other Kierkegaard works.

clusion. Ibsen was profoundly influenced by Kierkegaard in his early years, but most of Kierkegaard's influence was reserved for the 1870's.

There was another Danish poet-prophet who came to mean a great deal to Norwegian literary men. N. F. S. Grundtvig (1783-1872), historian and clergyman, hymnist and admirer of pagan mythology, founder of the folk high school and liberal theologian, was not as radical a force as Kierkegaard. But his views of teaching and his cheerful philosophy of life were fundamental in the thinking of men like Bjørnson and Kristofer Janson.

Simultaneously came the first realistic investigations of life among the lower classes in Norway, which laid the foundations of sociological research. Eilert Sundt (1817-1875) initiated a series of important studies of folk life which showed that the romantic picture had to be seriously revised. The "uncorrupted children of nature" were actually a good deal less admirable than was commonly believed by the romantics. Statistics and scientific observation showed that drunkenness, immorality, uncleanliness, and poor agricultural methods were more widespread than had been imagined. The political tactics of the agrarian bloc in the parliament also alienated some of their friends, showing as they did that the farmers often lacked a cultural horizon and were more interested in pinching pennies than in promoting great causes. It became fashionable to look with skepticism on the rural population, and its role as carrier of the national soul.

The 1850's were transitional in more than one way. The steamship traffic really set in during these years. The first railroad was built, modern roads were established, industry began to appear. But poets of the older school still dreamt about the idyllic life of an earlier generation. They looked away from the "prose" of their age and found refuge in an aesthetic view of life which deepened the cleavage between literature and life. Literary criticism was generally acid and negative, unable to give the writers any encouragement. Literature did not thrive, as the attention of the public turned to more practical affairs, particularly during the economic advance that coincided with the Crimean War. Those few who still loved poetry sought comfort in the writings of Andreas Munch. The years from 1850-1856 have been called "the Munchian interlude."

At the height of national romanticism there existed an intimate relation between the poets and those who cared about poetry and art at all. These included academic people and their ladies, but also some others of the so-called "cultured" class, socially the upper and middle classes. This circle had been in steady growth from the 1820's to 1850. But with the excessively good times came a stagnation in their literary interests. The prosy spirit of the capital and the dominantly negative attitude contributed to create the bitterness of Camilla Collett: "Oh big, little city." Vinje was fond of the capital because he learned so much there. But he had no chance to express himself freely and often was regarded as a fool. The negative attitude was the reason for Ibsen's having felt himself for many years as "a poet on the edge of his grave." Only Bjørnson dared to pitch his bold optimism against the spirit of the times. You can never get rid of the poets, he cried in 1855. "You can rattle with your pennies, scream at the top of your lungs in agricultural meetings and forestry commissions, make your trips by steamship and railroad. Nevertheless the lines of verse will irritate you in the newspaper you glance at, the book you thumb through. . . . You cannot kill poetry, you cannot even shake its thoughts out of your own mind. . . . The poets you cannot kill; for the poets are the good thought of the age."

If we examine what kind of literature Norwegians were reading in the first half of the nineteenth century, we find that just as in our day, novels were the most popular form. The farmers were still reading the old "folk books," late versions of the medieval romances. In the cities the ladies especially were reading foreign novels in frequently poor Danish translations, mostly borrowed at lending libraries. In the early years they were mostly German middle-class novels. Around 1850 they were mostly translations from English—Walter Scott, Bulwer-Lytton, Charles Dickens, Frederick Marryat, and Fenimore Cooper. The most popular French novels were those of Alexandre Dumas, Victor Hugo, and Eugène Sue, while among Germans there were Hackländer and Theodor Mügge. Danish authors like Mme Gyllembourg and Carl Bernhard and Swedish ones like Fredrika Bremer and Emilie Flygare-Carlén were eagerly perused.

But there were few Norwegian novels to choose from, and none of them good. The lyric was the only form of literature that had as yet reached a high cultivation in Norway. Mauritz Hansen's stories were "read in all cultured homes," but his novels were too improbable and unrealistic. Critics of the time often deplored the absence of Norwegian novels which could reflect the social life of the country. The answer to their demands came with Camilla Collett's novel *The Governor's Daughters* (*Amtmandens Døttre*).

Camilla Collett, born Wergeland (1813-1895), belonged to the age group of the national romantics, but her authorship fitted rather into that of

Ibsen and Bjørnson. She had many traits of the transitional personality. No one felt more keenly than she the contrast between the dreams and reality. It was the source of her inspiration and the undercurrent in her writing. At bottom she was a romanticist who never became wholly reconciled to reality.

She had many traits in common with her father Nicolai Wergeland, and her brother Henrik, including the melancholia and persecution complex of the former and the vivid emotional life of the latter. She had some of Henrik's imaginative capacity and his love of nature, together with his tendency to see his own experiences in a larger perspective. Just as Henrik identified himself with humanity, so she identified herself with womankind. The fact that melancholy predominated in her character, while optimism predominated in his, may be due to the bitter disappointment in love which she experienced in her youth. To Welhaven the affair with Camilla was a mere episode, but to her it became a fate. The fact that she loved Welhaven during the crucial years of controversy, and had to stand midway between St. Sebastian, as she called him, and her own father and brother, determined her development. Therefore we can read her diaries, letters, and notations from her youth as the great social novel of the 1830's. These documents, which were published at her own request after her death, surpass in dramatic intensity and passionate force anything she herself published.

In 1841 she was married to Peter Jonas Collett, one of the best men in the Intelligentsia, who gave her spirit a short respite and encouraged her to write. She wrote down folk tales she had heard and helped Asbjørnsen with some of the "frame stories" in his *Fairy Tales,* and wrote some sketches and short stories. But not until she became a widow did she complete *The Governor's Daughters* which appeared anonymously in 1854-1855.

This extraordinary book was the first novel of social purpose in Norway. It had a great influence on later Norwegian writing, on Ibsen's *Comedy of Love,* and some of Jonas Lie's stories. It was the first omen of the generation of writers who dominated the 1870's and 1880's, above all the writing of Alexander Kielland. When it appeared, it was not well received by the critics, but it gave to many of its woman readers a feeling of release and liberation, and it was later reprinted time and again.

The position of woman in home and society had been discussed in the novels of other countries from the 1830's on, by George Sand in France and Fredrika Bremer in Sweden. But in Norway it had never been discussed in any major work of literature. Henrik Wergeland had anticipated the theme in one of his sketches from 1833 about "Old Maids": "I thought that Mina would neither have been sour, lazy, thin, faded, wrinkled, prudish, malicious, hysterical, or finally consumptive and laid in an early grave if this confounded class difference, which is less founded in superior spiritual advantages than people think, had not forbidden her from attaining 'a woman's purpose.' "

In Camilla Collett's case, however, her own experiences were more influential than reading in opening her eyes to woman's need for a different education than the one that prepares her only for a socially desirable marriage. Her mission came to be a struggle on behalf of woman's right to love. Neither the man nor the woman shall choose, but the woman's love alone, to which she attributed mystic qualities. In *The Governor's Daughters* she did not primarily ask for practical reforms; her interests turned in this direction later. Instead she demanded a change of attitude, an understanding of the woman's heart. Into this cause she flung all her glowing passion, writing with bitterness and sympathy and an amazing boldness. She spoke of her novel as a "shriek," and many felt it to be just that.

The Governor's Daughters is not a perfect work of art, but still it is her most important contribution to literature. A more charming book is *In the Long Nights* (*I de lange Nætter,* 1862) with vivid pictures from her childhood and youth, above all of her father and brother. The rest of her writing was mostly agitation on behalf of the feminist cause, ironic and polemical, often bitter and aggressive. Camilla Collett felt herself to be persecuted and misunderstood, but on her eightieth birthday she was honored by men and women of all political persuasions. Henrik Ibsen was her escort at the great banquet that was held in her honor.

Her example helped to encourage other women to enter the literary arena, most of them minor though interesting figures. Not until Amalie Skram did one arrive who could equal or surpass the writing of Camilla Collett.

If we look at Aasmund Olafsson Vinje (1818-1870) from a sufficient distance, he may appear to be a typical representative of the transitional years around 1850-1860. He included within himself the contrasts of his time, between romanticism and realism, faith and skepticism, democracy and aristocracy, idealism and practicality. But he also had some of Holberg's classical desire of balancing between the extremes. Under closer scrutiny Vinje's character proves to be extremely complex. He was changeable as no one else, desultory, impulsive, emotional and cynical, warmhearted and tactless, radical and conservative, unreliable and faithful, half farm boy and half internationalist. Beneath all his sarcasm and irony there was a thin-skinned sensitivity which runs an undertone through his writing. He was a shy personality who protected himself by making fun of others.

He was born in Vinje in Telemark on April 6, 1818, the son of a tenant farmer or cotter who was known for a sharp tongue and keen wits. Aasmund himself early came to feel the stigma that was attached to being of the lowest social class, and never acquired that self-assurance which often goes with being a farmowner's son.

His outer life was a long and vain struggle to gain a footing in the society of his day. He had already had many experiences when he took to writing. He had been herdsboy and itinerant school teacher, distiller and brewer, maker of wooden shoes and cattle buyer. He went to school at Asker Seminary (1841-1843) and got a teaching position at the college in Mandal, where he taught the beginners' classes while he was still a student. All his life he thirsted for knowledge. But in spite of his brilliant head, nothing ever seemed to turn out for him. One time he thought of taking a seaman's examination, but was unable to climb a mast and got furiously seasick. He took out a merchant's license, and he had plans for emigrating to America. He went to Heltberg's prep school for university entrance where he met Ibsen. He also took a law degree and became an attorney. But his legal career was a failure also. He explained this himself by saying that he had been too kind. Others pointed out that he never had more than one case, and that one he lost.

His characteristic outlook appeared as early as 1851 in an article he wrote in *Andhrimner*, the periodical he edited together with Ibsen and Botten Hansen. Here he wrote: "Truth is nothing fixed and immutable, but a process, something fluid. God's kingdom is nothing one can point to and say: 'Here or there it is.' Only rather gross people wish to take the truth and put it in their pockets." Toward the end of the article he repeated: "Truth is nothing one can put in one's pocket and strut around the streets with, or pick up like a weight and place on the scales."

This conception of the relativity of truth made it a point of honor with him to change his mind as often as possible. Truth was in growth and he himself was developing. Could anyone expect that he would be a party man, feel himself bound by his earlier opinions, swear to a program? The same thing can be seen from many sides. Only stupid people have a one-sided view, claimed Vinje. What means something is to have "the two-sided view," the capacity to "see at one glance the right and the wrong side of life's web." For this reason he did not wish to praise anything without at the same time seeing the comical aspects of the same thing. He preferred to "cry with one eye and laugh with the other." This quality, which he shared with his friend Botten Hansen (and also with Heine and Goldschmidt), he found to be specially Norwegian. He found it in his great model Holberg, in Wessel, but no less in Shakespeare and the Norse skalds. His ideal was Thormod Kolbrunarskald who jested about his own wounds.

In spite of all aberrations and digressions in Vinje's authorship there was a certain purpose in it. He wanted to awaken his readers to thinking for themselves, criticize, stimulate, enlighten them. He worked to make education more popular and the people more educated. Through his journalistic activity he did more to present contemporary problems in a vivid and oral style than anyone else. All good journalism and scientific popularization in Norway owes something to him.

From 1851 to 1858 he was Oslo correspondent for the *Drammens Tidende*. His articles won favor, and he managed pretty well with his simple mode of life. But then he chose to abandon the standard Danish of the official press and follow Ivar Aasen's lead in writing Landsmål. The standard language had always felt like a strait jacket, and the Telemark dialect was his natural mode of expression. He mixed dialect words into his Danish, but was not satisfied until he started his own paper *Dølen* (*The Dalesman*) in 1858 and wrote it in his own language. The Language Cause was not just an idealistic program for him; it became a part of his personality. It gave him a chance to be himself entirely.

Ivar Aasen was about the only public personality of his times of whom he never made fun. Yet he did not adopt the aristocratic norm of Aasen's language, but followed his own head in this respect also. His language was as individual as his newspaper: "*The Dalesman* is a human being," he wrote, "and no dead paper." He wrote the whole thing himself, and practically every word has a personal slant. It is Vinje speaking, whether he is writing about philosophy, literature, politics, or methods of fertilizing. While his outlook was intellectual, he wished also to enlighten the country people. Now he was favorable to the government, now to the opposition. Only in his devotion to the Language Cause was he

consistent. His political program was one of co-operating with the agrarian bloc on one hand and the bureaucrats on the other. But in his day
this was impractical politics, and during his later years he gravitated
toward the new liberal party that was being formed.

Not until after his fortieth year did the vein of poetry blossom forth
in Vinje which made him one of the best lyricists of Norway. Nature
was not a subject for jesting, and he felt no "two-sided view" when he
faced it:

> Once more I had the joy of seeing winter yield to spring,
> The cherry tree so full of blossoms have its fling.
> Once again I had the joy of seeing ice-floes moving out to sea,
> The snow a-melting and the rivers rushing brave and free.

Whatever criticisms he might have of his people, he found nothing at
all to object to in nature, which called forth his reverence. Vinje's best
book is his *Travel Memoirs from the Summer of 1860* (*Ferdaminni fraa
Sumaren 1860*), in which he inserted a number of his nature lyrics. It
owes something to Heine's *Reisebilder* and other books, but expresses
Vinje's personality as nothing else he wrote. It is amusing, witty, deeply
felt. It is the highly personal account of his journey on foot from Oslo
to Trondheim where he was going to "cover" the coronation of King
Carl XV. Vinje used all of his keen observation and realistic outlook
in describing the valleys he traversed. But above all he extended himself
on the mountain districts. Vinje had grown up among mountains, and
his joy in meeting them again was one of recognition and reminiscence:

> Now once again I see such peaks and valleys
> As those my childhood knew so well.

There is an intimate mood in his descriptions of the mountains, "these
endless expanses with stone upon stone and ridges and edges and dales
like coagulated waves." The mountain heights have a personal message
to him. He feels no horror on meeting the glaciers and the barren wastes:
"The mountains have no ill will for me," as he said once when his
friends warned him against crossing a glacier. Many thoughts came to
him as he lay flat on his stomach in the "silk moss" and drank of the
"steel water": "When it can taste like this up here in the mountains, it
was no wonder that Mohammed who lived in a hot country installed
such springs in his heaven, or that the Bible also talks about the water
of life and of the hart who cries for water, though I can never believe

they have as good water in Arabia and Palestine as we have here in the mountains." A part of the charm in Vinje's descriptions of the mountains consists of the memories from his boyhood as herdsman which combine with the reflections of the mature and witty man. He feels liberated in the mountains, and his laughter as well as his lyrics flow more freely then; the bitterness and acidity are gone.

Vinje brought the high mountain expanses into Norwegian literature. He pondered all the problems that were connected with the mountains, their geology, their flora and fauna, the mountain fish and the mountain people. In his best descriptions one experiences the mountains in his company. There is more spirit in the people who live among the mountains than those who live in the lowlands, he claims. Even the animals show the difference: "Reindeer and goats are so spirited that they sparkle, and the mountain horse has almost human wit in comparison with his brother in the lowlands." Above all he became fond of Jotunheimen and its mountains; he gave them their name and made them a famous attraction.

Those of Vinje's lyrics which constitute his chief claim to renown, including some from his poetic cycle *Storegut* (1866), are not numerous, but have an unforgettable quality. Their images are simple, and there is often a touch of the ballad in them, but the main thing is their deeply personal tone. They reflect his longing for harmony.

Vinje was not taken too seriously during his lifetime, in spite of his reputation as a speaker and a wit. His economic circumstances were miserable during his last ten years. In 1862 he made a study tour of England, but the book he wrote in English about his observations, *A Norseman's View of Britain and the British,* won him little admiration, although it is still a document of great interest for the view it gives of England seen through the eyes of a Norwegian peasant critic. His stories and plays were not successful, lacking as he did the ability to create living figures. For three years he had a clerk's position in the Department of Justice, but lost his job because he wrote against the party in power. He married after this, but died on July 30, 1870.

On his sickbed in the hospital he often thought of his beloved Jotunheimen. "Can you remember the view from Skinegg that morning?" he said to Sars. "When the white mist drifted away among the peaks, and the glaciers shone like gold in the sun! Oh me, oh me, that I can't get up there this summer. . . . But now when I've been laid in my coffin, my spirit is going to take its abode up there among the mountains, and then I'll sit on Falketind and look out over Norway while the peaks rise row upon row before me . . ."

From National to World Literature

In 1896 BJØRNSTJERNE BJØRNSON PUBLISHED AN ARTICLE about modern Norwegian literature in the American periodical *The Forum,* in which he compared the literatures of Europe to fleets sailing across the Atlantic. Of the Norwegian he wrote:

It came from one of the smallest nations of the world, but one from whose people sprung Europe's oldest aristocracies and whose marvellously beautiful country has become a permanent world's exhibition for travelers. It was the Norwegian fleet, and it came with a rush. Something firm and compact about every vessel, as if each had an errand of its own. Not a single pleasure craft in the whole fleet. No movement outside the course. With one single exception no elegance in hull or rigging, but a solid reliability. Each ship looked a realm by itself. They came together, because they could not but do so, but each of them in his own manner . . .[1]

Bjørnson here succeeded in hitting off some of the traits which must have struck foreign observers when Norwegian literature first impinged on European consciousness. There was above all the seriousness of this literature, its rich freight of ideas, its definite purposes, and its lack of artistic playfulness. But at the same time the writers succeeded in giving expression to their individual artistic personalities. There was no standardized writing. Each of the great poets was a world unto himself, and made his appearance, not as a battler in a closed phalanx, but on his own artistic and ethical merits.

The great literary efflorescence of the last third of the nineteenth century was not unprepared, though it might look so to a foreigner. Its roots were to be found in the literature of the 1830's and 1840's, and its growth was stimulated by conditions in Norwegian society during

[1] Bjørnson, "Modern Norwegian Literature," *Forum,* XXI (1896), 318-29, 397-413.

this period. But it also owed a great deal to impulses from the outside. Many of the ideas and problems that seemed so new and created such a discussion throughout the civilized world had originated in those countries that welcomed Norwegian writing. But there the ideas had often been buried in scientific treatises on biology, sociology, or religion, while in Norway they found literary expression.

At the head of the young generation of writers stood Bjørnson himself. He turned against the national romanticists and prophesied that a new generation of poets would arise and create a revolution in the land of literature, a generation with new ideas and tasks, but still "with roots in this country from of old." From the beginning his life was a battle under the banner of Henrik Wergeland, though he owed Welhaven more as a versifier. He fought for Norway against Danish and Swedish hegemony, whether in culture or in politics, but also for Scandinavian unity, for Germanic understanding, and finally for world peace and the rights of all oppressed peoples. He demanded reforms in family life, in society, in the nation, in the relationships between nations. He always felt called upon to interfere when he thought someone was suffering an injustice, from the first day in school to the time when the world press was open to him. In his innermost self he was always a believer, even though his beliefs might change. He was a "poet politician" who made his influence felt in his immediate circle, but was also a dreamer who felt that "he never grasps the play of life, who brings no dreams into its strife." He was a born optimist, a lyrical leader type like his spiritual kinsmen Victor Hugo in France, Grundtvig in Denmark, Henrik Wergeland in Norway.

Ibsen was, by comparison, much less certain of his course in the beginning, vacillating as he did among impressions of Wergeland, Welhaven, and Oehlenschläger. But through all his doubt and distress he held fast to what he came to consider his "call" or "mission." He was an aristocrat and an anarchist at one and the same time, a stubborn individualist, a man of the absolute demand, a poet who loved ideas more than people, a fanatic logician and a merciless psychologist, a lonely fighter at the foreposts, an anatomist with the dissecting knife. He did not concern himself with a multitude of things like Bjørnson. His world of ideas was not a roomy one, but it was his own. "Be thyself" was his demand. This requirement he directed at every man, but he also held a "judgment day" on himself.

Jonas Lie was less of a battler, and more of a dreamer. But he, too, had a keen eye for details of reality and everyday life. His critique was subtler than that of the others, because he rarely expressed his ideas in the form of slogans or pointed speeches. Even while he was winning the confidence of his readers, he was tearing away the basis for antiquated views, undermining their prejudices so that they hardly noticed it. Above all he was concerned with the mysterious forces that slumbered in the depths of human nature, the "evil powers" as he called them, the world of the latent instincts.

Alexander Kielland was introduced by Bjørnson as "the most elegant vessel of the Norwegian fleet, or to tell the truth, its only elegant one." He compared him to a warship with rapid-firing cannon. The elegance of Kielland has become proverbial in Norway. The term refers primarily to his refreshing wit, which is as enjoyable today as when it was written. There is also a suggestion in it of his patrician background. But Kielland turned his wit against the stuffiness and hypocrisy of the social order with the same zeal as the others of his generation. His works reveal also a warmhearted sympathy with the oppressed and a lyrical quality which has given his works a universal appeal and an over-all kindly tone.

Arne Garborg came from the same part of the country as Kielland, but from rural stock. He was largely a self-taught man who went through a long development. Intellectually he was probably the sharpest of the writers in his generation. His keen eyes saw through everything and his logic penetrated to the heart of the problems he was concerned with. He had a noble and sensitive personality, was not highly creative, but with a sure artistic hand, half thinker, half leader. He came to be the personified national and international conscience of the Norwegian people, and the one most typical of his times among the writers of the eighties and nineties. Several of his works are like barometers of the cultural climate, registering as they do the intellectual development of his generation.

All of these writers had significance outside the borders of Norway. Ibsen became the great dramatist of the century, with influences far and wide. Norway became "Ibsen's country," as it later became Nansen's and Amundsen's. Bjørnson became a central figure in his time, partly through his work for oppressed peoples, but also through some of his plays. Lie won entry into the home, particularly in Germany where Norwegian literature won its first fame and was spread into other countries. Kielland was less known, but he had a considerable influence on a writer like Thomas Mann. Garborg's significance abroad was the smallest, but his naturalistic novels meant something to the German naturalists.

Norway was no longer just a recipient in the literary world; she had something to give back as well.

In Scandinavia the literature of these years gave Norway the literary leadership by the end of the century. Denmark had been the leader in the first half of the century, though Sweden also had had a great period during the romantic era. Sweden again came to the fore around 1900, through the writings of Strindberg, Selma Lagerlöf, Gustaf Fröding, and others.

The significance of the Norwegian writers was not merely the quality of their writing, but perhaps in just as high a degree the fact that they were able to shape the ideas of their times into artistic form. They were all reformers who wanted to change people's ideas. They were unanimous in their Wergelandian faith that artistic writing can open the way to new and better times. In spite of their social criticism and their polemic tone they were affirmative in their attitude. They had grown up in a romantic atmosphere and were all basically Christian-humanistic in their view, however much they may have attacked some phenomena of religious and social organization. If they made severe demands on humanity, it was because they basically had faith in man as a spiritual being, in the indwelling capacity of mankind for perfectibility.

Ibsen's Early Plays

THE LAST TIME the youthful Henrik Ibsen visited his birthplace Skien, he took a walk with his sister Hedvig to a hill behind the city where one could look out over the sea. He spoke to her then about his ambitions to reach "the greatest and most perfect of all that could be attained in greatness and clarity." "But when you have attained it, what then?" "Then I would die," he replied.

This episode sounds like a scene in an Ibsen drama, and reminds us of the ideas in his last play, *When We Dead Awaken*. It illustrates his ambitious dreams in the late 1840's, his absolutist demands and his sense of having a mission. But when we think of his situation at the time, it also gives us a picture of his extreme spiritual loneliness.

He was born on March 20, 1828, in Skien. His father, Knud Ibsen, came of a family of skippers from Bergen. He founded a business in Skien, but his speculations led to the loss of all he had in 1836, when Henrik was eight years old. Reminiscences of the father's wastefulness in the well-to-do period of his life recur in fantastic exaggeration in the figure of Peer Gynt's father, Jon Gynt, the hospitable and frivolous wastrel who "bought land in every parish" and "drove with gilded wagons." After his failure the father turned bitter, suspicious, and sarcastic toward his old friends, finally going entirely to the dogs. We find traces of him in the cutting remarks made by Daniel Hejre in *The League of Youth*. Henrik's mother Marichen, née Altenburg, is described as a self-sacrificing mother, introspective, deeply religious; in her later years she lived in almost complete seclusion. Ibsen used traits from her in the king's mother Inga in *Pretenders,* and "with necessary exaggerations" also in mother Åse in *Peer Gynt*. Of his four brothers and sisters only the sister Hedvig meant anything to him. She is reflected in the Solveig type, and he drew a childhood picture of her in the figure of Hedvig in *The Wild Duck*.

"One's home—is always far to the north; one's home—that word is always closed to the south," says the hero in the epic version of *Brand* which preceded the play. The words reflect Ibsen's feeling of not having had much normal happiness in his home. He was a shy boy, with many inhibitions and an exaggerated imagination. His craving for solitude was not diminished when the family moved to a house outside of Skien after the failure. He must have been deeply hurt by the social scorn that struck the family of a "bankrupt" in those days. He withdrew into himself, while he dreamed, read, painted, drew caricatures, and put on puppet shows.

After confirmation at the age of fourteen he was sent to Grimstad, a still smaller town down the coast, as an apprentice to the local druggist. The apothecary's shop became his home for six years. His satirical bent was intensified during his stay in Grimstad, along with his need for self-assertion. He felt as if he were at war with the small-town society around him. He wrote epigrams about the local citizens, expressed himself paradoxically and self-confidently about the problems of his time, and irritated his listeners by expressing scorn of the monarchy, of religion, and marriage. He called himself a freethinker and an adherent of Voltaire.

But in his own heart he was torn and insecure, alternating between feelings of guilt, inferiority, and faith. The poems he wrote during the years 1847-1850 were not very original, and their themes were the usual romantic ones of "resignation," "doubt and hope," "the ghostly ball," "a ride in the moonlight," "midnight moods." But he also wrote "Stella poems" in the spirit of Wergeland, dreamt of "overthrowing the pillars of tyranny" under the impression of the February revolution, and urged King Oscar to do battle for the cause of Scandinavia against the German invaders of Denmark.

His most interesting work is the drama *Catilina,* which was written in the winter of 1848-1849.[1] Here we meet the idea of mission in the very opening words: "I *must,* I *must,* so bids a voice within my soul, and I shall follow its commands." The play expresses for the first time the poet's bent for contradiction. He was annoyed while reading his schoolbooks by the scorn heaped on the rebel Catiline by Sallust and Cicero. There are also reflections of his own antagonism to the middle-class society around him. But the social problem is not prominent in this play.

[1] Tr. Anders Orbeck in *Early Plays: Catiline, The Warrior's Barrow, Olaf Liljekrans by Henrik Ibsen* (New York, 1921).

The real battleground is in the hero's own heart, where a struggle is raging between the forces of good and evil, symbolized in two women, the blond Aurelia and the dark Furia, prototypes of so many Ibsen women. Retribution falls upon the hero because of his own past, his "licentious pleasures." It is a drama of fate, but also psychological, which makes it a truly Ibsenian play.

Just before 1850 Ibsen came strongly under the influence of national romanticism. His play *The Warrior's Barrow* (*Kjæmpehøien*)[2] describes the struggle between heathendom and Christianity, wholly in the spirit of Oehlenschläger. After he arrived in Oslo that year for the purpose of entering the university, he came into close contact with the ideas of the times through his friendship with members of the incipient labor movement and literary men like Vinje and Botten Hansen. With these two he edited for a short time a periodical called *Manden* (*The Man*), later *Andhrimner*, where he published articles and a satirical opera called *Norma, or a Politician's Love*, on a theme he later developed in *The League of Youth*. He studied the aesthetics of Johan Ludvig Heiberg and formulated a program for national writing which he followed during the next few years: "The national author is the one who is able to give his work that basic tone which rings out to us from mountain and valley, from hillside and shore, but above all from our own hearts."

In the autumn of 1851 he was called to Bergen by Ole Bull, who had just founded a theater in that city. He was hired to "assist the theater as dramatic author," which meant that he was obligated to write a new play each year for the opening day of the theatrical season, January 2, besides helping to direct plays. The years of his residence in Bergen (1851-1857) were highly significant for his development, though he never became a good director, being awkward and insecure of manner. But he got valuable training in stage effects and served his apprenticeship as a dramatist. He had the experience of hearing his own words, seeing the creatures of his own imagination on the stage, and learning whether they sounded false or genuine. But he also got his chance to see foreign stages when the theater sent him to Denmark and Germany in 1852. On this journey he got acquainted with Hermann Hettner's book *Das Moderne Drama* (1852) which exerted a profound influence on him. Hettner maintained that even the historical tragedy must be psychological; the spectators of our day must be able to recognize themselves in the historical figures. Ibsen also received many impressions during

[2] *Ibid.*

these years from the historic memorials of Bergen and from the mountainous nature of western Norway. These often reappeared in his later writings, sometimes with symbolic significance.

One episode from his life in Bergen was the short-lived engagement, if such it was, with Rikke Holst, a lively sixteen-year-old. He wrote poems in her honor, and one of his jolliest and least typical songs, "We wander with merry hearts," dates from this period. They joined two rings together and threw them into the sea, like Ellida Wangel and the Stranger in *Lady from the Sea*. But the idyll was suddenly terminated one day when her father came upon them; Ibsen turned tail and ran. He confessed to her many years later, "Face to face I have never been a courageous man."

On his brief foreign journey he wrote the folk tale comedy *St. John's Eve* (*Sancthansnatten*), a literary satire in which he defended romantic naïveté against excessive sophistication. It was a failure, which is not strange. More surprising is the lack of appreciation shown his next play, *Lady Inger at Østraat* (*Fru Inger til Østraat*), performed on January 2, 1855.[3] This is a broadly conceived tragedy of character on a historical theme, the tragedy at once of mother love and mother country. For the first time he succeeded in creating living figures. He infused into the play his own characteristic theme of the conflict between life's mission and personal happiness, the idea that one's call demands the sacrifice of all else. *Lady Inger* was something new in Norwegian literature, even though the plot technique of misunderstandings and confusions was a formula learned from the French writer Scribe.

Ibsen now turned to the family sagas and conceived the first misty idea that led to *The Warriors of Helgeland*, particularly the two women who were later called Hjørdis and Dagny. But a love affair intervened and the tragedy turned into his only lyric idyll, *The Feast at Solhaug* (*Gildet paa Solhaug*, 1856).[4] The saga with its tragic overtones had to give way to impressions drawn from Landstad's ballad collection of 1853. The performance was a success, but the critics were cool. Ibsen was encouraged, however, to write another ballad drama, *Olaf Liljekrans*,[5] but this one was far below the first. He tried to defend it in a long essay "On the Ballad and Its Significance for Art Poetry."

Not until his engagement to Suzannah Thoresen did he start work

---

[3] Tr. Charles Archer, *Collected Works*, Vol. 1 (New York, 1908, orig. pub. London, 1890); R. F. Sharp, *Everyman* 729 (London, n.d.).
[4] Tr. William Archer and Mary Morison, *Collected Works*, Vol. 1 (New York, 1908).
[5] *Supra* note 1.

on his saga play. "She is a character of the kind I need," he later wrote about his wife, "illogical, but with a strong poetic instinct, a magnanimous mode of thought, and an almost violent hate of all petty considerations." We have his own word that she was the model of Hjørdis in *The Warriors* and of Svanhild in *Comedy of Love*. He started writing *The Warriors of Helgeland* (*Hærmændene paa Helgeland*) in verse,[6] but soon changed over to a prose in the manner of the sagas. In the world of the saga he recognized his own ideals, the stubborn self-assertion, the vigorous and whole-souled personalities, the indomitable will, the absolute demands on love. He succeeded in creating characters with clear and firm personalities, Hjørdis, Sigurd, Gunnar, Dagny. His old man Ørnulf is like Egil Skalla-Grimsson, but also like Ibsen himself, in being able to dissipate his sorrows by expressing them in poetry. The dramatic structure is surer than before, more integrated with the characters themselves. The dialogue is terse, stimulating, dramatic. But its concise and suggestive form was not merely an imitation of N. M. Petersen's Danish saga translation; it was also an expression of Ibsen's own nature.

By the time this play appeared, he had gone back to the capital to assume the artistic direction of the Norwegian Theater which had been founded in 1852 after the model of Ole Bull's theater in Bergen. But here it was not the only theater; it had to rival the previously established Christiania Theater and was consciously intended to offset the emphasis in the latter on Danish plays, actors, and pronunciation.

Ibsen's second residence in the capital (1857-1864) turned out to be the period of greatest distress in his life. He came with high hopes, and even applied to the Storting for an annual subsidy so that the theater would be able to educate its public and not be dependent on whims of taste. He wrote articles attacking the directors of the Christiania Theater and poems for various occasions in support of the national cause. He turned on the Danes in a poem called "Cries of the Seagulls." He went very far in the direction of the New Norse language these years, employing many Norwegian localisms in his writing. He insisted that Norwegian culture must free itself from the force of Danish influence. He found abundant support in this work when Bjørnson returned from Bergen in 1859 and became the editor of an Oslo newspaper, *Aftenbladet*. Ibsen then proposed the formation of a Norwegian Society to promote "nationality in literature and art." Bjørnson became its first president, Ibsen its

[6] Tr. R. F. Sharp, *Everyman* 552 (London, 1911); tr. as *The Vikings at Helgeland* by William Archer, *Collected Works*, Vol. 2 (New York, 1906, orig. pub. 1890).

vice president—as far as is known, the only time Ibsen ever joined a society or held an office. The two writers were great friends at this time, both being at once supporters of Wergeland's nationalism and Welhaven's Scandinavianism.

But alongside the believer in Norwegian nationalism there lived in Ibsen a skeptic as well, who gained nourishment from his many defeats. Ibsen got no fellowships. The performance of *Warriors* at Christiania Theater was postponed for a year. The finances at his own theater were miserable, and in 1862 it went bankrupt. *Christiania-Posten* wrote that he was one of "the minor poets," and as a dramatic author "a great nonentity, about whom the nation cannot with any enthusiasm plant a protective hedge." Even more mortifying, no doubt, was the rejection of *Warriors* at the Royal Theater in Copenhagen by J. L. Heiberg himself.

Ibsen reached his lowest point in 1861, ill and depressed, plagued by fever, inclined to nourish thoughts of suicide. In the very years when he was assisting Bjørnson in The Norwegian Society, it is characteristic that he was also a constant visitor among the men of the so-called "Hollanders' Circle." One of the leaders was Botten Hansen, his old friend, and the rest were clever and critical scholars, who cultivated Holberg as their model. Bjørnson was irritated at their negative and skeptical spirit, referring to them as "a gang of theoreticians and mockers." In this circle Ibsen could thaw out and playfully give expression to his paradoxical and contrary opinions. These men took neither the national romantics nor the middle-class society of their time too seriously, and we see the effects of their influence in the critical spirit of Ibsen's *Comedy of Love*.

"Not until I was married did my life gain a more substantial content," he wrote many years later. In the poem "Terje Vigen,"[7] which expresses a personal crisis, it says of Terje after he married and became a father: "It was said that Terje's spirit turned serious from that moment." But Ibsen himself was torn between conflicting desires. He also felt during these miserable years an urge to keep life at arm's length, to fly from the miseries of everyday life and seek shelter in the indifference to life that a purely aesthetic or artistic outlook could offer. The contrast between ideal and life, dream and deed, the poet's mission and the duties of daily life tormented him as never before.

[7] Tr. F. E. Garrett in *Lyrics and Poems from Ibsen* (London, 1912), 35-45; D. Svennungsen (Minneapolis, Minn., 1923); H. Hansen (Chicago, 1929).

In his poem "On the Heights" ("Paa Vidderne," 1859),[8] the first that clearly foreshadows the plays that were about to come, he created an imaginative expression of this contrast. In its central figure he depicted one who freed himself from human living, who split his personality between the human being and the artist. But he also showed the hardening of the heart which goes with the aesthetic outlook. In 1860 he started a play to be called *Svanhild*, using the name of a figure from *The Saga of the Volsungs*, in which he intended to contrast the artistic and the everyday views of life. Not until the bankruptcy of his theater was he able to complete it. Then he decided to do it in verse and changed the title to *Comedy of Love (Kjærlighedens Komedie)*. The verse form was at this time easier for him than prose and enabled him to give freer vent to his anger and his urge for freedom. At the same time he was also trying to break the stranglehold which the aesthetic view of life had upon him.

On the one hand *Comedy of Love* (1862)[9] is a witty idealistic attack on the bourgeois concept of love, in many ways a counterpart to *The Governor's Daughters*. The many engaged and married couples who appear on the stage are delightful types rather maliciously delineated. On the other hand it is also the tragicomic analysis of the relationship between a poet's mission and his responsibilities to others. The poet Falk has Ibsen's sympathy as long as he is mocking the bourgeois society with its stale compromises. But Falk is also an artistic egotist who represents the aesthetic view of life. When he meets Svanhild, his development enters a new phase. He wants to take part in life, do battle against lies and hypocrisy:

> My four-wall-chamber poetry is done;
> My verse shall live in forest and in field,
> I'll fight under the splendour of the sun;—
> I or the Lie—one of us two must yield!

Translated by C. H. Herford

The artistic egotist in him had at first wanted to reject Svanhild in order that their relationship might pass into memory as a source of his artistic inspiration. But in the end they agree to part because they both are

[8] Tr. as *On the Fells* by F. E. Garrett in *Lyrics and Poems from Ibsen* (London, 1912), 22-33.
[9] Tr. as *Love's Comedy* by C. H. Herford in *Collected Works*, Vol. 1 (New York, 1908, orig. pub. 1900); R. F. Sharp, *Everyman* 729 (London, n.d.).

doubtful of their capacity to realize a true and ideal love. But through his struggle with himself Falk has learned "to fight and renounce," and he now heads up into the mountains to strengthen his resolution. Now he perceives the ideal behind his activity, his life mission:

> I go to scale the Future's possibilities!
> Farewell! God bless thee, bride of my life's dawn,
> Where'er I be, to nobler deed thou'lt wake me.

Translated by C. H. Herford

Falk is only one of Ibsen's mouthpieces in this drama, for he grants some hearing to the representative of social duties, Guldstad, and even to the pastoral caricature Strawman. For the first time in his writing Ibsen does not take sides openly, but divides his blame and praise rather evenly among the opposing views, and for the first time he gives each character its own mode of expression. In spite of the verse form he succeeded in hitting off the special styles of speaking used by merchant, bureaucrat, parson, and sentimental spinster, without sacrificing poetic quality.

While he was working on *Comedy of Love,* Ibsen was just as poor as in the worst years of his youth. He had to get along on some vacation grants for collecting ballads and folk tales, which resulted in a journey through Gudbrandsdal and over the mountains to Sogn. Impressions from this journey are reflected in *Brand* and *Peer Gynt.* He kept his spirits up during this time because he was able to contentrate on his poetic work. But the reception of *Comedy of Love* was a disappointment. He was told that it was "pure claptrap," an attack on home and society, "immoral" and "unpoetic." When he applied for a grant from the government, it was said that he ought to get a whipping and not a grant. Nevertheless he did not let himself be entirely cowed. This was the time when he revised the poem "The Miner" into its final sculptured form and profound message, and when he wrote "With a Water Lily" and "Afraid of the Light," poems which express great mental anguish, but also an indomitable will.[10]

Nevertheless we can see from his next play, *The Pretenders (Kongsemnerne,* 1863),[11] that there were times when he doubted his own

---

10 A number of Ibsen's shorter lyrics are included in F. E. Garrett's *Lyrics and Poems from Ibsen* (London, 1912) and in *Lyrical Poems by Ibsen,* tr. by R. A. Streatfield (London, 1902).
11 Tr. William Archer, *Collected Works,* Vol. 2 (New York, 1906, orig. pub. 1890); R. F. Sharp, *Everyman* 659 (London, 1913).

mission as an artist. The original plan was conceived during his national romantic period, in 1858, when the theme interested him as an expression of rebellion. Skule then appealed to him as a man who, like Catiline, was unlucky enough to get his history written by his enemies. But by 1863 his attention had been focused on the doubter in Skule. The contrast between the skeptic and the believer as personality types was borne in upon him during a song festival he attended in Bergen together with Bjørnson. This journey enabled him also to gain some perspective on the worries of his everyday existence and an elevation of spirit which made it possible to create this drama. The magnificence of nature, the festive arrangements, all the lyricism of the Bergen temperament contributed to his satisfaction. He even enjoyed some personal recognition, possibly the most enthusiastic in many years, in the form of speeches and cheers in his honor. More important was the friendliness of Bjørnson, now the acknowledged leader of youth, who set him beside himself and inspired him with some of his faith. Bjørnson made a speech for Haakon, "Norway's best king." The parallel was obvious: here stood Haakon, and even Ibsen could feel the identification with both Bjørnson and himself. He gained faith in his own powers. In the drama we meet in Haakon the Ibsen who founded The Norwegian Society and stood by Bjørnson's side. In Skule we meet the Ibsen who was a member of the "Hollanders' Circle" and expressed his searching doubts of himself and society.

In spite of some weaknesses, *The Pretenders* is one of the masterpieces of Norwegian literature. It fulfills the program of Hettner in being a true historical tragedy of character, and it is less stylized and archaic than *The Warriors*. There is an inner connection with *Comedy of Love* in their common concern with a man's calling or mission. Haakon has the calling, and therefore luck is with him. Skule has the abilities and the will, but lacks the calling; he loses because he doubts himself. There are, as it were, three layers in the play—the struggle of the pretenders to the throne in the first half of the thirteenth century, a hidden reflection of Ibsen's relationship to his more fortunate colleague Bjørnson, and a dissection of himself. The profoundest and most beautiful passage in the play is the conversation between Skule and Jatgeir the Skald about the gift of sorrow which turns a man into a poet.

The Pretenders made a deep impression when it was performed at Christiania Theater. A short time earlier the poet had received a travel grant of $400 from the government, and Bjørnson gathered $700 more from private sources to help his friend go to Italy. Ibsen left Norway in 1864 and stayed away for nearly a generation.

The mood in which he left Norway was evoked by the events associated with the Dano-Prussian war of 1864. Ibsen took the failure of Norway to go to the aid of Denmark harder than most of his generation. To understand his rage during this period we must realize that to him the question of help for Denmark was not a political but a moral issue. His poem "The Murder of Abraham Lincoln" shows that he regarded the history of the world from an ethical point of view. He had been forced to give up one ideal after the other during these years of hardship, but one remained in which he pinned his faith, the mutual friendship of the Scandinavian nations. For years the academicians of the Scandinavian countries had held their annual festivals at which they had sworn undying brotherhood. When the government of Sweden and Norway decided to stand idly by while parts of Denmark were gulped down by the Prussian eagle, Ibsen's fury knew no bounds. His absolutist idealism found an almost hysterical expression.

But his protracted stay abroad stemmed more from his inferiority complex at the time of his humiliation. He wanted the revenge on his people of being able to return as a self-assured man at whom no one could shrug his shoulders. But he also felt a greater freedom when he was abroad. Just as he had withdrawn from his own parents and family, and cut down on the number of his friends, he could not stand in a relationship of half understanding to his country. Until late in his life he did not feel that he could be himself in Norway. He was afraid that he would be drawn into cliques and parties, or fall out with everybody. He had to be far away, needed distance and perspective to be able to tell his countrymen the bitter truth.

When Ibsen wrote his angry poem, "A Brother in Need" ("En broder i nød", December 1863), he still had some hope, in spite of the scornful words. But his anger grew as he journeyed southwards. In Copenhagen he wrote his acid indictment of the Norwegian army, "Well-Grounded Faith"; it was a kind of life insurance policy, he hinted, to join the Norwegian army. The crisis in his emotional life reached its climax in Berlin, where he saw the German mobs spitting in the captured Danish cannon. "It was to me a sign of how history will some day spit in Sweden's and Norway's eyes for that deed's sake." In this he was of course wrong, for our own time has become inured to betrayals of the same kind on an even greater and more vicious scale.

Ibsen now began to look at the relationship of Norwegians to their history in a new way. The whole business of national romanticism, he held, was merely a spree in which the Norwegians indulged themselves because they were ridiculous and impotent weaklings who could not face the realities of the present. He himself had worked to build a bridge between the old and the new Norway, had helped to whip up an interest in the old sagas and their heroes. In a letter to Bjørnson of September 16 he wrote: "We had better cross out our old history; for the Norwegians of today obviously have no more connection with their past than the Greek pirates have with the race that sailed to Troy and was assisted by the gods." At times he had an icy feeling that "for our people there is no eternity, only a short term."

When he first arrived in Italy, Ibsen had various plans in mind. But they were all laid aside because his anger demanded expression. The release came through his twin dramatic poems *Brand* and *Peer Gynt*. Like the bear in his poem "The Power of Memory," he had had his ordeal by fire:

> So let of that day but an echo sound,
> On a glowing grid I seem to be bound;
>
> As the quick of the nail to a stab must answer,
> I find my verse-feet and straight turn dancer.

Translated by F. E. Garrett

He burned with the crusader's zeal when he wrote *Brand* (1866),[12] which got its dramatic structure through the inspiration of St. Peter's dome. He embodied in his hero Brand impressions of idealists he had known, from the uncompromising lay preacher Lammers and the Danish writer Kierkegaard, to Christopher Bruun, the later folk high school teacher who volunteered in the Dano-Prussian war. He wanted to show the Norwegians how a real man should behave. At the same time he carried on his debate about the artist's role in life, embodied in such a figure as Einar, along the same lines as in "On the Heights" and *Comedy of Love*.

Above all, this is a drama about a man's calling, in which everything is demanded of the human personality. "Be yourself," cries the poet

[12] Tr. C. H. Herford, *Collected Works*, Vol. 3 (New York, 1906, orig. pub. 1898); F. E. Garrett, in *Lyrics and Poems from Ibsen* (London, 1912); M. M. Dawson (Boston, 1916); William Wilson, in prose (London, 1892).

pastor, realize your profoundest self, stay away from compromises. The high-minded personality must oppose his slogan of "all or nothing" to every common-sense utilitarianism. It is better to be in the clutches of sin than to be petty or mean in one's reasoning or irresolute in one's intentions.

> Grant you are slaves to pleasure: well,
> Be so, from curfew-bell to bell:
> Don't be some special thing one minute
> And something else the next, by fits!

But this poem is not merely a religio-ethical syllogism, written with apocalyptic eloquence and scathing satire. There is also a subtle psychology in the description of the inner struggles of the hero and his wife Agnes. In spite of its fanatical idealism and uncompromising evaluation of mankind, *Brand* is a deeply felt work, the tragedy of the merciless idealist. In Brand's heart there burns the poet's own love of the ideal. "Brand is myself in my best moments," he wrote in a letter. In his wife Agnes he created one of his finest feminine characters. As a woman she stands in a closer contact with life than her husband.

After *Brand* came *Peer Gynt* (1867)[13] "as if by itself," wrote Ibsen in a letter. He had found the motif in Asbjørnsen's collection of folk tales: "That Peer Gynt was something by himself. He was a regular fairy tale maker and storyteller you would have enjoyed. He always said that he himself had taken part in the stories people said had happened in olden days." Ibsen may also have heard something about Peer on his journey in 1862. But in reality he was glad that he had little to build on, "so that I have been able to play the more freely with the theme according to my own needs." The fantast Peer became the opposite of Brand. He represents all that Brand had fought against, the indecision, the mendacity, the self-deceit, the utilitarianism, the spirit of compromise. But the drama turned out to be a great deal more. It became also a self-searching analysis in agreement with Ibsen's later definition of poetry:

> To write poetry—is to hold
> Judgment day upon one's self.

[13] Tr. William and Charles Archer, *Collected Works*, Vol. 4 (New York, 1907, orig. pub. 1892); R. Ellis Roberts (London, 1912); Gottfried Hult (New York, 1933); Norman Ginsbury (London, 1946); R. F. Sharp, *Everyman* 747 (London, 1921); Paul Green, "American version" (New York, 1951); Richard Mansfield, "Acting version" (Chicago, 1906); Horace Maynard Finney (New York, 1955); selections by Isabelle M. Pagan, *The Fantasy of Peer Gynt* (London, 1909).

If he wished to be entirely honest with himself, he had to admit that he had not lived up to Brand's demands. He had not himself volunteered to fight for Denmark, as had his friend Christopher Bruun. To be sure, he could answer that his mission had been a different one, to teach his people "to think great thoughts." But this excuse did not entirely acquit him. In a letter to Bjørnson at this time he spoke of his "self-anatomizing": "You may be sure that in quiet moments I delve and probe and anatomize quite interestingly in my own innards, even at the points where it hurts the most." He adds that just as Brand was himself in his best moments, so he owes some of the traits of Peer Gynt to self-anatomy. In these quiet moments he could hardly overlook the fact that he himself had taken part in the national romantics' adulation of ancient heroism, had helped to deceive the Norwegian people with that which now seemed to him a lie. It is significant that the introduction to the epic version of *Brand* bears the title, "To my partners in crime." The self-anatomizing gradually made the liar and fantast more human. Ibsen had to endow Peer with all of his own imagination and poetic genius. He, too, often had difficulty in looking reality in the eye. With delicate irony he lets the other characters refer to Peer as "an abominable romancer." The word is *digter,* which means at once a poet and a prevaricator.

In a conversation with King Skule, Jatgeir Skald had said: "*I* needed sorrow; there may be others who need faith or joy—or doubt." Doubt had made it possible for Ibsen to write *The Pretenders.* The gift of sorrow had created *Brand.* But in the shaping of *Peer Gynt* the poet drew also from the other sources of inspiration mentioned by Jatgeir: faith and joy. Norway had given him sorrow and doubt, but faith and joy came to him in Italy. They came with the reports of the extraordinary success which *Brand* had had throughout Scandinavia. They came with the assurance that his economy was secure since the Storting had voted him an author's stipend. Impressions of Italian scenery also helped to bring him out of his shell. The same Ibsen who had written before the appearance of *Brand*: "I feel as if I am separated both from God and men by a great, endless wasteland," now wrote in May 1866, "It is marvelously lovely here. I have a capacity for work and an energy such that I could kill bears!"

In this way *Peer Gynt* became his merriest and most colorful work, full of malice and love, fantasy and prose, crackling wit and ringing lyricism. It is a central work in Norwegian literature, comprising elements from the nationalistic and romantic atmosphere of the preceding period and yet satirizing these elements in a spirit of realism akin to the period that was coming. It has been said that if a Norwegian were to leave his country and could take with him only one book to express his national culture, this is the one he would choose.

Brand brought the Norwegian mountains into world literature as symbols of the cold, relentless demands of an inhuman idealism. In *Peer Gynt* the nature symbolism is richer and more warmly experienced. The mist lies over Gjendin when Peer and the buck plunge down from the mountains and the seagulls scatter before them. The summer skies arch blue above the mountains of Rondane when Peer flees to the north. The huge fir tree shakes its crooked arm as Peer chops away at it. Peer Gynt brought the life of the Norwegian folk and their trolls into world literature, not only as national symbols, but also as basic forces in the human heart.

The Young Bjørnson

In a letter of march 30, 1866, to his Danish friend, the critic Clemens Petersen, Bjørnson wrote about *Brand*: "There is much that is powerful in this book, but it is not harmonized, it does not do good, except at the most on one or two points, and so it is no poem. . . . The whole thing is an abstract experiment, the maneuvers of an intellectual army. . . . I hate this book! I am ill from reading it. . . ." He prophesied that the book would be dead in two months. To Ibsen he wrote: "Now I wish you would design characters which do not in the final analysis, as in *Brand* and *Comedy of Love,* turn out to be mere ideas, abstractions." In the same letter he called Brand his "antipode."

The views here expressed are characteristic of Bjørnson and his attitudes. He was the diametric opposite of Ibsen's Brand, a man who loved humanity and abhorred a relentless logic: "Fie on this inebriation and mad enthusiasm over consistency, which makes French revolutions and German nonsense." He was repelled by all logical experiments that made life more difficult instead of consoling us with existence. This basic view is associated with his whole spiritual structure, the breadth and love and energy which characterized his generous heart. He placed his faith in a gradual evolution, in social progress, in the common people, and in humanitarian feeling. He was poet and politician, artist and educator, a man of action no less than of the pen.

Bjørnstjerne Martinius Bjørnson was born December 8, 1832, at Bjørgan parsonage in Kvikne. The parsonage is located just north of the watershed between Trøndelag and Østerdalen, though it is administratively a part of the latter. "From here two valleys could be viewed and much land," as he says in *Between the Battles.* His father, the pastor Peder Bjørnson, was a farm boy from Søndre Land, not brilliant, but solid and imperious, a fellow student of Henrik Wergeland. Bjørnstjerne was the oldest of six. His mother Elise, née Nordraak, was a merchant's daughter from Kragerø, cheerful and artistic of temperament. The poet once compared his father to a huge tree trunk and his mother to the twittering of the birds around it.

In 1837 pastor Bjørnson was assigned to the parish of Nesset in Romsdalen. Here the boy grew up, won friends among the farm boys of the community, and laid the foundation of his love for animals, as he has told it in some of his short stories. All his life he continued to keep in touch with this community and feel himself as a native of Romsdalen. He came to regard the colorful and multifarious qualities in himself, the gentle and the reckless aspects of his character, as somehow stemming from this region. This valley was the scene of his country novels, and many of his later works also bear the stamp of Romsdalen.

Childhood memories played a great role for him as they did for Ibsen. His childhood was not purely idyllic, as he has told us himself in accounts of a teacher who frightened him with hellfire or of an execution to which his father took him to put the fear of God in him. His description of the latter episode is a testimonial to his keen observation, but it also laid the foundation for his distrust of the law. In later years he distinguished himself by his many campaigns on behalf of individuals whom he believed to be unjustly accused; we may even see a stimulus here for his advocacy of the rights of small and oppressed nations.

Important for his development were also the years he went to school in Molde, where he quickly became the leader of his little group. He has given us the whole picture of the environment in *The Fisher Maiden*. He quickly showed talents for storytelling, to his playmates at school as well as the farmers in the community: "A worse boy for lying than the minister's oldest son was scarcely to be found in the whole valley" (*The Bear Hunter*). He was also quick to take a hand in local affairs. When the city fathers in their wisdom decided to economize by not celebrating the national holiday in 1848, he demanded in an article in the local newspaper that this decision be revoked. His article was written with all of Wergeland's rhetorical exaltation and bore the title, "The Speech of Freedom to the Citizens of Molde." In the autumn of the following year he left school in Molde because of a stupid punishment one teacher had decreed: he should "submit to the yoke." He would not be humiliated in this way, and his father agreed.

At Molde he may have acquired that love for the sea which so often recurs in his writing, and other impressions of its magnificent surroundings are reflected in many of his poems, not merely the beautiful poem he wrote "To Molde."

"What a happy time it was!" he later wrote about his years in Molde. He could no doubt have said the same thing about the years he spent at Heltberg's "Student Factory" (1850-1852), a preparatory course for students who were cramming for the university entrance examination. If the instruction he got earlier had been too systematic, he was now getting one that was much too unsystematic. But the important thing was the experience of human personality he was getting. "Old Heltberg" made a great impression on Bjørnson by his personality and his original method of teaching, as we can see from the poem he later wrote in his honor. More important, perhaps, was the fact that here he met Ibsen and Vinje, later Jonas Lie.

To begin with he was deeply impressed by Vinje, who was past thirty and far more mature than he, and in addition a country boy like himself. Vinje took a fatherly interest in him, but it was not long before Bjørnson rebelled. Bjørnson also had a certain contact with Marcus Thrane's labor movement. As an eighteen-year-old he made his first public speech in protest against the expulsion of a Danish revolutionist, Harro Harring. He was also active in the movement for a more Norwegian theater.

Bjørnson had early discovered that he wanted to be a poet. He handed in a musical play to the theater entitled *Valborg,* dealing with the same emigration theme as Wergeland's last play, *The Mountain Hut.* But no sooner had it been accepted than he withdrew it. His self-critique had been awakened, and he laid aside some other plays he had written also. From 1854-1856 he wrote theatrical and literary criticism in *Morgenbladet,* but also wrote for other papers, read and learned, developed his style and his capacity for observation, prepared himself thoroughly for a life of writing, while he was also living a healthy and lively student life in a circle of jolly friends. To help an impoverished printer he edited *Illustreret Folkeblad* from 1856. In this periodical his first country tales were printed.

While these were pictures of rural life, they were not idyllically romantic. He was a severe critic of Welhaven's romanticism and demanded "Nature! Truth and Nature!" He knew from his childhood that the peasants were no ideal characters. But he also wanted to protest against the negative view of them which was spreading during this period. He believed he knew a different kind of peasant from his life in Romsdalen than those which Eilert Sundt had described. They had their weaknesses of course, but these could be reduced by education and by pointing them out. He learned something from Asbjørnsen's "frame stories" in his folk tales and from the proverbs collected by Ivar Aasen.

But his real debut as a writer came in 1856, after an excursion to a student gathering in Uppsala during the summer. He has told about it himself in an essay entitled "How I Became a Poet." The underlying stimulus was one of national self-assertion against a superior foreign culture, the same as in his work for a Norwegian theater. In Uppsala he saw the monuments of Swedish history, in Stockholm the Riddarholm Church, all testimonials to Sweden's great past. He was gripped by "historical envy." He wanted to create a Norwegian "ancestors' gallery" so that Norwegians might become just as secure in their national feeling as the Swedes and the Danes. When he stood on the dock the last day in Stockholm, a little girl stepped forth and handed him a laurel wreath. He placed it on his head as if it had been handed him in a dream, and felt this as the consecration of his poetic mission.

He left at once for his parents' home and wrote *Between the Battles* (*Mellem Slagene*) in two weeks, having revised it from a modern play into a historical one from the time of King Sverre. There is some influence from Andreas Munch's *An Evening at Giske* which had appeared the year before, but Bjørnson was superior in his psychological insight. Sverre is a lightly disguised version of himself, his joy in battle, his sensitive heart, his faith in himself. The king bears a heavy treasure of good advice for his people, but is not heard. Nevertheless he stands firm "in spite of all the pangs of Hell." "He clenches his teeth and swallows the pain, tosses scorn and jests in all directions, stands on his own bloody ramparts delivering merry funeral speeches, and laughs the harder the more men he loses, and rises in the council with dignity and calm in his voice," because he is so "strong of soul that he can stand firm long enough to make both God and men see that he willed to do the good." The other figures are also good studies of character. The embarrassment at showing one's feelings, a trait he himself was free from, appears again in stories like *Synnøve Solbakken* and "The Father," in plays like *A Bankrupt, The New System, Paul Lange and Tora Parsberg*. The dramatic technique of *Between the Battles* is that of an intrigue much like Ibsen's *Lady Inger*.

In the autumn of the same year he left for Copenhagen "to be where understanding was the greatest, where art had made its greatest advances."

His association with Clemens Petersen and his energetic studies taught him to demand greater seriousness in writing. In a short story called "Thrond," dealing with childhood and the development of an artist, he reached artistic maturity and found his own personal style. In a letter to Botten Hansen he wrote, "I respect no grammar-Norwegian. I use chest-Norwegian!" His short, saga-like sentences and the terse, pregnant style are indeed related to the breath groups of natural speech. In 1857 he also wrote his most famous novel, *Synnøve Solbakken*,[1] and started the saga play *Lame Hulda* (*Halte-Hulda*).

The years from 1857 to 1859 when Bjørnson was stage director in Bergen were stormy years in his life. The theater was passing through a difficult period with a continual conflict raging between Ole Bull and his board of directors. Bjørnson threw himself into the battle on Bull's side, "galloped" into the fight like a "trumpeter's horse that has been standing in the stable all winter." "Ah, what life, this life in the papers. Murdered one day, resurrected the next!" But he managed to bring order into the affairs of the theater. He became an outstanding director, inspiring and with an eye for mass effects. He was also active as a speaker and lecturer, and for the first time as a politician. In December 1858 he took over the editorship of *Bergensposten* and carried on a lively political feud against the laws proposed in order to regulate the relationship between Norway and Sweden; he feared a tendency toward complete amalgamation of the countries in these proposals. He threw himself into the election campaign of 1859, although he himself had no vote because of the property requirements of the times. It was in part due to his agitation that the conservative representatives were defeated. The new members of the Storting were two old friends of Wergeland and two young liberals. He made the national policy toward Sweden a problem of party politics, tied the national problems together with the democratic ones and cleared the path for the Liberal party (*Venstre*) which began to take shape a short time later.

In the fall of 1858 he married Karoline Reimers, an actress at the Bergen theater. He had many friends, among them a circle of New Norse sympathizers. He developed a lyrical vein during this period and included many of his poems in the country tales, particularly *Arne* (1859).[2] His

[1] Tr. as *Sunny Hill* (New York, 1932); as *Synnöve Solbakken* by Julie Sutter (London, 1881), R. B. Anderson (Boston, 1881), E. Gosse (London, 1895-1898); tr. as *Love and Life in Norway* by A. Bethel and A. Plesner (London, 1870); as *Trust and Trial* by Mary Howitt (London, 1858).
[2] Tr. Augusta Plesner and S. Rugeley-Powers (London, 1866); R. B. Anderson (Boston, 1881); W. Low (London, 1890).

activity as a speaker led him on to the writing of patriotic songs. His best-known ones stem from these years, "There Lies a Land Toward the Eternal Snows," and the one which became Norway's beloved national anthem at once after its appearance, "Yes We Love This Land Forever."[3] While Ibsen in his lyrics usually wrote "I," Bjørnson preferred the plural "we," encompassing as he did the whole nation in one common emotion.

During the years from 1856 to 1872 Bjørnson carried on his curious "crop rotation," which meant that he worked alternately at country tales and saga dramas. The purpose was to show the kinship between the peasant of today and the heroes of the saga. He found some of the same qualities in both—restrained strength, emotional reserve, desire for adventure, inability to speak out. The saga dramas were to strengthen the national backbone of the people, so that they could assert themselves against their brother nation. The rural tales were a link in the social and political conflict of the times. They were not merely intended to oppose skeptical opinions concerning the peasant, but also to give the latter self-confidence and the courage to take his proper part in the building of the country.

There was also a personal message in his writing. He felt in his own character the conflict between, on the one hand, savagery, force, unscrupulousness, vengefulness, vanity, and on the other, the humanitarian impulse to live for others, to seek harmony and a social, ethical, and religious subordination of self. He wished to strengthen the forces for good:

> Love thy neighbor, thou Christian soul,
> Crush him not with iron heel,
>   Though in the dust he be lying!
> All that lives is subject to
> Love's creative power true,
>   If only we keep trying.

The theme of all his writing in this period is the idea that every talented individual must pass through a school of suffering. All his heroes are robust fellows who have to overcome some weakness of character to be useful in life. Thorbjørn in *Synnøve Solbakken* has a hard struggle to overcome the savagery in his own nature. But he wins

3 Tr. R. B. Anderson, *Norway Music Album* (Boston, 1881); A. H. Palmer in *Poems and Songs by Björnstjerne Björnson* (New York, 1915); W. E. Leonard, in Mark van Doren, *Anthology of World Poetry* (New York, 1939).

out through persistence and with the help of Synnøve's love. In the same way Arne has to overcome his desire to emigrate and his dreamy romanticism. Øivind in *A Happy Boy* (*En glad gut*, 1859)[4] is hampered by his ambition and his self-love. The same fundamental idea occurs in the masterful short story "The Father."

All the country tales end happily. The church holds a high position in them; in Bjørnson's words, "the church in a Norwegian valley stands in a high place." Religion is to teach people to turn from self-love to neighborly love. But the saga dramas usually end tragically. Here Christianity and culture combine in order to tame the viking spirit and create a social attitude, force the viking nature under the laws of love and life. But the savagery is too powerful, and the hero is destroyed. The young, vital Sigurd Slembe has more than enough abilities, and the world is open to him, but he fails to win the throne of Norway because he cannot conquer himself.

Bjørnson did not want his rural folk to be "Sunday peasants" like those in Tidemand's paintings. We sometimes feel that they are idealized, while his own times accused them of coarseness. Actually, they are neither. They do not tell us a great deal about the daily problems of the farmer, but then they were not intended to be primarily pictures of folk life. They are studies of character. As such they certainly do not lack realistic details; we need only think of Nils the Tailor's tragedy in *Arne* or the story of Aslak in *Synnøve Solbakken*.

The most important literary impulses for the writing of *Synnøve Solbakken* were Asbjørnsen's folk tales, the sagas, and Hans Christian Andersen's fairy tales. But the style was felt as something entirely new. The whole rhythm and tempo was a break with the more circumstantial style of an earlier generation of writers. There was a more Norwegian choice of words, short, vigorous sentences, bold images, and usually something unspoken to be read between the lines. If we read the stories without prejudice, we can still feel the freshness of the style. It is a masterful story, fully worthy of inclusion in world literature. *Arne* is more uneven, but has splendid passages like the opening chapter about "clothing the mountain." It gives a kind of perspective on Norwegian history, and its anti-emigration theme ties up with his play *Valborg* and Wergeland's *Mountain Hut*. *A Happy Boy* is the most cheerful in tone

[4] Tr. Mrs. W. Archer (New York, 1931); R. B. Anderson (Boston, 1881); tr. as *The Happy Boy*, by H. R. G. (Boston, 1870); as *Ovind* by S. and E. Hjerleid (London, 1869); as *The Happy Lad* (London, 1882).

and lyrical in form. It may seem almost too idyllic today, but it is genuinely poetic and has considerable historical interest. It gives us valuable glimpses of Ole Vig's work for popular education and Gisle Johnson's revivalism, as well as the activities of the first agricultural schools. In general, all the country tales were received well or even enthusiastically by critics and public alike, in Norway as in Denmark. These stories won Bjørnson a name as the outstanding living writer in Scandinavia.

The saga dramas were more uneven. *Between the Battles* was a fine beginning. *Lame Hulda* was weaker, reminiscent of Oehlenschläger with its iambic pentameter and its theme of the conflict between paganism and Christianity. The play *King Sverre* (*Kong Sverre,* 1861) was a complete failure and was badly received by the critics, to Bjørnson's great distress. But he recovered and wrote the best of his saga plays, the trilogy *Sigurd Slembe* (1862).[5]

The background of this play includes Bjørnson's experiences in Norway and abroad. During the winter of 1859-1860 he lived in Oslo, busy with plans for writing and politics. He edited *Aftenbladet* with Ditmar Meidell and Ole Richter, and made it an organ of the new Liberal party through his attacks on *Morgenbladet* and his defense of the Reform Society. When he had to step out of the editorial position in January 1860, he decided to go abroad. This was his first long stay abroad, lasting until 1863; it meant an enormous enrichment of Bjørnson's interests. Rome made him into a classicist. It is characteristic that Ibsen was most fascinated by the baroque and the Roman portrait busts, Bjørnson by Greek sculpture. But both were deeply affected by Michelangelo. Bjørnson always thought of Norway when he was abroad, and his association with the historian P. A. Munch strengthened his historical feeling, at the same time as his life in the eternal city gave him a deeper and wider perspective. *Sigurd Slembe* was created under the impression of Schiller's *Wallenstein* trilogy. Here is pictured the entire background of world history, the European Middle Ages, the spirit of the crusades. Because of the reverses Bjørnson had met with, there is also something of the spirit of Ibsen's *Pretenders* in it. Like Skule, Sigurd lacks the spiritual right to be king. Both are driven by a desire for power and both prepare the path for the true ruler. Ibsen's drama has a more profound character analysis, but Bjørnson's has greater historical perspective and better mass scenes.

Bjørnson's lyrics also gained a more classic form during these years, and he reached his height as a lyric poet, chiefly under the influence

[5] Tr. William Morton Payne (Boston, 1888).

of Goethe and the classics. He wrote poems like "Olav Trygvason," "Bergljot," "Monte Pincio," and he gave his earlier national hymns their final form. When P. A. Munch died in 1863, Bjørnson wrote a monumental memorial poem. Another fruit of the Rome years was his play *Maria Stuart in Scotland* (*Maria Stuart i Skotland*), written in 1863.[6] It was a Renaissance drama, with interesting studies of characters like Darnley and John Knox and effective group scenes, but it was still a basically lyrical play.

Like Ibsen, Bjørnson was zealous on behalf of the Danish cause in 1864. In verse and prose, in writing and speech he fought for Norwegian and Swedish aid to Denmark. Like Ibsen he was deeply depressed when Denmark had to fight alone. He was unable to concentrate on any major work at this time and could not understand that others were able to do so. But he did not let these events sap his courage, and he chose, like old Grundtvig, to preach the hope of a stronger generation to come. He became interested also in Grundtvig's religious ideas and he made himself acquainted with the ideas of education behind his folk high school. There is none of this in his slight play *The Newlyweds* (*De Nygifte,* 1865),[7] but in *The Fisher Maiden* (*Fiskerjenten,* 1867),[8] the influence of Grundtvig is apparent. This story advocates a "cheerful Christianity" and attacks the narrow religious views which held art to be sinful. The story is one of Bjørnson's freshest and liveliest, filled as it is with optimism and springtide spirit: "I give my poem to spring." The basic theme is the development of an artistic personality. Petra may have some traits from Magdalene Thoresen, an authoress whom he knew from his Bergen days, but she is drawn above all from Bjørnson's own character. The story is notable for its descriptions of childhood and nature and the rich imagery of its style.

For several years Bjørnson was the director of Christiania Theater, and from 1866 to 1871 he edited *Norsk Folkeblad* while taking an active part in the great forward push of the Liberal party. The years from 1868 were particularly productive for his lyric poetry; in 1870 appeared the

[6] Tr. as *Mary, Queen of Scots* by A. Sahlberg (Chicago, 1912).
[7] Tr. as *The Newly-Married Couple* by R. F. Sharp, in *Three Comedies* (New York, 1914); S. and E. Hjerleid (London, 1870); as *A Lesson in Marriage* by G. I. Colbron (New York, 1911).
[8] Tr. R. B. Anderson (Boston, 1882); M. E. Niles (New York, 1869); tr. as *The Fisher Lass* by E. Gosse (London, 1896); as *The Fishing Girl* by A. Plesner and F. Richardson (London, 1870); as *The Fisher Girl* by S. and E. Hjerleid (London, 1871); as *The Fisher Lassie* by W. Low (London, 1890).

first edition of *Poems and Songs* (*Digte og sange*)[9] and the epic poem *Arnljot Gelline*,[10] the latter dedicated to "the Folk High Schools of the North." Bjørnson's lyrics are among the finest in world literature. It would be difficult to find anywhere a tribute to home that equals his "My Companions." His "Arnljot Longs for the Sea" is fully the equal of Byron's and Heine's sea poems. No other Norwegian poet has his vigorous touch or his visionary plasticity. Many of his poems suggest the folk song and are eminently singable, e.g. "Olav Trygvason." There is a marked difference between the supple and gracious poems of his younger days and the clarified, resonant poetry from the time of his journey to Rome.

Most of Bjørnson's poetry is characterized by a combination of the musical and the plastic, with a touch of the dramatic also. The poet does not describe the sea itself, but Arnljot's and his own longing for it:

> For the sea, the sea, my spirit is yearning,
> Where wide it heaves in its calm majestic.
> Bearing its burden of mountainous fog-banks,
> Eternally rolling in self-communion.
> Though the heavens bend down, and the shores are calling,
> It is restless ever, and knows no yielding.
> In the nights of summer, the winter tempests,
> It voices ever its plaint of longing.

Translated by W. M. Payne

Bjørnson did not equal Wergeland in wealth of imagery, and he was more concerned with people than with nature. No Norwegian poet has drawn such a gallery of the great men of his time as Bjørnson in his poems to P. A. Munch, Johan Sverdrup, Ernst Sars, and others.

Even in his boyhood he was fascinated by the figure of Arnljot in Snorri's *Heimskringla,* the Swedish highwayman who came to St. Olaf on the eve of his last battle and offered his services to the king. He asked himself: what lay between the two occasions when he is mentioned— the first time when he saved the lives of the Norwegian tax collectors in Jämtland, and the second time when he came to the Christian king. Bjørnson had been working on this since 1859, and had also gained impulses from Runeberg and Grundtvig. There is also a connection

[9] Tr. A. H. Palmer (New York, 1915).
[10] Tr. W. M. Payne (New York, 1917).

with the saga plays and the country tales. Arnljot is compelled to suffer before he can begin serving the forces of good. The nature descriptions of this poem are excellently integrated with the character study, as in the matchless account of the royal army on the eve of the battle of Stiklestad. In his description of the coming of spring in the mountains the poet has symbolized the victory of the forces of light.

In 1872 Bjørnson "rotated his crops" for the last time. He wrote the story *The Bridal March* (*Brudeslåtten*)[11] as the text of a series of folk life paintings by Tidemand, inspired by a folk tune he had heard from Anders Reitan. In the same year he wrote a saga play, *Sigurd the Crusader* (*Sigurd Jorsalfar*), which has proved extremely popular. In both of these the theme is patriotic and is directed against emigration, which was growing in strength every year. Bjørnson had a keen eye for the adventure-someness that led people away from their country, but at the same time he expressed his sympathy most strongly for King Eystein who built inns and roadmarkers and set up lighthouses, while his brother Sigurd was filled by the romantic dream of the viking and the crusader. The theme is expressed thus in the final song: "Clear one's land, elevate one's people, do you call that sluggish and cowardly?"

[11] Tr. R. B. Anderson (New York, 1882); J. E. Williams (London, 1893); E. Gosse (London, 1896).

Realism Comes to Literature

THE GREAT PHILOSOPHIC SYSTEMS, such as Fichte's idealism, Schelling's romantic philosophy of nature, and above all Hegelianism, had dominated German science and philosophy in the years before 1870, and the same was to some extent true in Scandinavia. But about this time a change took place in European thinking. The philosophic systems began to crumble and lost their hold on people's minds. It grew more difficult to organize facts into systems, to build bridges between pure thought and reality, to harmonize faith and science.

For Idé og Virkelighed (*For Idea and Reality*) was the characteristic title of a Scandinavian periodical which a well-known representative of the dualism of his times, the Danish philosopher Rasmus Nielsen, edited together with his pupil Rudolf Schmidt, Bjørnson being the Norwegian member of the editorial board. Many new attempts to build philosophic systems represented a desperate effort to save the abstract mode of thought. There was a neo-Kantian and a neo-Hegelian trend, and there was the Swedish Boström's "rational idealism." Monrad tried to be a Norwegian Hegel, while G. V. Lyng wished to unite Hegelianism with what he called "realism." But Marx's application of Hegelian ideas to social development awakened no interest in Norway at this time.

In general terms the development was away from idealistic modes of thought to more materialistic ones. Instead of bold metaphysical constructions there arose various views of life having a closer association with the natural sciences.

The teachings of Charles Darwin led to a new conception of nature. The poets of romanticism had thought of nature as good and beneficent, very different in this respect from mankind. This was one of Wergeland's favorite ideas. But this conception was destroyed by the doctrine of the struggle for existence and the survival of the fittest. Nature was no longer

[196]

held to be idyllic. The conception of man was also changed. The doctrine of heredity came to be emphasized, and man was regarded as a product of heredity, education, and environment. At the same time the biological concept entered the field of the humanities. Social conditions, history, and religion were increasingly viewed from the point of view of natural science.

The philosophical doctrine founded by the Frenchman Auguste Comte under the name of positivism also tended away from the mystical and religious. This philosophy was in part built on English empiricism of the eighteenth century, and its supporters maintained that the metaphysical lies outside the grasp of human intellect. It would therefore be advisable for men to use their brains to improve life on this earth rather than be forever preparing for the hereafter. The English philosopher Herbert Spencer applied this view to education, and his ideas won a response from many Norwegian writers, above all Bjørnson. Along with these currents came English utilitarianism, which Kielland professed to support. The founder of this school was Jeremy Bentham, who taught that the standard of all values must be utility, not philosophic speculations like Kant's doctrine of absolute duty. Utility even became the criterion of truth, since man cannot establish any absolute truth. The purpose of social control must therefore be the greatest possible happiness for the greatest number of people. One of the members of the school was John Stuart Mill, who applied its doctrines to the position of women in society and became the chief advocate of feminine emancipation. Ibsen expressed his scorn for Mill in 1873, but a few years later he was paralleling some of Mill's ideas in his plays.

These ideas, combined with the growing industrialization of Norway, turned the interests of writers in the direction of society. From a concern with personal and national problems they turned to social and international ones. The writers took part in campaigns for specific social issues, or at least discussed social problems. They felt it part of their task to espouse the cause of those who were oppressed and in distress. They debated the position of labor, the cause of women, or the education of children. Following the model of Zola, they sometimes sacrificed the purely aesthetic for the sake of realism. The most extreme even went so far as to regard it as their task to gather "human documents" and operate more as scientists than as creative artists. Life itself was to speak through their books, and they often had a particular fondness for the darker sides of life. In order to emphasize their opposition to the supernatural and their documentation of nature, they sometimes made use of the rather confusing term "naturalists" to describe themselves.

Hegelianism had been challenged in Norway even before 1870, for example by Schweigaard, who had opposed German philosophy since his youth, no doubt influenced by Heine. The new ideas had found occasional supporters like Asbjørnsen and Vinje, or the historian Ernst Sars. Sars's view of the orderly development of social phenomena and of causality in Norwegian history showed the effects of positivist thinking. But in general Norway was untouched by the ideas of the new age. It was even fashionable to boast that Norwegian thinking was not "corrupted" or "depraved" like that of other European countries.

In 1871 Georg Brandes initiated his lectures at the University of Copenhagen on the "main currents of nineteenth-century literature."[1] In these he used his intimate acquaintance with contemporary literary, philosophical, and political currents to unsettle the conservatism of Scandinavian thinking. He passed judgment on the whole romantic movement, branding it as a reaction which had smothered the ideas of the French revolution. In all spheres of life he called for liberation from prejudices, whether national or religious, and he opened the windows to many cultural impulses from abroad. With a genuine sense of artistry and a fierce one-sidedness he drew vivid and fascinating portraits of the great leaders in philosophy and poetry. He gave to literature a different task than that of embroidering memories from the past. He wanted it to enter into the struggle of its times, work actively for new ideas: "A literature in our day shows that it is alive by taking up problems for discussion."

These oft-quoted words were only a partial truth, and Brandes did not himself maintain them in later life. But they were spoken at the psychologically right moment and they became highly influential, not least in Norwegian writing. His lectures were published in six volumes, but there were also others of his books that had considerable influence, particularly his book about Søren Kierkegaard (1877). In addition he entered into a direct relationship with the Norwegian writers through his stimulating letters. He had himself been inspired by Ibsen, and he in turn stimulated and defended Ibsen over a period of many years. He irritated Bjørnson to begin with, but was then for a few years his friend and father confessor, until the relationship once more cooled. He was a close friend of Jonas Lie in spite of their difference in temperament. He probably meant the most to Kielland, who always referred to him

[1] Printed as *Main Currents in Nineteenth Century Literature* (New York–London, 1902).

as the "field marshal." To some extent he also determined the outlook of Kristian Elster. Even in the younger generation which included Arne Garborg, Amalie Skram, Gunnar Heiberg, and Christian Krohg, he was often a stimulus to independent thinking.

The influence of Brandes's views may not have been entirely fortunate, because of his failure to understand many national and religious values, much of folk art and folk poetry, of nature and emotion generally. But it was greatly to his credit that he extended the cultural horizon, wiped out prejudices, and forced the poets to take a stand with respect to the problems of their generation. Through his critical essays on Norwegian writers he did more than any other single person to make these men known abroad.

The chief trait of Norwegian writing in the seventies was its trend toward liberalism and individualism, its passionate demands for freedom, the right of the individual to be himself and follow his convictions without hindrance from society. With blue-eyed optimism the writers advanced to their attack on authoritarianism in all fields, especially in church and state. They spoke on behalf of the poor, and they demanded the right for women to choose their own vocations. But no matter how critical these writers were of all forces that wanted to constrict life, among which they reckoned church, state, and school, they were not consistently extreme in their criticism. Several of them wanted liberation for women, but also an inviolable marriage. They demanded democratic reforms, but were themselves cultural aristocrats. They maintained Norway's rights in the union, but never intended to break out of it. The point of departure for their criticism was an optimistic and idealistic view of life. The force that imbued their agitation was a feeling of being in harmony with the future. The poets, even Ibsen, had confidence that it was possible to improve social conditions by encouraging greater freedom and truth, by abolishing abuses, overcoming prejudices and hypocrisy, creating greater happiness for people and raising their moral standards.

Typical of the spirit of the seventies and a leader in its movements was Kristofer Janson (1841-1917). His early stories imitated Bjørnson's but were written in New Norse although he was a city boy. He never became a great writer, and all that has lasting value of his work is the historical novel *From the Danish Era* (*Fraa Dansketidi*, 1875), *Our Grandparents* (*Vore Bedste-forældre*, 1882), a couple of stories from America, some poems, and his memoirs *What I Have Experienced* (*Hvad jeg har oplevet*, 1913). The optimism of the age lives in his many books, in his work as a folk high school teacher, his break with orthodox Lutheranism, his labors as a Unitarian minister in Minnesota, and his activity as a lecturer in Norway. The same humanistic philosophy recurs in Georg Fasting (1837-1914), a noble cultural personality who tried his hand at belles-lettres only a couple of times. In his writings he tried to unite impulses from Kierkegaard with a Grundtvigian view of life. He was a great art enthusiast, who fought bravely against the narrowness of money-minded merchants for a restoration of the Bergen Theater, and he was zealous in the work for humane school reforms and the peace movement. We find some of the same spirit in several literary schoolmen, such as Kristian Gløersen (1838-1916) who attacked pietistic education and shocked some people by his unsentimental portrayals of women in such novels as *Sigurd* (1877). There is also a strain of socialism in the period, but it is of an individualistic rather than a collective type. A characteristic advocate of the movement was Olaus Fjørtoft (1847-1878), a dreamer and agitator, an idealistic critic of his own times but a believer in the future. Like Aasta Hansteen he was a supporter also of the New Norse movement, more for democratic than nationalistic reasons.[2]

In the writing of the seventies some of the spirit of romanticism lived on under the mask of realism. The most typical writing of the eighties went farther in its realism, was crasser and more aggressive, and with a darker coloration. It was more consistent and probed its problems more deeply, but showed less humanity and wisdom. Attacks now extended to some of the institutions that earlier had been accepted, such as family life, marriage, and Christianity. Philosophies like positivism and determinism were proclaimed as objective truths. Artistically, too, the program of the eighties was a further development of the theories of the seventies. But the literature of the extreme naturalists rarely got beyond a purely mechanical enumeration of details, so that it may be doubted whether the theories of the eighties were beneficial in Norwegian writing. The passion which was generated in the discussions of the times, however, found expression in genuinely artistic writing during the 1890's and early 1900's, in the plays of Gunnar Heiberg, the poetry of Nils Collett Vogt, and the fiction of Hans E. Kinck.

The spirit of opposition which characterized the eighties found its

[2] A minor writer of the period whose descriptions of life in the far north were translated was J. A. Friis: *Sporting Life on the Norwegian Fjelds*, tr. W. G. Lock (London, 1878); *Laila, or Sketches from Finmarken*, tr. Henry John, Earl of Ducie (London, 1883), also tr. as *Lajla, a tale of Finmark*, by Ingerid Markjus (New York, 1888); *The Monastery of Petschenga*, tr. H. Repp (London, 1896).

most violent expression in the discussion of Hans Jæger's *From the Christiania Bohème* (1885), Christian Krohg's *Albertine* (1886), and Arne Garborg's *Menfolk* (1887).

Hans Jæger (1854-1910) was the leader of a homeless group of artists and intellectuals, the "Bohème," who despised and abhorred the society to which they belonged. They wished to prepare the way for completely new social conditions. Its members were almost entirely urban. Jæger himself had gone to sea in his youth, but in later years devoted himself to the study of philosophy, including Kant, Fichte, and Hegel, as well as naturalistic theories of art. He had a penchant for theory and was relentlessly logical, but at the same time a fantast and an original. He was honest in the extreme, sincere in his hate of hypocrisy and in his love of truth, but was neither a good psychologist nor an artist.

Jæger opened his campaign during a discussion in the Workers' Society in 1881 concerning the repeal of legalized prostitution. He maintained that under present conditions the state should demand respect for the prostitutes since they have an important function in society, and he proposed a radical revision in the relationship of the sexes. He asserted that the causes of immorality were the institution of marriage and economic exploitation. He flung out the paradox which stirred up enormous indignation and was quoted and misinterpreted *ad nauseam,* namely that as things now are, men are cheated of nineteen twentieths of their life happiness because of the requirement that they practice monogamy. He carried on his agitation in the Student Society, declaring that he was a supporter of determinism and an opponent of morality and religion. He tried to give expression to his ideas in two unsuccessful plays, *Olga* and *An Intellectual Seduction* (*En intellektuel forførelse*). But in 1885 he published a novel which created a sensation, chiefly because it was suppressed by the police, *From the Christiania Bohème* (*Fra Kristiania-Bohêmen*).

The novel is, as Jæger admits in his preface, "a monstrosity both artistically and socially." It is quite unartistic, much too lengthy, and would scarcely have been read by many had it not been suppressed. It contains indelicate attacks on known persons and distasteful elaborations of detail. But while the author was obviously obsessed by sex, the book was not written for pornographic purposes. Jonas Lie was one who perceived the serious conviction and deep suffering which had produced it: "It is a dreadful book. . . . It is written by one who is holding a revolver to his temple. Here this poor man has risked his entire social existence, his entire life, just to say, no, to scream out, all the terror which we others of course have been too refined to notice. It is a cry of distress, a cry from the ugliest and most profound distress, a cry of terror from those who are sinking." Later generations have benefited from the novel because it opened the way for a freer discussion of sexual problems.

The fact that *From the Christiania Bohème* was suppressed and the author condemned to 60 days in prison by the Supreme Court for "blasphemy and violation of modesty and morality" led to a violent controversy during the next few years. Not only Jæger's friends, but the entire radical intelligentsia looked on the suppression as a violation of freedom of speech. The Liberal Student Society passed a resolution of censure. Jonas Lie, who was anything but bohemian, wrote that to fight against ideas with the help of the police was like "trying to stop the Gulf Stream with a cork." The controversy grew even sharper when Krohg's *Albertine,* which is a genuine work of art, also was suppressed. When Garborg the same year published *Menfolk,* he wrote to the Department of Justice and demanded that he be prosecuted under the same law that had been used against Jæger and Krohg. He was not prosecuted, but his stand in this affair caused him to lose his position in the State Auditor's office.

Jæger himself left for France where he lived most of the rest of his life, ill and depressed, but teeming with ideas. His later writings, including *Sick Love* (*Syg Kjærlighed,* 1893), *Confessions* (*Bekjendelser,* 1902), and *Prison and Despair* (*Fængsel og fortvivlelse,* 1903), are confessions in a kind of novel form, depressing because of their pathological contents, but moving as human documents. His political views approached most nearly the anarchism of Prince Kropotkin. In his semimetaphysical, uneven, impulsive and original *The Bible of Anarchism* (*Anarkiets bibel,* 1906) he returned to the philosophical interests of his youth.

None of the writers who were then of the first rank sided entirely with the Bohème. Ibsen was repelled by their crudeness of manner and stayed out of the controversy. Bjørnson led the opposition on behalf of his ideals of purity in family life, education to self-restraint, and continuity of evolution. He traveled around the country lecturing on "monogamy and polygamy," and also introduced the problem in some of his writings. Kielland expressed his sympathy for some of Jæger's views in his letters to Bjørnson. But he was too much of an aristocrat to appreciate the tone of the bohemians, and too much of an artist to accept their view that the novel should be a kind of autobiography.

Ernst Sars once jestingly made up the word "poetocracy" concerning

the political position of the poets in Norwegian history. The expression
fits the Wergeland period, and also the period from 1875-1890, perhaps
still later. There are of course other forces that determine the course of
history, and literature is an expression of historical processes. But the
writers were a real force, not only through their art, but also through
their contributions to the controversies of their day. It is characteristic
that even Ibsen, half against his will, was drawn into politics. After *The
League of Youth* (1869), which satirized political phrase-mongers and
was hissed by the Liberals, he was regarded as a conservative writer. After
Pillars of Society (1877) he was considered a liberal writer, until he
declared his aversion for both parties in *An Enemy of the People* (1882).
Bjørnson was the stormy petrel of Norwegian political life. From 1879
on he was constantly engaged in controversy, being both hated and applauded for his advocacy of a republican form of government in Norway.
It was a great victory and a symbolic occasion for him when he was asked
to deliver the speech at the unveiling of the Wergeland statue in Oslo
on May 17, 1881. No less zealous was he in the cause of parliamentary
reform, and the break of the Swedish-Norwegian union in 1905 is hardly
thinkable without him. Kielland's novels were also generally praised in
the Liberal press and condemned in the Conservative. The question of
whether he should be given a poet's salary like the other "greats" added
fuel to the controversy about his name during the years from 1885-1887
and was one of the main factors in the split of the Liberal party.

The writers of this period touched upon innumerable social problems
in their works, but sometimes they also supported specific programs of
reform directly. In 1884 Ibsen, Bjørnson, Kielland, and Lie submitted
to the Storting a proposal for the improvement of the economic position
of married women. In the same year Hans Jæger's friend Gunnar Heiberg
raised the first demand for full social justice in his play *Aunt Ulrikke*:
"The geniuses lead the way—and after them an endless parade of the poor
and wretched."

Ibsen's Social and Psychological Plays

IT WAS AN ESSENTIAL PART of Ibsen's dramatic talent that he embodied the problems and conflicts of his own personality in the characters of his plays. He did not often attempt a solution of the problems raised, for, as he put it in a poem: "I prefer to ask; 'tis not my task to answer." But we can often perceive by the way in which he distributed light and shade in his plays where his sympathies must have lain. His personal indignation at all forms of compromise and hypocrisy breathes through such plays as *Brand, Peer Gynt,* and *The League of Youth.* Some of the same militant air is found in several of the so-called social dramas. He is most obviously present in *An Enemy of the People,* but he steps out of his objective role in other plays also and speaks directly to his contemporaries. We hear his own voice speaking in such programmatic statements as these: "The spirit of freedom and truth, these are the pillars of society," or "Freedom with responsibility."

In the 1850's and 1860's Ibsen was mostly concerned with personal and national problems arising from his own sense of guilt. He circled about the problem of the "contrast between ability and desire, between will and possibility," between the world of the ideal and the sorry reality. It was the problem of one's calling in relation to the real world.

When Ibsen in the middle 1870's turned to the writing of realistic social plays, he was not primarily interested in the social problems as such. He was concerned about the opportunities for growth on the part of the individual, his right to unfold his personality and attain the "joy of life," unhampered by society and its prejudices. For this reason all his "social dramas'" are really antisocial dramas. Society appears as an obstacle to the development of the individual into a free and courageous personality. Individual personality is the crucial element, now as before. Personality creates all valuable culture; where it is lacking, as he wrote in a poem of 1870, "the whole business is nothing but the dry bones of a skeleton."

As in *Brand* and *Peer Gynt,* the first command in the social plays is: "Be yourself!" When Consul Bernick in *Pillars of Society* has freed himself from lies, humbug, conventional morality, the thousand and one considerations, his old flame Lona Hessel says to him: "Now you have finally won yourself back!" Bernick is jubilantly grateful: "You have saved the best in me and for me." He had intended to educate his son as a pillar of society and make him his heir. But now he says: "You shall be yourself, Olaf, and then the rest will have to take care of itself."

The same basic view underlies Ibsen's attitude to the cause of women, from *Comedy of Love* to *Lady from the Sea.* He expanded the demand for personality and applied it to women also. Solveig in *Peer Gynt* is of course a romantic type and no feminist, yet she breaks with her background in order to be herself. Selma in *The League of Youth* threatens to rebel because she has always been excluded from responsibility. Ibsen sometimes amused himself by asserting that he had no idea what the "woman cause" was; he knew only of the "human cause." He was not doing battle primarily for the social and political rights of women, and still less for equality of the sexes. On the contrary he demanded that woman's nature be respected as different from man's. In a draft of *Pillars of Society,* which started out as much more of a feminist play than it finally became, he defined in clear words the woman's task in social life. She ought to bring to men "an insight from that incoherent, illogical mode of thought which a man may not be able to make use of in his work, but which can be stimulating and purifying to his whole thinking." Her views are less conventional, thought Ibsen, more individualistic. She has more intuition, or as he put it in a speech to the Scandinavian Society in Rome, "that brilliant instinct which unconsciously finds the truth." Therefore Nora in *A Doll's House* says: "I have to find out who is right, society or I." In the drafts of this play the idea is even more pointed: "A woman cannot be herself in present-day society."

In 1868 Ibsen moved from picturesque Italy to the plain city of Dresden in Germany, from artistic freedom to "a boringly well-ordered society." No longer was he the distant Savonarola who launched his "all or nothing" thunderbolts from on high. Now he wanted his writing to play a part in the society he was describing. In Dresden he wrote *The League of Youth*

(*De Unges Forbund,* 1869),[1] the comedy of Peer Gynt as politician. Although this play, like the preceding ones, grew out of Ibsen's annoyance at many phenomena in contemporary Norway, it has practically none of the lofty pathos that rings through his great dramatic poems. Although it is an attack on social hypocrisy, it has none of the force that marks the attack in his later social plays. Its plot reflects memories from Ibsen's childhood, but also from his first years in Oslo.

The League of Youth is one of the best comedies in Norwegian literature, with witty dialogue, keen characterization, and amusing situations. In this play Ibsen created modern Norwegian prose dialogue. Each character has his own style. We observe Stensgård's bombastic and rhetorical oratory, Aslaksen's suspicious and anxious petit-bourgeois style, the Chamberlain's reserved, cultivated formality, and Daniel Hejre's quick, malicious comments, accompanied by his dry, creaking laughter.

Ibsen's *Poems (Digte,* 1871)[2] appeared the year after Bjørnson's *Poems and Songs.* Only a few of his early poems were included, and these only after thorough revision and concentration. Ibsen's poems are characteristically different from Bjørnson's, in that they are not as singable or as elevating and colorful as his. The youthful poems included are those that express Ibsen's loneliness, his fear of life and his inhibitions, e.g. "Afraid of the Light" ("Lysræd"), or "Bird and Bird Catcher" ("Fugl og fuglefænger"). Some of them contain in embryo form the ideas of later dramas, e.g. "On the Heights" ("Paa Vidderne"). Others give a profound insight into the author's brooding personality, like the matchless "The Miner" ("Bergmanden"). The more extroverted and contemporary poems, like "Abraham Lincoln's Murder" ("Abraham Lincolns mord") and the magnificent "Balloon Letter," give us wide perspectives, imaginative views of world history. There are witty poems, like "Complications" ("Forviklinger"), but also tender ones like "Gone" ("Borte"). In his brilliant "Rhymed Letter to Mme. Heiberg" ("Rimbrev til fru Heiberg") the great dramatist employed the Wergeland line for a spirited characterization of dramatic art as the "offspring of fragrance, of inspiration, of a mood, a person, and a fantasy."

One of the poems bears the title "Balloon Letter to a Swedish Lady" ("Ballonbrev til en svensk dame"); it reflects a journey Ibsen made to Egypt in 1869 when he represented Sweden and Norway at the opening

[1] Tr. William Archer, *Collected Works,* Vol. 6 (New York, 1906); R. F. Sharp, *Everyman* 729 (London, n.d.).
[2] Some of these appear in F. E. Garrett, *Lyrics and Poems from Ibsen* (London, 1912) and in *Lyrical Poems,* tr. by R. A. Streatfield (London, 1902).

of the Suez Canal. He later referred to his visit in Egypt as "the most interesting and instructive period of my life." He was impressed by the remains of ancient Egyptian culture, and by the oblivion into which this culture had fallen in the modern world. The reason for this, he thought, was that the gods of Egypt, unlike the gods of Greece and Rome, were not living flesh-and-blood personalities. In the same way, he prophesied, the Prussian military machine, which just then had won its greatest victory in defeating France, was condemned to oblivion. General Moltke had murdered "the poetry of battle," while Bismarck did not know that "the age is yearning for beauty." This victory of machine culture, of arithmetic and ciphers, would never be celebrated by poets.

The invitation to Egypt was only one of the many honors that were showered on Ibsen during these years when he suddenly became the most feted author of Scandinavia. His outer manner changed entirely from that of a somewhat bohemian poet to that of a respected citizen, with medals and decorations to adorn his chest. He sardonically expressed the opinion that now his countrymen would think twice as well of his writing!

But at the same time his ideas grew if anything more radical. He expressed opinions which approached those of the anarchists. Under the impression of the defeat of France he wrote to Georg Brandes: "The state is the curse of the individual. . . . The state must go! That is a revolution I can agree to. Undermine the concept of the state, establish voluntary participation and spiritual kinship as the only basis for association—that would be the beginning of a freedom that is worth something." But alongside his revolutionary views he also harbored an aversion to the "internal dissolution" which the agitation of the Liberal party brought with it. This made him write that "the liberals are the worst enemies of freedom." Well known are his words in the poem directed to the Swedish liberal Adolf Hedin, "To my Friend the Revolutionary Orator":

> Your changing pawns is a futile plan;
> Make a sweep of the chess-board, and I'm your man.
>
> *Translated by F. E. Garrett*

In the same years he also expressed opinions that pointed in other directions. He had said that Italy had been taken away from the people and given to the politicians, but at the same time he could not help being impressed by Cavour. He attacked Bjørnson as the "priest of Pan-Germanism," but shortly after he spoke of his own view as having expanded to include all the Germanic peoples. He professed the most uninhibited individualism, but wrote a poem in honor of the millennium of the kingdom of Norway (1872) in which he emphasized admiringly the trend to national unification represented by such figures as Cavour and Bismarck. His views during these years were inconsistent, and were undergoing constant flux and fermentation.

The outcome was his drama about the "third empire." He embodied his philosophical reflections in a figure that had long attracted him, the Emperor Julian of Byzantium, also known as the "Apostate" because of his renunciation of Christianity. His first plans had been laid in 1864, but the play was not begun until 1870, and was published under the title of *Emperor and Galilean (Keiser og Galilæer)* in 1873.[3] His first intention was apparently to picture Julian as a pagan counterpart to Brand, a rebel and an idealist who was angered by the weaknesses of the Christian priesthood. But in the meanwhile a great many new impressions had stimulated him: the Franco-Prussian war, the Communard rebellion in Paris, Bismarck's struggle with the Catholics, the pessimistic philosophy of Schopenhauer and Eduard v. Hartman, the Bible criticism of Strauss and Renan, as well as Brandes's *Main Currents.* He studied the historical accounts of Emperor Julian thoroughly, but he was also familiar with neo-Platonism, ancient and modern gnosticism, Hegel's ideas of a synthesis of paganism and Christianity, and Heine's dream of the union of spirit and flesh. On every hand Ibsen saw a world struggle going on between the forces of paganism and Christianity, between the joy in life of the former and the martyr spirit of the latter. "There are three empires," proclaims the mystic Maximos. "First there is that empire which was founded on the tree of knowledge; then there is that empire which was founded on the tree of the cross. The third is still a secret empire, which will be founded on the tree of knowledge and the tree of the cross together."

In a letter to his publisher Ibsen had written in 1871: "This book will be my most important work. . . . The philosophical affirmation which critics have been demanding from me for so long they will now get." He often maintained in later years that *Emperor and Galilean* was his best work, possibly because it cost him the most labor. He returned to

[3] Tr. William Archer, *Collected Works,* Vol. 5 (New York, 1907, orig. pub. 1890); tr. as *The Emperor and the Galilean* by C. Ray (London, 1876).

the idea of the "third empire" several times later. As late as 1887 he concluded a speech in Stockholm with a toast "to that which will come." His work on the play had meant a great deal for his own development. But there are parts of it which also have a high artistic value, particularly in the first part, *Caesar's Apostasy*. Ibsen's conception of the contrast between the pagan joy in life and beauty and the martyr mentality of the Christians is dramatically portrayed in the encounter of two processions, the worshipers of Apollo and the Christian prisoners. There is tragic grandeur in the picture of Julian as a young man, when he was still an idealist in a corrupt world, a living and suffering human being.

But the second part, where Julian is portrayed as emperor, is weighed down by historical details. It is as if the author had lost interest in his hero. He describes very well how Christianity wins new life by martyrdom. But the "philosophical affirmation" turns out to be extremely airy; the dream of the "third empire" is misty. Ibsen's synthesis did not become the masterpiece it was intended to be. It turned out to be a Kierkegaardian "either-or" which was transformed into a Hegelian "both-and." But it was received with respectful admiration by the critics.

From philosophy Ibsen turned back to society. His intention of satirizing the rottenness of his times was foreshadowed in a poem he wrote in 1875 to Georg Brandes, called "A Letter in Rhyme." He compared Europe to a vessel sailing into the future with "a corpse in the cargo," an omen of coming tragedy and destruction.

Pillars of Society (*Samfundets støtter*, 1877)[4] takes place in a small town not unlike the Grimstad where Ibsen was a druggist's apprentice. But the ideas in it were those of his own times, suggested by impressions from his visit to Norway in 1874. This play was the first of the series of social plays that carried Ibsen's name to world fame. The technique is an improvement on that of *The League of Youth;* no longer is the plot advanced by mere coincidences. The real force in the action is the character of the persons involved. In *Pillars of Society* he utilizes also in an effective way his retrospective technique by letting a memory of the past become a vital part of the action. As the plot unfolds, the perspective to the past is revealed. This technique was further developed in later plays, and reaches a climax in such plays as *Little Eyolf, John Gabriel Borkman,* and *When We Dead Awaken.*

---

[4] Tr. William Archer, *Collected Works,* Vol. 6 (New York, 1906, orig. pub. 1888); R. F. Sharp, *Everyman* 659 (London, 1913); tr. as *Pillars of the Community* by Una Ellis-Fermor, *Three Plays by Ibsen* (London, 1950).

A Doll's House (*Et dukkehjem,* 1879)[5] stirred up a vigorous discussion. It appeared in German before the end of the year, and in the next few years made its way to the stages of all civilized countries. It was applauded and condemned, criticized and misunderstood; sequels were made in which the ending was changed so that Nora, instead of leaving her husband and children, decides to stay. Ibsen even made a revised conclusion himself for German use in order to prevent others from making one. But it was not long before everyone realized that the original ending was the only right one. Today the idea in the play is of less significance than its profound analysis of character. A number of the sentences that once were flung at the audience are now spoken in a quiet tone. Very few plays in world literature have offered a part at once so demanding and attractive for actresses as the part of Nora.

Ghosts (*Gengangere,* 1881)[6] was even bolder in its challenge to accepted opinion, but also a greater work of art. It is a stirring fate tragedy and a psychological masterpiece. Like so many of Ibsen's titles, *Ghosts* has a twofold meaning. On the one hand it refers to the ghosts of the past, the sins of the fathers which are avenged on their children, here in the form of a syphilitic condition that is passed on from father to son. On the other hand it refers to all the dead ideas, habits, and prejudices which dominate society and haunt the brains of men, like the "corpse in the cargo" referred to above. Mrs. Alving fights her hopeless battle against these: "It is not just what we have inherited from our father and mother that haunts us. There are also all kinds of old, dead ideas and a lot of old, dead beliefs and the like. They are not alive in us; but they cling to us just the same, and we cannot get rid of them."

The passionate protests at the radical ideas of *A Doll's House* were mild compared to the storm that broke over *Ghosts*. It was called blasphemous and corrupting; theaters in Europe refused to play it. It is a curiosity of stage history that the first performance was by a private Dano-Norwegian theatrical group in Chicago (1882). The poet had expected some opposition, but he was enraged when he discovered that even the liberals, who called themselves lovers of freedom and progress, would have none of the play. Only a few dared to defend it in Norway, and among

[5] Tr. William Archer, *Collected Works,* Vol. 7 (New York, 1906, orig. pub. 1889); R. F. Sharp (London, 1917); Norman Ginsbury (London, 1950); tr. as *Nora, or A Doll's House* by T. Weber (Copenhagen, 1880) and H. F. Lord (London, 1882).
[6] Tr. Havelock Ellis (London, 1888); William Archer, *Collected Works,* Vol. 7 (New York, 1906, orig. pub. 1891); H. F. Lord (Chicago, 1890, orig. pub. 1885); Norman Ginsbury (London, 1938); R. F. Sharp, *Everyman* 552 (London, 1911); adapted A. H. Leverton (New York, 1937).

these most prominent was Bjørnson. "He has in truth a great royal heart, and I shall never forget it," wrote Ibsen in a letter.

Ibsen's relationship to Bjørnson was ambivalent throughout his life, and like his relation to Norway a feeling that might be called love-hate. He was alternately attracted and repelled by his brother poet. They had been on the outs since the appearance of *The League of Youth*. But when Bjørnson lectured in the United States during the winter of 1880-1881, he spoke of Ibsen as the greatest dramatist of the period. When Ibsen heard that Bjørnson had been in danger of his life, he wrote in 1882: "Then I recognized vividly how very much you mean to me as to all the rest of us. I felt that if anything should happen to you, it would be so great a misfortune for our countries that all joy in my work would depart." At the twenty-fifth anniversary for *Synnøve Solbakken* (1882) he wrote: "Your works are among the first rank in the history of literature and will always remain there. But if I should decide what was to be inscribed on your memorial monument, I would choose these words: 'His life was his best poem!' " He sympathized with Bjørnson's campaign during these years and delineated his features in the noble profile of Doctor Stockmann.

It had become a kind of principle ever since he wrote *Pillars of Society* that two years would pass between each play. But in 1882 he departed from this principle. He could not wait to express his opinion of the people who had attacked him because of *Ghosts*. *An Enemy of the People* (*En folkefiende,* 1882)[7] became his most personal confession since *Brand*. Its central idea had been expressed earlier in his writing, but was evoked anew by the discussion of *Ghosts*. His old aversion for liberal politicians, for the party press, for the plebeian ways of public life combine with his contempt for the "stagnationists." His own efforts to clean up the evils of society had only earned him a campaign of abuse and nasty insinuations. So he let Stockmann fling out his wild paradoxes, asserting that the minority is always right, not the stagnant minority, but the advance guard, the radical intellectuals, who stand at a point which "the damned, compact, liberal majority" has not yet reached. Once the majority has managed to catch up, the truth is still in a minority, for "a normally built truth lives, shall we say, as a rule some 17-18, at the most 20 years."

In this play Ibsen borrowed traits from his birthplace Skien, and his

[7] Tr. William Archer, *Collected Works,* Vol. 8 (New York, 1907, orig. pub. 1890); Arthur Miller (New York, 1951); R. F. Sharp, *Everyman* 552 (London, 1911); Norman Ginsbury (London, 1939); as *An Enemy of Society* by Eleanor Marx-Aveling (London, 1888), same title originally used by Archer.

hero was modeled not only on Bjørnson but also on his friend Jonas Lie. But the opinions Stockmann expressed were his own, as he wrote in a letter to his publisher: "Doctor Stockmann and I get along so splendidly; we agree in many respects, though the doctor has a somewhat more muddled head than I." *An Enemy of the People* was the last play in which Ibsen spoke in the first person.

The plays that followed were largely concerned with individual problems, psychological studies without obvious preaching. Ibsen probes the conflict within the individual between the urge to happiness and the demands of conscience, between egotism and self-sacrifice, between age and youth. From a severely realistic technique he turned to the use of symbols for the expression of ideas.

The Wild Duck (Vildanden, 1884)[8] contained a reaction to the one-sided insistence on truth in human relations which had characterized some of Ibsen's earlier plays. The question posed is fundamental for the whole life work of the author: What value does truth have in human life? The pessimistic conclusion is that mankind is too weak to bear the truth and needs its "life lie" to make existence bearable. Gregers Werle is a well-meaning but wrong-headed idealist, a kind of caricature of Brand, who creates nothing but harm by his demands for truth. Like Doctor Stockmann he suffers defeat in his campaign for truth in human relations, but this time the sympathies are turned around. This is done by letting his "rectitudinitis" lead to the tragic death of the adolescent girl Hedvig. Gregers is not the only psychotic character in this play: Old Ekdal has some of the traits of Ibsen's derelict father. Most vividly portrayed is the hollow charm of Hjalmar Ekdal, a younger brother of Peer Gynt and Stensgård, but far shallower and more contemptible than they. *The Wild Duck* is one of Ibsen's most fascinating plays. It was received with bewilderment by the critics, and is still interpreted in various ways.

Rosmersholm (1886)[9] reflects contemporary events in Norway more directly than the preceding plays. Ibsen had visited Norway in 1885 and heard the parliamentary debate on Kielland's author's salary, which he himself had helped to propose. On the next day he said to Bjørnson's

[8] Tr. Mrs. F. E. Archer, *Collected Works,* Vol. 8 (New York, 1907, orig. pub. 1891); R. F. Sharp (London, 1910); E. Marx-Aveling (Boston, 1890); Una Ellis-Fermor, *Three Plays by Ibsen* (London, 1950).
[9] Tr. Charles Archer, *Collected Works,* Vol. 9 (New York, 1907, orig. pub. 1891); R. F. Sharp, *Everyman* 659 (London, 1913); M. Carmichael (Boston, 1890); L. N. Parker (London, 1889); E. Marx-Aveling (London, 1890).

son Bjørn: "Give my greetings to all who are young in Norway, and tell them that I wish to join them on the left flank, as their left guard." He refused to receive a torchlight procession of the Student Society because he did not feel akin to its conservative spirit. He even encouraged the members to repudiate their chairman, thereby stirring up a feud which led to the organization of a new Liberal Student Society and Ibsen's election as its honorary member. He encountered narrow-mindedness, but on the other hand he also caught sight of the ambitious liberal politician who took shape in his Mortensgård, the man who can live his life without ideals. He was repelled by the political fanaticism which tore family bonds into shreds, as reflected in the story of Rosmer and Rector Kroll.

In a speech delivered during his Norwegian visit Ibsen expressed it as his opinion that it was necessary for "a noble element to enter our national life, our government, our parliament, and our press. I am of course not thinking of a nobility of birth or of money, nor even one of knowledge or ability. But I am thinking of a nobility of character, of will and heart." This became the central idea of *Rosmersholm,* embodied in Rosmer's ill-fated effort to create what he called "happy noblemen" in his country. The attempt to synthesize happiness with nobility of character is a new version of the "third empire."

Nature had been virtually absent in the social dramas, but with *The Wild Duck* and *Rosmersholm* it creeps back in symbolic guise. Ibsen was inspired by his renewed impressions of the sea during his visit in Norway to make its mystic force a factor in his chief female character, Rebecca West. Her origin in the northernmost Norwegian province of Finnmark suggests her bewitching qualities—Ulrik Brendel, the bohemian in the play, calls her a mermaid. Rosmer himself has his name from a Danish ballad about the merman, but the model for his character is the Swedish poet Count Snoilsky whom Ibsen had met during his visit.

The most significant aspect of this moving drama is its portrayal of character. It is a story of the psychological conflict between Rosmer's sense of guilt, his fear of life, instilled by education and conventional morality, and Rebecca's flaming passion, the savagery which is ennobled by her love, only to end by destroying her will to live. The Rosmer view of life may ennoble, but it kills happiness. Family tradition, family fears, family scruples—these are stronger than Rosmer; but even he is in the end stronger than she.

The trend toward mysticism and the interest in the workings of the unconscious which became a commonplace in Norwegian writing of the 1890's was already present in Ibsen's *Wild Duck* and *Rosmersholm*. It was even more evident in the study of woman in marriage which Ibsen called *The Lady from the Sea* (*Fruen fra havet*, 1888).[10] Ellida Wangel carries on the mermaid motif by centering her daydreams on an absent sailor lover instead of her husband. For once Ibsen has provided a happy solution, and incidentally anticipated the principles of psychoanalysis. Ellida's return to a mature reality is in some ways parallel to Svanhild's in *Comedy of Love,* as pointed out at the time by Camilla Collett.

Another study in female distempers, Ibsen's most famous, is *Hedda Gabler* (1890).[11] While there is no apparent mysticism in this play, the mysteries of Hedda's psychology are fully the equal of Ibsen's other plays. The subtle analysis of her complexes is one that has been confirmed by modern psychology. There are connections here with Strindberg's contemporary writing, but the theme of the woman who cannot love is one that recurs frequently in Norwegian literature also during these years, in the writings of Amalie Skram, Kielland, and Garborg. In the summer of 1889 Ibsen had met and been fascinated by a young lady from Vienna, Emilie Bardach. While she probably meant more for the portrayal of Hilde in his next play, some of the "vulture-like" traits he found in her seem to have gone over into Hedda as well. He called her "the May sun in a September life" and corresponded with her for some months.

In 1875 Ibsen had moved to Munich, though he spent many of his summers at Berchtesgaden and Gossensass in the Alps. From 1880 to 1885 he lived in Italy, chiefly Rome, but then returned to Munich where he lived until his return to Norway in 1891. On his sixtieth birthday he was honored throughout Germany, where he was now as firmly established as if he had been a native German writer. To the artists who founded the "Freie Bühne" in Berlin in 1889, he was the great prophet of the age. He was often present at the premières of his plays in Germany, but the greatest pleasure he had was the dedication of an Ibsen Square in the little town of Gossensass. Here he led the parade himself. Meanwhile his works were penetrating into other countries, everywhere to the accompaniment of controversy. The first performances of his plays

10 Tr. Mrs. F. E. Archer, *Collected Works,* Vol. 9 (New York, 1907, orig. pub. 1891); Clara Bell (Boston, 1890).
11 Tr. E. Gosse and William Archer, *Collected Works,* Vol. 10 (New York, 1907, orig. pub. 1891); Una Ellis-Fermor, *Three Plays by Ibsen* (London, 1950); Eva Le Gallienne (London, 1953; New York, 1955).

in England around 1890 shocked the conservative theater world, but aroused the vigorous enthusiasm of young men like Gosse, Archer, and Shaw. Ibsen had become a citizen of the world.

Yet in 1891 he returned to spend his declining years in the city that had rejected him and sent him away a generation earlier. In his imagination he had lived in Norway all the time; all but one of his plays had their scene in Norway. But he found it difficult to live in the atmosphere of his homeland, though his isolated mode of life was not essentially different in Norway from that he had pursued in Germany and Italy. In either place he was a tourist attraction, an oracle, a sphinx, though not at all unwilling to receive the homage that poured in on him.

The meeting with Norway became also a meeting with his own youth. The old problems from 1857-1864 bobbed up again, the relation of art to life, which he had dealt with in "On the Heights" and *Comedy of Love*. To this was added an impulse from Nietzsche's doctrine of the superman, though indirectly. But Ibsen's nobleman is very different from the superman. He has nothing of the brutality associated with the latter. On the contrary, if he ruthlessly tries to make space for himself by destroying others, as do Solness and Borkman, he is inevitably destroyed.

One of Ibsen's first experiences was his meeting with the new generation of Norwegian writers, in the shape of the arrogant young Knut Hamsun, who proclaimed that old men like Ibsen had served their time and should now yield to youth. Ibsen saw the dramatic force of this encounter and reflected it in the tragedy of *The Master Builder* (*Bygmester Solness,* 1892).[12] He expressed in this play a genuine sympathy for the younger generation, but also the frustration of the older man who feels his powers waning but still wants to reach the heights. In this story of artistic ambition and human happiness Ibsen gave a masterful expression of his own earlier themes. He called it "a poetic confession" and found room in it also for a portrayal of marriage. This theme was carried on into *Little Eyolf* (*Lille Eyolf,* 1894),[13] a low-pitched, gentle, almost unreal play. Most impressive is the portrayal of child psychology in the crippled boy Eyolf, who compensates for his physical weakness by pride in other advantages. The play is another one with a "happy" ending, in so far as Rita and Almers return to their marriage, after she has agreed to sublimate her passion into a humanitarian work for poor children. The

[12] Tr. E. Gosse and William Archer, *Collected Works,* Vol. 10 (New York, orig. pub. 1893); Eva Le Gallienne (New York, 1955).
[13] Tr. William Archer, *Collected Works,* Vol. 11 (New York, 1907, orig. pub. 1895).

urge of nature is transformed into an ideal force, lifting the soul "toward the peaks, toward the stars, and toward the great silence." But the basic idea is one that Ibsen often touched upon, and which arose from his sense of guilt, as expressed in *Comedy of Love*: "There is a retribution that runs through life."

In *Lady from the Sea* and *Hedda Gabler* marriage was seen largely from the woman's point of view, as it had been in the social dramas proper. From *The Master Builder* on the man takes the center of the stage. He sacrifices the woman to his calling, and has to suffer the consequences. She is no longer his best helper, but an enemy of his work, a theme that was launched in *Hedda Gabler*. This is the theme that connects *John Gabriel Borkman* (1896)[14] with the preceding works. This is the powerful drama of the former bank director, who had the artist's nature that permitted him to hear the metals singing in the mountains, a man who believed in his mission and after his defeat felt like a Napoleon who had been crippled in his first battle. Like Earl Skule and Consul Bernick, Borkman had betrayed love for the sake of his calling; this is his greatest sin, for which there is no forgiveness. This theme became the chief burden of the next, and last, play.

Ibsen's fame on his seventieth birthday had reached its climax during his lifetime. Greetings poured in from all parts of the world; books and articles were published about him. Theaters performed his plays, and students honored him with torchlight processions. He was dragged about from celebration to celebration, to Copenhagen and Stockholm. Princes came to see him, and King Oscar II spoke to him of "we two kings." More decorations descended upon his breast. While all this tickled his vanity, it did not make him happy. *When We Dead Awaken* (*Naar vi døde vaagner,* 1899)[15] was subtitled "A Dramatic Epilogue," and gives the effect of a formal conclusion to his writing, in which he passes merciless judgment on himself and his activity as an artist. He asks: Was all my life work really worth those sacrifices of living values which it has required? Even more profound is the question: Would not my writing also have had more truth in it if I had taken an active part in life? His words here have to an even greater degree than earlier a double set of meanings. Everything becomes symbolic. This is a poem about death, life, art, and love. Though it is one of the least transparent of his works, it is also one of the most fascinating.

---

[14] Tr. William Archer, *Collected Works,* Vol. 11 (New York, 1907, orig. pub. 1897).
[15] Tr. William Archer, *Collected Works,* Vol. 11 (New York, 1907, orig. pub. 1900).

His last years, which were spent in Oslo, were unproductive; he died on May 23, 1906. The funeral address was given by Christopher Bruun, one of the models for Brand. The obelisk on his grave symbolizes his uncompromising and lonely personality; it is engraved with a hammer, the symbol of the miner's profession.[16]

[16] Some of Ibsen's letters and speeches are published in *Letters,* tr. J. N. Laurvik and Mary Morison (New York, 1905), and in *Speeches and New Letters.* tr. Arne Kildal (Boston, 1910).

Björnson and the Problems of Realism

THE SEVENTIES PROVED TO BE the greatest period of controversy in Bjørnson's life. He was still concerned with nationalism, the Swedish union, Scandinavianism, democratic reforms, language problems, the theater, and education, to name a few of his favorite topics. But when new problems arose, Bjørnson had to attack them also, whether they were political, moral, or religious. His campaign in the seventies was directed entirely against conservatism on all sectors, but in the eighties he had to open a new front against the extreme radicals on his left. While he was still battling the conservatives in politics and religion, he had to fight both the conservatives and the bohemians on the issue of morality. The current feuds were taking so much of his time that he scarcely found the peace of mind to create.

In 1870-1871 Bjørnson, like Ibsen, was deeply disappointed at the defeat of France. For a French bazaar held in Oslo in 1871 he wrote the poem "To the Wounded" which begins with the words: "Through all the din of battle a quiet train is passing with prayers in every language." Yet he was also critical of certain aspects of French culture, its "piquanterie," its "mock ideas," its positivist philosophy. His feelings for Denmark cooled as he discovered that his Grundtvigian friends in Denmark did not share his Christian forgiveness for Germany's actions toward their native country. He disappointed and startled many of them when he delivered a speech at the grave of Grundtvig in which he asked that they turn the other cheek and make friends with their old enemy. But Bjørnson's Pan-Germanism was never a support of German aggressiveness; it was a transitional phase through which he passed on the way to his work for international understanding.

In 1873 he finally fled from Norway to find peace once more in Rome. The plays he wrote during this second exile were highly significant in the development of Scandinavian drama. They brought into this genre for the first time the new devotion to realism and social problems which Brandes had been urging upon his fellow Scandinavians. Their titles were *A Bankruptcy* (*En fallit*)[1] and *The Editor* (*Redaktøren*)[2] and both appeared in 1875.

The one that awakened the greatest popular interest was *A Bankruptcy,* which quickly penetrated to Denmark and Germany, and from there to the stages of many other countries. Never again was Bjørnson to win as much international acclaim as he did with this play. One reason was the novelty of the topic: business had not been considered a proper theme for literature. Another reason was its frank appeal to popular sentimentality. The theme was one that had suggested itself to Bjørnson in his Bergen years, when there were many bankruptcies. The parallel to Ibsen's *Pillars of Society* which appeared two years later is obvious. But in Bjørnson's play the attack on hypocrisy and dishonesty was made on behalf of society and the family, while in Ibsen's it was directed against society. Bjørnson wished to say that the individual who operates according to an egotistical and irresponsible code of business ethics is injuring a healthy society, his family, and himself. The characters are clearly and interestingly drawn, and several scenes are excellent. But the final act, with its Bjørnsonian harmonization, weakens the artistic effect of the play. The purpose is to show that misfortune had reunited the family: "A family that sticks together cannot be beaten."

Bjørnson himself thought more highly of *The Editor,* probably because there is more of his own personality in it. He pictured in it his own relationship to the poet Wergeland, as well as some of his controversies with the conservative editor Chr. Friele, the chief model of the leading figure. The play caused a great hubbub because it was taken to be a personal attack on the editor, an act of vengeance. But there is a genuine effort to make his actions humanly understandable, and the whole tenor of the play is a plea for political tolerance. It was generally overlooked that in spite of its scenic weakness, there is much good writing in it.

Bjørnson's coolness toward the Grundtvigians led to his finding other friends, among them the Swedish liberal editor S. A. Hedlund in Gothenburg, the Swedish poet Victor Rydberg, and the Norwegian historian Ernst Sars. These and other friends stimulated him to read Charles Darwin and the new writers who were advocating ideas that had so far

---

[1] Tr. as *The Bankrupt,* by R. F. Sharp, in *Three Dramas* (New York, 1914).
[2] Tr. R. F. Sharp in *Three Dramas* (New York, 1914).

seemed abhorrent to him. But as late as 1874 he bought himself a home at Aulestad in the Gausdal parish of Gudbrandsdal in order to be near the Grundtvigian folk high school conducted by Christopher Bruun. He dreamt of working with them to introduce Grundtvig's ideas in Norway, in a union of national, democratic, and religious faith which would harmonize all Scandinavia. His first book from Aulestad was a novel situated in Italy, *Captain Mansana (Kaptein Mansana, 1875)*,[3] one of his weaker efforts.

The time was coming when a quiet growth of personality and the gradual progress of mankind no longer satisfied him, a period when he fell in love with ideas almost as much as with humanity. In the early seventies he was devoting much more attention to religion than before. But while his Christianity was growing more personal, he also became more critical of the official hypocrisy which characterized a so-called Christian society. He became more aware of the discrepancy between the practice and the ideals of Christianity. He was also annoyed by the fact that every time he advocated some new reform, the theologians were invariably arrayed against him. He began to discover that there was more of the Christian spirit in Victor Hugo, who fought for world peace and neighborly love, than among the theologians who asserted that liberalism was the work of the devil.

From the middle seventies the new ideas fermented so strongly in him that he began to re-evaluate many of his opinions. He made friends with Brandes and wrote to him in 1878: "I now understand Ibsen's *Brand* better. I did not understand it before. . . . Not until now have I been grateful to Ibsen for it." The demand of "all or nothing" had acquired a new appeal for him, especially after his great speech of 1877 when he addressed the Student Society on "Being in Truth." "If I were a minister in our times," he said, "I would begin and end everything by saying: . . . 'For each individual the most important thing is to be in truth.' . . . But precisely because something is being concealed here, we are being botched, botched in our will, our sincerity, and our truth, corrupted already as young people in our noblest self."

This demand for truth is the theme of the bold play *The King (Kongen, 1877)*,[4] which he had just published. Here he scoffs at the idea that we are all Christians and live in a Christian society, much as Kierkegaard had done in Denmark some years earlier. Everyone thinks of himself as

[3] Tr. E. Gosse (London, 1897), R. B. Anderson (New York, 1884).
[4] Tr. R. F. Sharp in *Three Dramas* (New York, 1914).

a Christian, but what happens to the Christian ideals in this society? Are they realized? No, says the king: "I tell you, Christianity has laid aside its ideals. Christianity is living on dogmas and formulas instead of ideals." "If there were a strong Christianity in this country, the whole salvation business (the state church) would fly up to heaven like a bad stench." But unlike Kierkegaard, Bjørnson demanded that Christianity should create, not just "lonely believers," but also a new social spirit. *The King* is effective on the stage without being one of his best plays. Its attack on the monarchy is elevated by the noble personality of the monarch himself.

The angry conservatives, who regarded *The King* as *lèse majesté*, were no more pleased with his story *Magnhild* (1877).[5] The scene is the same as in his country tales, but now looked upon from an entirely different point of view. He no longer accepted the idea of a single divine call for each human being; his heroine has artistic abilities, but is able to find a satisfactory life in other fields. More offensive to the moralists was his open defense of divorce, which some took as an attack on marriage. It seems incredible in our day that anyone should reject divorce as the only reasonable escape from a husband like Skarlie. But the nationalistic advocates of rural culture were also outraged by his more pessimistic view of the country folk. In reply to an attack by Garborg, Bjørnson in his abrupt manner declared: "We have entertained far too much peasant worship. . . . There must be an end to our boasting. But not to our hopes, our work, our truth."

In the long run the rural environment and the folk high school atmosphere became too confining for Bjørnson. He had not been at Aulestad long before he changed his mind about Bruun and his noble idealism. Bruun, he wrote, "loves overexertion in mankind." He found this preacher of love defending the Old Testament gospel of divine vengeance. In 1877 they broke, and Bjørnson declared he could no longer endure life "among long-haired, red-bearded, heavy-booted, homespun-clad pietists and apostles of virtue." Victor Rydberg had convinced him that asceticism was oriental and pietism unsuitable to the Germanic temperament. In 1877 he read John Stuart Mill, Robert Ingersoll, Brandes on Kierkegaard, and the history of dogma and religion. He was convinced that "Christianity is either of Kierkegaard's kind, which is an impossibility, an insanity, or else it is the renewer of the world." From here the step was short to the conclusion that since it has not renewed

[5] Tr. E. Gosse (London, 1897).

the world, it must be likened to the "mad" teachings of Kierkegaard.

Bjørnson's religious crisis in 1878-1879, which led to his rejection of the church dogma, was a terrible strain, and often depressed him deeply. But it did not alter his basically religious nature and in no way changed his ethical principles. He merely accepted Darwinian evolution and reshaped it into an expression of divine "order and harmony." He made his own an idea that Wergeland too had entertained, though in a somewhat more metaphysical spirit. He transplanted his old optimism in a new soil. His new faith even caused him to burst into poetry, which took the shape of hymns in honor of evolution: "Honor the undying springtide of life, which all has created!" He believed in the God of light as an illumination in each individual:

> Oh, but be Thou who thou wilt;
> For I know that Thou art,
> As the undying cry in my soul, it is Thee!—
> The cry for justice and light,
> The cry for victory's right
> Of the new-revealed forces, it is Thee, it is Thee!

He also believed in the God of light as a force against the destructive powers, the darkness in the world. His cosmological picture and his concept of God changed; but his faith in life was the same.

In the midst of his crisis he wrote *The New System* (*Det ny system,* 1879),[6] a play to show how difficult it is in a small country to tell the truth. There is much of the same spirit as in *An Enemy of the People* and other typical writings of the period. It contains sharp attacks on the clergy, the state church, the bureaucracy, and the prudish upbringing of his times. The play *Leonarda* (1879)[7] showed that the crisis was over. He had joined the moderns completely, and even let his bishop say that the "unbeliever" Leonarda had acted from a nobler morality than he and his congregation. Like *Magnhild* this play discusses a woman's right to divorce, but in spite of many fine and effective scenes, it was overshadowed by Ibsen's *Doll's House* which came in the same year.

During the next years Bjørnson was too much engaged in political affairs to do any serious writing. In 1882 he removed to Paris and stayed away from Norway for five years. Even so he was constantly involved

[6] Tr. E. Björkman in *Plays,* First Series (New York, 1913).
[7] Tr. R. F. Sharp in *Three Comedies* (New York, 1914); D. L. Hanson in *The Drama* (Chicago, 1911), 16-76.

in Norwegian affairs, having taken the initiative in the impeachment of the cabinet which in 1884 produced a peaceful revolution in Norway and ensured the triumph of the Liberals. In 1887 he angrily resigned his author's salary because the Storting refused to give one to Kielland. In 1889 he raised the demand of full equality or an end to the union with Sweden.

Bjørnson's writings during the eighties were his contribution to the liberation of the human mind from dogmas and prejudice, in the spirit of Brandes's proclamation. His first major effort was the excellent short story *Dust* (*Støv*, 1882),[8] in which the falling snow is a symbol of the conventional ideas of society which obliterate the sharp outlines of truth. Its purpose is akin to Herbert Spencer's ideas of education, to show that it is dangerous to educate children to the belief that everything is so much better in heaven than on earth. The story is notable for its descriptions of nature, particularly the scene of a forest which shakes off the snow and straightens out its branches.

In the play *A Gauntlet* (*En hanske,* 1883)[9] Bjørnson ventured into the field of sexual relations, this time with an attack on the so-called "double standard." His heroine Svava throws her glove in the face of her fiancé when she learns that he is not as pure as herself. When she learns that her own father is no better than her fiancé, she collapses. The ideals of purity on which she has been nourished turn out to be unrealistic and exaggerated. But oddly enough, Bjørnson does not here draw the conclusion he did concerning religion, that the standards should be relaxed. Instead, he set up an equally high standard for both sexes, which led to violent attacks from the bohemian writers, and Bjørnson's equally spirited defense, plus a revision of the play which made it less humanly and psychologically satisfying.

Some months later he published his dramatic masterpiece, acknowledged as one of the best plays written in Norway, *Beyond Our Power I* (*Over ævne, første stykke*).[10] This expressed Bjørnson's own fear of becoming unrealistic in his insistence on an ideal. He wrote in a letter of July 16, 1878, about the trend in his time to "vault over the real," a tendency to go "beyond our means," "not merely in the economic sense, but in our relation to our ideals." The expression *over ævne,* which Bjørn-

8 Tr. E. Gosse (London, 1897); R. B. Anderson (New York, 1884).
9 Tr. R. F. Sharp in *Three Comedies* (New York, 1914); E. Björkman in *Plays,* First Series (New York, 1913); H. L. Brækstad (London, 1890); Osman Edwards (London, 1894).
10 Tr. E. Björkman in *Plays,* First Series (New York, 1913); tr. as *Pastor Sang* by W. Wilson (London, 1893).

son used in this letter, came to be the title of two separate plays; it may be freely rendered as "beyond one's means" or "beyond one's ability." The theme of the first play by this name, wrote Bjørnson, was "over-exertion in mankind," the danger of "overextending oneself" in order to reach the impossible. While Bjørnson said that he had chosen his friend Kristofer Janson as a model for his main figure, he clearly equipped him with even more traits from himself. The Reverend Sang is a warm-hearted, optimistic believer, who spreads joy and sunshine about him wherever he goes, and shares with Bjørnson a naïve faith that anything is possible. Yet the point of the play is that this is not true.

The structure of the play is superb, and its richly varied mixture of comedy and tragedy, faith, hope, and fear is superior to anything else Bjørnson wrote. The chorus of pastors, as has been well said, is reminiscent of the choruses in the Greek drama, just as the central idea is not unlike that of the Greek "hubris," or pride which brings on tragedy. Lyric passages alternate with others which portray small human weaknesses. The plot itself is unlikely to say the least, but its scenic effect is remarkable because the author has succeeded in conjuring up an atmosphere in which even the impossible seems probable. The impressions of nature in northern Norway, where night is day and day is night, have combined with lyric prose to suspend the spectator's disbelief. In Gunnar Heiberg's words, the work is that of a genius, "because the author compels the spectators to see what he wants them to see." During the battling, prosaic eighties the play was not appreciated at its full value; only in the nineties did it win a response.

The psychological crisis which had sharpened Bjørnson's sense of the contrasts in life made him a better dramatist. But as a theme of positive doctrine the idea of beyond-human-power is rather prosaic. This may be a reason why his novels during this period do not measure up to his early novels. The stories *Flags Are Flying in Town and Harbor* (*Det flager i byen og på havnen*, 1884)[11] and *In God's Way* (*På Guds veie*, 1880)[12] are marred by lengthy discourses on topics that the author burned to expound.

The first of them is a pedagogical novel and deals with a subject that had interested Bjørnson from the start. He was warmly concerned about the schools, as the seedbeds of all the progress which he wished for society. From the country school teachers of the early novels and the

[11] Tr. as *The Heritage of the Kurts* by Cecil Fairfax (London, 1890).
[12] Tr. Elizabeth Carmichael (London, 1890).

Grundtvigian folk high school teachers of his later books he now turned
to the progressive schoolteaching of Herbert Spencer. Bjørnson looked
on the schools as a means of ennobling mankind. Jonas Lie, who thought
of Rousseau's *Émile* when he read the book, wrote to him: "You have
always had a touch of the great and enthusiastic schoolmaster in you
with your visions about the future needs of our people."

Bjørnson also ran other errands in his pedagogical novel, including
an attack on the bohemian program of morality. This theme is also
involved in the witty and lighthearted play *Geography and Love* (*Geo-
grafi og kjærlighed*, 1885),[13] where he satirized a tendency (which was
also his own) to become overly absorbed in one's own interests and
enthusiasms. The geographer in the play neglects his family and practically drives it out of the house with his maps, but in the end the near
tragedy is averted and turned into comedy. The theme of education is
prominent here also, as it is in the novel *In God's Way*. But in the latter
the main subject is religious tolerance, and the book is one long debate
between an unbelieving physician and a believing pastor. The two of
them agree in the end that "where good men walk, *there* is God's way."
In this book he advocates a school system in which boys and girls are
educated together. In his second play with the title *Beyond Human
Power II* (*Over ævne, annet stykke*, 1895)[14] Bjørnson returned to the
theme of education. The play deals with the conflict of labor and capital,
and both sides come to realize that their demands are unreasonable. Here
Bjørnson points out that the dream of social justice cannot be realized
without a new spirit in the schools. His credo is spoken by one of the
characters who says: "Begin with the schools, for in the schools they
must learn to live for one another."

This untiring interest in youth and in schools shows us something
central in Bjørnson—the educator and teacher of his people, the warmhearted spokesman of the best ideas of his day. But it also reflects his
feeling for the connection between new and old, the continuity of tradition,
the union of the radical and the conservative in his nature. As Dag says
to his son in the play *Daglannet* (1904): "In all you have said to me,
I miss one word, the word for continuity. The experience of the old and
the fire of youth—or their faith, if you will. What binds these together.
Joins what was to what is to what will be. Continuity."

[13] Tr. as *Love and Geography* by E. Björkman in *Plays*, Second Series (New York, 1914).
[14] Tr. as *Beyond Human Might* by E. Björkman in *Plays*, Second Series (New York, 1914);
tr. as *Beyond Human Power* by L. M. Hollander in Dickinson, *Chief Contemporary Dramatists* (Boston, 1915).

After 1890 Bjørnson grew more conciliatory in the union controversy. This was connected with the fact that the work for international understanding gradually came to be his most important activity. He wished the union with Sweden to be loosened gradually, without a sharp break that might lead to war. He was in the pacifist's dilemma of wanting both independence and disarmament. He had faith for a long time in arbitration as a means of settling conflicts between the major powers, but the Bobrikoff affair in Finland in 1898 made him feel that the small nations had to take the lead in the peace movement and become the core of a league of nations. He was continually active during these years on behalf of all the oppressed nationalities of Europe, and had the gratification of being listened to respectfully on behalf of the Slovaks, the Ruthenians, the Czechs, and the Finns.

During these years Bjørnson usually called himself a socialist, though he had no sympathy for the class struggle. He expressed his social views in the delicate story *Mother's Hands* (*Mors hænder,* 1892), and in the play *Beyond Human Power II,* where Nietzschean and anarchistic ideas clash. His other writings in the early nineties included the oratorio *Peace* (*Fred,* 1891), the antibohemian but brutal story *Absalom's Hair* (*Absalons hår,* 1894), and the university cantata *The Light* (*Lyset,* 1895) in the spirit of Wergeland. Bjørnson's campaign for peace even led to his being accused by some newspapers in Norway and Sweden of acting as an agent of the Russian government.

Two distinguished plays still were to be written by him. The first of these was *Paul Lange and Tora Parsberg* (*Paul Lange og Tora Parsberg,* 1899)[15] on the theme of political intolerance. The plot reflected an event in which Bjørnson himself was involved, leading to the suicide of the political figure Ole Richter. Bjørnson's male lead is a weak but noble personality, a lover who cannot decide, a politician who cannot act. The woman Tora Parsberg is unforgettable in her healthy womanliness, proud but humble, untiringly inventive in protecting his diseased mind. She is near victory again and again, but is defeated at last.

The other was his last production, *When the New Wine Blooms* (*Når den ny vin blomstrer,* 1909),[16] a highly effective stage play. As so often before, he spoke out on behalf of the family. The title sounds as if it was chosen in reply to Ibsen's *When We Dead Awaken,* the conclusion of which is "Then we discover we have never lived." The conclusion of

---

15 Tr. H. L. Brækstad (London, 1899).
16 Tr. L. M. Hollander in *Poet Lore,* Vol. 22 (1911), 1-78.

Bjørnson's title is "Then the old wine ferments," a clear affirmation of life even for those who are aging.

When Wergeland was on his long deathbed, he sent packets of seed throughout Norway in order that they might grow and blossom. When Bjørnson was about to die, paralyzed on one side, he wrote his grand cantata "Norway's Weal," in which he described the life-giving spring rains, no doubt in allusion to Wergeland's poem "A Good Year for Norway." This symbolizes the relationship between them. Wergeland was the great sower in Norwegian history. Bjørnson carried on a life-long battle to make the seed sprout and bear fruit.

Bjørnson was awarded the Nobel Prize in Literature by the Swedish Academy in 1903. He died on April 26, 1910, in Paris. The last days of his life he was working on a poem to be called "Good Deeds Save the World."[17]

[17] Bjørnson works not mentioned above, but translated into English are the plays *The New System* (Björkman, *Plays,* First Series, New York, 1913), *Laboremus* (Björkman, *Plays,* Second Series, New York, 1914, and a tr. in London, 1901). Other novels and short stories are included in the R. B. Anderson (Boston 1881-1882) and the E. Gosse (London, 1895-1909) translations of his novels.

Novelists of Realism

JONAS LIE

IT WAS CHARACTERISTIC OF JONAS LIE'S AUTHORSHIP that he did not build his writings on theories, even though he was constantly buzzing with ideas. Through his visionary imagination and his impressionistic technique he succeeded in making his characters share the reader's intimacy, so that the reader feels with them and sees them through the author's eyes. Precisely because there was no direct agitation in his books, he could, in Bjørnson's words, act as "the sliest, laughing subverter of all the ideas that were highly respected but no longer deserved to be so."

Lie's skill in making characters and things come alive was due to his feeling for characteristic details. He had a sharp eye at close quarters. But he also had an intuitive capacity which made him see connections immediately and without reasoning.

He was a realist in so far as he wished to portray reality. But he rejected the naturalistic theory that it was necessary to enumerate the details as precisely as possible. He best expressed his conception in a letter to Garborg: "What the deuce good does it do for an author to swear to a chunk of casual reality; all that matters is that the spirit in the reader's breast should testify that it *is* reality. . . . It is nonsense to think that we would be interested in having a hundred life stories written down in all their details and facets. The important thing is to distill the hundred into one; that is art, the intervention of spirit in matter." Therefore he criticized the naturalist Zola and added: "But to raise reality out of the realities, that is art."

He was not as simple or uncomplicated as Bjørnson. Alongside the realist in him there dwelt a dreamer and a fantast. He had a capacity for looking at the world with reflective eyes, a religious wonderment and respect for life, which appeared already in his first novel, *The Visionary,* and in his old age reappeared in the two volumes of *Trolls* and other fairy tales. He was convinced that the primitive and elementary aspects of human psychology, the "troll" stage, were still potent in the civilized age. He saw the causes of social abuse and individual conflict in irrational forces within man himself.

His culture had its roots in the age of Wergeland and the bureaucratic tradition. He was tolerant, with an aversion to all kinds of fanaticism and attempts to force life into certain paths. Even in Bjørnson he found too much of an "either-or." He sometimes felt that Norwegian intellectual life consisted of little else than one fanaticism after the other.

Geographically his writing embraced large parts of Norway, from Tromsø to Stavern, from Bergen to Kongsvinger. Socially, too, he was highly inclusive, since his characters were not only members of the upper classes, but also sailors, fishermen, and workers. He portrayed family life, the problems of daily existence, conflicts between social groups. The country and its people emerge clearly from his writing.

He was born at Hokksund in Eiker on November 6, 1833, but lived most of his childhood in Tromsø where his father was a city judge. It was the boy's wish to become a naval cadet, but his nearsightedness caused him to be rejected. He then attended school in Bergen a short time, and continued at Heltberg's "student factory" in Oslo, taking his entrance examination in 1851. After completing a law degree he married his cousin Thomasine Lie and settled at Kongsvinger to practice law. But he got involved in disastrous financial enterprises connected with the lumber industry and made a thunderous bankruptcy in 1868.

At this point he decided to give up entirely the life of affairs and turned to the life of letters. It was his dream to be able to repay his creditors, in spite of the fact that he had a wife and two children to support. The wife courageously supported his venture, even to the extent of guiding and pruning his writing. His exuberant imagination may have led him astray at times, but Bjørnson was probably right in considering her much too conventional and prosy. There were no "trolls" in her character.

Jonas himself had inherited the most from his mother, an impulsive and culturally minded woman, enthusiastic and complex; he believed or hoped it was true that her slight, dark figure represented a strain of either Lappish or gypsy blood. His boyhood in the North left indelible impressions on him of its magnificent nature and exotic folk life; his fantasy was stimulated by the rich stock of folklore communicated to him by the servants. In his student days he made a fast friendship with Bjørnson. Even while he was a practicing lawyer, he wrote numerous and surprisingly independent articles about national and international problems. In 1866 he even published a collection of poems of Wergelandian form, but he never became a lyricist.

When Bjørnson in 1869 made a visit to Nordland, he made a speech in Tromsø where he called attention to Lie and prophesied that he would become the epic writer of that region. This encouraged his friend to publish his first novel, *The Visionary or Pictures from Nordland (Den Fremsynte eller Billeder fra Nordland,* 1870).[1] This charming book is not merely an imaginative and pretty little love story. In its pages the sea rolls into modern Norwegian writing, and that with a force which makes one think of Petter Dass's *Trumpet of Nordland.* David Holst, the student who has come from up north, complains bitterly about the nature around Oslo, a grimy, gray, waveless sea where you sit in a flat-bottomed boat and haul up a few miserable perch with a flimsy fish line, while up north the spouting whales swish through the deep sea channels. In Oslo people talk about birds and mean something they can eat. In Nordland there is a screaming, teeming snowstorm of birds over the hatching places and the bird mountains. In Oslo there is now and then a little squall and some "damage in the harbor." Up north the storm falls upon you from the mountains, so that reefs and skerries vanish in the foam, and vessels are smashed against the cliffs. In this novel the whole mysticism of the North found its way into Norwegian literature, the hidden but seductive forces of nature, the sea monster in its half boat that haunts the storm-doomed fishermen, the darkness that lasts for so many months, the short but hectic summer with its midnight sun; all this Bjørnson described later in *Beyond Human Power I,* Ibsen in *Lady from the Sea,* and Hamsun in *Pan.*

The Visionary was a great success and appealed to the public as something entirely new. He made it his immediate goal to "reflect the nature, the folk life, and the social spirit of that region which is my beloved land." In *The Barque 'Future' (Tremasteren 'Fremtiden,'* 1872)[2] he wrote the first Norwegian sea story and story of business life, while in *The Pilot and his Wife (Lodsen og hans Hustru,* 1874)[3] he wrote the

[1] Tr. Jessie Muir (London, 1894); cf. also *Weird Tales, infra* note 6.
[2] Tr. Mrs. Ole Bull (Chicago, 1879).
[3] Tr. Mrs. Ole Bull (Chicago, 1876); G. L. Tottenham (Edinburgh and London, 1877).

first Norwegian novel of marriage. The latter is a story depicting jealousy and feelings of social inferiority, but it is also a vivid description of life at sea.

In the latter half of the seventies Lie's efforts did not measure up, though he tried hard and published novels, poems, and plays. He was slowly absorbing the new ideas, more intuitively than intellectually, but it took him time, as he said, "for his conscience to catch up." In 1880 he suddenly erupted, as was his nature, with a new freshness of spirit in the salty sea story *Rutland*. In the novel *Go Ahead!* (*Gaa paa!* 1882) he took a stand on behalf of youth against the dominance of the old men. His introductory chapter describes a valley quite enclosed by mountains and intellectually just as circumscribed. Even the trout are malformed because no one fishes in the streams, and the cows are degenerate because there is no renewal of blood. The women in the community all have a depression in the forehead. Generations of intermarriage have led to stagnation. This description of a community is also intended as a symbol of Norway, where new ideas and young blood are needed. The hero of the story is Rejer Jansen Juhl, the man with courage and persistence, whose initiative puts an end to the stagnation and breaks the traditional customs of the valley.

The novels that followed were marked by the ideas and techniques of naturalism, without being aggressively radical. *The Life Convict* (*Livsslaven*, 1883)[4] is the story of a lad born out of wedlock whose temperament and social misfortune combine to destroy him. Although this was probably his most naturalistic story, it does not preach directly, only as life itself speaks. The same is true of the novels that describe the position of women. It would never occur to Ma in *The Family at Gilje* (*Familien paa Gilje*, 1883)[5] to rebel or to toss off political aphorisms; yet few figures in literature have done more for the liberation of women than she. When her daughter Inger-Johanne refuses to enter into a marriage of convenience, it is not because of any social or political doctrine.

This story, *The Family at Gilje*, is a classic work in Norwegian literature. It is a first-rate sociological study from a mountain valley in the 1840's, borne by an intimate poetic feeling, and characterized by subtle psychological analyses. An example is the remark by one of the girls about her father, the home tyrant Captain Jæger: "Father was terribly amusing whenever company was present." In *A Maelstrom* (*En Malstrøm*,

---

[4] Tr. as *One of Life's Slaves* by Jessie Muir (London, 1895).
[5] Tr. S. C. Eastman (New York, 1920).

1884) he described the dramatic episodes of a bankruptcy such as the one he himself had experienced. His most penetrating psychological study is the novel *A Marriage* (*Et Samliv*, 1887) in which he showed how two people slowly move apart until an economic catastrophe brings them together again.

Lie's naturalism was to some extent a sacrifice to the spirit of his times. His wife had often had to cut out digressions in which his rebellious imagination found its outlet. He was never a determinist, and believed in the power of spirit over matter. In 1890 he published another story of business life, *Evil Powers* (*Onde Magter*), which to some extent reflected the break between himself and Bjørnson in 1887 over the moral issue of the bohemian writers. In this novel he wrote, "Might there not be a tiny, piquant, incalculable troll hidden somewhere far down in us?" This was the motif he elaborated in his two volumes of fairy tales called *Trolls* (*Trold*, 1891-1892).[6]

In keeping with the new romantic emphasis of the 1890's he was able to give a freer and more artistic expression to his view of life in these stories. This view included a fondness for mysticism and love of the fantastic, coupled with an all-inclusive tolerance and a noble, often paradoxical, but always humanitarian outlook. Several of the stories return to the theme which had occupied him in his first novel, the problems of the unconscious and the clairvoyant. Yet Lie never turned to the spiritualistic experiments of some of his contemporaries. His novels in the nineties are interesting for their descriptions of his life and times, but they are artistically weak. The most original of his later novels was *When the Iron Curtain Falls* (*Naar Jernteppet falder*, 1901). In this moving story he tells of a number of persons who happen to be on board an Atlantic liner when a time bomb is reported to be hidden somewhere in the hold of the ship. The fear of death brings out hidden thoughts and unsuspected traits of character. In the end it is not the "trolls" who win out, but the divine spark in humanity.

Jonas Lie had lived abroad for twenty-eight years, mostly in Paris. In 1906 he returned to Norway, and in the following year he and Bjørnson were once more reconciled. Lie died on July 5, 1908.

In one of the fairy tales that appeared after his death he had written

---

[6] Some of the stories appear in R. N. Bain, *Weird Tales from Northern Seas* (London, 1893). Other Lie novels that have been translated are *The Commodore's Daughters* by H. L. Brækstad and Gertrude Hughes (London, 1892) and *Niobe*, by H. L. Brækstad (London, 1897). Also *Little Grey: The Pony of Nordfjord*, tr. Mrs. Arbuthnott (Edinburgh, 1873).

these words: "It was truly my need and my passion to picture forth all of Norway with my pen."

ALEXANDER KIELLAND

When the *Family Hope* came sailing into the fjord with a lively breeze and settled at anchor, Skipper Worse waved his hat where he stood on the bridge and shouted so it could be heard all over Sandsgaard, "We're getting in late, Mr. Consul, but we're getting in good!" Kielland himself could have said the same when he anchored up in Norwegian literature as "the most elegant ship in the Norwegian literary fleet," to use Bjørnson's expression.

Alexander Lange Kielland was born in Stavanger on February 18, 1849. This city and the nature in its environment provided the basic chord in all his writing. On his father's side he belonged to a merchant family with a long cultural tradition, with Norwegian roots and a dash of the international, reflected in his portrayal of the Garman family. His mother's family were government officials. Though he lost his mother when he was thirteen, he has pictured her in Mrs. Wenche Løvdahl who appears in the novel *Poison,* along with the school Kielland attended in his youth. Kielland studied law in Oslo, but never took his studies very seriously. He returned to Stavanger, married, and bought the Malde Brick Works, which he ran for nine years. There was nothing in his career so far that indicated he would become a writer.

In his student days he had not been prominent, but he had read writers like Heine and Kierkegaard who had made an impression on him. During his years as "a doubt-ridden, malcontent brickmaker," ideas began to ferment in him. He read Kierkegaard with growing absorption, but also oriented himself in the ideas of his time by reading Mill, Darwin, Georg Brandes, Dickens, and the French writers. He dreamt of becoming a popularizer of philosophy like John Stuart Mill. In 1878 he tore himself away and left for Paris, where he wrote a couple of short stories and a play. In Paris he met Bjørnson who was completely charmed by his talent and his personality. The year after he published his *Novelettes* (*Novelletter*), which captivated the public by their new style and their elegance.[7] He was thirty years old; he got there late, but "he got there good."

[7] Some of these appeared as *Tales of Two Countries,* tr. William Archer (New York, 1891), others in *Norse Tales and Sketches,* tr. R. L. Cassie (London, 1897).

His form combined an ironic and jesting tone with an almost romantic sensibility. Yet a purpose was evident even in these early stories. He was out to break a lance against the injustices of the world. His opinions were democratic and liberal, though his personality and way of life were those of an aristocrat. His later books brought out his purpose even more clearly. He prided himself on making his books socially useful, not just entertaining: "It is my pride to be an honest believer in utilitarian literature; be sure you bring this out if you are going to write about me." These were his words to Edvard Brandes, a brother of Georg. He refused to write objectively, and when anyone accused him of being one-sided, he answered, "When people sleep soundly, you don't whisper into their ears: 'Please get up and be about your business'; no, you scream 'Fire!' and when they get their sleepiness and their anger rubbed out of their eyes, they thank you for having screamed. . . . He who wants to awaken people, must exaggerate. . . . That sugar water which they call an objective impartial description is bosh and pap." To Georg Brandes he wrote, "In the center I light a bonfire, as it were, where I plan to burn some social evil, and around this fire a number of people are grouped; on these the sparks from the fire fall more or less vigorously, but always the illumination [is] from the fire and nothing else."

Kielland tried in his writing to combine thinkers who were as different as Kierkegaard and Mill. Kierkegaard's demand for personal participation led Kielland to attack all forms of hypocrisy and dishonesty. Among his favorite targets were the state church and its pastors, but never Christianity itself. On the contrary, he liked to contrast the lofty ideals of Christianity with the term-serving, worldly parsons of the state church. He contended that in so doing he was acting in behalf of true Christianity, and wrote to his brother who was a pastor, "I think, without mocking your God, that He will be grateful to me if I rid Him of that pack of official lies which are the reason His name is being scoffed at among the heathen." He also attacked jurists and teachers, the memorization of Latin in the colleges, old-fashioned methods of education, and the lack of social conscience among the rich. But he had considerable sympathy for the old merchant artistocracy; they were men who had felt a patriarchal responsibility for their workers.

Kielland often expressed his scorn for "psychologizing" literature, and he cared little for the praise of aestheticians. But he loved his own weapons, his cool and supple style, his elegant language and his eye for composition. He was aware that his purpose would remain unfulfilled if it were not borne by an artistic form and a convincing psychology. But he also digressed from his purposes and created purely lyrical moods, in his short stories as well as in his novels. Such passages are the description of the sea and the birds in *Garman and Worse,* the birds of passage in *Working People,* or Morten W. Garman in his garden in *Skipper Worse.* These show his gifts as a writer of lyric prose.

In the novel *Garman and Worse (Garman & Worse,* 1880)[8] he portrayed the life of his native Stavanger. The story combines vivid descriptions of nature with an ironic view of his fellow men. Two worlds are here contrasted: the merchant aristocracy and the common people. Between them stand the ministers, who use their "patent felt" to prevent all conflicts between idealism and reality, whose task it is "to smooth out all doubts and to put the damper on all vigorous life of the individual." With tart irony the author sends two of his leading characters to the cemetery on the same day, the rich Consul and the poor Marianne whom he had once seduced: "There were three kinds of hearses, so that one could ride to the graveyard just as on the railroad, in first, second, or third class carriages. . . . Consul Garman rode first class with angels' heads and silver adornments."

Kielland felt that his novel was too tame, and after some more short stories and plays, he published his most argumentative novel, *Working People (Arbeidsfolk,* 1881), an unrestrained attack on the bureaucracy, especially the lawyers in government offices. Although there are brilliant passages, the purpose overwhelms the artistry; and besides, Kielland was out of his depth in describing the Oslo scene. Much more effective was the little "Christmas story" *Else* (1881),[9] in which he ridiculed a hypocritical charity and gave a naturalistic portrayal of social misery. In his second masterpiece, *Skipper Worse* (1882),[10] he returned to the familiar scene of his own environment, but this time projected back to the generation of 1840. As a counterweight to this charge he here portrayed the Haugean pietist Hans Nielsen Fennefos as a fine and noble personality, contrasting the lay, revivalistic religious activity favorably with that of the official church. He has given a masterly description of

[8] Tr. W. W. Kettlewell (London, 1885).
[9] Tr. as *Elsie* by M. M. Dawson (Chicago, 1894).
[10] Tr. Henry John, Earl of Ducie (London, 1885).

the gradual decay of his bold and merry skipper. Through the whole novel blows a fresh wind, even in the stuffy meeting houses, with a salty tang of sea and herring.

The novels *Poison* (*Gift*, 1883) and *Fortuna* (1884) reflect Kielland's conception of his contemporaries.[11] Primarily they are sharp attacks on antiquated educational methods and social hypocrisy, which he described as a poison instilled into the young. These two novels have a common gallery of figures grouped around the young Abraham Løvdahl, and the best part of them is their description of the spiritual degeneration of this promising lad, who had started out as a brave boy with the ideal of truthfulness in him. In the novel *Snow* (*Sne,* 1886) the author attacked the fusion of Christianity and conservative politics, much in the vein of Bjørnson's *Dust.*

The story of Abraham Løvdahl was continued in *St. John's Festival* (*Sankt Hans Fest,* 1886), Kielland's sharpest and most satirical book. Here he made hypocrisy the leading theme, and returned some of the barbs that had been leveled at him in the controversy over his author's salary. The leader of the "moderate liberals," a local pastor with great power, was the unmistakable model of the Elmer Gantry-like figure who dominates this book. Much lighter was the satire with which Kielland amused himself in such plays as *Three Couples* (*Tre Par,* 1886), *Betty's Guardian* (*Bettys Formynder,* 1887), and *The Professor* (*Professoren,* 1888), in which he poked fun at some of the topics commonly discussed in his day.

In the course of ten years Kielland had tossed off eight novels, two collections of short stories, six short plays. As a writer of fiction he was now in a leading position. No one could write with such grace as he or hit the mark more precisely. But in spite of the controversy about his name, he was disappointed with the results of his struggle against the bureaucracy and the conservatives. In the shadow of democracy and liberalism a generation of *nouveaux riches* had grown up; something vulgar and mean had appeared which made the aristocrat in him react. He tried his hand as editor of a local paper in 1889 in order to counteract the vulgarization of the times. The same purpose is apparent in his last novel *Jacob* (1891), the story of the poor boy Tørres who starts his business career by stealing a dime from his employer's cash box and winds up as an all-powerful businessman and politician.

Kielland had written in order to realize his dream of intellectual and political freedom, and to express his demand for social justice and truth.

[11] Tr. as *Professor Lovdahl* by Rebecca Blair Flandreau (Boston, 1904).

He admitted that much of his writing had its ultimate root in a bad social conscience. Though he was often one-sided, he had succeeded brilliantly in varying his basic themes. But now his sympathies were divided. He did not like the extremities in which the bohemians indulged, and even less the romantic reaction of the 1890's. It has been guessed that these were the reasons for his abrupt exit from the literary scene. He could not, like Bjørnson, do battle on two fronts.

In 1891 he was appointed mayor in Stavanger and in 1902 district governor in Møre. During these years his only literary efforts were some essays entitled *People and Animals* (*Mennesker og dyr,* 1894) and a rather unsuccessful book about Napoleon in 1905.[12] Otherwise he limited himself to private correspondence, much of which was published after his death. Kielland's letters give us the best insight into the man himself. Ibsen's letters were usually dry and businesslike, Bjørnson's lyrical and impassioned, while Jonas Lie's reflected his independent and unprejudiced spirit. Only Kielland cultivated letter writing as an art, and produced epistolary gems which rank with the best in Norwegian literature.

He died April 6, 1906.

KRISTIAN ELSTER

It tells us something about the prevailing climate of the seventies and eighties in Norwegian literature that this delicate and original writer first aroused attention by the novel *Dangerous Folk* (*Farlige Folk,* 1881). This novel had a clear and indubitable purpose, viz., to attack small-town life and caricature the clergy. Old man Holt and his son are "dangerous folk" in the eyes of the village because they advocate modern ideas. Unhappily for Elster this recognition came too late, for he died before the publication of the book. It was generally overlooked that the book is a true work of art and contains profound studies of character. Few were aware that he had previously written stories and novels that entitled him to serious respect.

Kristian Elster (1841-1881) was born in north Trøndelag, but accompanied his father, a judge, to Sunnfjord in western Norway at the age of twelve. Although he later lived in various parts of Norway, the Førde valley in Sunnfjord became his real home to which he always longed to return. In his moving story called *Sun Clouds* (*Solskyer,* 1877) he portrayed his nostalgia: "I sometimes long so that my breast hurts and

---

[12] Tr. as *Napoleon's Men and Methods* by Joseph McCabe (London, 1907).

my blood is feverish to be back in the moist air and the delightful summer fragrance of wet trees and wet grass in those western regions. I long for the wild, foaming torrents, for delicate, fresh, green grass, for black pine woods, for the tiny white houses with gardens and the gray paths of the valleys. I long for high mountains with snow on their peaks, for the smell of the sea, for the sound of long, faintly breathing summer waves, and the sight of waving seaweed and billowing boats. I long for sailing vessels, for big storehouses with barrels, for talk about herring and sailing. I long for a narrow patch of sky and flaming colors of the sunset; I even think I long for the smoke smell of the farm houses, the tiny churches, and the old-fashioned hymn singing."

One of Elster's favorite topics was the problem of uniting Norwegian national and folk traditions with European currents of thought. In his novel *Tora Trondal* (1879) this was one of the leading ideas. He joined this problem with the idea of the contrast between East and West Norwegians, whom he regarded as complementing one another in a higher Norwegian unity. But western Norway and its people were his primary interest, and most of his stories deal with these. His characters are often individuals who live halfway outside of society, whose tender and eccentric natures cause them to live mostly in their dreams and fantasies. Such persons are the central figures in his best stories, *Sun Clouds* and *A Strange Bird* (*En fremmed Fugl,* 1881). The problems he deals with are mostly the contrast between the ethical and the aesthetic points of view, between participation and observation of life. Among his teachers were the Danes Kierkegaard and Goldschmidt, but also the Russian Turgenyev and the German Spielhagen.

Elster's development was slow and difficult, and due to his early death he never reached full artistic stature. His literary work showed a cast of sadness, even though he could be lively enough as a journalist. There is a delicate flavor in his best writing, something restrained and genuine, and there is a profound understanding of individuals and of folk types. His voice drowned in the clamorous discussions of the times. But he created unforgettable figures, like Eline Holt and her uncle in *Sun Clouds* or the mother in *A Pilgrimage* (*En Korsgang*). In the history of the Norwegian novel he has a small but secure niche.

AMALIE SKRAM

That Elster won his fame as a poet after he was dead, can be attributed to the fact that he was not "modern" enough. But the opposition that held Amalie Skram back was due to her being altogether too modern, too crass for the taste of her public. Many people were particularly offended that a woman would write like this. Camilla Collett had idealized female love and maintained a woman's right to make her own decisions. Amalie Skram tried to give an unadorned picture of the inner life of women, and particularly of women who are unable to love. Camilla Collett had stirred up discussion, but Amalie Skram caused consternation.

The keynote of her writing was pessimistic. Her favorite Bible passages must surely have been "the wages of sin is death" and "the misdeeds of the fathers are visited upon the children." Throughout her books runs a feeling that life is a hopeless struggle for sensitive individuals and a bottomless morass for most human beings. Nevertheless the best of her writing is not depressing because it is infused with a sympathy that elevates the spirit and gives a deeper understanding.

Some of her novels, particularly those that grew out of her personal experiences, are direct attacks on individuals and institutions. But when she herself was not so directly involved she tended rather to explain than to condemn. As a pure naturalist she was content to document, and did not wish to be understood as a writer with a purpose. When the last volume of her main work, the four-volume *People of Hellemyr,* appeared, she was bitterly attacked on the grounds that her novel was an accusation. Then she answered, "I have never portrayed evil, for I have never met it on my path. That which superficial and doctrinaire persons call evil is to me a necessity, a result. If I have had any purpose whatever in my writing, it has been to make one or another understand, and to moderate their judgments." She was convinced that heredity, education, and environment were what caused people to stagnate and made them vicious and petty. Above all she attributed it to poverty and the joylessness of life. Very few of her characters avoid this fate, and happiness is rare in their lives once they have reached adulthood.

Amalie Alver was born in Bergen on August 22, 1846, as the daughter of a huckster and unsuccessful speculator. Her childhood years were marked by the disharmonious home life that is so prominent a feature of her books. She was fond of school and of the novels she devoured, which opened her eyes to the pettiness of real life and stimulated her social ambitions. In many respects she became a disappointed romantic. The decisive disappointment in her life came when she married a sea captain nine years older than herself named Müller; this was in her eighteenth year. Many of her heroines look forward to life as young girls, but are cruelly disappointed by marriage.

Some years later she contracted a second marriage, more harmonious and satisfying, with the Danish writer Erik Skram. He encouraged her to write, and in the year after her marriage she published her first novel, *Constance Ring* (1885). The book was praised by Arne Garborg and the radicals, but branded as immoral by the conservatives. A more direct contribution to the sexual discussion of the times was *Lucie* (1888). A third novel, *Mrs Inés* (*Fru Inés*, 1891), showed an artistic advance. Her mastery in this field came with the sea story *Betrayed* (*Forraadt*, 1892). Here, the relationship between the very young girl and her older, "experienced" husband is not seen exclusively from the girl's point of view. Ory drives her husband to insanity. Bjørnson wrote about this tragic tale that it "leaves an impression as if you were out at sea and look down into the water and there you see a pair of eyes, large, large eyes in a head that cannot be discerned, but the eyes keep opening and closing, opening and closing, cold as the sea itself."

But it would be a reduction of Amalie Skram's talent to speak only of her depiction of feminine psychology. She is also a student of the child. No Norwegian writer has had a deeper understanding of the defenselessness of the child's position in an adult world, whether in childhood, adolescence, or the transition to adulthood—its religious difficulties, its relationship to parents and the other children in the family. No one has understood better the influence of social circumstances on the child's mind. In her portraits of childhood we often find a brighter atmosphere than otherwise in her writing. When children and young people are allowed to be together without thinking of the grownups or their homes, or when brother and sister share their deepest intimacies, the atmosphere can be lighthearted and free. Such traits go back to her friendship with her brother Ludvig in the days when she played in tomboy fashion with the boys in the street.

The novel that tells the story of the relation between generations, of family ambition and inferiority feelings, of a family in decay is *People of Hellemyr* (*Hellemyrsfolket*, 1887-1898). This is one of the masterpieces in Norwegian literature, a work that has gathered no dust. Much of it can indeed be better understood today, in the light of modern psychology, than in its own time. The first volume, *Sjur Gabriel*, pictures a fisherman's family at the farm Hellemyr, some few miles north of Bergen.

It is marked by poverty, illness, drink. The description of Sjur Gabriel himself and his incredibly vital but alcoholic wife is particularly notable. The second volume, *Two Friends* (*To Venner*), is the liveliest sea story in Norwegian literature from the time of the sailing ships. It tells the story of Sivert, the grandson of the fishing folk in volume one. Here the atmosphere is brighter and sunnier, aside from the dark shadows cast on his life by the boy's grandmother. Volume three, *S. G. Myhre*, is a study of life in old Bergen, dramatic and intense, but less profound as a social analysis. The fourth volume, *Offspring* (*Afkom*), is the most dismal, but also perhaps the most moving Norwegian novel. In this book comes the final catastrophe for both the third and fourth generation.

She also tried her hand at playwriting, but never became a master of dramatic form, in spite of the dramatic scenes in her novels. In Copenhagen she received treatment for nervous disorders, and she succeeded in writing vivid descriptions of her experiences in the novels *Professor Hieronymus*[13] and *At St. Jørgen's* (*Paa St. Jørgen*), both of which were published in 1895 and stimulated much discussion. Less naturalistic and more conciliatory toward religion were her novel *Christmas* (*Julehelg*, 1900) and the unfinished *People* (*Mennesker*). She died on March 15, 1905.

Amalie Skram was not a fastidious stylist or a great artist. But the profound humanity which fills her best works, the passion that burns beneath the surface, the intense psychological analysis, and her incomparable pictures of the life of her times—all of these contribute to the unmistakable effect of reality and genuineness which keeps these books alive.

ARNE GARBORG

Thoughts make unrest; thoughts make grief.
From thinking them through there is no relief.

There are scarcely any lines in Garborg that express more precisely the heart of his personality. In religion, politics, nationalism, or art—everywhere he had to think his thoughts through, follow them to the end of the road, sometimes to the edge of the precipice. But this was not the result of any lack of intellectual balance, and nothing could be more misleading than Bjørnson's description of him as the "hysterical man

---

[13] Tr. A. Stronach and G. B. Jacobi (London, 1899).

in our literature." Garborg was driven by intellectual passion and curiosity, an honesty which drove him to a conscientious testing and doubting of everything. The fact that he did not lose his balance is due to his healthy common sense and keen peasant's insight, a certain self-irony and humor, a sharp eye for what was practical and attainable.

Garborg lived through the crisis of the Norwegian farmer in the second half of the nineteenth century, the transition from a self-contained to a money economy, the great transformation of the social order. He experienced more strongly than Aasen and Vinje the conflict between rural and urban culture, and he feared the victory of capitalism in the country communities. But at the same time as he knew and understood the peasant, he absorbed in himself the intellectual crises of Europe. Because he had such deep roots in Norwegian soil and also a strong sympathy with the new ideas of the European intellectual world, he reached the rural youth as no one else. Ivar Aasen also knew the peasants, but more as a class and less as individuals. He regarded it as his task to present the peasant's view to the city man. Vinje as a cotter's son lacked an appreciation of the good sides of farm life, and wanted to educate the peasants by teaching them to improve their farms and to acquire the city man's culture, elevate their thoughts. In Garborg these two currents met and joined into one stream.

His elasticity of mind and his capacity for insight were such that he succeeded in creating studies of Oslo life that render brilliantly the specific traits of urban behavior in his day and age. The same catholicity of approach made him a better critic than writers like Bjørnson and Wergeland. He could write with equal insight about Ibsen and Jonas Lie, about Nietzsche and Tolstoy. His severe logic and psychological keenness also made him a witty and vigilant participant in numerous political, linguistic, and literary debates. Bjørnson had greater power in his argumentation; he rode his opponent down like a troop of cavalry, using good and bad arguments indifferently. Garborg was more softspoken in manner, but he had a surer eye for his opponent's weaknesses.

Arne Garborg was born in Time parish of the Jæren district January 25, 1851. His father was an intelligent and capable farmer. But when Arne was eight years old, his happy childhood was disturbed by a religious revival which stirred the community and changed his father's outlook. From now on life was darkened by fears of hellfire, and everything that smacked of the world was taboo. Arne had to do his reading in secret, and got an early impression of the mentality that dominated what he was later to call "the dark continent." But alongside his memories of this world, which he depicted in the novel *Peace,* he also retained memories of the old pre-pietistic Jæren, as we see from the poetic cycle *Haugtussa.* The broad lines of the landscape appealed to the intellectual in him, which demanded a wide horizon; while its gloomy gray skies above the lonely heaths called forth a mystic form.

While he was attending the teacher's seminary at Holt, there came the message that his father had committed suicide in a fit of religious melancholy. Garborg called this period of his life "the darkest of my life history." He never quite rid himself of the feeling that he was guilty of his father's death, because he as the oldest son had refused to take over the farm. This became his great sin and "a lifelong pang of conscience." He repeatedly tried to free himself of it by writing about it.

Dreams of writing had haunted him from his earliest youth, and his great model was Henrik Ibsen. But he was slow in finding himself, and spent some years as teacher and editor, frequently being also the printer and only contributor of the papers he edited. He then starved himself through a preparatory education and took his entrance examination in Oslo with top grades. Shortly before he had published a penetrating and original study of Ibsen's *Emperor and Galilean* (1873). For several years he had struggled to achieve a religious philosophy and had clung to Kierkegaard's teaching about the paradox, his faith in the absurd. Sometimes he felt that he was entirely liberated and could fill his lungs with air: "All this business that the preachers and the sermon books talked about was bosh. There was no such old fire-eater of a Lord who was eagerly waiting to see if he could throw us into Hell." He developed a marked antipathy to the theologians, and fell upon them with Kierkegaard's weapons in a little pamphlet called *Jaabæk and the Pastors (Jaabæk og Præsterne).*

But he was still a believer in authority. When the university in contravention of all good academic custom refused to permit Georg Brandes to lecture, Garborg defended the university. Not until 1878 did he lose his faith in authority and cease to ask the theologians for answers to the questions that troubled him: "No one can actually believe anything except what he himself has found the truth of." At this time he wrote his first major story, *A Freethinker (Ein Fritenkjar,* 1878),[14] a novel about Eystein Hauk who becomes a martyr for freedom of thought and is condemned

14 An extract, tr. by W. H. Carpenter, appears in Warner's *Library of the World's Best Literature,* Vol. 11 (New York, 1897), 6185-94.

by his own son. It is a sharp attack on theological intolerance and religious narrowness, but without deep psychological penetration. It is also his first book in *Landsmål,* or New Norse language, whose leading champion he soon became.

With the publication of *Peasant Students* (*Bondestudentar,* 1883) Garborg took his place as one of the significant writers of his time. Its theme was one of the leading problems in Norwegian social life. Many had maintained that when country youth left for the capital and studied at the university, eventually finding positions of influence, this was a great democratic advance. The peasant students infused new blood into the upper classes, and as pastors, judges, etc., they would understand the people better than the urban students could. Most of the country lads we meet in Garborg's novel either go to the dogs because of hunger and illness, or they are spiritually damaged by city life, losing their roots and their culture, becoming contemptuous of the peasant's life and language. The leading character, Daniel Braut, is a victim of the cultural conflict in Norway. He has grown up in poverty, but has learned to scorn his own class, and has lost his bearings because of the contrast between the ideal he nourishes of student life and the harsh reality in a snobbish and undemocratic city. But, as Garborg wrote to Brandes, the book has an economic purpose; poverty is the factor that weakens the moral and cultural backbone of many peasant students. The conditions of student life are described with all the intensity of personal experience, and without an equal in Norwegian literature. In this deeply moving picture of social conditions in Oslo he even introduced well-known personalities like Heltberg, Vinje, Fjørtoft, and others, without reducing either the psychological or artistic value of his novel.

Garborg's running feud with the theologians drove him still further to the left. He became convinced that religion "was outside the borders of necessary conclusions"; all that mattered was to make this life livable by reforming society. He grew more and more interested in the ideas of anarchism and socialism, participated in the discussions of sexual freedom, and made fun of Bjørnson's *A Gauntlet* in a witty story called "Youth." He regarded himself as a member of the outcast bohemians, though he did not agree that free love would solve all problems. He pointed out the social and economic problem which resulted from the fact that so many men in the cities had to remain unmarried until they were 35-40 years of age, and then had to betray their real love when, more or less burned-out, they sought refuge in the port of marriage.

His stringent search for the causes of misery and sexual deviation led him to write two more novels in a naturalist vein. *Menfolk* (*Mannfolk*, 1886) and *With Mother* (*Hjaa ho Mor*, 1890) were more thoroughgoing in their documentation of life's tragedy than *Peasant Students*. His insistence on "mere" photography was so conscientious that he had scruples whenever he thought he had idealized or retouched his picture to eliminate anything ugly. He felt as if he had written bogus checks. *Menfolk* is a well-considered, farsighted discussion of the moral problem, but bores the reader with its overly detailed descriptions. *Menfolk* provides a collective analysis of male sexuality against a social background, while *With Mother* does the same for female sexuality. But the latter lacks inspiration and warmth, and won little attention in Norway. It was praised by several Swedish critics, however, and won him a literary prize in Germany from the periodical *Freie Bühne*.

The demand for social reforms and a strengthening of the national backbone were the chief poles of Garborg's interest in the eighties. Politics became his religion. He suffered a number of sharp disappointments, first of all the loss of his position on account of *Menfolk*. Then Sverdrup's Liberal party, the party of progress and national enthusiasm, split on the issue of Kielland's author's salary. The worst reactionaries in this matter were Garborg's beloved peasants. In the play *Irreconcilables* (*Uforsonlige,* 1888) he wrote about them: "If there is anything that is moldy and fusty and clerical and antagonistic to all freedom, it is these old clodhopping peasants with their inherited West Norwegian stinginess and their puritanical pietism."

Irreconcilables was written in Garborg's mountain cabin at Kolbotn after he had married Hulda Bergersen. He wrote letters from his retreat to the newspaper *Fedraheimen* and published these in 1890 as *Letters from Kolbotn* (*Kolbotnbrev*). Here we learn about his varying moods in his most amusing, most deeply felt, and most gracious book. There is something of the philosopher, but above all we meet him as a nature lover. He had never before attained the verbal artistry of his descriptions from the mountain heights and his intimate fellowship with nature. In the woods and the high plateaus, which he describes in all seasons and weathers, the problems of politics, society, and morals are all happily remote.

But the intellectual currents of his times never left him alone for long. Around 1890 he again entered upon a crisis, as the superficiality of the evolutionary optimism of the eighties became obvious to him. Nor was his artistic and psychological intuition satisfied with mere external description. He had imagined that if he only limned every detail as precisely as possible, the resulting description would be true. But human psychology was not as simple as the naturalists thought. From pure naturalism he was moving toward an impressionism in which reality was not to be presented as it was but as it impressed the artist's eye. It took him some time before he reached a clarified point of view. He lived in Germany for some years, but in the summers he retreated to Kolbotn, weary of politics, feeling that his ideals had been betrayed. For a time he leaned toward Prince Kropotkin's anarchism, and in religion he vacillated from the Buddhist doctrine of life's insignificance to Nietzsche's doctrine of the superman. For a long time he even half jestingly tried his hand at spiritualistic experiments. He also took to reading Tolstoy, with whom he had many points in common.

In 1891 came *Weary Men* (*Trætte Mænd*), a novel in diary form, written in a soul-searching mood, but sparkling with his best ironic wit. The theme is the decadence of his generation, its psychological debacle, and inability to meet the problems of life. Questions concerning the meaning of life and death haunt him, and the answers are always the same: "Is there a God? We don't know. Does life have a meaning? We don't know. Why do I exist? We don't know. Do I exist at all? We don't know. What do we know then? We don't know." The protagonist, Gabriel Gram, is a typical decadent, who combines a Nietzschean philosophy with a life of dissipation. He doubts everything, shrugs his shoulders at all ideals and similar nonsense. He laughs at science: "This systematic 'we don't know' is called science!" It ends with his giving it all up and laying his head in the roomy lap of the church.

Garborg stated his intentions with this novel in a letter he wrote to Jonas Lie: "If I had any practical purpose with my novel, it was this: to combat dogmatic free-thinking, or rather to deliver our good people from their latest sophomoric enthusiasm, and I have had the opportunity to discern that there is more than enough of that in our blessedly young and naïve people."

Weary Men was a turning point in Garborg's production, in one sense his farewell to urban life. Its theme was one that characterized urban culture in western Europe generally, and was in no way peculiar to Norway. But Garborg's interests from now on turned back to his own peasant origin, though it was not correct to say as Bjørnson did that he had bought an intellectual round-trip ticket. He came to his analysis of the peasant with all the sophistication of his new-won urban culture, but also with an understanding born of love and sympathy. His novel *Peace (Fred,* 1892)[15] did not accept or condone the religious fanaticism which he had abandoned in his youth. But it was a deeply understanding analysis of the psychology of the West Norwegian peasant, his fear of hell and his fanatical otherworldliness, which are not assuaged by his growing economic difficulties. The title is ironic, for if there is anything Enok Hove, Garborg's portrait of his father, does not find, it is peace. He broods night and day, wrestles with the Lord, is pressed down by the yoke of sin, tortures himself and his family. This picture of the Jæren peasant and his struggles with God is set in a framework of magnificent nature description.

One aspect of Enok Hove's religion did have Garborg's sympathy: Enok took the Christian ethics seriously and tried to realize the words of scripture about selling his goods and giving them to the poor. His Christianity demanded an active attitude, a positive program of action. Garborg was gradually regaining his interest in getting things done also, and re-entered public life. In an article entitled "Faith in Life" he wrote that in practice it is impossible to think of a meaningless existence: "Life is there. Entirely unmotivated, completely contrary to reason. It is a mere postulate, but an energetic postulate which we cannot bypass. A postulate so superior that it scorns even a proof of its own existence." We are forced to create our own meaning in existence, because we ourselves have a purpose in existing. Here religion can "strengthen one in life's battle" and develop "psychological depths and subtleties." "Faith in life" is the religion of those who think.

At this time the old peasant grows stronger and stronger in him: "We peasants are bound to the soil in a special kind of way; if we tear ourselves loose from this basis of our lives, we always get some kind of a stoppage or malformation of our growth. The city street may be resplendent. But it is not made to sink one's roots into." He even found that Kolbotn with its mountains was no longer for him; he had to get back to the seacoast where he was born: "My longing for the sea awoke. Memories of the sea drew me back; I felt imprisoned among the mountains. . . . I had traveled halfway round the world looking for a home; now I felt that I would never be at home anywhere—except at home."

In the poetic cycle *Haugtussa* (1895), one of the masterpieces of Norwegian literature, both the thinker and the peasant have found artistic

15 Tr. P. D. Carleton (New York, 1929).

expression for their deepest concerns. First and foremost these poems, to which Grieg has set magnificent music, are a deeply felt hymn to nature, though in a minor key. It is dedicated to the melancholy nature of Jæren:

> To you, pale heath and bleak, grey moor
> With thornythong,
> Where hooded crane and heron soar,
> I give my song.

But faith in life is also proclaimed here:

> But larks rise from forgotten graves
> With victor's song;
> The wind sweeps from across the waves
> So fresh and strong.
>
> And though we sorrow, groan and grieve
> And feel fear's sting,
> We still the larksongs must believe,
> Which promise spring.

Translated by K. G. Chapman

In *Peace* and *Weary Men* the poet had pictured those who lost out in the struggle with the life-destroying forces, the trolls. In *Haugtussa* the girl who is his leading figure overcomes these forces. Gabriel Gram with all his European decadence ended in a weary resignation. Enok Hove with his Norwegian piety found no other peace but death. But poor Veslemøy, who had read neither Nietzsche nor Tolstoy, or even religious tracts, defeated the trolls because she was loving and kind.

Garborg's following books, *The Teacher, The Lost Father,* and *The Returned Son,* formulate his program for the good life. His doctrines are in no way metaphysical, and it is impossible to speak of any conversion back to Christianity. This is a religious-ethical humanism, a Christian program of living: "All that is told us about the life hereafter is dark speech and imagery which we can have no idea about."

In the powerful play *The Teacher* (*Læraren,* 1896), Paulus Hove, a son of Enok in *Peace,* breaks with pietism. This man is a radical thinker in the tradition of Tolstoy, to whom Christianity means a social and spiritual revolution. But because he tries to realize the ethical ideals of

Christianity, he gets into conflict with "Christian" society. The play is akin to *Brand* and *Beyond Human Power I*: Paulus has Brand's will to sacrifice and his force as an agitator, combined with some of Sang's optimism, but he is more realistic than either. In spite of some weaknesses, the play is scenically effective. The second part of the trilogy, *The Lost Father (Den burtkomne Faderen,* 1899),[16] is a prose poem of the highest merit. This is the most personal of all his writings, perhaps his master-piece stylistically. While *The Teacher* had portrayed altruism, the theme of *The Lost Father* is the bankruptcy of egotism. Gunnar, a brother of Paulus Hove, has been out in the world where force rules. But he loses his wealth, returns to his home, and is filled with longing for the farmer's tasks and the God of his childhood. The ideas are more pro-found, more beautiful, and weightier in content than in any of his other books. Here he contrasts the fear of life, the sense of guilt, the gnawing of conscience on the one hand, and on the other the harmony of a quiet, laborious life without brooding over insoluble problems.

Garborg was not prepared to lay aside the many problems that inter-ested him. He was continually engaged in the controversies of his day over national, social, and religious problems. While he had his moments of doubt, his faith in the rural culture was restored and his writings circle largely around this theme. A sequel to *Haugtussa* called *In Hell's Home (I Helheim,* 1901) is a symbolic poem dealing with the evil forces of life. His *Letters from Knudahei (Knudaheibrev,* 1904) discuss many national and social problems. He had faith in the ability of a rural society to meet the problems of the new age, but worried about the influ-ence of the new capitalistic mentality. The question of how one could secure the peasant's soil against the power of money and speculative enterprise occupied him more and more as the years passed. He thought he had found a solution in Henry George's doctrine of the single tax. At the same time he worked with his religious problems. In his book *Jesus Messiah (Jesus Messias,* 1906) he tried to restore the figure of Jesus as he had appeared to the first Christians. He wanted to cut away every-thing the church had added, including such dogmas as the teachings of salvation and redemption. He worked for a humane, earthly religion, both in this book and in *The Lost Messiah (Den burtkomne Messias,* 1907). In the third part of his trilogy about the Hove family, *The Returned Son (Heimkomin Son,* 1908), he combined his cultural and religious philosophy in a noble and deeply personal book. But none of

[16] Tr. Mabel J. Leland (Boston, 1920).

these later writings show an artistic force equal to that of his best work.

Garborg continued to work at literary tasks until shortly before his death on January 14, 1924. He spent ten years of his life translating Homer's *Odyssey,* and in 1922 he published a translation of the Indian epic *Ramayana.* Personally Garborg was a quiet, unobtrusive man. When he reached his sixtieth year, his wife Hulda wrote about him: "The only pleasure he really cares for is to jolt along on a safe road that is free from automobiles in a cart pulled by a kind horse that doesn't talk to him." When he turned seventy, a gift of honor was given him, a "Nobel Prize" from the Norwegian people. A part of this gift was a Norwegian fjord pony, which honored him by not talking to him.

The Neoromantic Reaction

IN THE 1890'S NORWEGIAN LITERARY LIFE became more abundant and varied than before. Young voices and old expressed many new ideas and made new demands upon life, all the way from pessimism and decadence to a new optimism and faith in life. Above all, there was an insistence on artistry as the touchstone of literature.

In the first issue of *Samtiden,* a new magazine of opinion founded in 1890, Knut Hamsun wrote an article entitled "From the Life of the Unconscious." In this article he formulated the program for a new kind of literature.

Among more and more people who live a strenuous intellectual life and who are sensitive of temperament, strange kinds of psychological activities often arise. These may be quite inexplicable sensory states: a dumbfounded, causeless rapture, a breath of psychic pain, a perception of having been spoken to from afar, from the air, from the sea; a cruelly delicate sense of hearing which causes one to suffer from even the whisper of unseen atoms; a sudden, unnatural revelation of hidden kingdoms; the intuition of an approaching danger in the midst of a carefree hour—all of them phenomena which have the very greatest significance, but which coarse and simple hucksters' brains cannot grasp.

Hamsun demanded that the poets make it their task to learn more about "the secret movements that go on unobserved in the remote locales of the soul . . . these voyages of thoughts and feelings into the unknown, footless, trackless journeys by brain and heart, strange activities of the nerves, the whisper of the blood, the prayer of the bones, all the unconscious life of the soul."

In the same summer Arne Garborg wrote in the newspaper *Dagbladet* concerning "The Idealistic Reaction": "People are tired of superficial facts and their orderly sequence; they are eager to learn 'what is behind them,' and to hear about the exceptional, the mystic." He wanted to give the new movement a hearing: "Let us in the name of God have the neo-idealism! If it can produce good art, it has the same right as other isms."

The previously mentioned volume of *Samtiden* also contained an article by Garborg on Nietzsche, the fashionable philosopher of the period. Even Kielland wrote about dreams, a subject we might not have expected from him. There were poems by Vilhelm Krag, including "Fandango" which had created a sensation when it was read in the Student Society by the young art historian Jens Thiis. The poem was the fanfare of a new romantic era in Norwegian poetry. Here was an exotic luxuriance, strong and foreign words, Circassian women and music of the janissaries, a "trickling tinkle of gems and jewels." There was no longer the march of heavy rhythms, but "humming, cooing, caressing tones, smiling, resting, whispering tones." But there was also youthful pessimism and *Weltschmerz*:

> Withering. Withering.
> The world is withering, and roses and women,
> My body and all its vibrating nerves
> Are withering!

A whole battery of critics supported the new signals in literature by their attacks on naturalism, positivism, and materialism. Most notorious of these were Knut Hamsun's arrogant attacks on the four great classics, Bjørnson, Ibsen, Kielland, and Lie, or the "four-headed idol" as he put it. He proclaimed the end of the "literature of ideas" and the European "boulevard literature" in Norway.

The new interests of writers during the years 1890-1892 were abundantly reflected in such books as Jonas Lie's *Evil Powers* and *Trolls*, Arne Garborg's *Weary Men* and *Peace*, Kielland's *Jacob*, Gunnar Heiberg's *King Midas*, and Knut Hamsun's *Hunger*. In each of these there was some degree of reaction against the doctrines of the preceding generation.

If we turn to the most promising of the younger writers, we can characterize the change in this way: the authors turned away from social problems and debates, often left the city, and produced ecstatic descriptions of forest, sea, and mountain. They searched for a vital connection with things and people, gave themselves over to dreaming, sensed life as a mystery, and tried to develop their own special artistic talents. Some became clearly antisocial and glorified the supremacy of the one, the rare and eccentric personality. Many picked up the slogan of art as a goal in itself, "art for art's sake." Lyric verse and prose flourished, and the impersonal narration of the realists gave way to diaries and other personal forms. Gunnar Heiberg attacked Bjørnson's moral preaching, while Hamsun expressed his distaste for Ibsen's problem plays. Hans E. Kinck was cool toward both Ibsen and Bjørnson.

The change came suddenly. But it was prepared by the disappointments of the writers at the liberal politicians, by the weakening of the bureaucratic class, by the rise of capitalism, and a feeling that the old ideas had been dragged in the dust and vulgarized. Ibsen himself had helped to prepare the change by his trend toward mysticism in *The Wild Duck* and especially *Rosmersholm*. Zola's program had demanded that a corner of reality should be described as seen through a temperament. The emphasis at first was on reality, on the scientific objectivity of the individual, but it shifted gradually to the temperament, giving impressionism in art. It was the impressionistic style of works like *The Family at Gilje* which made the bohemians accept Jonas Lie. The journal published by Jæger and Krohg for the bohemians was called *Impressionisten* ("The Impressionist"). From this point the step to expressionism was not great. Art burst the confines of external reality and the expression of the artist's temperament became everything. This was the path from bohemianism to a poet like Obstfelder. The same took place in the development of art from naturalism to the works of Edvard Munch and Gustav Vigeland.

The new spirit of literature around 1890 was part of a general European trend. In France the symbolistic school had won a prominent place with such names as Baudelaire, Verlaine, Rimbaud, and Mallarmé. The writings of the Belgian writer Maeterlinck were mystic and symbolic in nature. The philosophy of Nietzsche had suddenly become popular in many circles. In Denmark there was the lyric poet Holger Drachmann and his novel *Condemned* (*Forskrevet*, 1890), as well as Johannes Jørgensen and his periodical *Taarnet* ("The Tower"). One of the strongest impulses came from Russian literature, in part from Turgenyev, but to an even higher degree from Tolstoy and Dostoyevski. In these writers they learned of a more profound psychology, which showed a greater understanding of the irrational forces of the mind. Around 1890 Swedish poets also began to play a role in Norwegian literature. Strindberg had already had some influence on the naturalists, but now he too turned mystic. Heidenstam's critical essay *Renascence* (1889) had the effect of a trumpet signal. He pursued it in the theoretical discussion which he wrote with the poet and critic Oscar Levertin, *Pepita's Wedding* (1890). On top of this came the poetic impulses of Fröding's luxuriant lyric verse and Selma Lagerlöf's charming, romantic novel *Gösta Berling's Saga* (1891).

The general trend was one in which ideas had to give way to psychological and artistic considerations. But this did not mean that every writer immediately changed from one outlook to the other. Nor did it mean that all realism immediately disappeared; in fact, the writers of folk life carried on this tradition throughout the nineties. Amalie Skram's highly naturalistic novels were written in part in the nineties. Garborg and Bjørnson continued to express religious and political ideas in their writings; and in 1891 the young writer Per Sivle wrote a social novel entitled *Strike*. Some of the writers whose work belonged to the nineties acknowledged their admiration for and indebtedness to the ideas of the eighties. Among these were Gunnar Heiberg and Nils Collett Vogt, to some extent also Hans E. Kinck.

GUNNAR HEIBERG

Gunnar Heiberg (1857-1929) was the greatest dramatist of the younger generation. In spite of his attacks on the moral preachments of the age, he was himself a moralist, possibly the most moralistic of recent Norwegian writers. His roots went back to the seventies to the struggles for intellectual and national freedom of that period. But he was too much of a skeptic to become a party man.

He was born in the capital and always had something of the special tone of the Oslo man, a tendency to conceal a warm heart behind a reserved exterior. He abhorred all bombast and pomposity, but had withal a lyric vein of his own. He was a friend of Hans Jæger and developed his talents as a wit in debates with Jæger and other young bohemians. In 1878 he and Jæger issued a joint publication, including his didactic poem "A Soirée Dansante" and Jæger's essay on Kant's *Critique of Reason,* surely one of the strangest publications in Norwegian literature. The poem is reminiscent of Byron, Shelley, and Wergeland, but also of Kierkegaard's writings. In the same year he published the poem "Genesis of Man" which is akin to Wergeland's famous cosmic poem. But Heiberg's sympathies are with Cain, and he praises rebellion as having a value in and of itself.

Heiberg felt himself drawn at an early period to the writings of Ibsen, in whom he recognized his own idealism, his passionate desire for consistency, his individualism and spirit of contradiction, and his admiration for greatness whether in good or bad. The influence is obvious in a play like *Aunt Ulrikke* (*Tante Ulrikke,* 1883), a play with considerable scenic effectiveness. The play reflects the dawning socialist ideas of the times, the struggle between a passion for justice and the narrow prejudices of middle-class society:

"Justice," cry the leaders. "Justice, justice," echoes like a melody throughout the whole army, and they will receive, they will seize justice. If you can hear songs like that when you listen, you don't mind if they laugh at you; then you can bear to stand on your outpost and shiver, and you can be crazy and queer and halfwitted and let the others be wise.

The play is in all respects typical of the eighties, but it was not performed until 1901.

In his next drama, *King Midas* (*Kong Midas,* 1890), there were no party politics. His satire was directed at the passion for reform, the demands for truth and morality in public life, which were particularly associated with Bjørnson. The idea is similar to that of *The Wild Duck,* but Ramseth is more egotistical than Gregers Werle and "the sacred relativity" of this play is not identical with the "life lie." It is an attack on a rigorism which the author regarded as harmful and hypocritical, and a defense of happiness, the human and original kind, the "unorthographic." The play stirred up a great controversy, bringing protests and demonstrations from the bohemians when Christiania Theater refused to perform it, and fights between those who hissed and applauded when it was played at the Tivoli. It was taken to be a satirical description of Bjørnson.

The technique of *King Midas* is a departure from Ibsen's method. Instead of his detailed retrospection, there is a one-sidedness of presentation which is deliberately adopted in order to serve the author's purposes. In his other plays Heiberg tried further experiments. He wrote two plays in a lyric-satiric vein, *Artists* (*Kunstnere,* 1893) and *Gert's Garden* (*Gerts have,* 1894), conversation pieces with little action, but so much the more beauty and wit of expression. In 1894 he published also *The Balcony* (*Balkonen*),[1] erotic in theme, but deeper in its probing than the earlier ones. The problem in this play is not a social one; it is that of one woman's relationships to three men, the materialist Ressman, the idealistic worker Abel, and Antonio who is just a lover. The tone of this

[1] Tr. E. J. Vickner and Glenn Hughes, in *Poet-Lore,* Vol. 33 (Boston, 1922), 475-96.

symbolistic play distressed many, and became the occasion for an attack on the new literature by Christen Collin, who was then a young man, a university fellow. He was a devoted follower of Bjørnson and Wergeland and wanted writers to take an active hand in political and social problems of their times. Many of the newer writers opposed him, maintaining the right of the poet to choose his own themes. It became a conflict over the purpose and freedom of art which helped to clarify the understanding of art in Norway.

One of the motifs of *The Balcony* was elaborated in the magnificent and moving play *The Tragedy of Love* (*Kjærlighetens tragedie*, 1904).[2] This was the conflict between a woman's love and a man's work, and the battle of the sexes which results from the fact that love cannot be "civilized." The play is less lyrical, less ecstatic than *The Balcony,* but is more vivid in its portrayal of character and more valuable as a drama. In both plays there is a strong intellectual strain in the erotic experience. The untamed passion of the bohemians is united with a neoromantic metaphysical worship of love. But Karen does not pass from man to man as did Julie in *The Balcony*. She is monogamous and prefers death when she perceives that Erling has lost the edge of his first passion and turns back to his life work. The character of Hadeln is that of a young poet not unlike our image of Obstfelder. He expresses Heiberg's conception of love: "Be proud, Erling Kruse. Paint a cross above your door. A bloody cross. For love has visited your house."

Heiberg's ideas in politics were no less uncompromising than his ideas on love. In 1895 he published *The Great Lottery* (*Det store lod*), a play dealing with a labor leader who grows wealthy and loses his spirit of rebellion. It does not help that he turns philanthropist and gives away his wealth. He becomes nothing more than "a poor kind man who needs to be a link in a chain, to be the son of a dead mother, to bear his guilt and responsibility together with all the strangers." While the scene here is indefinite, his next plays have a direct connection with Norwegian events. He was uncompromisingly behind a nationalistic policy in the problem of the union with Sweden, which was becoming acute during these years. In a bitter dramatic sketch *His Majesty* (*Hans Majestæt,* 1896) he attacked the Swedish monarchy; in *The People's Council* (*Folkeraadet,* 1897) he derided the cautious policy of the Norwegian parliament. It is characteristic that a woman, Ella, should be the one who

[2] Tr. E. Björkman, in Dickinson, *Chief Contemporary Dramatists,* Second Series (Boston, 1921).

represents a purely impulsive moral integrity and a scorn for humbug and stagnation. In *Harald Svan's Mother* (*Harald Svans mor,* 1899) he produced another comedy in the spirit of Aristophanes, but this time a satire on the press. Here, and again in *Love thy Neighbor* (*Kjærlighet til næsten,* 1902), it is a woman who shows an uncompromising idealism and has the healthy instincts. In the latter he ridicules an altruism and a philanthropy which is a kind of hypocrisy because it has its foundation in the escape of the individual from himself and because it is used as a cover for egotism.

Heiberg's national idealism appeared most clearly and passionately in his drama about the events of 1905, when Norway and Sweden parted company, scornfully entitled *I Will Defend My Country* (*Jeg vil værge mit land,* 1912). Heiberg felt that Norway had yielded too much in the settlement that followed the break with Sweden. He criticized what he held to be the opportunism shown, the business mentality, the small cynicism of the new capitalists. In the same vein he wrote *Lit de Parade* (*Paradesengen,* 1913), a comedy about the difficulty of being worthy descendants of a great man. The sons of the dying hero haggle outside his door about film rights for the death scene. The sardonic wit of this play was understood by its contemporaries as directed at the sons of Bjørnson, who had died in 1910; yet none other than Bjørn Bjørnson directed its first performance at the National Theater in 1924.

It would give an inadequate picture of Heiberg's authorship if one were to omit his essays. In these we meet his personality most directly, his respect for courage and his disrespect for everything that lacked inner strength and personality, his faith and his skepticism, his contempt for "popular movements," and his deep respect for the human being. His articles are clear, witty, and wise, and can rise from dry skepticism to high pathos. His splendid *Letters from Paris* (*Pariserbreve,* 1900) deal chiefly with the Dreyfus affair, and portray sharply the power of mass suggestion. But most of his essays deal with art and the theater, collected in such volumes as *Seen and Heard* (*Set og hørt,* 1917), *Ibsen and Bjørnson on the Stage* (*Ibsen og Bjørnson paa scenen,* 1918), *Norwegian Theater* (*Norsk Teater,* 1920), and *Salt and Sugar* (*Salt og sukker,* 1924). Many of his essays testify to an underlying warmth, particularly his speech on Obstfelder.

PER SIVLE

While Heiberg lashed his people with scorpions, Per Sivle (1857-1904) tried to hearten them by retelling the story of their ancient heroes. Heiberg was a poet of the radical intelligentsia, while Sivle was in every sense a man of the people. He was no less of a nationalist than Heiberg, and his songs came to be an important factor in the events of 1905 because of their wide popular acceptance. But he also had a personal problem in the destructive forces that harried his sensitive spirit.

Sivle was born in Aurland in Sogn but grew up at Stalheim, and struggled most of his life against hunger, poverty, and ill health. Early poems won no response, and not until his collection of stories *Tales (Sogur,* 1887) did he find his form. His special qualities were those of the story-teller, with a warm interest in children and animals, and genuine folk humor. His sense of humor is best expressed in the tales he wrote in his native dialect of Voss, which are matchless in their evocation of the local atmosphere and ways of thinking.

As an editor for some years he tried to defend the policies of Sverdrup, and in the nineties he wrote many of the nationalistic poems that made him most famous. He had a capacity for giving his poems monumental form, and infusing the old episodes with a new meaning. While his nationalistic poems usually show an optimistic attitude, his personal lyrics seesaw between the blackest melancholy and glimpses of awakening joy. In the end the defeats accumulated and the melancholy overcame him so that he took his own life.

THE LYRIC RENAISSANCE: VOGT, KRAG, OBSTFELDER

The characteristic forms of literature in the eighties had been the novel and the drama. Most writers had followed Ibsen's lead in regarding verse as a dying form of literature. Never since have the lyric poets been as completely silenced as they were between 1870 and 1890. In the nineties the new doctrines of individualism in art released the veins of poetic composition. The fashionable poet of the nineties was Vilhelm Krag, but Nils Collett Vogt had a more original talent and a more enduring effect.

Nils Collett Vogt (1864-1937) came from a conservative family of government officials, against which he rebelled from his earliest youth. Speeches by Bjørnson and other liberal leaders fired his young, enthusiastic spirit. For a time he even joined the bohemians, more because of his rebelliousness than because he had any deeper kinship with them. His novel *A Grief to His Family (Familiens Sorg,* 1889) was intended to be a bohemian book, but was rather a description of idealistic youth in rebellion against a social order dominated by old men.

Stubborn and argumentative, he rushed out into the dangerous but bracing air of the eighties. He might at times feel "a child of my age," as "a will-less slave of my age." Puzzled he might ask: "What does the age wish to use me for?" But he learned to harden his will and steel his mind:

> If I were but a spruce-tree in the forest,
> Who, when wintry storms are coming
> —The air is pale, the snow is falling—
> Sway above the wooded hallways
> Like a wide extended banner,
> Till the leaves turn green next summer!

He became a poet who expressed the need of the age for confession, its joy, its pain, and its indignation. A large portion of his writing deals with the conflict of the generations, not merely the novel *A Grief to His Family,* but also *Harriet Blick* (1903), the two plays *Anxious Hearts* (*Spændte sind,* 1910), later reworked as *The Maimed* (*De Skadeskudte*), and many poems. Because he was in tune with the times, he felt a strong sympathy for the workingman's cause, not because of any Marxist theories, but because he had a warmhearted sense of justice. He had the intellectual's aversion to the narrow-minded, smug, and money-minded middle class. Therefore he gave the workers his fiery battle song: "This earth, it was ours, it was ours." But he never became a party poet.

Collett Vogt wrote several good novels and short stories, as well as some psychological plays, including *The Mother* (*Moren,* 1913) and *Therese* (1914). But above all he was a lyric poet in the vein of Henrik Wergeland, jubilant in the pride of youth, erect in adversity. The strength of his lyricism is its stamp of reality, the genuineness of his outburst. The deeply felt union of poetry and realism which is the mark of his poetry never permitted him to write anything he did not feel very strongly. There are no phrases or stereotypes in his lyrics, no trace of sing-song routine. He was a poet of the nineties who never forgot the demands of the eighties for truth.

After a residence in Italy he published *From Spring to Autumn* (*Fra vaar til høst,* 1894). These are poems about his meeting with the South of Europe, a dizzying joy of life, but above all about Norway. The collection *Music and Spring* (*Musik og vaar,* 1896) had a deeper tone, including poems about his Norwegian landscape. But there are also poems composed "in the company of the tenderest yearnings of spring," exposed to love and nature, from the little flowers to the star over Oslo's hills. He recalls his spiritual kinsman Wergeland:

> He lay in the sunshine
> His visage at rest,
> His eyes a-gazing,
> His hand under chin . . . .
> A spring brook was trickling,
> A lark was a-trembling,
> A dandelion flaming
> Into his heart.

He reached equal heights in his collection *The Precious Bread* (*Det dyre brød,* 1900) and *September Fire* (*Septemberbrand,* 1907). Many of his poems deal with revisiting the scenes of his youth, e.g., the match-less "The Poplars in Eidsvold Square" ("Poplerne paa Eidsvold plads") in which he says to an old friend who has become a "pillar of society," "correct, worthy, with a father-of-his-country mien":

> My hair is grayed, my feet are weary,
> Yet beckon still to me the poplars of our youth,
> The upward-striving ones.
> Tell me, why this smile every time we meet?

No less attractive are his poems about other poets, which tell us more about the poets than do similar poems by Wergeland, which tell us more about himself, or than do poems by Bjørnson, which tell more about his times. Vogt's patriotic poems have less festive bombast than any others in Norwegian literature; they are the manliest and most personal of all:

> Here would I grow, here would I die,
> But first would I scatter in thy soil
> My wealth, though it be but a tiny seed . . .
> Perchance 'twill be a tree some day
> Through which your songs will blow.

When Vogt began to feel old, his poems acquired a touch of frosty September, a clear-eyed atmosphere of understanding. He was still the radical of the eighties, but had now gained a greater respect for the integrity of the older generation. In "Homecoming" ("Hjemkomst") he meets his father once more in his thoughts:

> Now here we walk once more, the two of us,
> And talk about the time that passed,
> The air about us is so clear and deep,
> A peacefulness, a quiet of eternity,
> In which he reaches forth his hand
> With greetings to me from our common home.

There is a clear and deep atmosphere also in his later collections of poetry, *Down from the Mountain* (*Ned fra bjerget,* 1924), *Wind and Wave* (*Vind og bølge,* 1927), and his last poems, *A Life in Poetry* (*Et liv i digt,* 1937). He has lost the blue-eyed faith in progress of his youth, but wishes that he still had it. He looks toward Germany and finds the spirit of humanism in decay. He looks toward Russia and wishes that he could believe in bolshevism, as he once believed in the ideas of his age. But no, he is an individualist. As he writes in his intensely interesting memoirs of his life, *From Boy to Man* (*Fra gutt til mann,* 1932): "The struggle of my generation was for intellectual freedom, and how could I ever voluntarily relinquish the advantages we laboriously had attained?"

When Vilhelm Krag (1871-1933) finally, after many travails both in Oslo and Copenhagen, got his collection *Poems* (*Digte,* 1891) published in Bergen through Gerhard Gran's assistance, he became at one stroke the lyrical voice of his age. His songs were so melodious that composers, such as Grieg and Sinding, competed for a chance to set them to music. Even in our day this collection has its charm. We may be repelled by the purple patches in his rhetoric, by the fairly thick sentimentality of his outlook. But we can still enjoy the atmosphere he evokes, his "sable hounds" running on the highways, the bell that rings toward eventide and tolls the day to its death. A poem like his "There Cried a Bird" ("Der skreg en fugl") gives a brilliant picture of the hopelessness of youthful dreams, but in its moving portrayal of a melancholy scene it calls upon painters and composers. There are also expressions of the beauty and loveliness of the world, as in his poem:

> All the world shall sing on your wedding day,
> And the cherry on the hillside shall blossom.

While Vogt had become a poet of the conflict between generations, Krag gradually became the poet of the traditional connection between them. He gave up his early romantic world weariness, which still speaks in *Songs from the South* (*Sange fra Syden*, 1894), and tried in *The Merry Lieutenant* (*Den glade Løitnant*, 1896) to attain a more ethical view of life. But the chief escape from the atmosphere of the nineties came to him through his special South Coast sense of humor.

The humor is displayed along with a vivid feeling for an old tradition in his many volumes of stories and novels from the South Coast. One of the best known is his *Major von Knarren and his Friends* (*Major von Knarren og hans Venner*, 1906). His folk characters with their sly humor and imperturbable exteriors meet us also in his comedies, e.g. *Baldevin's Wedding* (*Baldevins Bryllup*, 1900).

He is chiefly remembered, however, for his lyrical poems. There is a fervor of local patriotism in his *Songs of the Westland* (*Vestlandsviser,* 1897) which made him the national poet of the region to which he gave the name Sørlandet, "the Southland," in 1901. His humorous ballads show the influence of the Swedes Fröding and Karlfeldt, but have an even closer association with the "penny ballads" which were a favorite form of entertainment in the old days. The high point in his lyric writing came with the poem "The Island" ("Øen") introducing his collection *Songs from My Island* (*Sange fra min Ø*, 1918). In this there is vivid realism and romantic solitude, humor and nature piety. God seems to be just about within reach:

> He came down here with the sun,
> He's sitting just around the point.
> The hem of His cloak is sparkling
> Like smouldering mother-of-pearl
> Right in the sea-weed here.

Vilhelm Krag did not escape some of the parodic effects to which romantic verse is subject in a cynical age. Some of his earlier poems were ridiculed by critical friends in a collection called *Rhythmic Gurgles* (*Rytmeskvulp*, 1895) under the pseudonym Adolescentius Olsen.

Among those who were parodied in this collection was also Sigbjørn Obstfelder (1866-1900), which is understandable enough. But if one reads his own verse in *Poems* (*Digte*, 1893),[3] it is easy to see that he stays

---

[3] Some of these appear in a collection called *Poems* (London, 1920), with original text and translations.

always on the right side of the thin line that separates the sublime from the ridiculous.

He was born in Stavanger; but there is little of the local in his writing. While the poet of local color, Vilhelm Krag, dreamt of becoming a painter, Obstfelder wanted to become a musician. His ambition was to express the inexpressible. His verse is more auditory than visual, and he listened particularly to the voices in his own heart. When he looked, he felt that "it is so strange here," and he had a panic-stricken feeling of having "arrived on the wrong globe." He had the new-born child's capacity for wondering at the world, a capacity which is the ultimate source of all religion and art. His original, moving, often hectic verse and prose poetry are the words of a man who feels that he is a stranger on earth, a melancholy pantheist, an inquiring dreamer.

Obstfelder never acquired any definite position in society. His life was a restless and usually planless migration, in fear of life, in the hope of meeting happiness. He studied the Old Norse language for a time and wrote an amusing little parody on philological learning. He got some training in mechanical engineering in Milwaukee, but was utterly unsuited to the practical life. He dreamt about studying music and becoming the great composer and musician of the age, but had to give it up. His writing also bears no evidence of definite plan or program. He was as far removed as one could be from the literature of ideas of the previous generation, though he defended the rights of the naturalist group; but he was deeply impressed also by Kierkegaard, Jens Peter Jacobsen, Strindberg, Maeterlinck, Walt Whitman, Dostoyevski, and the German pessimistic philosophers Schopenhauer and von Hartmann. Yet he was always himself and no one else, oddly mature from the first moment. Already in "Snowbells," a prose lyric of 1887 not printed until after his death, he had found his special kind of prose style.

The collection of his poems was published in 1893 by John Grieg in Bergen, in spite of the latter's comment to Vilhelm Krag who brought them to him: "Just as surely as your poems were the wildest nonsense, these are absolute insanity." In these poems we find some of the more significant traits of Obstfelder's poetry, his notable ability to create a basic mood with the help of humble and everyday words, his simple yet suggestive symbolism, the loneliness of his psyche, his tone of solitary mysticism:

> Can the mirror speak?
> The mirror can speak!

It asks and it greets you with dark blue eyes:
'Are you pure?
Are you true?'

No one has drawn a simpler picture of solitude than he does in "Christ-mas Eve" ("Julaften"). Never has humility been more intensely ex-pressed than in "Nameless" ("Navnløs"). The basic theme in these poems is the relation of man to the universe, the soul in relation to the cosmos.

It would be erroneous to call all of Obstfelder's writing remote. He followed the events of his time with great interest and wrote an excellent article about "The Joy of Newspapers." In the play *The Red Drops* (*De røde draaber,* 1897) he took up one of the great problems of our time, the conflict of the soul and the machine. He also had a vivid love of nature, expressed in the intense joy in flowers which we see in his short story "The Plain" ("Sletten") in *Two Novelettes* (*To Novelletter,* 1895). But he always saw something spiritual behind things. In his stories of love, including the preceding and his masterpiece *The Cross* (*Korset,* 1896), woman is both Eve and Mary, an elemental primitive force, but also a divine mystery. *The Cross* tells about a woman who has passed from man to man, but nevertheless is psychologically monogamous.

Obstfelder died young of tuberculosis, as do some of his best female characters. After his death appeared a fragment called *A Pastor's Diary* (*En præsts dagbog,* 1900). In this we hear a lonely man's monologue about religion and longing, life and death, the individual and society. It is a deeply personal book, but also an expression of the restless, inquiring spirit of the nineties, a book that has an inner kinship to Garborg's *The Lost Father.*

The trend to lyric poetry is apparent in the nineties not only in the poets here mentioned, but also in the plays of Ibsen and Heiberg, in Garborg's *Haugtussa,* in Sivle's national lyrics, in Kinck's short stories, in Hamsun's *Pan* and *Victoria,* in many of the local poets. A new awareness had come to the writers of the possibilities Norwegian nature offered to the sensitive poet.

Critics and Storytellers

NOT ALL REACTION IS BAD. It was unquestionably a healthy reaction when the neoromantics turned away from universals, which had dominated literature for so long, and sought out individuals, whom they portrayed because they found them original and interesting. They were exercising their undoubted poetic privilege when they permitted themselves to dream or invent without forever thinking of society. If they now and then went out of their way to turn somersaults or cartwheels, that too could be a healthy gymnastic exercise. All of these things were expressions of the experimentation and play which go with the freedom of art. Nor can it be denied that it was a healthy criticism that writers like Heiberg, Kinck, Bojer, Nils Kjær, and others directed against democracy and parliamentary government.

Even the influence of Nietzsche which was so decisive during these years was not always harmful. In many cases the German poet-philosopher stimulated writers to think independently and encouraged them to attack the stodginess of the bourgeois and all expressions of vulgarity. The influence was dangerous only when it led to a break with the European cultural tradition as this had been represented in Norway since the time of Wergeland. Reaction against the universal became unhealthy when the doctrine of the superman, a poet's dream, masqueraded as a science, allied itself with vulgar misinterpretations of Darwinism and with racial prejudice, glorified the primitive instincts and proclaimed a gospel of hate. Hamsun's paradoxes about "a qualified crime" and "a distinguished sin" might be no more than jesting expressions of his romantic annoyance at the "ridiculous and middle-class ABC error." But when they were combined with the dream of the superman and an "Anglo-Saxon complex" they could be dangerous. It was the tragedy of his life that he lived to see his own words put into effect.

THOMAS KRAG

Beside Obstfelder, Thomas Krag (1867-1913) was the typical dreamer and mystic of the period. Like his younger brother Vilhelm he was strongly attached to the Kristiansand of his childhood and to the South Coast country. As in the case of his brother, old traditions were deeply significant to him. But in contrast to Vilhelm he dwelt mostly on the gloomy and melancholy aspects of nature. There is something morbid about his landscapes, with their pantheistically colored mysticism, whether he is picturing the sea, the dark forests, a lonely moor, or an old manor house.

Thomas Krag was successful in his portrayal of feminine psychology in several of his novels, e.g. *Ada Wilde* (1896) and *Gunvor Kjeld* (1904). But most of his characters are strangely artificial. His forte was the lyric mood he created by means of his prose poetry which often could be highly melodious and suggestive. Most of his characters were lonely beings, as in *Tubal the Outlaw* (*Tubal den fredløse,* 1908) and the auto-biographical novel *Frank Hjelm* (1912). His religious views were in-fluenced by Kierkegaard and the Danish poets of Johannes Jørgensen's circle. He was deeply concerned about the "holiness of suffering," the "sublime madness of original Christianity." He saw the danger to Chris-tianity not in unbelief, but in the dogmatic orthodoxy which kills the spontaneity of religious expression. He was not one-sided in his views of the purposes of literature, and like Obstfelder he insisted on the author's right to portray all aspects of human life. Poetry, he thought, should create "the great understanding" and be "a temple to the eternally human." Poetry he held to be akin to the great religions.

TRYGGVE ANDERSEN

Another novelist who partook of the intellectual climate of the nineties was Tryggve Andersen (1866-1920). He had some traits in common with the numerous regional writers whose work footed on folklore and local dialects, but he stood artistically head and shoulders above them. He went to work like a most conscientious historian and folklorist when he gathered the materials for his masterpiece *In the Days of the Chancery Councilor* (*I Cancelliraadens dage,* 1897). He copied out passages from old documents and wrote down the words of old people. He sifted his materials in order to reach the core of truth and the significant parts of the tradition. In these respects he was a realist, but at the same time he was a romantic who suffered from neurasthenia, who felt himself destined to misfortune, a mad dreamer and a fantast in the grip of his own hallucinations, a poet of the degraded outcasts. Like the poet he admired most, the German romantic, E. T. A. Hoffmann, he had a split personality, being on the one hand a sober office worker and a talented scholar, on the other hand absorbed in his dreams and fantasies.

He was born on the farm Kinnli in Ringsaker; he grew up near the city of Hamar where his family home became a center of intellectually awakened youth. He rejected the spirit of the eighties very early, admiring only Jens Peter Jacobsen of the Scandinavian authors. His interests turned to the German romantics, not only Hoffmann but also Novalis, Lenau, and Adalbert von Chamisso, in whom he found the riotous imagination, the mysticism and melancholy he was looking for. As a student at the University of Oslo he turned to the study of Egyptology and was looked upon as a promising scholar. But he also took part in the dissipations of the age and collected young literary neoromantics around him. One day he disappeared from the capital and turned up in Mandal where he recovered his balance by office work; later he worked for a brother in Hamar. In both places he worked on his writing after hours, planning novels and gathering materials for them.

Tryggve Andersen reacted against the Norwegian boasting about the saga age and the scorn for the Danish period. He declared that it was evidence of an inferiority complex, an expression of the newly rich person's lofty disregard of his parents. He made it his task to bring to life the inner history of Norway by portraying the cultural tradition that led from the Danish period into the modern period. He picked up the tradition from around 1800 and tried to show the clash of the upper-class bureaucratic culture with the peasant culture. *In the Days of the Chancery Councilor* is one of the masterpieces of Norwegian literature, both for its picture of the period and for its psychological insight. It is more artistic and better rounded than *The Family at Gilje,* to which it is related.

The novel is a series of episodes centering around one figure, the chancery councilor, and occurring in a common setting. Several of the officials portrayed are historical, and nearly all have some connection with real events. Their bitter enemy, the well-to-do peasant Dahlby, is modeled on one Halvor Hoel, a leader of the agrarian opposition in the early 1800's. Most of the officials are disintegrating culturally because they have lost contact with the culture they were brought up in. Only the chancery councilor himself and the pastor's son Nicolai Lind realize that it is necessary to fuse the general European and the Norwegian, the official and the peasant culture. The impressions of nature are artistically interwoven with the psychological portrayal, never described for their own sake, but as seen through the eyes of the characters. The style is transparent, oral, sober, and impressionistic. What the characters say is of interest primarily through the state of mind they reveal.

The theme of intellectual disintegration was only a minor motif in his first novel, but became the chief theme of his second, *Towards Evening* (*Mot kvæld*, 1900). This was not historical but contemporary in its scene, and told of a man who tried to escape from a barren intellectualism by associating with the people in his little town. But he does not succeed in "converting himself to people," and his melancholia turns into hallucinations, while the novel ends with judgment day breaking upon the characters.

In 1902 he lost his first wife and a son, and sought forgetfulness on a long sea voyage. While the voyage restored his health, it did not provide him with the materials he had wanted for a sea story. Instead, he kept a diary which was published in 1923, after his death, and is the most vivid description of the sea between Amalie Skram's *Two Friends* and Nordahl Grieg's *The Ship Sails On*. Andersen was most impressed by the gloomy aspects of the sailor's life, but the book gives above all a vivid picture of the author's own unhappy soul.

Tryggve Andersen worked very slowly, not because he lacked materials, but because his artistic honesty set such high standards. He could spend weeks hunting for a single word which would express his intentions precisely. His favorite form was the short story, and his collections of stories contain some of the gems of Norwegian literature. Among these were *Old Folks* (*Gamle folk*, 1904), *The Bishop's Son and other Stories* (*Bispesønnen og andre fortællinger*, 1907), *Homeward Bound* (*Hjemfærd*, 1913), *Fables and Happenings* (*Fabler og hændelser*, 1915). It may be questioned whether any Norwegian short story surpasses the title story in *Old Folks*. Some of these stories are connected with those about the chancery councilor; most of them have an intensely eerie effect, particularly those from the sea and the coast. We have here a vivid realism combined with madly romantic motifs, wraiths, murders, ghosts. His fables were wholly romantic, but often with an ironic mood. A personal confession appears to be contained in the story "The Great Success" ("Den store suksess"), which tells of the struggle in an artist's soul between the ideals of art and the temptation to write for the public.

All his life he had been sickly, and he died of tuberculosis. Collett Vogt applied to him the words of Wergeland cited above, "Is it not to kind-heartedness, genius, and unhappiness that God gives his fairest wreaths of immortality?"

NILS KJÆR

One of those who added a new perception of Norwegian nature was the essayist and dramatist Nils Kjær (1870-1924). But he also illustrated the reaction of neoromanticism in other respects, particularly its critique of the evolutionary optimism which had flourished in the preceding generation. He was the witty *causeur* of his period, who smiled at the naïve faith in reforms and inventions. He was convinced that all advance in technology was a retrogression in culture and humanity. He was a humanist in his appreciation of the classical-Christian tradition. He looked with ironic tolerance on many events in contemporary life, cultivating such ironists of earlier literature as Cervantes and Holberg.

He began as an essayist and was one of the leading literary critics, alongside Carl Nærup and Sigurd Bødtker. In 1895 he wrote about the "Freedom of Art," and in a series of witty articles in 1896-1897 he attacked the moral rigorousness of Collin and the latter's insistence on a socially optimistic literature. From the very first he looked spiritually and individualistically at existence, which appears from the essay collection *Foreign Authors* (*Fremmede Forfattere,* 1895) with analyses of François Villon, Dante, Pascal, and Rydberg. A result of his years in Italy was *Books and Pictures* (*Bøger og Billeder,* 1898), in which he praised the religiosity and the joy of life which characterized the South Europeans, spoke highly of Strindberg (particularly the *Inferno*) and rejected Ibsen (except for *Peer Gynt*).

His first success as an imaginative writer came with the play *Day of Reckoning* (*Regnskabets Dag,* 1902), a profoundly serious attack on the moral relativism of his day, and the liberalism which leads to a hollowing out of the personality and the dissolution of a cultural tradition. The same theme runs through the plays *Mimosa's Homecoming* (*Mimosas Hjemkomst,* 1907) and *For the Tree There Is Hope* (*For Træet er der Haab,* 1917). A more direct reference to contemporary controversy is found in *The Successful Election* (*Det lykkelige Valg,* 1913), a witty and amusing political comedy with sharp attacks on language reformers, feminists, temperance advocates, and the general parliamentary confusion.

Nils Kjær is best approached through his collection of articles and epistles, the latter having more in common with Holberg's than just the title: *In Passing* (*I Forbigaaende,* 1903), *Small Epistles* (*Smaa Epistler,* 1908), *New Epistles* (*Nye Epistler,* 1912), *Lost Summers* (*Svundne Somre,* 1920), and *Last Epistles* (*Sidste Epistler,* 1924). The most valuable of his essays are his descriptions of nature along the South Coast, gems like "Letter about South Coast Wind and Weather," "The Lobster," "Gray Weather Epistle," and "Letters from Brekkestø." His comments on Norwegian conditions and the trends of his age are disrespectful and amusing, while his attacks on the West Norwegian pietistic puritanical spirit are witty though superficial. He claimed he had met the personification of this spirit one rainy evening near Finse: "He looked like a prayer meeting that had shriveled up and stuck together into a single figure of dankness and mold. . . . "

Nils Kjær's attitude to most phenomena in his day was negative, often to excess. But he had a profound respect for intellectual integrity, a religiously humanistic idealism, and a vivid sense of cultural values.

Hamsun and Kinck

KNUT HAMSUN

IF WE TURN TO KNUT HAMSUN'S NOVELS from the reading of Tryggve Andersen's artistically wrought short stories with their mood of annihilation, from Thomas Krag's melancholy and dreamy mysticism, or Nils Kjær's disrespectful contributions to contemporary discussion, we cannot avoid noticing a certain kinship. Hamsun has all of these elements, but a richer imagination, greater inventiveness, and a wider sweep.

Knut Hamsun was born August 4, 1859, at the farm of Garmostræet in Lom; his parents were of peasant stock in that Gudbrandsdal community. When he was three years old, his family moved to Hamarøy in Nordland. The nature up north, its bright and hectic summers, the autumn days with their brittle atmosphere, the woods and the mountains awakened an intense love of nature in him. He was only eighteen when he began writing stories, mostly imitations of Bjørnson's country tales; but they are little more than boyish exercises, even though he succeeded in getting them printed. He was thirty when he wrote *Hunger* (*Sult,* 1890)[1] his first masterpiece. Like the spring in Nordland, his literary youth came late, but also like the Nordland spring, it came with an overwhelming force.

He had tried practically everything, had struggled and starved for many years when he stepped—or rather catapulted—into literature for good. He had been a shoemaker's apprentice and a store clerk, a peddler and a roadworker, had been to the United States twice, and had there been secretary and assistant to the Norwegian Unitarian minister and author Kristofer Janson. He had worked as a streetcar conductor in Chicago, as a farmhand in North Dakota, had delivered lectures both

[1] Tr. George Egerton (pseud.) (New York, 1920).

in America and Norway. He had written a good many articles in the papers, had published a brazen little book misnamed *The Intellectual Life of Modern America* (*Fra det moderne Amerikas Aandsliv,* 1889), and a witty but scurrilous attack on the discredited politician and leader of pietism in Norway, Lars Oftedal (1890). As we have seen above, Hamsun had a literary program which aimed at nothing less than the renewal of Norwegian literature. The literature of ideas lacked a soul; the authors should now probe more deeply into the unconscious life of man.

The novelty of *Hunger* appears most clearly if we compare it with Garborg's *Peasant Students* seven years earlier. In Garborg, too, the theme was the hopelessness of starvation, the atmosphere of stuffy attic rooms and smoky bars. Garborg, too, portrayed all the phases of hunger and poverty down to hallucinations of fragrant wheat loaves. But the difference is much greater than the similarity. In Hamsun the man who does the starving is a genius. His starvation is not a social problem, and no complaints are directed at society. *Hunger* is individualistic in its entire cast. In the midst of misery there is a wealth of fantasy, the overpowering force of inspiration. Our hero is nervous and irritable, but also generous, and his temperament is humble and arrogant at once. Hamsun's hungry genius is a totally asocial individual. He will put his vest in hock to enjoy the luxury of helping a beggar, but he does not care a hoot for society. There is often a kind of realism in *Hunger,* even crass and ugly realism. But the accent is on the psyche of the genius, the nervously spontaneous actions of the starving young man, his emotional fluctuations from piety to rebelliousness, from pride to humility. He slaves unmercifully at the writing for which he is paid a measly ten kroner. But when the inspiration is upon him, he weeps in joy and pain.

Hunger introduced a new period in the history of the Norwegian novel. Its lyrical, almost incoherent style, with its subtle and unexpected transitions created a furore, and made Hamsun the literary lion of Scandinavia. But as a personal document and an intellectual expression *Mysteries* (*Mysterier,* 1892)[2] is at least equally rewarding. Here the author reveals the recesses of his soul through the characters. There is something compulsive in this novel, with its strange figure Nagel in his eccentric yellow suit, who is called a "halted wayfarer," an "outsider of existence," "God's fixed idea," who is characterized by his sudden fluctuations of temper, his mysterious relationship of open friendship and secret hate to Minutten,

[2] Tr. A. G. Chater (New York, 1927).

his shy and irritable personality, his love for Dagny Kielland, and his curious attraction to the white-haired old maid, Martha Gude. There is a close affinity to *Hunger,* but all that is irrational and inexplicable, the day dream, the "feverish progeny of pitching brains," "the great and the bizarre and the marvelous," the unsocial and exaggeratedly individualistic —all this is even more sharply in evidence here than in *Hunger.*

In this novel Hamsun aired his antipathies for the first time in his creative writings, the same antipathies he had recently expressed in his challenging lectures. He let Nagel speak his mind about the great names in literature, Ibsen, Victor Hugo, Leo Tolstoy. He does so from "the subjective logic of his blood," from the feeling that they are old and he is young; he does so from an antipathy toward that which is completed and recognized. Basing himself on the same illogical feeling, he turns on the recognized politicians of the day, from Gladstone down to the local lights in Norway. All their activities were mere trifles in the perspective of Nagel's (and Hamsun's) Nietzschean exaltation. Bjørnson alone wins his approval: "He makes noises like a living body on our globe and he needs forty elbowrooms. . . . Bjørnson's insides are like a forest in storm; he scraps, he is active everywhere, and he magnificently injures his standing with the public at Grand Café. He is built en masse, he is a commanding spirit, one of the few rulers." These words point forward to his magnificent poem to Bjørnson on his seventieth birthday and the equally sublime "Bjørnson's Death" (1910). But they also point up his admiration for the superman.

In his next two novels the satirist took the upper hand: *Editor Lynge* (*Redaktør Lynge*) and *New Soil* (*Ny Jord*)[3] (both 1893). The first was directed against the press and the politicians, the second against writers and artists. Both books are written in a realistic style, with little of the youthful and giddy brilliance which marked the preceding novels, though here too there are some outbursts of his baroque wit and delicate psychological tracery.

In *Mysteries* he had attacked the older writers. In *New Soil* he finished off the young ones. His character Coldevin says: "Just take a peek at our youth, look at the authors too, they're clever, but . . . yes they're clever, they work and work at it, but *the spirit isn't in them.*" The last words are the only ones that are italicized in the whole novel. Hamsun's demand of his fellow writers was that they should show signs of the overpowering inspiration, the lyrical exuberance, the lavish spirit that scatters gold on

[3] Tr. as *Shallow Soil* by C. C. Hyllested (New York, 1914).

its path. This is the basic nerve in his creation, the lyric fire which he calls "the glowing irons," the exuberant source of inspiration. His mood calls forth sonorous effects, "linguistic flukes," rare and curious words, his own personal words, words of twilight. Gradually the images come also, first as colors, then as situations. The word of the moment tumbles into his mind in much the same way as when the young genius of *Hunger* meets the young lady and his lips form the word "ylajali."

This lyrical quality recurs throughout the best of Hamsun's writing. Words of mood and visions of poetry make *Pan* (1894)[4] and *Victoria* (1898)[5] magnificent poems in prose. His female psychology is that of a lyrical romanticist. All the women in his books are seen in relation to men, and almost exclusively in this relation. Lieutenant Glahn in *Pan* pictures Edvarda as follows: "She stepped forward and gave me her hand in a girlish way. 'We were here yesterday, but you were out,' she said." It is lyrical psychology when Glahn notices "the chaste girlishness of her thumb." It is the lyricist in him that makes Hamsun a poet of love. The love he describes may be of many kinds, "a wind that whispers through the roses and then dies away," or "an unbreakable seal that lasts through life, lasts unto death," as in *Victoria*. It may be a madness in the blood, as in the plays *Game of Life* (*Livets Spill,* 1896), *Queen Tamara* (*Dronning Tamara,* 1903), and *In the Grip of Life* (*Livet ivold* 1910),[6] or just a muted melody, as in his books about the Wanderer, sometimes childlike and touching, sometimes brutal. But always there is jealousy at work bringing on the sudden shifts of mood, the mad attacks on the beloved, the unexpected actions, as when Glahn throws Edvarda's shoe into the sea.

The lyric mood is infused in the nature descriptions from Nordland, sometimes as an ecstasy, sometimes as a quiet whispering in fervent communion with woods and mountains. The soul vibrates in harmony with nature's rhythm, with the changes of season. At times the poet's feeling for nature has a religious undertone which may give rise to a pantheistic feeling of "God's murmur among the trees." No sound escapes the poet's ear, no note in nature's organ, the scream of the magpie, the cry of the loon, the song of the swans, the buzzing of insects. His senses have an unbelievable capacity for perceiving the tiniest details. An inchworm creeps "like a piece of green thread sewing a seam with

[4] Tr. W. W. Worster (London, 1920).
[5] Tr. A. G. Chater (New York, 1923).
[6] Tr. G. and T. Rawson (New York, 1924).

slow stitches along the branch." He sometimes gets a feeling of pre-existence in his meeting with nature: "Perchance I was a flower in the forest, perchance I was a beetle and had my home under an acacia tree" (*Under the Autumn Star*). The idea appears also in one of the poems in his little collection *The Wild Chorus* (*Det vilde Kor*, 1904):

> Perhaps 'twas here
> In early ages
> I lived a time
> As a white spirea.
> I know the fragrance
> As once I knew it,
> I tremble now as
> In old remembrance.

In most of Hamsun's books there rambles a lonely figure, the Wanderer, the writer's brilliant contribution to world letters, in many ways his own flesh and blood. He is a hunter and a nomad in *Pan*, an adventurer and rebel in the world drama *The Monk Vendt* (*Munken Vendt*, 1902), a little student in *Rosa*, a telegrapher with a budding pussywillow in his buttonhole in the charming little story *Dreamers* (*Sværmere*, 1904).[7] But when the author approached his fiftieth birthday, the Wanderer too began to age. He now lives *Under the Autumn Star* (1907) and he *Plays With Muted Strings* (1909).[8] He appears as the poet himself in *The Last Joy* (*Den siste Glæde*, 1912).[9] He is no longer overpowering and ecstatic, but rather brooding and melancholy. He feels sorry for mankind, but is too proud to show it. Nearly always he is in love with a proud and unapproachable but nevertheless devoted woman. He scorn city life and civilization.

Hamsun's fondness for the asocial wanderer led him to deprecate all aspects of the society in which he lived, the West European and American liberalist-capitalist industrial society. He was morally upset by the expressions of social change around him, the rise of the newly rich, the scramble for money, the tourist traffic, the emancipation of women, the use of canned goods, the organization of labor unions. These and other phenomena were attacked in essays as well as in such novels as *The Last Joy, Children of the Age* (*Børn av Tiden*, 1913),[10] and *Segelfoss*

[7] Tr. W. W. Worster (New York, 1921), pub. as *Mothwise* (London, 1921).
[8] Both stories tr. together as *Wanderers* by W. W. Worster (New York, 1922).
[9] Tr. as *Look Back on Happiness* by Paula Wiking (New York, 1940).
[10] Tr. J. S. Scott (New York, 1924).

Town (*Segelfoss By,* 1915).[11] These are social satires in which the small-town societies of northern Norway are cruelly delineated as semi-barbarous, uprooted cultures whose people have lost the old virtues without acquiring any new ones.

The positive gospel which Hamsun wished to preach to a sick generation was contained in his masterpiece *Growth of the Soil* (*Markens Grøde,* 1917),[12] which won him the Nobel Prize and a world reputation. The ideas in it stem back to the years around 1912 when he ceased his own wandering and settled down to the simple life. At first he bought himself a farm near his childhood home in Nordland, but he found the climate strenuous and moved to the estate Nørholm near Arendal in southernmost Norway. His hero was no longer the wanderer, but the peasant, the man of the soil, who still possessed all the simplicity that modern civilization had taken away from its victims. In a beautiful, subtly suggestive, often dithyrambic style he cries in the accents of Rousseau: Go back to nature, or rather, to the true and primitive culture. His Isak is the one utterly self-sufficient man, the breaker of soil:

There goes Isak, sowing, nothing but a mill-wheel of a figure, a stump of a man. He wears homespun clothing; the wool comes from his own sheep, the boots from his own calves and cows. He walks worshipfully bareheaded while he is sowing; the top of his skull is bare, but elsewhere he is shamefully hairy; there is a wheel of hair and beard about his head. That is Isak the margrave.

Hamsun returned to his attack on contemporary society in his postwar novels *The Women at the Pump* (*Konerne ved Vandposten,* 1920)[13] and *Chapter the Last* (*Siste Kapitel,* 1923).[14] In these bitter satires society is portrayed as utterly corrupt and impotent, without a gleam of hope. But four years later he revived the Wanderer in a new version, and returned to a happier, more humorous vein in the trilogy which began with *Vagabonds* (*Landstrykere,* 1927)[15] and continued with *August* (1930)[16] and *Life Goes On* (*Men Livet lever,* 1933).[17] The central figure, August, is an adventurer and liar in the Peer Gynt tradition, who has dragged his roots with him from country to country, and in his zeal for new enterprise has lost his soul. Hamsun no longer admired the

[11] Tr. J. S. Scott (New York, 1925).
[12] Tr. W. W. Worster (New York, 1921).
[13] Tr. A. G. Chater (New York, 1928).
[14] Tr. A. G. Chater (New York, 1929).
[15] Tr. E. Gay-Tifft (New York, 1930).
[16] Tr. E. Gay-Tifft (New York, 1931).
[17] Tr. as *The Road Leads On* by E. Gay-Tifft (New York, 1934).

Wanderer, but looked at him from the point of view of the resident farmer:

Never a mother or a father, never a table to gather around, never a grave to cherish, never the divine voice of one's mother country through one's heart. A machine constructed for externalities, for industry and trade and mechanics and money. A life but not a soul.

Nevertheless, the author cannot forget that he himself was once a wanderer, and he tells about him in an imaginative and affectionate way. In his novel *The Ring is Closed* (*Ringen sluttet*, 1936),[18] Hamsun again played through his wanderer theme, but this time more faintly and with an attempt at psychological explanations.

Hamsun's reaction against the social order and the ideas of progress advocated by the preceding generation was more violent than that of any of the other writers of the nineties. In his case the antidemocratic and asocial ideas were reinforced by a specific hate for Englishmen and Americans which led him to side with Germany even after his own country had been attacked and occupied by German soldiers. The tragedy of Hamsun's support of one of the most vicious tyrannies the world has seen in modern times is not diminished by his attempt at an explanation in his one postwar book *On Covered Paths* (*På gjengrodde Stier*, 1949). But the book does show that he was still, in his ninetieth year, one of the greatest masters of style in Norwegian literature. Norwegians cannot afford to exclude his works from their literature.[19]

HANS E. KINCK

The range of the Norwegian psyche is measured by such contrasts as those between Wergeland and Welhaven, Bjørnson and Ibsen, Hamsun and Kinck.

Although Hamsun and Kinck were both concerned with the unconscious and the irrational in the human mind, it is as if they came from different worlds. The contrast is not merely that one was of peasant stock, the other of the bureaucracy. Nor that the one came from a helterskelter vagabondage, the other from learned studies. They were different in temperament and their inmost traits of character. While Hamsun fixed his gaze on the external phenomena and interpreted them in a radical but also reactionary way, Kinck was always looking behind them to search out their cultural roots. The basic difference is also

[18] Tr. E. Gay-Tifft (New York, 1937).
[19] Other Hamsun books translated into English are *Benoni*, tr. A. G. Chater (New York, 1925), *Rosa*, tr. A. G. Chater (New York, 1926).

apparent in their styles. Hamsun's is lyric and emotional, often chatty and studded with little witticisms and tricks. Kinck's language is more concentrated, full of meaning, massive but also colorful. He favors certain repetitions that sometimes have the effect of a refrain, and he likes to press his ideas into baroque images which remind one of woodcarving.

Kinck's writing has also a reflective quality which sets it apart from Hamsun's. Yet he is more the artist and visionary than a theoretician. His writing has a strong association with the art of painting, and he has been compared with Edvard Munch. But he is more reminiscent of the Spanish painter Goya; his art is akin to the baroque. While he has an awareness of reality, he prefers to describe his characters in distorted positions, and he has a great inclination to draw caricatures. He is like Hamsun in being unable to portray psychological development. The figures he portrays usually stand out against a background of nature and culture from which they are inseparable, like a windblown pine or a crippled juniper in the landscape.

He was the psychological anthropologist in Norwegian literature. He was not so much interested in the characters themselves, their actions, their dreams, or their opinions, but in all that lay behind these phenomena, the psychological and cultural basis, the life of the instinct, the historical and psychological forces that conflict in people. He analyzed the vitality in his characters, the interplay between animalistic fear of life and the ability to overcome this fear, the clash between patriotism and humanism, between Christianity and paganism, between what he calls the medieval and the modern. At times he also showed his desire to influence his own age by means of burlesque satire.

Hans Ernst Kinck was born at Øksfjord in Finnmark on October 11, 1865, and came of an educated family with branches in various parts of the country. When he was six, his father became a physician in Setesdal so that Hans spent some happy years of his childhood there, until his tenth year. Then the family moved to Strandebarm in Outer Hardanger. As he put it himself, the transition from the romance of the valley of ballads and folklore to the salty rationalism of the fjord country was like a box on the ears. He never forgot this box, and it started him brooding on the subject of folk psychology. From the starting point of his familiarity with the peasants of Setesdal and Hardanger he extended his interest to the entire people, and the insight he gained he then applied to problems of European culture in the great periods of conflict and innovation.

Though he studied at the university in the eighties, the problems then being discussed failed to interest him. He never had much respect for generalizations, and turned to Moltke Moe's lectures on Norwegian folklore. He joined a small circle which met at the home of the original but quite unproductive professor of literature, Cathrinus Bang, of whom Kinck later said: "He saw life in everything, even the tiniest drop of dew had its reflection." After his philological degree examination he competed for a prize with an essay on "The Relation between the Ballads of the Middle Ages and the Ancient Mythical-Heroic Poetry." He did not win the prize but the work he did on the essay extended his perspective of the national psychology. At the same time he was writing poems in Hardanger dialect and descriptions of folk life in prose.

Kinck's first novels *Huldren* (1892) and *A Young People* (*Ungt folk,* 1893)[20] show a thorough familiarity with West Norwegian rural life and foreshadow the treatment he gives it in his later writing. In the first we read of an illegitimate boy whose sensitive mind is unsettled by the influence of his environment. Kinck here describes the sneers, the backbiting, the inverted and repressed sexuality of the rural community in somewhat the way we find them in so many of his later stories. The other is a country tale from the eighties. The leading figure, Sigurd Bjørntveit, is an up-and-coming social climber, an uprooted scoundrel who elbows his way ahead, portrayed with poisonous malice. We are shown also the clash of the two cultures, the officials and the peasants, a theme which occupied the author all the way to his novel *The Avalanche Broke*.

Kinck's first two books were written in the sober style of naturalism. Not until his meeting with Jonas Lie in Paris in 1894 did he dare to let his imagination loose. The short-story collection *Bat's Wings* (*Flaggermusvinger,* 1895) is one of the most beautiful books of the neoromantic age, with a magic of mood, a compelling and suggestive style, a colorful and primitive lyricism, a tragic and burlesque humor. There are stories like "The Fiddle in the Wild Woods," about art and love, "Tore Botn," about the poet's struggle with his fear of nature, "White Anemones in the Meadow," about some old fellows who go up in the mountains and behave like madcap youngsters. More extreme are several of the stories in *From Sea to Mountain* (*Fra hav til hei,* 1897), with such stories as "The New Chaplain" ("Den nye kapellanen"), "This Stool" ("Denne krakkjen"), and "The Great Heart" ("Den store hugen"). These are

[20] Tr. B. Ten Eyck (New York, 1929).

not just funny, they are uproariously funny. In reality they tell about a crushing loneliness, about poverty and psychological disintegration, about a dream and a yearning for something great and extraordinary, about a need for happiness that is inverted into destructiveness, about the victory of irrational forces over the utilitarian view. In his later peasant stories the tone is usually more bitter, with scorn and the wildest caricature fused in a macabre mood. Only when he writes about the peasants in the interior does his mood relax into sympathy.

The path from *Bat's Wings* led in the direction of his love stories and portrayals of youthful emotion in *Birds of Passage and Others* (*Trækfugle og andre,* 1899), *Spring Nights* (*Vaarnætter,* 1901), *When Love Dies* (*Naar kjærlighed dør,* 1903), *The Spirits of Life* (*Livsaanderne,* 1906), *The Church Is Burning* (*Kirken brænder,* 1917), and others. Among his outstanding stories of this type may be mentioned "The White Little Lady" ("Den hvite lille dame"), the story of a little boy on a lonely farm who is impelled to emigrate because of the memory he carries with him of a childhood infatuation. One can find a good many stories in which the author expresses his love of children. "Be careful with the smallest thing Our Lord created" is a basic idea in his writing. Even in the love stories his best descriptions are those of the adolescent years, the transition from childhood to adulthood, when the mind is tortured by vague desires or by a bad conscience. There is often an infantile quality in the love he describes. His stories contain many lyric passages, but for the most part there is a macabre effect in them, of repressed eroticism which is tortured and often on the verge of insanity.

Kinck reached his artistic peak in the short stories. But his own personality comes out most clearly in the novels. At the same time as *Bat's Wings* he wrote a novel which was later combined with *The Adder* (*Hugormen,* 1898) in the novel *Herman Ek* (1923). He wrote in the preface to the latter: "In this book I have been digging for the 'national,' not understood as the colors of the flag or the foreign service, but as temperament. I have been looking for the mystery of the people, fragments of that powerful thing we may gather under the term 'medieval' and which was once the discovery of Romanticism." The lawyer's son Herman Ek grows up in a South Norwegian valley, clearly intended to be Setesdal, which cuts its way into the country like "the furrow of a giant's plow." In later years he always treasures the whisper of the pines on the moors. As a student he gets into the midst of the clash between the literature of discussion and the neoromantic reaction. He does not believe in the possibility of "changing values by discussion," and in the midst of a debate in the Student Society he cries out: "Fresh Air! Opinions make life barren around us, barren in this hall, barren in our hearts." As a mature man he tries to realize his dream of raising up again the country people, taking care of them, making them happy, reaching down to their level. Unhappily he is divided in his feelings toward them: "I am so fond of these people, but I can't endure them." This becomes his tragedy. The romanticism in him turns into a mad passion for destruction. He turns the beautiful valley into an industrial inferno, and is himself destroyed by it. But in the mentality of the country people there is also a dualism which is fatal for them, their mixture of the "horse trader" and the "mountain soul."

The same basic problem recurs in the following novels in various forms: *Mrs. Anny Porse (Fru Anny Porse,* 1900), *Doktor Gabriel Jahr* (1902), the sarcastic and bitter *Emigrants (Emigranter,* 1904), and *The Minister (Præsten,* 1905). Everywhere the author is looking for the cultural roots, "the veins of the two cultures in the people." He loves that which is rooted and genuine and abhors the leveling of modern society.

His chief work is the great three-volume novel *The Avalanche Broke (Sneskavlen brast,* 1918-1919). Here the theme is the meeting of the peasant and official cultures, spiced with nature mysticism and distorted minds. The novel is set in the 1870's. As a whole it is not successful, but there are excellent parts, particularly in the first volume. Here we have passages like the description of the country people who are looking for the fjord, and one of sheep that have been snowed in, the rattle of ice particles in the avalanche, the hopeless tracks in the snow. The work is written with grotesque humor, though the themes would not seem to be humorous: distorted love, envy and sadism, repressed initiative that finds an expression in nasty tricks and jests, outbursts of energy that alternate with complete inactivity.

There is a close kinship between Kinck's stories and novels on the one hand and his dramas on Norwegian themes on the other. The chief work here is the verse drama *The Drover (Driftekaren,* 1908) with its continuation *At the Rindal Camp (Paa Rindalslægeret,* 1925). *The Drover* is the synthesis of all Kinck wrote about Norwegian folk psychology and Norwegian nature. The protagonist Vraal is the poetic genius who is cut out to lead the people, but he is a capricious personality, filled with poetry and irony, split in his love and in his attitude to country and people. He has left his home to conquer life, intoxicated by spring and his vast abilities. He has visited in all parts of the country, knows the whole of it; but at the age of fifty he begins to feel a nostalgia. The mountains and the fjords call him back, and so do the people, though he can never come to rest among them. In this beautiful and nobly conceived drama the poet wishes to describe a people who live too far to the north, their state of torpor in the winter, their vigorous enterprise in the intoxication of spring, the dissolution of autumn. He delineates Norwegian folk character as he sees it, the horsetrading logic and the card player's eye, the insecurity behind the piousness, the adventurousness of the old Dublin kings as it still lives among the people. As in many other works, he is trying to disentangle the various layers of folk character.

In the works with Norwegian motifs he usually describes the seamy sides of the folk character. On Italian soil, where he lived many times from 1896 on, he studied the mixture of races. In his moving tragedy about aging love, *Agilulf the Wise* (*Agilulf den vise*, 1906) with a motif from Boccaccio, he created his characteristic form of versification. His verse does not move on ballbearings, like Krag's or Hamsun's, and it avoids the crackle of rhyme. The rhythmical principle is based on expiration and inspiration; the verses are like a breathing chest, now short and now relaxed.

At the same time Kinck was studying Italian history and art, folk character, and literature. He published some essays in *Italians* (*Italienere*, 1904), and in 1907 came *Old Soil* (*Gammel jord*). For several years he rotated his publications, producing now a learned article or essay and now a drama on the same theme. He was fascinated most particularly by two types, the man of principle and the opportunist. Machiavelli was the great man of principle in an opportunist age, who had to use his genius and his enterprise to arrange carnivals; Pietro Aretino was the opportunistic journalist, the unprincipled scandalmonger. These were the themes of his historical studies *A Quill Driver* (*En penneknekt*, 1911), *Men of the Renaissance* (*Renæssanse-mennesker*, 1916), and to some extent *The Voice of the Tribe* (*Stammens røst*, 1919), but also the plays *The Last Guest* (*Den sidste gjest*, 1910) and *Towards Carnival* (*Mot karneval*, 1915), in part also *The Wedding in Genoa* (*Bryllupet i Genua*, 1911) and *Lisabetta's Brothers* (*Lisabettas brødre*, 1921). Kinck's renaissance dramas have their technical weaknesses as plays, but they sparkle with the brilliance of his spirit.

Kinck used philology and history to clarify the hidden forces in the growth of nations, the mystic reality, traces of the migrations of peoples, "vague and light as the marks left in new-fallen snow by the wings of the ptarmigan," or "heavy and sad as the lonely tracks of the moose." Therefore he also studied the old sagas and wrote incisive psychological studies of "Characters the Saga Did Not Understand" and "Love in Kormak's Saga," appearing in *Many Kinds of Art* (*Mange slags kunst*, 1921). He wrote the ingenious study *Age of Greatness* (*Storhetstid*, 1922), in which he tried to show that Haakon Haakonsson's age was a period of cultural decadence because of the foreign influences that seeped in. But his studies of Norse literature also led to the writing of short stories, above all the masterly "Towards the Ballad" which was directed against Sigrid Undset's and Fredrik Paasche's conception of the role of Christianity in the old period.

In spite of his learned studies Kinck was a man who kept in touch with the life of his own times. He often sallied forth to heap scorn on those phenomena that seemed to him an expression of vulgarity or superficiality. In some of the stories in *The Golden Age* (*Guldalder*, 1920) and *Spring in Micropolis* (*Foraaret i Micropolis*, 1926) he ridiculed the get-rich-quick spirit that followed the First World War, and in articles in *Helmsman Overboard* (*Rormanden overbord*, 1920), dedicated to the students of Norway, he urged them to preserve the national values, the inner strength, and not give up their "capacity for dreaming." In *Places and People* (*Steder og folk*, 1924) he described the places that interested him most, Setesdal, Hardanger, Italy. But he did not like the political development in Italy, and was one of the Norwegians who spoke out most sharply against Mussolini. He sometimes used the word "race," but turned against the German generalization of racial theories: "People are not as far apart as some think. Nor are peoples" (*Italien og vi*, 1925).

Kinck was incredibly productive. He wrote book upon book, sometimes two in a single year. When he died on October 13, 1926, he still had some uncompleted works left. While he is not one of the favorites of the general public, he has shown a remarkable capacity for winning the enthusiastic admiration of individuals and small groups. His writing has evoked an almost religious loyalty among some, for the profundity and visionary quality of his thinking, and the intense artistic delight which his style can evoke in the connoisseur.

Regional Writing

THE URGE TO ESCAPE FROM CITY LIFE was a general European phenomenon in the nineties and later. Many of the denizens of Europe's megalopolitan beehives were sated with industrialism and capitalism. The primitivism of a Hamsun or the nostalgia of a Garborg were not the only forms this reaction could take. It could also find expression in an intense love of one's local community which called on the best powers of writers to picture its people and customs. The search for roots did not only go back into Norwegian history, as in Tryggve Andersen and Kinck, but also into the local regions, where a new generation of writers grew up and made their contribution to the national symphony.

There are traces in this writing of the new spirit of exploration and sports, as we find it in Fridtjof Nansen's bold voyages and his books *On Skis Over Greenland* (*På ski over Grønland*, 1890),[1] *Fram Over the Arctic Ocean* (*Fram over Polhavet*, 1897),[2] and later his *Outdoor Life* (*Friluftsliv*, 1916).[3] Writers were stimulated to make more room in their writing for winter life, ski trips across the barren mountains, the winter storms, and the coming of spring. But they were also stimulated by cultural and folkloristic voyages of discovery, such as Moltke Moe's studies of folklore, collections of historical and local traditions like Ivar Kleiven's volumes from Gudbrandsdal and Johannes Skar's from Setesdal. In the same period were also founded the leading folk museums of Norway, the collections of Sandvig at Maihaugen near Lillehammer and those of Norsk Folkemuseum at Bygdøy near Oslo.

This interest carries on the tradition of the topographic literature from the Renaissance on, but it also falls into the romantic tradition of

---

[1] Tr. as *The First Crossing of Greenland* by H. M. Gepp (London–New York, 1890).
[2] Tr. as *Farthest North* (New York, 1897).
[3] Tr. as *Sporting Days in Wild Norway* (London, 1925).

the nineteenth century in which the chief contribution was Bjørnson's country tales. But the best of the regionalists had their insight sharpened and their style hardened by impressions of the realist period. It cannot be denied that regional writing often seems narrow and parochial, without an adequate feeling for the universally human. But there is also very commonly a thread of protest against puritanical restrictions which can be traced back to the folk high school. There are, of course, some writers who have grown out of their environment and reached out to universal problems beyond those of the locale and the folk high school.

Every region, and practically speaking every valley, is represented in the literature. But the literary mapping of Norway is not just due to the regionalists proper. Garborg, Hamsun, Kinck had their part in it, as did older writers like Bjørnson, Lie, and Kielland.

The South Country has its special group in the brothers Krag, Gabriel Scott, Olaf Benneche, and others. The North Country writers are no less characteristic, including besides Hamsun such authors as Andreas Haukland, Regine Normann, Bernt Lie, Carl Schøyen, Matti Aikio (the only Lapp in Norwegian literature), and Andreas Markusson. The West Country has a multitude of variegated writers, from Hans E. Kinck to Jens Tvedt, Hjalmar Christensen, O. W. Fasting, Rasmus Løland, Anders Hovden, Kristian Elster, Jr., Gro Holm, Theodor Dahl, Hans Seland, and many others. The Trøndelag group includes names like Johan Bojer, Peter Egge, Olav Duun, Kristofer Uppdal, Magnhild Haalke, Inge Kro-kann, Ola Setrom, and Johan Falkberget. The valleys of the East Country are also richly represented in Hans Aanrud, Jacob Bull, Sven Moren, Ragnhild Jølsen, Ingeborg Refling Hagen, and Olav Sletto. Even the emigrants to America have received their epic in O. E. Rølvaag's books.

While most of these belong properly to the twentieth century, the period when regional writing first began to flourish on a great scale was the years after 1890. Among those who entered Norwegian literature then one of the most realistic was Jens Tvedt (1857-1935). His story *Misfortune* (*Vanheppa,* 1891) was the first of a series of masterpieces from folk life on the Hardanger Fjord. His books are far from idyllic, picturing an abundance of coarseness and the harsh distress of life. But at bottom there is a harmonious outlook, wisdom, and humor in his writing, without any attempt at penetrating psychology. His types are genuine all the way through, like the poor Per who is saved from his folly through marriage, the touching Madli for whom things turn out well in the end, and many others. His books are generally without a social program, though one can note here and there an antagonism to urban culture.

Rasmus Løland (1861-1907) was not interested in the rural life and society around him, but rather in those individuals whom the social group rejects. Tuberculous himself, he felt a deep sympathy for shy and lonely personalities whom he pictured in *Guilt* (*Skuld*, 1892) and other books. His understanding of children was reflected in a number of stories that have become well-known classics of childhood. In some of his books he discussed the problems of art and culture in Norway, and the position of the artist, as in the story *Aasmund Aarak* (1902). His religious faith was sincere, but he opposed all puritanism and dogmatism. In a story "Times of War" ("Ufredstider") he portrayed the events of 1814 and their impact on a rural community. He was a sensitive, imaginative writer who had a good sense of humor and self-irony, but illness and difficult circumstances made it impossible for him to reach full artistic maturity.

Vetle Vislie (1858-1933) was another who interested himself in the folk culture, though he also was in touch with current social problems. He was born and reared in Telemark, taught school, studied theology, wrote for the papers, taught at a teacher's seminary. His early stories were attacks on the puritanism which had "made our race homeless." He was influenced by Ibsen and Vinje, but in the story of folk life *The Ghost* (*Gasten*, 1895) he showed full artistic maturity. Other novels deal with religious and ethical problems, and the meeting of rural culture with industrialism. Like so many of the writers in this period he was afraid that the traditional culture of the rural folk would be destroyed by an uncultured proletariat and a power-mad capitalism.

The oldest of the regional writers was Jacob Breda Bull (1853-1930), a zealous patriot and an angry opponent of the naturalistic and bohemian writings of the eighties. He wrote a great many stories, novels, and poems, besides plays and popular biographies. But the only really valuable productions were some of his vigorous and picturesque descriptions of life in the eastern valleys of Østerdalen and Rendalen, and the mountain heights of that region. All of these are from the nineties; most of his later stories were poor.

Hans Aanrud (1863-1953) was one regional writer whose artistic standards were high. His discriminatingly written stories from the lowland valleys of the East have a quality of humor and humanity that has made them classic in Norwegian literature. Some of his novels, like *Sidsel Longskirt* (*Sidsel Sidsærk,* 1903)[4] and *Sølve Solfeng* (1910), are so idyllic that they are best suited for juvenile reading, but his short stories are often keen and penetrating studies of the quirks of rural character. Aanrud also dipped his pen in satire in a series of three comedies, *The Stork* (*Storken,* 1895), *Riding High* (*Høit tilhest,* 1901), and *The Cock* (*Hanen,* 1906). Like Holberg he warned his times against extremities and fanaticisms. He wanted the country people and the official class to compose their differences in the name of common sense, and he warned against the dangers of dissolving the old traditions in the superficialities and humbugs of modernity. In the last of his three comedies he let neither priest nor theologian into heaven, only simple, honest, kind people. Aanrud was at his best in his intimate portraits of family life, and in his portrayals of nature, where we get unsurpassed pictures of frosty East Country winters, rime-bedecked spruces in the wintry light: "Here and there a frosty tassel let go, fell, pulled others with it, so that they were sprinkled like cold, gleaming specks of snow and made the soft light quiver."

But the poet of the forests above all others is Sven Moren (1871-1938). Johan Falkberget once wrote about him: "Sven Moren descends from the old fairy tale kings of the eastern woods." He had his realistic aspects, and he was a nationalist on the same lines as Arne Garborg and others. But whenever he pictured the woods, he turned mystic. In his youth he was deeply stirred by Obstfelder, and the lyric strain is basic in his writing. Only through his adherence to the national cause did he save himself from the decadence of the period. He found his own form in the story "Lost" ("På villstrå," 1898), reached a large public with the story *The Great Forest* (*Storskogen,* 1904), and produced his best portrayal of nature and people in *From Eastern Woods* (*Aust or markom,* 1905). He wrote other novels, but only the lyric parts of these are above average.

The most original of the eastern regionalists is Ragnhild Jølsen (1875-1908), who belongs in the tradition of Asbjørnsen, Kinck, and Tryggve Andersen. She came of a family devoted to folklore, and gathered stories from an early age, not only at home but also among her neighbors in the Romerike communities. She was most deeply attracted by fantastic and gruesome elements, the grotesquery of folk imagination. In her first major work *Ve's Mother* (*Ve's mor,* 1903) we meet an old family

[4] Tr. as *Lisbeth Longfrock* by Laura E. Poulsson (Boston, 1907), as *Lisbeth Longsark* (Oxford, 1918), as *Little Sidsel Longskirt* by Anna Barwell (New York, 1924).

estate in dissolution, echoing with the footsteps of people who have loved and suffered. Her artistic grasp increased with books like *Rikka Gan* (1904) and *Fernanda Mona* (1905), in which old estates also play important roles. While we catch glimpses of a life that was once lived in gaiety, the dominant impression is one of old aristocracy in decay. Suggestive and powerful is the grotesque story *Hollas's Chronicle* (*Hollases krønike*, 1906) from around 1500, a book about evil but written with wild humor. While these books are predominantly romantic, her *Stories of the Sawmills* (*Brukshistorier*, 1907) are sharply realistic in their portrayal of the conflict between the old paternalistic life of the sawmills and the new industrialism. Ragnhild Jølsen was a first-rate artist and her early death was a great loss to Norwegian literature.

The mysticism of the North Country which first found expression in Jonas Lie's early stories reappears in the best books of Regine Normann (1867-1939). But she was more immediately influenced by Asbjørnsen's *Fairy Tales* and by Tryggve Andersen, to whom she was married a number of years. Her feeling for superstition and legend appears already in her first book, *Krabvaag, Pictures from a Small Fishing Station* (*Krabvaag, Skildringer fra et lidet fiskevær*, 1905), which also gives a depressing picture of the influence of a revivalist in a poverty-stricken society. Some of her other novels plead for a healthy, harmonious religiousness and attack an inhuman and tyrannical form of Christianity. She portrayed the Nordland of her childhood with great historical understanding in *In those Days . . .* (*Dengang . . .* , 1912) and *Eiler Hundevart* (1913). In her last years she published some collections of folk tales from the North, retold with vivid imaginativeness.

The most learned of the regionalists aside from Kinck was Hjalmar Christensen (1869-1925), a nephew of Kristian Elster Sr. and born in Førde, Sunnfjord, the only fixed point in his varied life. His authorship was voluminous, including as it did literary criticism, literary history, and cultural history, as well as books on Norwegian and world politics. He wrote about the regionalists of his time in *Young Norwegians* (*Unge nordmænd*, 1893) and *Scandinavian Artists* (*Nordiske kunstnere*, 1895). As a cultural historian he wanted to rehabilitate the Age of Enlightenment and point out the connection between the eighteenth century and the generation from 1840 to 1870 in Norway. The same program was apparent in his literary work also. In his deeply personal and semiautobiographical novel *A Life* (*Et liv*, 1900), he found his way back to nature, to the family, and the soil which he felt as a part of himself. In a series of historical novels *The Sheriff's Home* (*Fogedgaarden,* 1911), *The Brothers* (*Brødrene,* 1912), *The Old Community* (*Den gamle bygd,* 1913), and *The New Community* (*Den nye bygd,* 1914), he portrayed officials and peasants against a broadly conceived background of the decades from 1840 to the industrialization around 1910. Possibly more valuable are his stories from the eighteenth century, *The Sacred Tree* (*Tuntræet,* 1917) and *Dawn* (*Dæmring,* 1918). Christensen was no great psychologist, and was possibly too intellectual to be a first-rate artist. But by virtue of his intelligence and profound learning he became a master in the portrayal of a culture. He also had a gift for satire.

Although they were not regionalists, Ivar Mortensson (Egnund) (1857-1934) and Anders Hovden (1860-1943) were writers deeply in sympathy with the national movement of which the regionalists were one expression. Mortensson was a fantast and dreamer, at once a theologian and a supporter of the Russian anarchist Kropotkin. In poems and plays he tried to reproduce the spirit of the primitive Norse life that he found in the *Poetic Edda.* But he is better known for his translation of the *Edda* than for anything original he wrote. Anders Hovden was another theologian, who was also active in the religious and cultural life of his country. He was a sympathizer of Bjørnson and Sverdrup in the political conflicts and an opponent of the bohemian radicals in the literary world. His influence was exerted on behalf of the folk high schools and in opposition to puritanical sectarianism. His verse erects a memorial to the fishermen and their courageous struggle with natural forces. He is also known for his hymns with their touches of folklore and national sympathies. His prose stories are weak, but his autobiography *Looking Back* (*Attersyn,* 1928) reflects interestingly the writer himself and the spiritual forces which he promoted in an attractive and tolerant way.

The 1890's were thus not exclusively decadent or even pessimistic, but contained many elements of growth and optimism. They were years of intense germination, in which the foundations were laid for the enormous expansion of literary activity that characterized the twentieth century.[5]

---

[5] Writers not discussed above: Dikken Zwilgmeyer (1867-1913), *Johnny Blossom* (Boston, 1912), *What Happened to Inger Johanne* (Boston, 1919), *Four Cousins* (Boston, 1923), *Inger Johanne's Lively Doings* (Boston, 1926), all tr. by Emilie Poulsson; Elias Kræmmer, pseud. of Anthon B. Nilsen (1855-1936), *Dry Fish and Wet,* tr. W. Worster (London, 1922).

The New Realism

THE GREAT EVENT IN NORWEGIAN LIFE during the early years of the century was the peaceful but dramatic dissolution of the union with Sweden in 1905. For more than a generation the writers of the nation had been leaders in preparing this event. Bjørnson had been the most vehement in his insistence that Norwegians build up their "pride of independence." But his fellow writers had been practically unanimous in their support of this plank in the Liberal platform. There was little difference on this point between older men like Kielland or Garborg and younger men like Hamsun or Kjær. The writers also had their share in preparing European public opinion for the emergence of Norway as an independent nation. After Ibsen and Bjørnson Norway was no longer a blank spot on the cultural map of Europe.

The writers who made their entry into literature during these years were indelibly stamped by the rapid progress of their country and the air of optimism which then prevailed. The national enthusiasm was reflected in a generation that turned to the task of describing a new nation, the newest and yet one of the oldest in Europe. The gloomy vapors of neoromanticism were dissipated in the rosy dawn of the new century. Individualistic introspection gave way to the portrayal of social forces, presented with broad and incisive strokes by writers who were convinced that a new society was emerging. General literacy brought new circles of readers, and the rapid progress of democracy promoted an emphasis on universal human values. Realistic techniques of writing came back into fashion, along with a huge expansion of the writing fraternity.

These were also the years when heavy industries were first established in Norway, thanks to the harnessing of water power for the production of electricity. The growth of an urban proletariat led to the rise of labor problems, as it already had in other European countries. A third force thus came into being, alongside the farmers and the civil servants, which was destined to play an enormous role in the further development of the country. Many of the older writers looked with suspicion and antagonism at the new industrial development as a potential threat to the old culture, whether that of the peasants or the bureaucracy. But the laborer himself also made his appearance in literature, and his voice was heard through writers like Uppdal, Falkberget, and Oskar Braaten. There is a bustling activity in the writing of these years which contrasts strangely with the static quality of the writing of the 1890's.

Two forms of literature showed special vitality, the novel and the lyric. No dramatist of consequence appeared, and the essays or short stories written were incidental to the main interests of their writers. Most of the important work done by this generation appeared after the First World War, but the years of their youth and their début fell in the prewar period, and there is a common tone which marks them as members of a generation that was still firmly anchored in that period.

JOHAN BOJER

Possibly the most popular, if not the most significant novelist of the generation was Johan Bojer (1872–1959). Born in a coastal fishing-farming community like those he has repeatedly described in his books, at Orkdalsøra near Trondheim, he won an international circle of readers by presenting the problems of early twentieth-century Norway in entertaining fictional form. He established himself in Norway with *A Procession* (*Et folketog*, 1896), in France and Italy with *The Power of Faith* (*Troens magt*, 1903),[1] in England and America with *The Great Hunger* (*Den store hunger*, 1916).[2] These works revolved around rather simple themes, e.g., that many politicians are rascals, that idealists are often self-deceiving egoists, and that material success does not of itself bring happiness. But they were widely acclaimed, even by such prominent and various writers as Brandes, Romain Rolland, Rabindranath Tagore, John Galsworthy, and Joseph Hergesheimer, who found Bojer stimulating and praised him for his realism, his vigorous style, and his original ideas.

Norwegian critics, however, refused to recognize him as a major writer, on the grounds that his ideas interfered with his art, his characters were insufficiently motivated, and his style lacked artistic cultivation.

[1] Tr. as *The Power of a Lie* by Jessie Muir (New York, 1909).
[2] Tr. W. Worster and C. Archer (New York, 1918).

They were won over to a somewhat grudging admiration only by his epics of folk life, *Last of the Vikings* (*Den siste viking*, 1921),[3] which dealt with the Lofoten fishermen, and *Folk by the Sea* (*Folk ved sjøen*, 1929),[4] a story of the poverty-stricken tenants among whom Bojer spent his boyhood. These works, along with some of his fairy tales and the fantasia entitled *The Prisoner who Sang* (*Fangen som sang*, 1913),[5] certainly seem to show the best promise of enduring value. Interesting, but less intimate in its understanding, was his attempt to portray Norwegian emigrants in the United States, *Our Kinsmen* (*Vor egen stamme*, 1924).[6]

Within his own generation Bojer's grasp on his public was predicated on the immediacy of his writing to the problems that agitated the civilized world. Nowhere else outside the public press could one find so detailed and entertaining a panorama of all the surface aspects of Norwegian life through a generation of postwar and prewar adjustment. Practically every major event and every topic of discussion between 1890 and 1925 turned up here: the status of women, the relation of labor and capital, the return to the soil, national defense, munitions manufacture, war profiteering, and many others. The characters in his books (in contrast, e.g., to those of Hamsun) are such as one might conceivably have met in the rapidly advancing Norway of that day, a generation of hard-working and progressive people (the engineer is Bojer's favorite character), nationalistic and enthusiastic, liberal and somewhat inclined to over-optimism about the future. This purely sociological value of his writings is fortified with a remarkable skill of observation, which enables him to reproduce creatively the manners and mannerisms of real people, with their quips and anecdotes, their foibles and self-deceptions, as well as their unconscious heroisms. He does not delve deeply into the mechanism of their being, but marches them firmly along toward a dramatic dénouement. The ideas that he advocates through them are never profound, for his views were practically a barometer of liberal bourgeois opinion in his

[3] Tr. Jessie Muir (New York, 1923).
[4] Tr. Arni Heni, Louise Rourke, C. Archer (London, 1931), same translation as *The Everlasting Struggle* (New York, 1931).
[5] Tr. Sara Hélène Weedon (New York, 1924).
[6] *The Emigrants*, tr. A. G. Jayne (New York, 1925). Other Bojer translations are: *The Face of the World*, tr. Jessie Muir (New York, 1919); *Life*, tr. Jessie Muir (New York, 1920); *Treacherous Ground* [*Vort Rige*], tr. Jessie Muir (New York, 1920); *God and Woman* [*Dyrendal*], tr. A. R. Shelander (New York, 1921); *A Pilgrimage*, tr. Jessie Muir (New York, 1924); *The New Temple*, tr. C. Archer, J. S. Scott (New York, 1928); *The House and the Sea*, tr. T. M. Ager (1934); *By Day and by Night*, tr. Sölvi and Richard Bateson (New York, 1937); *The King's Men* (New York, 1940).

day. He was the mouthpiece of an idealistic individualism which now seems quaintly old-fashioned.

It is easy to see the many influences that have played on his thinking— the ethical idealism of Ibsen, the national and religious liberalism of Bjørnson, the poetic exaltation of Victor Hugo, the realistic techniques of Zola and Maupassant. He lacks the colossal vigor of these men, and his brew is to some extent a dilution of their doctrines. He lacks those mighty swings of the pendulum that terrify, bewitch, and inspire. His appeal lies in his humanism, his kindliness, and that undogmatic religion which fills his best characters with an abiding faith in the glory of hard work and the mysterious power of love.

PETER EGGE

However different they might be in temperament and interests, both Johan Bojer and Peter Egge (1869–1959) had many ties with the realism of the 1870's. Peter Egge had a hard time of it as a young man, but the effort strengthened his character and may have helped to give his writing its air of honest, manly authenticity, as well as its sympathy with the psychological problems of youth. He showed solid artistic quality from his very earliest short stories of 1894, which described folk life in the Trøndelag region. He also wrote a number of plays, some of them from the same scene, others satirically directed against phenomena in contemporary life of which he disapproved.

His major works, however, consist of the novels in which he depicts the life of his native region on a broad canvas. *The Heart* (*Hjertet*, 1907) was his first great success and reflects his best qualities. It is a moving story of life and art, of weaknesses concealed behind a brusque façade, of the happiness that comes from work. As is often the case in his books, it is the women who have the force of character necessary to rescue lives that are threatened by shipwreck.

Something new entered his writing in the novel *In the Fjords* (*Inde i fjordene*, 1920), dedicated to Georg Brandes. This is the story of the social conflicts in a Norwegian valley which arose in the 1870's and 1880's over the new political and intellectual movements of that period. The contrast between traditional peasant culture and the urbanized culture of the bureaucrats is here portrayed with deep understanding. *Jægtvig and his God* (*Jægtvig og hans Gud*, 1924) is a highly original story of a craftsman who tried to build a religious philosophy of his own, but suffered defeat because of his insistence on winning every argument.

Possibly his most valuable book is *Hansine Solstad* (1925),[7] the only one to be translated into English. In this novel he portrayed the consequences of gossip and malice in the life of a young girl. He has also told the story of his own life in well-written *Memoirs* (*Minner,* 1948, 1950), which include incisive pictures of his contemporaries.

GABRIEL SCOTT

A writer who has won for himself an assured niche among the well-beloved authors of his country is Gabriel Scott (1874–1958). He followed in the footsteps of the Krag brothers as a poet of the South Coast, for whose many queer characters he had a keen eye. He was a romanticist at heart, even a neoromanticist in his early books, but he approached realism in his later work. He is noted above all as a writer for children, and such books as *Aunt Pose* (*Tante Pose,* 1904), *Hollænder-Jonas* (1908), and *Sølvfaks* (1912), have won many youthful readers. At the same time he wrote witty comedies directed at the foibles of his times, such as *The Tower of Babel* (*Babel tårn,* 1910) about the Norwegian confusion of tongues.

Not until he wrote *The Ordeal* (*Jernbyrden,* 1915) was he recognized as a major writer. In this moving novel and its continuation *Enok Ruben's Life* (*Enok Rubens levnedsløp,* 1917) he produced a splendid historical study of life in West Moland in the 1770's. This portrayal of the social and political conflicts of that period is a colorful reflection of the coastal region with its lonely heaths, its naked skerries and open sea, but also its cozy inlets.

His masterpiece, however, is *The Spring, or the Letter about the Fisherman Marcus* (*Kilden eller brevet om fiskeren Markus,* 1918),[8] a poem in prose along the lines of Hamsun's *Growth of the Soil,* but entirely original. It reflects the author's mystical outlook, his love of folk wisdom, and his sense for the simple, pious life of nature, as well as his scorn for the busy haste of the city dweller. The fisherman Marcus is content with his meager subsistence. He is a gentle philosopher with a humble mind, and his eye "reflects all nature and takes up into itself all that is fine and good without asking about value or rank."[9]

KRISTIAN ELSTER JR.

Kristian Elster Jr. (1881-1947) is another contemplative author, whose

[7] Tr. Jess H. Jackson (New York, 1929).
[8] Tr. as *Markus The Fisherman* by S. and R. Bateson (London, 1931).
[9] The novel *The Golden Gospel,* tr. by W. Worster, appeared in English (1928) and one of his children's books, *A Story of Kari Supper,* tr. Anvor Barstad (New York, 1931).

chief themes are the relationship of individual to society and the dissolution of the old official (*embetsmann*) class. Like his father, Kristian Elster Sr., he considered himself a son of Sunnfjord in western Norway, even though he was born in Trondheim. Some of his writings portray life in this region, but he was primarily interested in character study. Even his first stories show psychological insight and a sure sense of artistry; by the time he wrote *The Young Hearts* (*De unge hjerter*, 1910), he was well started on his leading theme. In his novel-trilogy *Apprenticeship* (*I lære*, 1911), *On the Road* (*Landeveien*, 1912), and *Master* (*Mester*, 1913) he contributed a rich and vivid portrayal of character. He showed what happens when an *embetsmann's* son is made aware of the new sense of social responsibility. A novel that reflects impressions of the World War is *My Brother Harris* (*Min bror Harris*, 1917); written in diary form, it is a vigorous critique of the old individualism. Elster did his best work in *From a Race of Shadows* (*Av skyggernes slekt*, 1919), a novel that pictures the effect of the new age on the *embetsmenn*, and in *Farmer Weatherbeard* (*Bonde Veirskjæg*, 1930), a novel that does much the same for the farmer class. He also wrote good poetry and excellent literary essays.

JOHAN FALKBERGET

Among those who succeeded in giving monumental expression to the life of humble folk one of the foremost was Johan Falkberget (1879-). His scene was that part of Norway which lay farthest from the sea, the mountain regions around Røros, a mining town in the central eastern part of Norway not far from the Swedish border. His love of the mountains is apparent on every page, and one might even compare his style to the brisk air of the snow-capped peaks which meets the miner as he emerges from his dark shaft. Like Gabriel Scott he is close to the narrative art of the folk.

He was born near Røros where his father was a mineworker of Norwegian peasant stock and his mother was descended from a Swedish mining family. He himself started in the mines at the age of eight and did not give this work up until he was twenty-seven years old, in 1906. He had then already written a number of stories in the dime-novel class, but achieved artistic success with his book *Black Mountains* (*Svarte fjelde*, 1907). In this story and the following ones he added a new world to Norwegian literature by his description of the lives led by workers in the mines and on the railroads. Falkberget was not one who presented this life in a gray and depressing light, however realistic he might be in his portrayal. In spite of the rebelliousness expressed by his characters, and their antagonism to the settled farming community, he succeeded in giving his workers a festive air and a deep sense of traditional values. In their lives the Christian idea of brotherhood was more significant than the class struggle.

In Falkberget's eyes the workmen he describes have heroic stature, because they carry with them a dream, a star in their hearts. The author reveals his own humanism and faith in goodness through his characters, who often have a sense of secret sympathy with the powers that govern life. Most of them are projected back into earlier ages and can therefore emerge in greater relief as epic figures against a historic background. *Eli Sjursdotter* (1913) tells about the mountain folk during the Great Northern War (1700-1720), while *Lisbeth of Jarnfjeld* (*Lisbeth paa Jarnfjeld*, 1915)[10] tells of the enmity between the mountain folk and those who lived in the valley. *The Fourth Night Watch* (*Den fjerde nattevakt*, 1923) is an exciting and well-told story of life at Røros between 1807-1825. It tells of the minister Sigismund, who sins against his holy orders by falling in love with one of his parishioners, another man's wife. Through the tragic humiliations that befall him he learns that "God judges in love, men in malice."

After taking over in 1922 the farm his father had owned, Falkberget engaged in the studies that enabled him to write the epic series of novels that stands as one of the masterpieces in Norwegian literature between the wars. This was the novel of mining life from the 1720's entitled *Christianus Sextus* (1927-1935). His extensive source material entered unobtrusively into the structure of this novel, together with impressions from his own age. The events of World War I and the postwar depression are here projected two centuries back into the years that followed the Great Northern War. Volume I, *The First Journeymen* (*De første geseller*), has the clearest lines and the best epic form. Thirteen workers from Jämtland in Sweden cross the border in 1723 to Røros where they are looking for employment in a newly opened mine. For seven days they struggle across mountains and through forests with their bare day's rations of bread baked from moss. Some of them have been soldiers in the army of Charles XII, and the thunder of cannon is still in their ears. *In the Sign of the Hammer* (*I hammerens tegn*) is more lyric,

---

[10] Tr. R. Gjelsness (New York, 1930). A volume of stories by Falkberget appeared as *Broomstick and Snowflake*, tr. T. Welhaven (New York, 1933).

with its introductory poem in prose describing the mountain regions. This is unmatched in its kind in Norwegian literature, with the mountain portrayed in sunshine and in drizzle. In the third and last volume, *The Watchman* (*Tårnvekteren*), from about 1730, we get the richest and most varied contents. Possibly the most moving character is the watchman himself, the fantast and genius Erns-Ola, an amateur astronomer who people used to think was slightly mad.

Falkberget's second major work, *Bread of Night* (*Nattens brød*), was also planned as a trilogy, but promises to extend even farther. The first volume, *Ann-Magritt* (1940), describes a people laboring endlessly, but with a will to live and an energetic courageous determination which meant a real strengthening to readers during the years of German occupation. The second volume, *The Plow Share* (*Plogjernet,* 1946), is also highly imaginative and well told, with a symbolistic quality which may be thought to suggest the postwar reconstruction. Volume 3, *Johannes* (1950), carries the heroine Ann-Magritt into marriage, and shows her as the heroic symbol of the spiritual resources of her people. Falkberget's production includes also a great many efforts in the lyric, in essays, and memoirs, which testify to his rich surplus of imaginative capacity.

KRISTOFER UPPDAL

Another novelist of the worker is Kristofer Uppdal (1878–1961), like Falkberget influenced by the folk high school and with more individualism than Marxism in his philosophy. But while the former is an optimist and a prophet, Uppdal is more of a skeptic and a questioner. The problem in his books is the relationship between peasant and laborer, and between the common laborer and the one who is on his way up the social ladder. Born in northern Trøndelag, Uppdal worked as shepherd boy, as agriculturer laborer, journalist, railroad worker, and labor leader before he achieved his ambition of becoming a writer. His earliest published book of poems appeared in 1905. But he is best known for his novel in ten volumes, *The Dance Through the World of Shadows* (*Dansen gjenom skuggeheimen,* 1911-1924).

At the end of this uneven but remarkable work, the author wrote that its purpose was to give "a united perspective of the labor movement after its separation from the peasant class and down to our day." Uppdal was interested primarily in the psychological rather than the political aspects of this transition. But the volumes were not published in chronological order, and the connection is sometimes hard to observe. One of the leading motifs in the earlier volumes is the process of tearing oneself loose from the soil and entering upon the life of the migratory worker. Among these laborers there are some with artistic talents. The descriptions are often coarse, but lifelike. In the later books of the series, there are two motifs, the psychological development of his main character, Torber Landsem, and the relationship between the individual and the labor union. He gives us a vivid picture of the increasing radicalism of the labor movement between the wars. Among his best characters is the "cathedral builder" who wants to infuse the movement with religious idealism, while his fellow workers are obsessed by ambition and the hunger for power.

OSKAR BRAATEN

One of the few real proletarians in the prewar generation was Oskar Braaten (1881-1939), whose book *Around the Factory (Kring fabrikken,* 1910) introduced Norwegian readers to the life of the factoryworker. This collection of short stories was followed by *The Baby (Ungen,* 1911), a play from the life of working people in the least privileged parts of Oslo. Braaten himself was a worker's son, born in Oslo, and knew the feelings of envy and ambition which surged through the hearts of many workers' sons during these years. In his writing there is a powerful expression of the desire for better conditions which was basic to the growth of the labor movement. His plays and novels are marked by sincerity, and they show a deep understanding of the laborer's psychology, tempered by good humor and warm sympathy. His play *The Big Baptism (Den store barnedåpen,* 1925) has also proved to be popular, with its lively portrayal of folk life in the back streets of Oslo, and its expression of sympathy for the mother instinct of young girls who work in the factories. Of his many novels *The Wolf's Lair (Ulvehiet,* 1919) and *Matilde* (1920) are the masterpieces. These give a vivid insight into life in a big city tenement house.

* * *

The problems Camilla Collett had raised were taken up and developed by the great male authors of the 1870's. But Amalie Skram was the only woman who pursued the subject down to the turn of the century. Around 1900 Alvilde Prydz (1848-1922) discussed woman's position in a number of highly idealistic novels.[11] Some years later Barbra Ring (1870-1955) developed the theme in her novels, especially *Before the Cold Comes* (*Før kulden kommer,* 1915);[12] she won a wider audience through her children's books, especially the *Peik* and *Fjellmus* series (first collected in 1917-1918).[13]

But a woman who must be reckoned among the really notable writers of her generation was Nini Roll Anker (1873-1942), whose first significant book, *Little-Anna and the Others* (*Lill-Anna og andre,* 1906), showed a heartfelt sympathy with the conditions of laboring women. She was herself a member of the upper classes by birth and marriage, but she possessed an intellectual radicalism which joined hands on the one hand with the generation of the seventies and eighties, and on the other with the younger postwar generation. She combined intellectual curiosity with a warm heart, a tolerant liberalism, and a social conscience. She reached her artistic maturity in the novel *The Weaker Sex* (*Det svake kjøn,* 1915), in which she attacked the current education of women; her contention was that it tended to cripple their sexual potentialities. In her novel *The Church* (*Kirken,* 1921) she showed her anticlerical feeling in an attack on the blessings bestowed by the church on the armed forces of each nation. She demonstrated her interest in the history of culture and her feeling for the upper-class tradition of Norway in a series of novels entitled *The House on Shore Road* (*Huset i Søgaten,* 1923), *At the Governor's House* (*I amtmandsgaarden,* 1925), and *Under the Sloping Roof* (*Under skraataket,* 1927). She also issued three volumes of light fiction under the pseudonym Kåre P. and succeeded in making the identity of the author not only a well-kept secret but also something of a mystery in Norwegian literature. The last of her many novels was *Woman and the Black Bird* (*Kvinnen og den svarte fuglen,* 1945), a stirring appeal to mothers of the world to put an end to war.

THE LYRICISTS: WILDENVEY, BULL, ØRJASÆTER, NYGARD

The lyric writers after 1905 were like the novelists in meeting life with greater courage and optimism than their predecessors. They also turned

[11] *The Heart of the Northern Sea,* tr. T. Engdahl and J. Rew (London, 1907); *Sanpriel, The Promised Land* (Boston, 1914); plays *He Is Coming,* tr. Hester Coddington, in *Poet-Lore* (1914), 230-44, *In Confidence,* tr. A. Paulson, in *Twenty-five Short Plays International* (New York, 1925).
[12] Tr. as *Into the Dark* by W. Emmé (London, 1921).
[13] *Peik,* tr. L. M. Woodside (Boston, 1932); *The Tomboy Cousin,* tr. J. L. E. Aspinall (New York, 1927).

away from the romantic contemplation of nature to an interest in urban life, and they showed a strong philosophic trend.

The most popular and influential of them was Herman Wildenvey, whose verse brought a new, carefree air into Norwegian literature. His sun-filled, easy-going lines were like flowers planted in suburban gardens. The casual, colloquial manner was his stock in trade, and won him immediate attention. Olaf Bull was a seeker after perfection, whose verse required infinite polishing. Although he often described scenes from the Oslo he loved so well, much of his poetry was fraught with ideas; it was reflective in tone, and yet visually exquisite. Tore Ørjasæter carried on the tradition of the ballad and the folk-life lyric from Welhaven and Garborg. Øverland, too, had his debut before World War I, but his poetry changed so markedly in the postwar years that he belongs more clearly to the later generation.

Herman Wildenvey (1886–1959) is the troubadour of Norwegian verse, the tireless singer of youth, beauty, and summer. Born of farming stock in the community of Eiker, his real family name being Portaas, he attended college and then emigrated to America in 1904. He attended a theological seminary for a time, but returned to Norway three years later. That summer he wrote his first collection of verse Bonfires (Nyinger, 1907),[14] which at once established him as a popular idol and the standard-bearer of a lyric revival. He disclaimed all social purposes in his verse, and declared that he was a pagan worshiper of life and beauty: "I was washed into the world by a flood of sunshine, that's the word!" He built on the form and spirit of Hamsun's poetry, but developed an "ambling" verse line all his own, with an easy billowing cadence produced by the alternation of three- and four-syllable feet and by the enjambement of sentences over several lines. With this technique he was able to relieve Norwegian verse of its usual sobriety, and give it a lightness which was sometimes merely frothy, but could also be ingratiatingly charming, as well as witty and daring.

He enjoyed irritating the staid and the bourgeois, and he treated love with a flippancy that is reminiscent of Heine (whose Buch der Lieder he translated in 1929), though he lacks his tragic undertone. A colloquial, even slangy style, a sudden teasing quip at the end, a glittering, summery love of nature, a ready tenderness for children and the unhappy, these are the qualities his admiring public has come to expect. His autobiographical

[14] A selection of Wildenvey's verse appeared as Owls to Athens, tr. by Joseph Auslander (New York, 1935).

prose works have some of the same charm, but are trivial in comparison with his verse. Such collections as *Caresses* (*Kjærtegn,* 1916), *The Orchestra of Fire* (*Ildorkestret,* 1923), and *The Lyre of Autumn* (*Høstens lyre,* 1931), to mention only a few of his many volumes, reveal a true poet, progressively deepening his formal mastery and the seriousness of his themes. Eternity has begun to play a role in his verse, though still on a poetic, rather than a religious basis: "I believe in the human spirit, that it can reach the stars, and that it yearns for the stars." Much of his later poetry suffers from pretentiousness, but now and then we get a glimpse of the old spirit: "I cannot be profound without a merry smile."

Olaf Bull (1883-1933), a son of Jacob B. Bull, may justly be called the Keats of Norway. He was a dreamer, a pure artist, a passionate lover of truth and beauty, a master of concrete imagery, and a matchless workman who patiently wrought into imperishable form the full wealth of a pensive, restless spirit. His first collection, bearing the modest name of *Poems* (*Digte,* 1909), led to his being immediately recognized as a genius. His *Metope* (1927) might be compared to the "Ode to a Grecian Urn" for its classic tone and melancholy contemplation of the fragility of life. It is woven into a vivid setting which preserves in the "young, eternal alabaster of poetry" a mood like that of Keats's "still unravished quietness." His themes were those of all great lyric writers—nature, love, beauty, death, and the poet's self. He sang of the nature of Oslo and its environs, particularly the northern spring in its earliest, most auspicious moments, vivifying every nuance of color and light among the shadows. In love he sought the ideal beauty that is glimpsed but never won, dwelling much on memory, concretely and presently imaged, in which he found the true eternity.

His goal was to experience poetically the entire universe, and he pursued it by delving deeply into history, biology, geology, and other branches of learning, as well as by direct, acute perception of the outer world. This goal required an intense objectification of his experiences, expressed in life by a completely bohemian, asocial existence, in poetry by a constant veiling of the immediacy of experience in allusion, myth, or poetic imagery. He also hid behind a self-ironic humor which could often be utterly charming.

In his last years poems of less esoteric nature, showing a warmer contact with nation and society, came into being, e.g., *The Hundred Years* (*De hundrede aar,* 1928), *Ignis ardens* (1932), but in the midst of this new and fruitful development his life was cut short by illness. Bull is generally named in one breath with Norway's masters of lyric verse, Wergeland, Bjørnson, and Vogt. He lacks their social stature and their urge to action, but he shares their cosmic feeling and daring imagery, and exceeds them in chiseled perfection of form. Some of his most unforgettable poems deal with the laws of fantasy and the poet's difficult art, which he once described as "festively forging parted thoughts together." His sense of form extended beyond rhyme and rhythm into the very sound texture of his lines, which he wove together in a rich but subtle assonance. The aristocratic form of his poetry won him admirers among the fastidious rather than the multitude. It is occasionally overloaded with imagery and allusion to the point of unclarity, but is always imaginative, tender, yet virile in its unflinching view of the world. In form and spirit he has much in common with the French symbolists, especially Paul Valéry, and he has learned from Henri Bergson, but his own singular genius is apparent in every line.

Tore Ørjasæter (1886-) is the lyric poet of the mountains, among which he was born and has lived most of his life. The mountains have some of the same symbolic value to him as they had to Ibsen in *Brand* and other plays. At the same time he is drawn to the sea, which symbolizes harmony to him. This dual attachment reflects his position in the rural community where he was at once inside and outside the group. As the son of a school teacher from western Norway he did not really belong; at the same time he wanted above all to be a part of the farming community in Gudbrandsdal.

His early collections of poetry, *Heritage* (*Ættararv*, 1908) and *In the Valleys* (*I dalom*, 1910), express a passionate attachment to the life of the farm and its traditions. But we also see traces of wanderlust and a streak of religious reflection. He reached his maturity in the poetic trilogy *Gudbrand Langleite* (1913-1927), on which his reputation largely rests. This is a cycle of poems in loosely epic form, which deals with many psychological and cultural problems. He considers the clash of rural and industrial culture, the conflict between the individual and his heritage, the struggle of the artist to be himself in a materialistic culture. The figure of Gudbrand contains much of the poet's own personality, as does the fiddler and peasant artist Falkjom. One senses in these poems the difficulties which Ørjasæter experienced in gaining clarity concerning himself and his poetic form. He emphasizes the power of will in overcoming fate. While he is often unclear, his poetry is conceived in symbols of original beauty and grandeur of thought.

Most of what Ørjasæter has written can be seen in relation to his masterpiece. His views on the sexes are expressed in the collection *Man's Poems* (*Manns kvæde,* 1915), as in the following lines:

> Man must bear woman the way of the Cross
> Through thorns in the darksome wood;
> With shoulders squared to the burden sore,
> He bears his very own blood:
> Bears her suffering step by step,
> And just as a hero should.

A story in prose concerning the poet's own life, *The Traveler* (*Fararen,* 1922), can be regarded as a commentary on the first part of his epic. His plays also deal with the same themes, e.g., the story of the isolated mountaineer *Jo Gjende* (1917) and the "dream play" *Christophoros* (1948), in which the conflict between art and life is resolved with the help of a child. His allegorical cycle of poems *Song of the River* (*Elvesong,* 1932), expresses most beautifully his reconciliation with life in the symbol of a drop of water which is melted out of the ground by the sun and eventually reaches the sea. His later poems carry on this theme of harmony and optimism, even during and after World War II.

The poet Olav Nygard (1884-1924) had a basic kinship with Olaf Bull. His life work remained a torso because he died young, of tuberculosis, and he felt himself that he had never been able to write "my only poem":

> It is unwritten still;
> It found no words;
> It sails on visions
> And dreams in the earth.

He published four collections from 1913 to 1924. In the last of these there are poems that make one think of Wergeland's intense and bitterly beautiful poems written on his deathbed.

Sigrid Undset

SIGRID UNDSET (1882-1949), one of the two or three outstanding authors of the "interwar period," succeeded in reaching far greater international acclaim than most other Norwegian writers. When her early novel *Jenny* appeared, some critics hailed her as another Amalie Skram. Both portrayed the seamy sides of life with characteristic force and directness, but Sigrid Undset lacked almost entirely the attitude of protest which marked Amalie Skram and her predecessor Camilla Collett. Times had changed, but even more important: Sigrid Undset's attitude to sex was entirely different from theirs.

She was born in Kallundborg, Denmark, on May 20, 1882, of a Danish mother and a Norwegian father. Ingvald Undset, her father, had a name of his own as one of the pathfinders in Norwegian archaeological research. He died when she was eleven years old, but had already managed to leave a deep impression on her by his enthusiastic accounts of the historical researches in which he was engaged. She recalled in her delightful autobiography of childhood *Eleven Years* (*Elleve aar*, 1934)[1] how he took her along to the archaeological museum which he directed and let her play with Stone Age axes and figures from the ruins of Troy. At the age of ten he set her to reading the sagas. Her early life was spent amid varied and fascinating impressions of Denmark, Oslo, and Trondheim, in a family with wide intellectual and artistic interests. Her father was a Liberal and sent her to the school supported by Liberals, Ragna Nielsen's School. The teachers were advocates of liberal ideas, and she reports that they seemed to think "that God was a great and all-powerful Liberal who was in favor of coeducation and the pure flag."

The straitened circumstances that resulted from her father's death

[1] Tr. as *The Longest Years* by A. G. Chater (New York, 1935).

forced her to give up plans of becoming a painter and to take an office job
instead. For some ten years she worked in the same office and learned
to know intimately the life and circumstances of the girls who worked
in offices, their trivial and empty existence. In her spare time she studied
literature—English poetry, medieval ballads, German minnesingers, sagas
and legends. The Middle Ages had an attraction for her which was
unusual in her time, and her first attempt at creative composition was a
novel set in the middle of the thirteenth century.

This novel was rather brusquely rejected by the publishers, and she was
advised to try writing about her contemporaries. Strangely enough, she
succeeded in changing over and meeting the taste of her times, putting
aside her medieval interests until later. She wrote a series of novels from
the life she knew best, the middle classes from which she had sprung.
In all of these early novels women are the main characters, and most of
them are cheated out of the happiness they deserve. But Sigrid Undset
did not lay the blame on society, as had the writers of the eighties. She
laid it on the people themselves, making it a matter of individual responsibility. "I have deceived my husband," writes the leading woman in her
first novel; these are the opening words of *Mrs. Marta Oulie* (*Fru Marta
Oulie,* 1907). Many writers of the realistic school would have condoned
her unfaithfulness, but Sigrid Undset irritated a number of ardent
feminists by reasserting the significance of the marriage bond. Mrs. Oulie
writes: "In olden days I used to get angry when I read in books that a
woman was happy only when she became part of another human being.
Now I say yea and amen to this truth, just as I do to all the other outworn
and shabby truths which I rejected in my youth."

Sigrid Undset sympathized with the dreams and the yearnings of
her young women, but she insisted that it was their own fault (and
that of their times) when they were unable to find happiness in the
strife and struggle of everyday life. After the novel *Spring* (*Vaaren,* 1914)
children came to be the solution for more and more of her women. As
Uni puts it in *Images in a Mirror* (*Splinten av troldspeilet,* 1917) :[2] "No
human beings could live without being happy now and then, but we
never think of it when it is there. We grow aware of ourselves only
when we are unhappy. As long as I have my children, I know that I can
bear to live—gladly, no matter how things turn out in other respects."

There is a marked development from book to book, the style becoming
firmer and more personal, and the themes growing one out of the other.

[2] Tr. A. G. Chater (New York, 1938).

Uni in the story *The Happy Age* (*Den lykkelige alder,* 1908) we meet again in Mrs. Hjelde in *Images in a Mirror.* The urban environment of the novels reappears in a small collection of poetry *Youth* (*Ungdom,* 1910), treated in the same tender, understanding mood. She won the greatest attention and awakened considerable discussion by *Jenny* (1911)[3] because of her frank descriptions of erotic experience. It is the great realistic novel of its period, a profound psychological study, written with painful intensity. The story "Simonsen" in *Unhappy Fates* (*Fattige skjæbner,* 1912) is a climax in her realistic descriptions of folk life in Oslo. The novel *Spring* shows a growing concern with problems of morality, while *The Wise Virgins* (*De kloke jomfruer,* 1918) strikes the first religious note. The essays *A Woman's Point of View* (*Et kvindesynspunkt,* 1919) reflect her development over several years, but also point to her later production. They show that she recognizes to the full the struggle for woman's liberation, but refuses to accept the modern slogans. The main thing for her is solidarity, the home, the relation of mother and child. In a postscript she insists that the only possible basis for a deeper solidarity is religious faith.

Sigrid Undset's early stories of modern life portray a whole gallery of women, but most of them are doomed to a mean existence. She felt unable to picture life on a grand scale against the background of her own times. To do this she had to project them back into the past. The conflicts were much the same as in the novels of modern life, but the air was less confining, and the movement of life more vivid and colorful. The sense of moral guilt in her modern novels was derived more from inherited morality and respect for the laws of life, while in her medieval novels she added a dimension of the hereafter. But she did not for a moment relax her insistence on realistic detail. Her amazing scholarship enabled her to introduce realism into the historical novel.

She had never given up the plan she had formed for her first, rejected effort. Her studies of the saga had led to a saga imitation called *Viga-Ljot and Vigdis* (*Viga-Ljot og Vigdis,* 1909),[4] while her reading of medieval romances resulted in a retelling of *Stories About King Arthur and the Knights of the Round Table* (1915). But the medieval novels are most intimately connected with the preceding modern novels. Even though the externals are different, the human problems are, in Sigrid Undset's

[3] Tr. W. Emmé (New York, 1921).
[4] Tr. as *Gunnar's Daughter* by A. G. Chater (New York, 1936).

view, always and everywhere the same: guilt and responsibility, the relation of the individual to others, and of the soul to God.

Kristin Lavransdatter (1920-1922)[5] is one of the masterpieces of Norwegian and world literature. The novel takes place in the first half of the fourteenth century, a period that has not left many written documents, but nevertheless lives on in the architecture and other cultural forms of the valleys. By building on the cultural and linguistic survivals she avoided the air of unreality which usually attaches to modern imitations of saga style. She re-created history by reliving it in her mind. But the chief title of the novel to greatness is its portrayal of character, the author's skill in bringing to life all its figures and situations and making them memorable.

The first volume is the most dramatic of the three. *The Bridal Wreath* (*Kransen*) is the story of Kristin's childhood and youth, her self-willed actions, her sin against her father, and her struggle to win the man she loved. The high point is here the reckoning between Lavrans and his wife Ragnfrid. The second volume, *The Mistress of Husaby* (*Husfrue*), is the somewhat overly detailed account of Kristin's and Erlend's marriage. An unforgettable passage is the story of Kristin's pilgrimage to St. Olaf in the Nidaros cathedral, particularly when she stands on the hill that overlooks the city and sees it wreathed in the rays of the setting sun. *The Cross* (*Korset*) brings the conclusion of the story about Kristin and Erlend and their children, the love battle between the aging parents, Kristin's fears that her growing sons will come to resemble their frivolous but charming father. Wonderfully told is the passage about Kristin's trip to her husband to make up with him. No less moving is the conclusion with its description of Kristin's work as a nun to help the sick and dying during the Black Death.

While Sigrid Undset was working on her next novel, *Olav Audunssøn* (1925-1927),[6] she joined the Catholic church. The religious theme is even more prominent in this novel than in the preceding one. It takes place in the thirteenth century, and is built up around the same themes as *Kristin*—love, marriage, guilt. Its four volumes are overly loaded with details, but there are many passages that equal those of the preceding novel.

During the years that followed she turned back to her own age, speaking now from a definite point of view which she expounded not

[5] Tr. C. Archer and J. S. Scott (3 vols., New York, 1923-1927).
[6] Tr. as *The Master of Hestviken* by A. G. Chater (4 vols., New York, 1928-1930).

only in novels, but also in collections of essays. Some of these were propagandistic, like her *Norwegian Saints (Norske helgener,* 1937),[7] others historical and analytical. One after the other her second series of modern novels analyzed life as she saw it, with the same realistic clarity as before, but now committed to a solution which is carefully but unobtrusively placed before the reader. They bear such names as *Gymnadenia* (1929),[8] *The Burning Bush (Den brændende busk,* 1930),[9] *Ida Elisabeth* (1932),[10] and *The Faithful Wife (Den trofaste hustru,* 1936).[11] All of them are stories of family life, and they give her an opportunity to criticize the feminists, the evolutionary optimists, and the superficialities which she detected in the liberals. She was no more of a puritan than she had been, but she was now primarily concerned about the materialism of her times, for which she wanted to substitute an active faith in God. Since she firmly believed in the depravity of man's nature, she was skeptical of movements that proclaimed man's essential goodness and perfectibility on earth.

In 1939 appeared *Madame Dorthea,*[12] which was planned as the first volume of a historical novel from around 1800. She employed the same technique of intimate narrative here as in her medieval novels. She portrays customs and superstitions, food, architecture, child care, all in such vivid terms that one can see and smell them. Her pictures of childhood in this book belong to her very best efforts. But the occupation of Norway by the Nazis in 1940 caused an interruption in her writing such that she never got back to the story, and it proved to be her last novel.

When the German attack came, Sigrid Undset rallied to the support of her government and worked in its defense until she was forced to flee across the border to Sweden. She has herself told the story of this flight in her book *Return to the Future (Tilbake til fremtiden,* 1942).[13] Her journey did not come to an end until she had crossed Russia and Japan, and sailed across to the United States. She spent the rest of the war years in America, lecturing and writing on behalf of her war-torn country and its government in exile. One result of her stay was the charming book *Happy Times in Norway (Lykkelige dager,* 1942),[14] in which she remi-

[7] Tr. as *Saga of Saints* by E. C. Ramsden (New York, 1934).
[8] Tr. as *The Wild Orchid* by A. G. Chater (New York, 1931).
[9] Tr. A. G. Chater (New York, 1932).
[10] Tr. A. G. Chater (New York, 1933).
[11] Tr. A. G. Chater (New York, 1937).
[12] Tr. A. G. Chater (New York, 1940).
[13] Tr. Henriette C. K. Naeseth (New York, 1942).
[14] Tr. by J. Birkeland (New York, 1942).

nisces about the life she had known in happier days. The cloud that hung over her country gave the book an undertone of deep pathos.

After the appearance of her very first novel, her mother had inscribed a story by the Danish writer Steen Steensen Blicher to her with the words: "May you as an author look to him as your model, be as incorruptibly honest as he, look life fearlessly in the eye, and tell truthfully what you see." No one can question the fearless honesty of Sigrid Undset's writing, which sometimes borders on the oppressive. But she has also a sense of humor, which often enlivens her argumentation, and particularly her descriptions of children. Although her style tends to be severe, it has a lyric quality in many of her descriptive passages. Monumentality is perhaps the word that best characterizes her work. This is revealed not only in the epic proportions of her novels and their powerful climaxes, but also in her nature descriptions. The mountains are used in many of her novels both descriptively and symbolically; in *The Burning Bush* she lets Paul Selmer say: "Toward the mountains we Norwegians all have a religious feeling." On a summer night they are enveloped in the moon's silvery light, and the purling of water in the stillness is like "another life beyond the life of man."[15]

Sigrid Undset was granted the Nobel Prize for literature in 1928.

[15] Other Undset translations are: essays in *Christmas and Twelfth Night,* tr. E. C. Ramsden (New York, 1932, new ed., 1941); *Men, Women, and Places,* tr. A. G. Chater (New York, 1939); *Stages on the Road,* tr. A. G. Chater (New York, 1934); stories in *Sigurd and His Brave Companions* (New York, 1943); *True and Untrue* (New York, 1945).

Olav Duun

A writer of whom it was hoped in many quarters that he also would achieve the Nobel Prize was Olav Duun (1876-1939). While Sigrid Undset had given the Norwegian Middle Ages universal significance by her descriptions, Olav Duun did the same for Norwegian peasant life. He exemplifies some of the best qualities of Norwegian literature, the folk wisdom of Aasen, the skepticism of Vinje and Ibsen, the profundity of Kinck, the humor of Hamsun. To all of these he adds a deep sympathy with his characters, which causes one to experience his world as one in which art and reality, life and ideal are harmonized into a larger whole. His matchless style causes form and contents to fuse so perfectly in his best books that he stands as a remarkable synthesis of the Norwegian folk spirit and the European cultural form.

Olav Duun was born on November 21, 1876, on an island in the Namsen Fjord, where his parents farmed and fished. He himself spent a boyhood and youth like that of other youngsters in the community, herding cattle, fishing, and absorbing the proverbial lore of his ancestors. When he was twenty-five years old, he left to attend the teachers seminary at Levanger. A few years later, after he had started his work as a rural school teacher, he published his first book, a collection of short stories (1907).

Duun wrote a whole series of novels and stories before his masterpiece about the Juvik people. While these have been overshadowed, many of them are interesting even if they are in a minor format. There are lines of thought that lead forward from each of them to his later production. As early as in *Marjane* (1908) we glimpse the type he calls Lauris in his masterpiece, the man of malice and deception, and his counterpart, the Odin type. Among the other books of this period one should mention particularly *Good Conscience* (*Det gode samvitet*, 1916),[1]

[1] Tr. E. Björkman (New York, 1928).

which seems like a preview of the Juvik epic. It deals with the growth
of conscience through three generations.

   The People of Juvik (*Juvikfolke*, 1918-1923)[2] is an epic in six volumes,
a family saga from the life of a Norwegian farming community during
the century of 1814-1918. It was written against the background of a world
war and the years that followed it. The writer does not directly allude
to these events, but it can be sensed that he has sought refuge from
them in a search for national and human roots. His moral program is
expressed by one of the characters, who dreams of becoming a poet:
"I want to picture the people who came stumbling down through the old
days and the darkness and had nothing but the evil powers round about
them. I want to picture the one who wrestled with Satan and won, for
he is the greatest of them all. Yes, who won, so that others could
breathe and laugh as they pleased—that was a great day, which lasted
for centuries perhaps. . . . I want to picture for you the time when
they became aware of one another. And then the time when one or
another of them became aware of himself. And finally you shall get to
see the struggle, the great struggle, when they are all against one and
one against all. The one who loses everything but still wins."

   These half-mystic words refer to the psychological development of
the family pictured in *The People of Juvik,* but they suggest a similar
growth on the part of the whole Norwegian people. The first three
volumes, *The Juvikings* (*Juvikingar*), *The Blind Man* (*I blinda*), and
The Great Wedding (*Storbrylloppe*), tell about the old days, from the
beginnings in the mists of the past and down to the first hints of the new
industrial culture in the 1880's. The old clan of Juvik had consisted of
men who lived vigorously and instinctively, without reflection or regrets.
They were pagans at heart in the midst of a Christian community. The
last of these "wholehearted" characters was old Per Anders in the first
volume. The following generation was slowed down, inhibited by conscience and self-critique until it lost its capacity for action. But then
came Blind-Anders, who lifted himself above his forebears like a wave
after its trough; his wisdom and character are combined with an unquenchable good humor and a simple, straightforward patience. The
leading figure in the last three volumes is Odin Setran, whom we follow
from childhood to death. *In Fairyland* (*I eventyre*) is the story of his
early years, one of the finest descriptions of boyhood in Norwegian
literature. *In Youth* (*I ungdommen*) tells of a trip to Nordland by Odin

---

2 Tr. A. G. Chater (6 vols., New York, 1930-1935).

and his contrast Lauris. The essential theme is Odin's struggle to achieve a philosophy of life, and his gradual coming of age. In the powerful last volume, *In the Storm* (*I stormen*), Odin is the leader in a struggle against the community during the period of industrialization. He unites in his person the old days and the needs of the new age, but only by his death does he succeed in overcoming their opposition. There are many other fine figures in the epic, men as well as women. The whole novel has been well described as "a history of Norwegian character."

The novels and short stories that followed were an interlude leading up to a new major effort, the trilogy about the woman Ragnhild: *Fellow Man* (*Medmenneske*, 1929), *Ragnhild* (1931), and *Last Year* (*Siste leveåre*, 1933). The first of these is a masterly study of evil in the shape of psychopathic quarrelsomeness and a twisted sense of justice. The moral problem underlying it is a question that Odin had raised in *The People of Juvik*: Is it defensible to kill an evil human being in order to save another? Ragnhild is spiritually akin to Odin. She kills her satanic father-in-law Didrik Dale in order to save her husband Håkon from doing it. She acts in a half unconscious feeling that something must be done. But when her husband proves to be unable to bear the burden of this act, she turns herself over to the sheriff. The last two volumes deal with her relationship to her spiritually inferior husband and to the people of the community. The writer shows how the basic forces of good and evil in human character clash, but also co-operate. Here as in other books Duun makes full use of proverbs and other expressions of wisdom. His characters grow vividly out of the nature and the society in which they live.

Duun's later books show a tendency to symbolism and a form that is firmer and more concentrated. In the mid-thirties he expressed a feeling of approaching catastrophe which he projected into the life of a Norwegian community in such a novel as *Contemporaries* (*Samtid*, 1936). The conflict between the people on two sides of the bay, the distortions, the hate, the lies, the agitation—all of this is world history in brilliant concentration. This feeling is even more perceptible in *Mankind and the Powers* (*Menneske og maktene*, 1938), artistically perhaps his most satisfying work. The theme is not unlike Jonas Lie's *When the Iron Curtain Falls*, but it is handled far more intensely. It is a story of a group of people on a little island of which it is prophesied that it will be swallowed up by the sea. One night the sea begins to rise, and we are witnesses to the fears and tensions that spring up, but also to the courage, the will to live, and the unquenchable humor of the inhabitants. Old enemies become friends, repressed instincts are released, and people reveal themselves for what they are. The desire for revenge melts away in the face of death. The central figure is named Helmer, in many ways a spiritual kinsman of Odin and Ragnhild. He is a man with the gift for happiness: "He felt the gray cliffs singing within him, the bunches of seaweed that swayed in the waves, the birds asleep on their rocks, the sea and the infinite around him, the world of clouds above him and the sky above that—all the truth that met his eyes once he awoke and looked." In the end the human values win out over the blind powers.

When Duun died on September 13, 1939, the catastrophe had occurred that he had feared, but also had met with his faith in life. He let Helmer say: "Even if they took the earth from under us, and the heavens from above us, we are men just the same. We will freeze our way through. We ourselves don't know how much we can endure."

New Trends Between the Wars

NORWAY WAS ONE OF THE FEW EUROPEAN NATIONS that escaped the ravages of World War I. But the peace she enjoyed down to 1940 was not a complacent one, at least if we measure it by the reactions of her authors. We have already seen how the shock of world conflict affected the older generation of writers. Knut Hamsun urged a war-torn world to get rid of its lethal gadgets and return to the simplicity of the peasant's life. Gabriel Scott joined him in a plea for the wisdom of simple piety. Hans E. Kinck was stirred to dig more deeply into the sources of national character, and Sigrid Undset turned back to the Middle Ages for a rock on which she might stand. Olav Duun and Johan Falkberget also cast a long backward glance at the inner life of their people, one among the peasants, the other among the miners, and found strength in their enduring qualities. Writers like Johan Bojer, Kristofer Uppdal, and Nini Roll Anker caught in their works some of the sharpened tempo of the new age.

These were the men and women whose writings made the years just after the First World War memorable in Norwegian literature. The epics which they created stand as monuments to the new Norwegian nation which came into being after 1905. But they were rooted in the world that existed before 1914, and they were essentially molded by its thinking.

For in spite of all the cultural and political conflicts of the nineteenth century, Europe down to 1914 was essentially harmonious. Whatever opinions thinking people might have entertained in other matters, the great majority of them were agreed that the world was making rapid progress. Advances were being made in extending national and individual freedom, humanitarian and social ideals. The difference between radicals and conservatives was more a question of pace than of purpose. The

Norwegian prime minister, Gunnar Knudsen, was censured more than once for having declared in February of 1914 that the political skies were "cloudless." But English politicians were saying much the same thing. Only occasional warnings were heard, as when Christen Collin wrote in 1913: "Can we celebrate the centennial of Norwegian peace with a clear conscience?"

Then Europe was thrown into chaos and has never since returned to normal. The great revolution in Russia was followed by revolutions in central Europe with subsequent reactions. Crisis followed crisis. Fascism came into being in Italy and after the crisis of 1930 Nazism made great headway in Germany. These developments gave the lie to the optimistic faith in progress and evolutionary liberalism which had dominated European thinking. The new generation was suddenly thrown into a new world for which their elders had not prepared them, and they often showed their resentment by laying the blame on the older generation. In the half-mocking words of Sigurd Hoel's *Sinners in Summertime*: "You are a self-deceiver, and as such belong to the previous generation!" The young people were gripped by an anxiety that made them seek compensation in frenetic dissipation. Along with a rampant materialism there was a growing faith in intellectual patent medicines. One gospel succeeded the other, from the most extreme individualism to totalitarian collectivism. Religious, moral, social, and economic questions were debated in a cultural atmosphere chiefly remarkable for its hectic tempo.

The consequences of the war were, to be sure, much less prominent in Norway than in the warring nations, which brought forth a literature written by returned soldiers. It is also conspicuous that the artistic reorientation of the postwar period was less radical than in other European countries, even neighboring Denmark and Sweden. German expressionism left its traces in Denmark, but hardly in Norway; Sweden got a great proletarian literature, but not Norway. It may be suspected that the tradition of the golden period in the late nineteenth century inhibited the originality of Norwegian writers during these years.

Yet there was a new generation of writers who in some respects broke decisively with their elders. Those who came to maturity during and immediately after the war, and who were of age with the "lost generation" of European and American literature, felt that the old foundations had given way. They "cleared their desks of every fetish," to adapt a phrase from the poet Arnulf Øverland. They tested the ideals of their youth, and either rejected them or sought to reaffirm them in new ways. Science was here a dominant influence, but the names to be conjured with were no longer Mill and Spencer; they were Freud, Adler, Jung, and Einstein. What the writers lacked in scientific knowledge, they made up for in the fervor of their devotion to popularized ideas which they could understand.

The 1920's was the period of greatest fermentation and discussion, since it was also the period of the most rapid growth of political radicalism in Norway. The stormy development of socialistic or even communistic politics led to a vehement discussion which was reminiscent of the 1880's. The main trend was one of liberation from the prudish rigor and the moral hypocrisy of the Victorian age. Contrary to Freud's own intention, psychoanalytic theory was sometimes used in defense of sexual anarchy. But the same ideas led also to a growing interest in child psychology. While older writers had intuitively been tending in this direction, we find in Sigurd Hoel's *Road to the World's End* a happy combination of psychoanalytic theory and poetic insight. In less talented authors the results of a schematic psychology were not always as convincing.

Another important influence on literary development was the huge increase of the reading public that resulted from the abundance of money and the scarcity of consumer's goods. For the first time translations of foreign literature became a factor of consequence in the Norwegian market. Best sellers from the American and English world made their appearance along with the more valuable products of literature. The dominant trend in literature was realistic, and the German doctrine of "die neue Sachlichkeit" won some support in Norway. Reflections of the erotic primitivism of D. H. Lawrence could also be traced, and in the latter part of the twenties the new, realistic literature of America made its début through the efforts of Sigurd Hoel in his *Yellow Series*.

History and literary criticism were also influenced by the new trends. At the University of Oslo more or less Marxist views were propounded by influential historians like Edvard Bull (1881-1932) and Halvdan Koht (1873-). But alongside them there was a more liberal and humanist vein in the writings of historians like Jacob S. Worm-Müller (1884-1963), Wilhelm Keilhau (1888-1954), and others. The literary periodical *Edda,* founded by Professor Gerhard Gran in 1914, became a central organ for literary research. Gran's objectivity and humane historical outlook also characterized his successor, Francis Bull (1887-). His colleague Fredrik Paasche (1886-1943), with whom he collaborated on a great history of Norwegian literature, interpreted ancient and modern Norwegian literature against its European background. In the critical writing of the period the principal point of view was historical and psychological, though there were also scholars who maintained the necessity of a purely aesthetic analysis. Literary criticism flourished immediately after the war, thirteen collections appearing in 1919-1920. But interest declined in later years, and the 1930's were not notable for their critical activity.

The writers who most clearly exemplified the radicalism of the twenties and whose names came to symbolize the postwar generation were the lyric poet Arnulf Øverland, the novelist Sigurd Hoel, and the dramatist Helge Krog. However different these men might be, they had in common a critical and intellectual spirit that inclined them to social satire and criticism. They constituted a literary triumvirate, or in the opinion of some, a three-headed hydra, which determined the literary climate of the capital.

There was nothing in the earliest verse of Arnulf Øverland (1889-) which gave promise of his later career as iconoclast. Making his début before the war, he seemed like another young Ibsen in the collections entitled *The Lonely Feast* (*Den ensomme fest,* 1911), *The Hundred Violins* (*De hundrede violiner,* 1912), and *Advent* (1915). He wrote of his lonely heart, bitterly crying out against the vanity of all things, devoted to his dreams, which alone seemed to satisfy him. His poems were acclaimed by critics for their fastidious restraint of form, their elimination of all rhetoric, and their truly monumental use of simple, unadorned words. These qualities have remained characteristic of his verse, which is pale in coloration, with a glint of steel, yet passionately moving because of the angry fire in his heart.

The idea of making his poetry into a social weapon, of "forging a sword," as he put it, came to him after the peace of Versailles. He awoke to the existence of social injustice, and it made him cry out in *Bread and Wine* (*Brød og vin,* 1919) that "there are dearer things than life. You shall fight for them!" He turned away from the cultivation of his own soul and plunged into contemporary life as a rather obstreperous battler on the extreme left. The collections *Blue Mountain* (*Berget det blå* 1927), *Laws of Living* (*Hustavler,* 1929), and *I Conjure Thee* (*Jeg besverger dig,* 1934) are not one-sidedly social, for there is love and beauty in them too, but they are dominated by his growing faith in the value of sharing life with one's fellow men. A religious devotion to socialism became a substitute for the Christianity against which he turned all his acid scorn, using repeatedly its own vocabulary and form.

Many of his poems implied for himself a suffering to come, a crucifixion: "This is my body . . . nailed to the tree of passion; eat, ravens!" Prophetic was also his cry in the poem "Departure" of 1934: "Harsh times are coming, when each man bears a sword." He quickly found his leading target in Hitler, and his poems in the thirties were challenges intended to awaken his countrymen to the menace of fascism and Nazism. His poems in *The Red Front* (*Den røde front,* 1937) bore such flaming titles as "Spain 1936," "Guernica," and "You Must Not Sleep!" ("Du må ikke sove!").

When the German horde actually did invade Norway in 1940, his position was therefore clear. He wrote a series of poems which were anonymously and privately circulated; these became in his countrymen's hands the swords he intended them to be. Such poems as "We Shall Live Through All" ("Vi overlever alt"), "They Came as Friends" ("De kom som venner"), "To the Fallen" ("Til de falne"), and "To the King" ("Til Kongen"), established the pattern of Norwegian resistance by virtue of the simple but powerful poetic form in which they couched his demand for national integrity.[1] Øverland paid for his writing of these poems by spending close to four years in a German concentration camp, thus giving substance to his own line of 1929: "Words that cost something may long survive." His liberation came in May 1945, and the Norwegian government expressed the gratitude of the people by giving him the old home of Henrik Wergeland, The Grotto, as his residence.

Sigurd Hoel (1890–1960) is often regarded as the most representative writer of his generation. He was the son of a country school teacher in a valley in eastern Norway. It is therefore the more curious that he came to be one of the most urban among Norwegian writers, one who has written the Dano-Norwegian language with the greatest precision and elegance. He was deflected from his intention of teaching mathematics in 1918 when he won a Scandinavian prize for his short story "The Idiot." Other stories were added to make up the collection *The Road We Walk* (*Veien vi går,* 1922), which gave little indication of the role the author was going to play in Norwegian literary life. Another experiment

[1] Poems by Øverland are included in Charles Wharton Stork, *Anthology of Norwegian Lyrics* (Princeton, 1942) and *20th Century Scandinavian Poetry,* ed. Martin S. Allwood (Mullsjö, Sweden, 1950); "You Must not Sleep" was tr. by Einar Haugen in *The American-Scandinavian Review* (1943), 5.

was the novel *The Seven-Pointed Star* (*Syvstjernen,* 1924), a vigorous social satire on postwar morality. One immediate influence on his thinking during these years was Franz Kafka, but Hoel's next book shows that Sigmund Freud had taken the upper hand. This was the entertaining satire called *Sinners in Summertime* (*Syndere i sommersol,* 1927),[2] which popularized psychoanalytic catchwords and at the same time poked fun at overserious Freudians. It is one of the few gay books written in Norway, though there is also a serious strain in this picture of intellectual youth in the postwar period. Hoel warns youth that while they may scoff at the mustiness of their elders, they are liable to commit exactly the same errors as they.

The theme of self-deception, which he relied on psychoanalysis to untangle, grew to tragic proportions in the novel *One Day in October* (*En dag i oktober,* 1931).[3] The setting is a modern apartment house and the catalytic agent that unites its dwellers in common but hypocritical condemnation is the scandalous behavior of Mrs. Tordis Ravn, a doctor's wife whose love life is frustrated by her husband's devotion to science. In *Fourteen Days Before Autumn* (*Fjorten dager før frostnettene,* 1935) happiness is again the theme, as a successful career man of forty tries to analyze what has gone wrong with his life. Hoel appears to have embraced the doctrine of the Freudians that all our fears and complexes go back to the nursery. In his novel from the German occupation of Norway, *Meeting at the Milestone* (*Møte ved milepelen,* 1947),[4] he even traces the compulsive tyranny of Nazism back to the restrictions of childhood: "The old men lift their trembling forefingers and say: 'Sin and more sin! All that your body and soul want is sin! Remember that you are evil and what you want is evil. Therefore you must restrain yourself!'" The theme of freedom was one of Hoel's most important assertions during the years of growing menace from totalitarianism. He turned with equal vehemence against Nazism and Communism during the thirties, and carried on an active campaign for the Norwegian cause during his World War II exile in Sweden.

Some of Hoel's best and most convincing writing is to be found in his stories of childhood. His masterpiece here is *Road to the World's End* (*Veien til verdens ende,* 1933), a novel that portrays the happiness and frustrations that fill the life of a very small boy. This return to his own

[2] Tr. E. Spriggs and Claude Napier (New York, 1930).
[3] Tr. S. and R. Bateson (New York, 1932).
[4] Tr. E. Ramsden (London, 1951).

rural childhood gave Hoel a chance to release some of the emotional warmth that is only latent in his urban books. Most of his satire is reserved for the city and its banalities, as in the witty picture he gives of the literary circles of Oslo in *Open Sesame* (*Sesam, sesam,* 1938). Hoel himself has played a leading role in these circles through his activities as critic and publisher's reader. We have already mentioned his work on behalf of American and other foreign literatures in his five-foot shelf of great novels entitled *The Yellow Series* (*Den gule serie,* 1929–   ). Writers like Hemingway, Thornton Wilder, Steinbeck, Dos Passos, and Faulkner got their first introduction to Norwegian audiences through Hoel. As critic, novelist, and essayist the outstanding characteristic of Hoel has been his undogmatic and intelligent approach.

Helge Krog (1889–1962) is the *enfant terrible* of Norwegian literature, a charming critic who has regarded it as his task "to upset the public, for only when people are upset, can one hope they may begin to think." His plays stand in a direct line of descent from Ibsen by way of Gunnar Heiberg. His début work was a play entitled *The Great We* (*Det store Vi,* 1919), an entertaining attack on the venality of the press and the capitalistic exploitation of seamstresses by the great department stores. Social themes also filled his serious play *Jarlshus* (1923), but were almost entirely absent in the comedies that followed it. Most of these are witty but penetrating studies of the relation between women and love, or more precisely, the liberation of women as personalities. The first and most purely erotic of these is *The Conch Shell* (*Konkylien,* 1929),[5] the story of a woman who is more in love with love than with men. Krog's worship of woman as pure eroticism is carried on into the plays *On the Way* (*Underveis,* 1931),[6] the story of an unmarried mother, and *Break-up* (*Opbrudd,* 1936),[7] which tells of a woman who breaks out of conventional love in the hope of finding a cause to which she can devote her life.

Krog's plays are often overloaded with epigrammatic dialogue, and he is at his best in his society comedies *On Life's Sunny Side* (*På solsiden,* 1927),[8] *The Carbon Paper* (*Blåpapiret,* 1928),[9] and *Triad* (*Treklang,*

---

[5] Tr. as *Happily Ever After?* by Roy Campbell, in *Three Plays by Helge Krog* (London, 1934); as *The Sounding Shell* by Roy Campbell in *Scandinavian Plays of the Twentieth Century,* Second Series (New York, 1944).
[6] Tr. H. Yourelle (London, 1934), also in *Break-up, and two Other Plays* (London, 1939).
[7] Tr. Margaret Linge (London, 1939).
[8] Tr. C. B. Burchardt (London, 1939), also in *Break-up, and two Other Plays* (London, 1939).
[9] Tr. Roy Campbell in *Three Plays* (London, 1934).

1933).[10] These are unpretentious, but have proved popular on the stage. Even in these one can perceive the rebellious feelings of the author about the conventional good society from which he himself has sprung. His several volumes of critical essays are enjoyable for their keen analysis of contemporary and classical writers. An almost artistocratic sense of form combines in Krog's work with a relentless demand for honesty.

The three writers so far discussed had close contacts with the radical social and political movements of their time, but could hardly be regarded as party hacks. The vigorous intellectual radicalism of the *Mot Dag* group attracted them, but did not hold their interest. *Mot Dag* ("Towards Day-break") was the name of a periodical launched in 1921 by Erling Falk, and also of a band of revolutionary idealists, who were united by the magnetic personality of their leader Falk.

The only truly proletarian writer of the period was the lyric poet Rudolf Nilsen (1901-1929), whose early death cut short a highly promising literary career. As the son of a laborer and himself a resident of the workers' quarters in Oslo, he knew firsthand the problems that faced the proletariat. Much of his poetry (appearing in three collections 1925-1929) was mere agitation, but no one succeeded as he in expressing the mingled love and hate for city streets that filled the lives of its less privileged citizens. We sense in his poems a passionate longing for a world without poverty and inequality.

The social critics were carrying on the tradition of the 1880's, though often along new lines and with different accents. But there were also writers who carried on the traditions of the 1890's in mystic, romantic, or nationalistic writings.

The novelist who most distinctly joined issue with the social critics on behalf of traditional values was Ronald Fangen (1895-1946). He formed a kind of conservative counterpart to Sigurd Hoel, but lacked the latter's spirited style and his ability to concentrate action into entertaining plots. He made an early début with the novel *The Weak* (*De svake*, 1915), tried his hand at dramatic writing, and partook actively in the literary life of the capital. His first significant novel was *Some Young People* (*Nogen unge mennesker*, 1929), which like Sigurd Hoel's novel *Nothing* of the same year gave a vivid picture of the unsatisfied longings of youth. Both of these stories reflect prewar rather than postwar conditions, but in the novel *Erik* (1931) he turned his searchlight on the period of wartime profiteering. It is characteristic of Fangen, however,

[10] Tr. Roy Campbell in *Three Plays* (London, 1934).

that the problems discussed are not social but personal. The same is true of *Duel, A Woman's Way,* and *The Man Who Loved Justice,* which are his best novels.

Duel (1932)[11] is the story of a friendship between two men, the one a harmonious, successful personality, the other split and dissatisfied. Their friendship turns into a hidden rivalry, as suggested by the title of the book. *A Woman's Way* (*En kvinnes vei,* 1933) is another study of individual psychology, this time of a woman whose ability to give herself wholly in love has been destroyed by a loveless childhood. *The Man Who Loved Justice* (*Mannen som elsket rettferdigheten,* 1934) is projected back into an eighteenth-century German environment, but it, too, deals with the problem of self-understanding. A man whose ruling passion is justice becomes himself the victim of injustice and has to go through many sufferings before he realizes that he has been egotistical and has only himself to blame for the injustices he has suffered. The self-examination to which Fangen's characters are subjected is of a Christian nature, but Fangen did not publicly adhere to a religious philosophy until 1934 when he announced his membership in the Buchmanite group, the so-called Oxford Group movement.

Although this appears to have been conducive to his own personal happiness, it did not enable him to produce more convincing literary products. As in the case of Sigrid Undset's conversion to Catholicism a few years before, it led to a number of novels in which the element of sermonizing took the upper hand. Dialogue turned into long conversations on religious themes, so arranged as to present the author's ideas in rather barefaced form. Fangen's religiosity was not pietistic or otherworldly. He showed by his vigorous attacks on the puritans in the Norwegian church, as well as on the totalitarian trends of his times, that he was essentially a religious liberal who believed that religion should lead to humane goals. The clearest expression of this idea is found in his novel *An Angel of Light* (*En lysets engel,* 1945),[12] which attempts to analyze Nazism as an idealism that has gone wrong. The religion in this novel is a social gospel, a fighting faith which takes up the struggle against evil in this world.

Another novelist whose emphasis on traditional values and psychological individualism placed him outside the stream of social criticism was Sigurd Christiansen (1891-1947). His environment both personal

11 Tr. Paula Wiking (New York, 1934).
12 Tr. as *Both are My Cousins* (London, 1949).

and aesthetic, was that of the provincial town, with its petit-bourgeois life. He won the attention of the general public by a prize-winning but superficial novel *Two Living and One Dead* (*To levende og en død,* 1931),[13] the story of a post-office robbery which made a hero of a coward and darkened the life of the real hero. Most of his novels are serious, and rather lengthy, analyses of psychological problems, particularly the problem of guilt and atonement. Christiansen owes much to Ibsen, whose idea of "being oneself" had a deep influence on his writing; but his attempts to follow in the master's footsteps as a dramatist were not successful, aside from the play *A Journey in the Night* (*En reise i natten,* 1931), the most Ibsenian of modern Norwegian plays.

His first major novel was the trilogy about the carpenter and manual-arts teacher Lauritsen and his family, bearing the titles *The Entrance* (*Indgangen,* 1925), *The Swords* (*Sverdene,* 1927), and *The Kingdom* (*Riket,* 1929). Lauritsen is a quiet, humble craftsman, whose life is filled with religious conviction. The novels tell the story of how he brings up his three sons and how their father's example gradually leads them back from pride to self-understanding. The artist Helge returns from the sophisticated environment of the city to his small-town background and discovers anew the values of religion. *Chaff in the Storm* (*Agner i stormen,* 1933)[14] and *The Man in the Gasoline Station* (*Mannen fra bensinstasjonen,* 1941) deal with similar themes, but the real masterpiece of his writing was the trilogy which began with *Dream and Life* (*Drømmen og livet,* 1935) and carried on into *The Lonely Heart* (*Det ensomme hjerte,* 1938) and *Man's Lot* (*Menneskenes lodd,* 1945). This trilogy is the story of Jørgen Wendt, a boy whose development is analyzed against a broad canvas of his life and times. It is a moving picture of the awakening to self-consciousness of an artist and the many difficulties which his devotion to the "inner world" causes in his relation to himself and others. In the end he is driven into greater participation in life and gains an understanding of people which enables him to create his first work of art. In clarifying to himself what he wants to create, he says he would like it to be "a novel, a drama, a poem about the innermost, sacred reserves of mankind—about the hidden resources which well up in the hour of distress, even in the weak, and give them the capacity of overcoming life, so that it can be lived in spite of everything."

The hidden resources of man play a great part also in the writings of

---

[13] Tr. E. Björkman (New York, 1932).
[14] Tr. as *Chaff Before the Wind* by Isaac Anderson (New York, 1934).

Tarjei Vesaas (1897–). This novelist and short-story writer of Telemark has departed from the accepted realistic pattern by introducing symbolism and allegory in many of his books. Although his characters are rural, their problems are universally human. He is widely regarded as the heir of Olav Duun in his interpretations of the Norwegian psyche. There is a subdued quality in his books, a restrained accent which permits one to eavesdrop on subtle movements of the soul. Vesaas is a good listener, and one has the impression that sound plays a great part in his books. In his novel of the German occupation, *House in Darkness* (*Huset i mørkret,* 1945), he has embodied Norway in the image of a house surrounded by an ominous, stormy darkness. The storm causes the house to creak and groan, but does not succeed in destroying it, in spite of the forebodings of its denizens. They do become highly sensitive to the noises caused by forces they cannot see. Their main problem, however, is to avoid being seduced by the dangerous bright arrows which point inward to the middle of the house, where dwell the forces that have brought on the darkness. The studied understatements of this book become highly effective against the background of terrorism and heroic resistance that brought it into being, but it may be questioned whether the book is comprehensible without this background.

Even in his earlier books, which awakened much less attention than *House in Darkness,* Vesaas combined this awareness of danger in the air with a quiet confidence in the existence of protecting powers, expressed in the smile of a child or a woman, or a message from the world of animals. A tetralogy written in 1930-1938 is centered around the figure of Klas Dyregodt and is the story of a man who is on the verge of being destroyed by loneliness and fear of life, but is saved by the quiet words of one who restores his confidence in himself. Here, too, there is a structure that trembles, in this case a dam, and nothing less than a human sacrifice is required to close the crack that threatens destruction to many. The symbolic struggle between fear and faith is one that recurs frequently in Vesaas's writing. In his two novels about Per Bufast, entitled *The Great Game* (*Det store spelet,* 1934) and *Women Call Home* (*Kvinnor ropar heim,* 1935), the forces of good have the upper hand. They deal with man and earth in the rhythmic play of seasons on a Norwegian farm and are a worthy counterpart to *Growth of the Soil.* These books are also notable for their portrayal of children.

Vesaas began reflecting on the events of his times in the novel *Germination* (*Kimen,* 1940), a picture of the force which mass suggestion could exert in whipping up hate. But the thesis of the book, symbolically expressed, is that it is man's duty to resist barbarism in all its forms. When liberation from barbarism finally came to Norway, *House in Darkness* was the first novel to express the feelings of the people. He followed up his success by other symbolic novels, *The Bleaching Place* (*Bleikeplassen,* 1946), *The Tower* (*Taarnet,* 1948), and *The Signal* (*Signalet,* 1950). The first of these is the best. It pictures a man in agonized conflict with himself and his feeling of inferiority; life becomes unbearable to him because no one loves him. Vesaas has also tried his hand at poetry and drama, but is most highly regarded for his prose style. It is monumentally simple, and yet subtly suggestive. His collection of short stories *The Winds* (*Vindane,* 1952) won an international prize at Venice.

It will not be possible here to discuss in detail the rich harvest of writers who have come out of the valleys during this generation, many of whom have been stimulated by the folk high school movement. Most of them have made their contribution as purveyors of local color; few have transcended the local point of view either in outlook or in literary skill. Their use of dialectally colored idioms and the New Norse language has tapped the vigorous sources of folk life, but has often hampered the writers from reaching an urban or international audience. Head and shoulders above the rest stands a novelist like Inge Krokann (1893–), whose historical cycle from early modern times in the valley of Oppdal has been compared to Sigrid Undset's *Kristin Lavransdatter.* The central character in this family saga might also be said to be the Dovre mountain range itself, which affects the lives of the characters in a multitude of ways. Its stubbornly defiant peaks are symbolic of the countrymen's resistance to foreign domination during the Danish period. This is especially apparent in the last volume of the tetralogy, *Under the Omen* (*Under himmelteiknet,* 1941), which was much read during the occupation.

Krokann and the other writers of rural and conservative background have found much of their inspiration in the poems of Olav Aukrust (1883–1929), who is universally acclaimed as the greatest modern poet in the New Norse tongue. If we should compare him to Øverland, we would have a measure of the contrast between urban and rural cultural traditions in Norway. Øverland is crystal-clear, while Aukrust is mystical and involved. Øverland is sparing in his imagery, and his words often have a restrained quality, occasionally ironic and scornful. Aukrust favors vigorous words and bold images. Øverland's manner is academic, while

Aukrust's is marked by the folk high school, and often includes a distaste for urban life. His models are to be found in the poetry of medieval Norway and in the ballads, especially *The Dream Ballad,* but also in Wergeland and the youthful Bjørnson. He is a dualist with ecstatic visions of heaven and hell.

Aukrust's masterpiece was the cycle of poems *Cairn of Heaven* (*Himmelvarden,* 1916), an imaginative and visionary description of a human soul battling against forces of evil and gaining at last its victory with the aid of divine light. Aukrust's concern with the inmost quality of national feeling was intimately tied up with his experience of the nature and folk of his native valley of Gudbrandsdal. Its high peaks symbolized the aspirations of man toward the heights, and its people seemed to him the foundation of Norwegian nationality. He had planned a series of works tying local patriotism together with nationality and building further into the universally human, but he never succeeded in writing more than fragments of this series. His originality is unquestionable, and his poems show many glimpses of humor, while primarily concerned with problems that can hardly be expressed except in poetic terms. His combination of visionary power and fragmentary but highly lyric form is occasionally reminiscent of Wergeland.

Another writer with close attachment to folk tradition and mystical interpretation of national psychology is Ingeborg Refling Hagen (1895-), lyric poet, short-story writer, and novelist. In her best writing there is a powerful current of love for the common folk of the Hedmark district where she was born, and a passionate feeling for the great forest and its mysteries. Her development led her from the creation of eerie moods and crass realism through fairy tale themes to an imaginative reconstruction of Norwegian folk life. In her case, however, the cultural conservatism was combined with political radicalism, though of a motherly kind, which aimed at the creation of a better life for the poverty-stricken people whom she knew so well. Among the high points in her voluminous writing may be named the poems in *I Want to Go Home (Jeg vil hem att,* 1932), and the novel-trilogy *Three Days in the Great Woods (Tre døgn på storskogen,* 1937-1939). In these her combination of the fantastic and the realistic, her kind heart and concern over current causes as well as her religio-mystical outlook find their finest expression. Her immediate master is Hans E. Kinck, but she regards Wergeland as the great model of her writing.

A writer strongly influenced by the folk high school is Olav Sletto

(1886-), whose novels, essays, short stories, and plays have been appearing since 1901. His most notable work is the novel in five volumes called *The People of Røgnald* (*Røgnaldsfolket*, 1943-1950), which describes the folk culture in monumental terms, and its meeting with the urban culture of the twentieth century. Among the numerous minor writers one might mention Ola Setrom (1895-1946), poet and novelist of Oppdal. There is the writer of animal stories from Valdres, Mikkjel Fønhus (1894-),[15] and the describer of farm women from Hardanger, Gro Holm (1878-1939). There is the fantastic Hans-Henrik Holm (1896-), whose voluminous poetry from the Setesdal valley, especially his *St. John's Night* (*Jonsoknatt*, 1933), is acclaimed by some, but sharply denounced by others. There are the superficial but entertaining writers of popular novels from the valleys, Olav Gullvåg (1885-) and the highly inferior Trygve Gulbranssen (1894-).[16]

The social critics and the national mystics do not by any means exhaust the possibilities of Norwegian literature in this generation. Among those who cannot be labeled as belonging either in one camp or the other are such writers as Cora Sandel, O. E. Rølvaag, Magnhild Haalke, and Aksel Sandemose. While each one has his special physiognomy, they have in common an interest in telling stories.

Cora Sandel (pseudonym of Sara Fabricius, 1880-) tells the story of a woman's human and artistic development in her trilogy *Alberte and Jacob* (*Alberte og Jacob*, 1926), *Alberte and Freedom* (*Alberte og friheten*, 1931), and *Just Alberte* (*Bare Alberte*, 1939). This intimate and unrelentingly honest picture shows her unusual feeling for milieu and details, her delicate style and psychological insight. Her novel *Krane's Sweetshop* (*Kranes Konditori*, 1945) is more concentrated and therefore more intense; it was also turned into a successful play by Helge Krog. She has published several collections of short stories and a charming book entitled *Animals I Have Known* (*Dyr jeg har kjent*, 1945). She fits well into the tradition of intense, realistic woman authors in Norway—Camilla Collett, Amalie Skram, Sigrid Undset.

Although Ole E. Rølvaag (1876-1931) was an American, the books that made him world famous were written in Norwegian and first published in Norway. Born in Helgeland, Norway, of a fisherman's family, he emigrated at the age of twenty; ten years later he became professor of

---

[15] *The Trail of the Elk*, tr. S. H. Weedon (New York, 1923); *Jaampa, the Silver Fox* (New York, 1931); *Northern Lights*, tr. E. Jayne (New York, 1931).
[16] *Beyond Sing the Woods* (New York, 1936), *The Wind from the Mountains* (New York, 1937), tr. Naomi Walford.

Norwegian at St. Olaf College. His first published novel was *America Letters* (*Amerikabreve,* 1912), but he was not widely known until 1924, when *In Those Days* (*I de dage—*) appeared, followed by *The Founding of the Kingdom* (*Riket grundlægges,* 1925). When these were translated together under the title of *Giants in the Earth* (1927),[17] the novel was recognized by American critics as the most powerful epic yet written about the immigrant pioneer. While it is a story of heroism, it is also a story of the cost of emigration; the former is embodied in Per Hansa, the latter even more compellingly in his wife Beret. Rølvaag's storytelling is in the tradition of Bjørnson, Jonas Lie, and Knut Hamsun, rather than of American models. The sequels *Peder Victorious* (1928)[18] and *Oh Blessed Day* (1931)[19] carried on the story of the immigrants, but with less fire.

Magnhild Haalke (1885–) was a fifty-year-old school teacher when she published her first novel, *Alli's Son* (*Allis sønn,* 1935).[20] This is the story of a boy who was different from other children, more imaginative and sensitive than they, but with a tragic end because his mother was unable to understand him, frightened by his oddness. She, too, wrote her trilogy of woman's fate in a narrow and perverse environment, the novels *The Yoke* (*Åkfestet,* 1936), *Twinkle of Day* (*Dagblinket,* 1936), and *Red Fall?* (*Rød haust?* 1941). But this woman does not rebel, like Cora Sandel's Alberte; she is patient to the point of being left with no life of her own. The stories *Karenanna Velde* (1946) and *Kaja Augusta* (1947) have greater breadth than the earlier novels. Like most of her writing they deal with the problem of bringing up children and of finding a place for oneself in life even when circumstances are petty and adverse.

A much more glittering but also more uneven author is Aksel Sandemose (1899–), born in Denmark of a Norwegian mother. He decided to become Norwegian in 1930, after he had begun his career in Denmark. His first novels, *A Sailor Disembarks* (*En sjømann går iland,* 1931) and *A Fugitive Crosses His Tracks* (*En flyktning krysser sitt spor,* 1933),[21] are the story of Espen Arnakke, a young sailor who has committed a murder in Newfoundland. The theme is the repression that society exerts

---

[17] Tr. Lincoln Colcord (New York, 1927).
[18] Tr. Nora O. Solum (New York, 1929).
[19] Tr. as *Their Father's God* by T. M. Ager (New York, 1931). Other translations of Rølvaag books are *Boat of Longing* (1921, tr. 1933 by Nora O. Solum); *Pure Gold* (1920, tr. 1930 by S. Erdahl).
[20] Tr. A. G. Chater (New York, 1937).
[21] Tr. E. Gay-Tifft (New York, 1936).

on the individual and the crime and tyranny which result. All those who have been made unfree have an urge to subdue others because they will not endure that anyone shall be different. Later novels are drawn from life at sea, such as *The Klabauter Man* (*Klabautermannen*, 1932) and *Horns for our Adornment* (*Vi pynter oss med horn*, 1936)[22]; their outspoken reporting of seamen's life and language was shocking to some readers. Sandemose has a remarkable capacity for saying startling things and cutting through the usual paths of thought and conventional ideas. He alternates between sarcasm and melancholy, tosses out the most baroque ideas, but sometimes he also lands in banalities while attempting to perform somersaults. Sandemose published a novel while he was an exile in Sweden, *The Past is a Dream* (*Det svundne er en drøm*, 1944, Oslo 1946), picturing the events of the German invasion of 1940. His experimental, chaotic technique, and his bizarre, Strindbergian temperament have made him a much discussed author, on whom general agreement has not been reached.

There are many other writers who have turned out valuable books, too many to mention. One would like to speak in more detail about Arthur Omre (1887–), whose studies in the psychology of criminals are outstanding.[23] There is the delicate but strangely mystic author Ernst Orvil (1898–), and the aristocratic, almost classic novelist Johannes Thrap-Meyer (1898-1929). Masters of style like Gunnar Larsen (1900–) and Johan Borgen (1902–) have written stories and novels of urban life. There are poets like Gunnar Reiss-Andersen (1896–), Jacob Sande (1906–), and Louis Kvalstad (1905-1952) whose verses bid fair to enter into the corpus of Norwegian literature. Novelists like Bjørn Rongen (1906–) and Nils Johan Rud (1908–) express problems of the times, combining the social with the psychological view.

But of all the writers who streamed into Norwegian literature between the wars, none was more typical of the age than Nordahl Grieg (1902-1943). In his indomitably lyric soul we meet the faith and the desperation of the times, their hopes and their doubts. He was a town patriot from the city of Bergen, but also a citizen of the world. He was an enthusiastic Norwegian nationalist, but also globetrotter and an adherent of Stalinist Marxism. He was vital and aggressive, whether he was fighting for pacifism or for Norwegian independence. His tragic death in an Allied plane over Berlin on December 2, 1943, has given him a halo which his

[22] Tr. E. Gay-Tifft (New York, 1938).
[23] *Flukten*, tr. as *Flight* by S. and R. Bateson (New York, 1940).

literary efforts hardly warrant. But he was a great lyric poet, who created some of the finest poems of modern Norwegian literature, and a dramatist who brought an original turn to the Norwegian drama. In all his work he was a courageous, noble-minded personality. He was a lyricist above all, the poet of the grand emotions, the eternal youth.

His first collection of verse, *Round the Cape of Good Hope* (*Rundt Kap det gode Haab,* 1922), resulted from a year at sea interspersed among his studies. It is romantic, both in its view of the sea and in its strongly expressed sympathy with the sailors. The novel that followed, *The Ship Sails On* (*Skibet gaar videre,* 1924),[24] was so realistic in its picture of the sailor's life in foreign harbors that many were offended, even though its purpose had been to call attention to the need for improving the sailor's lot. At the same time Grieg had his eyes opened to the "tragedy of the chief," "the immense loneliness he must wrap himself in if he is to rule over all." Grieg was something of a hero worshiper, and fell under the spell of Rudyard Kipling's poetry during a year of study at Oxford. He admired the wholehearted, unabashed patriotism of Kipling, on whom he wrote a thesis, and resolved to express some of the same enthusiasm for Norway in his own poems. A new collection, *Stones in the Stream* (*Stene i strømmen,* 1925), appeared at the same time as he took his advanced degree at the University of Oslo. But the patriotic note did not come fully into its own before his great collection *Norway in Our Hearts* (*Norge i vore hjerter,* 1929). These poems are often verbose and pompous, but at their best they are matchless expressions of national feeling. He pays homage to nature and the people, to the postman and the pastor who cross the mountains on their rounds of duty, to the sailor and the fisherman and all who contribute to the welfare of their nation.

In the meanwhile he had embarked on a journalistic career, and actively sought the stages of great world events. He went to the Far East as foreign correspondent and wrote up his experiences in the Chinese civil war in *Chinese Days* (*Kinesiske dager,* 1927). He also wrote plays that were suggested to him by the dramatic developments of the age and that posed the problems to which he returned again and again in his later writing. In *A Young Man's Love* (*En ung manns kjærlighet,* 1927) he asked the question: Goodness or brutality? In *Barabbas* (1927) it was Jesus versus Barabbas, pacifism or force, the cross or the sword. He was deeply concerned about finding an answer to the question: Can anything good be created through the use of evil means? A third play,

[24] Tr. A. G. Chater (New York, 1927).

The Atlantic (*Atlanterhavet,* 1932), a satire on the effects of publicity, was less successful. A volume of critical essays on English poets, *The Young Dead* (*De unge døde,* 1932), brought this period of his life to an end. With a premonitory concern he probed the lives and poetry of Keats, Shelley, Byron, and three poets of World War I, Brooke, Sorley, and Owen.

From England he now turned to Russia, where he spent the years 1932-1934 and found the optimism and faith in the future which he had missed in the western democracies. He adopted the techniques of the Russian theater and produced one of his most successful plays *Our Power and Our Glory* (*Vår ære og vår makt,* 1935). The title comes from a poem of Bjørnson's in honor of the Norwegian merchant fleet, but the theme is a violent attack on the owners of that fleet for their disregard of human lives during World War I and their scramble for profits. The proletarian theme is carried on into the play *But Tomorrow—* (*Men imorgen—,* 1936) and *The Defeat* (*Nederlaget,* 1937),[25] both of which are attacks on the pacifistic humanism of the western world. Grieg's intense sympathy with the Republican government of Spain during the Spanish civil war inspired *The Defeat,* which deals with the Paris Commune of 1870 and is generally held to be his best play. His enthusiasm for Soviet Russia even survived the Moscow trials and the Trotsky episode, as we see from his novel *But Young the World Must Be* (*Ung må verden ennu være,* 1938), in which there are scenes from England, Russia, Spain, and Norway. While other Norwegian radicals had recoiled over the Moscow trials, Grieg attempted to justify them and even gave a psychological explanation of the confessions made. It is a fascinating book, enthusiastic, but loosely composed and hardly convincing.

The German invasion of Norway found Grieg in uniform, protecting Norwegian neutrality in Finnmark. He happened to be on leave in Oslo and immediately joined the Norwegian forces that rallied to defend the country. He accompanied the Norwegian government on its disastrous retreat through Norway and then over to England. While actively on duty as an officer of the armed forces, he used his literary talents in the service of his country. His poems and his radio speeches reached the Norwegian people and heartened them in their distress. His war poems included "May 17, 1940," "Good Year for Norway" ("Godt år for Norge"), "The King" ("Kongen"), and many others.[26] In these poems the primary

25 Tr. in *Scandinavian Plays of the Twentieth Century,* Second Series (New York, 1944).
26 Poems by Grieg are included in Charles Wharton Stork, *Anthology of Norwegian Lyrics* (Princeton, 1942) and *20th Century Scandinavian Poetry,* ed. Martin Allwood (Mullsjö, Sweden, 1950).

theme is a warmhearted love for Norway which harks back to his earlier period, but now with an emphasis on the humanistic values her civilization represented. It is clear that in spite of the support Grieg gave to the use of force on behalf of good, he remained at heart the pacifist he had always been. In his poem "The Nature of Man" ("Den menneskelige natur"), he insisted that war was not a goal, not even a permanent part of human nature. Typical of the kinship between himself and older poets like Wergeland and Bjørnson are these lines from his first war poem:

> Slowly the land we conquered
> With oar and axe and hoe,
> And toil made it sweet to live in
> And tender for life to grow.
> We followed not the new fashion,
> On peace we founded our state,
> So those whose deeds are destruction
> May treat us with scorn and hate.

Translated by C. W. Stork[27]

[27] Other writers from this period, not discussed above, are: Sven Elvestad (1884-1934), *Man who Plundered a City,* tr. F. H. Martens (New York, 1924); G. af Geijerstam (1888-   ) *Northern Summer* (New York, 1937), *Storevik* (New York, 1938), *Iva* (New York, 1939), *Northern Winter* (New York, 1940), all tr. by Joran Birkeland; Marie Hamsun (1881-   ), *A Norwegian Farm* (London, 1933), *A Norwegian Family* (London, 1934), both tr. by M. C. Darnton; Andreas Haukland (1873-1933), *The Norns are Spinning,* tr. by B. Ten Eyck (New York, 1928); Haakon Lie (1884-   ), *Ekorn,* tr. C. Hultgren (New York, 1931).

The Occupation and After

THE GERMAN INVASION of April 9, 1940, fell upon a nation that was militarily and spiritually unprepared for war. The warnings of an Arnulf Øverland or a Nordahl Grieg that "you must not sleep" had gone comparatively unnoticed. Many of those who favored rearmament were lukewarm toward the Nazi menace, while those who had most to lose by German aggression were often pacifists who wished to keep armaments at a minimum. When the war broke out in Poland and swiftly drew a large part of the world into its vortex, Norwegian leaders hoped that their luck would hold through another world war, as it had in the first. Their hopes proved false, and they were put to the awful test of a war they had not asked for and a five-year occupation which they abhorred. The armed resistance they were able to put up in 1940 was a token of what they would have done if their military might had been greater. When the war in Norway was over in the summer of 1940, they could take comfort in the record of their swiftly rallied divisions and of their heroic king and government, first in the Norwegian campaign and later in London as exiles. But the first effect was one of paralyzing the literary productivity of the Norwegian people.

The first to rally, as we have seen, were lyric poets like Nordahl Grieg, who accompanied the government to London, and Arnulf Øverland, whose secretly circulated poems soon landed him in a German concentration camp. Sigrid Undset issued appeals for resistance to counter the discordant note of Knut Hamsun's calls for acceptance of German rule. Like some of the population, some of the writers fled to Sweden while others stayed and took part in the growing resistance movement. The attempts of the Nazis to clamp totalitarian controls on the cultural life succeeded only in driving the writers underground. Regulations were met by strikes and sabotage; subtle means were found to express opposition even in those books that were innocent enough in appearance to pass the increasingly severe censorship.

None of the books published in Norway during the Occupation can be reckoned as significant in the history of Norwegian literature. The people turned to the classics, and read them now as never before. The flowering of Norwegian literature in the nineteenth century had given them a treasure on which they could draw in adversity. The values proclaimed in this literature had become a force in the minds of the people and helped to stimulate the will to national survival. It created a counterforce to barbarism by keeping alive ideals of humanity, democracy, and justice. Behind the blackout curtains were read Wergeland, Bjørnson, Aasen, Garborg, Sivle, Collett Vogt, Fridtjof Nansen, not to speak of Ibsen's *Brand* and *Pretenders* with their heroic reminders. Many modern writers were banned from the bookshops and the libraries, but the classics remained, and they took part in the struggle just as surely as the living writers.

Not until liberation came and books could again be printed and circulated freely did much of the literature become known that had been written during the Occupation. The year 1945 was like a bursting dam, when a flood of books poured out, nearly all of them occasioned by the war itself and its innumerable tragedies. Many of these were straightforward accounts of military events, underground experiences, concentration camp memoirs, defenses and attacks, few of which have any title to literary merit. But a real literary harvest also began appearing in this year.

There were posthumous collections of Nordahl Grieg's poetry, *Freedom* (*Friheten,* 1945) and *Hope* (*Håbet,* 1946). Other collections appeared by Arnulf Øverland, Gunnar Reiss-Andersen, Tore Ørjasæter, Inger Hagerup, and many others. One can say of a good share of these poems, as Øverland did of his own war poems, that "they have done their deed." But one's chief impression of these poets is that they turn their gaze forward to the future. They express a hope for better times and a love of country which occasionally reaches the sublime, as in Øverland's lines in the poem "Back to Life":

> Strange it is to feel—
> This salty grayish strand,
> These sheepdowns bare and cropped
> Are now a sacred land.

No less moving than the poetry are some of the accounts from prison camps and underground. The outstanding example is the monumental *From Day to Day (Fra dag til dag,* 3 volumes, 1946)[1] by Odd Nansen, a son of Fridtjof Nansen. This extract from the writer's secret diary written in various camps in Norway and Germany reflects the noblest humanity face to face with the most repulsive evil. It is written with a compelling style. A counterpart to the depiction of mass fates is *Petter Moen's Diary (Petter Moens dagbok,* 1949),[2] a human document of the highest quality. Young Moen was the editor of an underground newspaper, *London News,* until the end of 1943 and was then head of all the "illegal" newspapers in Norway until he was arrested; he died on the way to a German camp. In his book, which was mostly written in solitary confinement, we learn to know the scrupulously honest individual in a situation of terror, his pangs of conscience and his quiet heroism.

Among novels dealing with the war a high rank is held by Sigurd Evensmo's *Travelers to England (Englandsfarere,* 1946),[3] which achieves a great human insight in spite of its half documentary character. Evensmo views the struggle in Norway as a phase of the larger struggle of mankind for freedom from tyranny. Others emphasize the conflict within the individuals who took part in the war, their struggle with the psychological effects of Nazism, with the problem of hate and love, and with the adjustments that followed the war. As Inge Krokann put it in his novel *Out of the Shadow (Ut av skuggen,* 1949): "It seems that when the war is over on the general front, it goes on as a duel within the individual." We have already seen how Vesaas symbolized the Occupation as a darkness that settled on the country so that it became difficult to see what was right and what was wrong. We have also mentioned Hoel's explanation of Nazi tendencies as due to an authoritarian education, while Fangen attributed them to a lack of true religion. Younger writers take up the same problem in novels like *The Circle Round the Well (Ringen rundt brønnen,* 1946) by Odd Bang-Hansen (1908–), *To the Bold (Til de dristige,* 1946) and *Walter the Peaceful (Walter den fredsommelige,* 1947) by Finn Havrevold (1905–), and the experimental novel *The Great Crossroads (Det store veiskillet,* 1949) by Kåre Holt (1917–). In the latter the same person is pictured in three alternative stories as coward, villain, and hero. Even in novels that do not directly refer to the war,

[1] Tr. Katherine John (New York, 1949).
[2] Tr. B. Kofoed (New York, 1951); also by K. Austin-Lund (London, 1951).
[3] Tr. as *Boat for England* by S. and R. Bateson (London, 1947).

like Falkberget's *Bread of Night* and Sigurd Christiansen's *Man's Lot,* one can feel its presence in the background.

It will be noticed that most of the names mentioned so far are those of authors who were well established when the war broke out. The war did not bring out any new talent, aside from a very few like the lyric poet Inger Hagerup or the novelist Sigurd Evensmo, and did not change any reputations, except that it made novelists like Tarjei Vesaas and Inge Krokann better known. It made Nordahl Grieg a hero and Knut Hamsun a villain, on human rather than literary grounds. But the question that now presses for an answer is whether we can speak of a new literary epoch during and after the war.

There is no doubt that a great many new names have appeared in the literary world during the years since the outbreak of the war. But it is impossible at this stage to predict whether they are going to continue the traditions of their forerunners or break new paths. So far there has been little sign of any revolutionary developments. The tradition from the nineteenth century is still strong, and the experimentation with new forms which has been so characteristic of Swedish poetry in recent years has not been transplanted to Norway.

Even so, lyric poetry has been the field in which one can feel most clearly the pulse of the age. The anxieties and unrest of the postwar years are expressed by the poets in the form of struggles to overcome their pessimism, their disillusionments, their apocalyptic mood. They are seeking for a new basis on which to live their lives. This is especially noteworthy in one of the finest lyric writers, Halldis Moren Vesaas (1907–), in her collections *Speech of a Dark Age* (*Tung tids tale,* 1945) and *The Tree* (*Treet,* 1947). There is brooding on the problems of the times in the young Jan-Magnus Bruheim's (1914–) *Surface and Depths* (*Yta og djupe,* 1945) and *On The Scales* (*På skålvekti,* 1947). We glimpse the unrest of the age behind Claes Gill's (1910–) extraordinary lyrics in *Fragments of a Magic Life* (*Fragmenter av et magisk liv,* 1939) and *Words in Iron* (*Ord i jærn,* 1942). Gill is akin to the German poet Stefan George, but even more to the Irish W. B. Yeats. Even in the charming and extroverted nature poetry of Einar Skjæraasen (1900–) we perceive touches of seriousness. Per Arneberg (1901–) is reminiscent of Walt Whitman whose verse he has translated, while Paal Brekke (1924–) has done the same for T. S. Eliot. Tor Jonsson (1916-1951), poet and essayist, showed more promise than most in his brief, lamented life. Beyond these it would be futile to discuss individually such names as Gunvor Hofmo, Astrid Tollefsen, Paal Brekke, Tormod Skagestad, Emil Boyson, André Bjerke, or Ernst Orvil. Each of them has contributed valuable verse without becoming rivals to the great poets of the preceding generation. Their position is still to be established.

The restrained but troubled note which the poets strike is characteristic also of the prose writers. It is symptomatic that the intellectual radicalism which leaned on Marxist doctrines and raised so many furious controversies between the wars has now quieted down. The war brought many closer together than before, adversaries who discovered in concentration camps and underground activity that they had more in common than they had imagined. Yet the two streams persist, with the more humanist-liberal view represented in a literary periodical like *Vinduet (The Window)*, the more metaphysical-conservative view represented in *Spectrum*. Sociological and psychological points of view are being asserted, but the dogmatism of the Freudians is no longer fashionable.

Symbolistic trends were reinforced by the necessary concealments of the Occupation, as in Bjørn Rongen's harrowing novel *Night of Nights* (*Nettenes natt*, 1940) or Nils Johan Rud's *Courage, Man* (*Godt mot, menneske*, 1940) or Ragnar Vold's *As Your Days Are* (*Som dine dager er*, 1941). Novelists like Vesaas and Sandemose have adopted some techniques from surrealism in letting dreams and action run parallel in their stories. But most of the novelists have followed traditional lines, as in Hans Geelmuyden's (1906–) *Open Sea* (*Åpent hav*, 1945), a trilogy about life in the merchant marine, or in Arne Vaagen's (1878–) stories. Arne Skouen (1913–) has shown his understanding of the psychology of youth in such books as *Festival in Port des Galets* (*Fest i Port des Galets*, 1947)[4] and in *Street Urchins* (*Gategutter*, 1948). Johannes Heggland (1919–) has pictured old family feuds in the secluded environment of a west Norwegian fjord.

The period of the Occupation and after has not been a great, creative era in Norwegian literature. The quality of writing is not proportionate to its volume, and the youngest generation has not yet won its spurs. The drama has been particularly neglected. We must therefore leave the question of whether this is a new epoch for the future historians of literature to decide.

We can be assured, however, that in the future as in the past, a central factor in the writing of Norwegians will be the nature of their country— the sea, the mountains, and the forests. In their contemplation of these

---

[4] Tr. as *Stoker's Mess* by J. Birkeland (New York, 1948).

they will almost inevitably continue to be influenced by the tradition of literature that we have portrayed and which constitutes a vital part of the literature of the western world.[5]

[5] Short stories by Norwegian authors of various periods may be found in *Norway's Best Stories*, ed. Hanna Astrup Larsen (New York, 1927); poems in *Anthology of Norwegian Lyrics*, tr. C. W. Stork, with an introduction by C. J. Hambro (Princeton, 1942), and in *20th Century Scandinavian Poetry*, ed. Martin Allwood (Mullsjö, Sweden, 1950).

Additional Readings

The following list will include only readings in English, and does not claim to be all-inclusive; it is mostly limited to books. The reader who masters the original Norwegian will naturally turn to Paasche, Bull, Winsnes, and Houm, *Norsk Litteraturhistorie* (Oslo, 1924-1955) in six volumes, and for further bibliography to J. B. Halvorsen, *Norsk Forfatter-Lexikon* (Christiania, 1885-1908) and Reidar Øksnevad, *Norsk Litteraturhistorisk Bibliografi* 1900-1945 (Oslo, 1951).

NORWAY AND HER LITERATURE. In English the following more or less complete surveys exist: Illit Grøndahl and Ola Raknes, *Chapters in Norwegian Literature* (London, 1923); Theodore Jorgenson, *History of Norwegian Literature* (New York, 1933); Theodore Jorgenson, *Norwegian Literature in Medieval and Early Modern Times* (Northfield, Minn., 1952); Halvdan Koht and Sigmund Skard, *The Voice of Norway* (New York, 1944). See also Carl J. B. Burchardt, *Norwegian Life and Literature* (London, 1920). In French a useful survey is Jean Lescoffier *Histoire de la Littérature Norvègienne* (Paris, 1952). Brief, sketchy surveys may be found in Giovanni Bach, *The History of the Scandinavian Literatures* (New York, 1938), E. Bredsdorff, B. Mortensen, R. Popperwell, *An Introduction to Scandinavian Literature* (Copenhagen, 1951), H. G. Topsöe-Jensen, *Scandinavian Literature from Brandes to our Day* (New York, 1929).

FROM ANTIQUITY TO THE VIKINGS. Various aspects of the history and literature of the viking period in Norway are treated in the following works: A. W. Brøgger, *Ancient Emigrants* (Oxford, 1929); Haakon Shetelig and Hjalmar Falk, *Scandinavian Archeology* (Oxford, 1937); T. D. Kendrick, *A History of the Vikings* (New York, 1930); Karen Larsen, *A History of Norway* (New York, 1948); Laurence M. Larson, *The Earliest Norwegian Laws* (New York, 1935); Henry Goddard Leach, *A Pageant of Old Scandinavia* (New York, 1946); Axel Olrik, *Viking Civilization* (New York, 1930); Magnus Olsen, *Farms and Fanes in Ancient Norway* (Cambridge, Mass., 1928); Bertha Phillpotts, *Edda and Saga* (New York, 1931); G. Turville-Petre, *The Heroic Age of Scandinavia* (London, 1951); Mary W. Williams, *Social Scandinavia in the Viking Age* (New York, 1920).

THE POETIC EDDA. A systematic account of Old Norse mythology is available in P. A. Munch and Magnus Olsen, *Norse Mythology* (New York, 1926); a more popular account is found in Katharine Pyle, *Tales from Norse Mythology* (London and Philadelphia, 1930). Problems concerning the dramatic form of the *Edda* are treated in Bertha Phillpotts, *The Elder Edda and Ancient Scandinavia's Drama* (Cambridge, Eng., 1920). For a discussion of the heroic poems and stories see Sophus Bugge, *The Home of the Eddic Poems* (London, 1899) and Axel Olrik, *Heroic Legends of Denmark* (New York, 1919).

POETRY OF THE SKALDS. See p. 31, note 1.

THE SAGAS. General books about the sagas are Halvdan Koht, *The Old Norse Sagas* (New York, 1931), Knut Liestøl, *The Origin of the Icelandic Family Sagas* (Oslo, 1930), W. A. Craigie, *The Icelandic Sagas* (Cambridge, Eng., 1913), Bertha Phillpotts, *Edda and Saga* (New York, 1931). Among studies of special topics relating to the sagas, the following are of interest: H. R. Ellis, *The Road to Hel* (Cambridge, Eng., 1943); M. Jeffrey, *The Discourse in Seven Icelandic Sagas* (Bryn Mawr, Pa., 1934); G. D. Kelchner, *Dreams in Old Norse Literature* (Cambridge, Eng., 1935). See E. Haugen, "Snorri Sturluson and Norway" *The American-Scandinavian Review* (1953), pp. 119-27.

FOREIGN CULTURE AND NORSE TRADITION. The literature of this period is discussed in Henry Goddard Leach, *Angevin Britain and Scandinavia* (Cambridge, Mass., 1921) and in Margaret Schlauch, *Romance In Iceland* (Princeton and New York, 1934). See the analysis of *The Dream Ballad* by Knut Liestøl. For background see Sigrid Undset, *A Saga of Saints* (London, 1934).

BALLADS AND FOLK TALES. The Norwegian ballads have been collected in Knut Liestøl and Moltke Moe, *Norske Folkevisor* (Oslo, 1924), 3 vols. Aside from *The Dream Ballad,* referred to above, only a few of these have been translated into English. The backgrounds and origins of Norwegian folklore have been discussed in Moltke Moe's *Samlede Skrifter* (Oslo, 1935-1937), 3 vols.; English summaries are provided. Much information concerning the collection of Norwegian folklore is found in

S. B. Hustvedt, *Ballad Books and Ballad Men* (Cambridge, Mass., 1930).

REFORMATION AND HUMANISM. For readings see the general histories of literature listed above.

PETTER DASS AND THE BAROQUE AGE. See general histories listed above.

LUDVIG HOLBERG. Oscar James Campbell, *The Comedies of Holberg* (Cambridge, 1914; Harvard Studies in Comparative Literature 3); B. J. Hovde, *The Scandinavian Countries, 1720-1865* (Boston, 1943), pp. 103-14.

HOLBERG'S SUCCESSORS. See the general histories of Norwegian literature listed above.

A YOUNG STATE AND AN OLD KINGDOM. B. Hovde, *The Scandinavian Countries 1720-1865* (Boston, 1943), pp. 447-52, 458-60; Karen Larsen, *A History of Norway* (New York, 1948), pp. 373-422.

THE AGE OF WERGELAND. Introductions by Francis Bull and G. Gathorne-Hardy to Henrik Wergeland, *Poems* (Oslo-London, 1929); Agnes M. Wergeland, *Leaders in Norway* (Menasha, Wis., 1916), pp. 38-63; Elias Gordon, *Wergeland, the Prophet* (New York, 1938).

DISCOVERY OF A NATIONAL CULTURE. Oscar J. Falnes, *National Romanticism in Norway* (New York, 1933); Einar Haugen, *Linguistic Development of Ivar Aasen's New Norse* (Publ. Mod. Lang. Assn., 1933), pp. 558-97.

DREAMS AND REALITY. Agnes M. Wergeland, *Leaders in Norway* (Menasha, Wis., 1916), pp. 64-101 (on Camilla Collett). See Grøndahl and Raknes, *Chapters,* pp. 113-26, 140-54.

FROM NATIONAL TO WORLD LITERATURE. Bjørnstjerne Bjørnson, "Modern Norwegian Literature" (*Forum,* 1896, pp. 318-29, 397-413).

IBSEN'S EARLY PLAYS. On Ibsen's life see Halvdan Koht, *The Life of Ibsen* (2 vols., New York, 1931), which has superseded all earlier biographies. New and previously unknown material is presented in Bergliot Ibsen, *The Three Ibsens,* tr. G. Schjelderup (New York, 1952); anecdotes not elsewhere available are collected in A. E. Zucker, *Ibsen, The Master Builder* (New York, 1929). The backgrounds of Ibsen's thinking are analyzed in Brian W. Downs, *Ibsen, The Intellectual Background* (Cambridge, Eng., 1946); three plays of this period are analyzed in his *Study of Six Plays by Ibsen* (Cambridge, Eng., 1950). A thesis on one aspect of the plays is A. Anstensen *The Proverb In Ibsen* (New York, 1936). A full but uneven book is Henri Logeman *A Commentary on*

Henrik Ibsen's Peer Gynt (The Hague, 1917). Many other items of Ibsen criticism will be found with the aid of Annette Andersen, "Ibsen in America" (*Scandinavian Studies*, Vol. 14, pp. 65-109, 115-55), now supplemented by Sverre Arestad for 1936-1946 (*Scandinavian Studies* 24, pp. 93-110).

THE YOUNG BJØRNSON. Harold Larson, *Bjørnstjerne Bjørnson, A Study in Norwegian Nationalism* (New York, 1944); see also Sigmund Skard and Halvdan Koht, *The Voice of Norway*, pp. 235-59, Grøndahl and Raknes, *Chapters*, pp. 155-70.

REALISM COMES TO LITERATURE. Georg Brandes *Main Currents in Nineteenth Century Literature* (London, 1901-1905); Georg Brandes, *Henrik Ibsen, Bjørnstjerne Bjørnson, Critical Studies* (London, 1899); Georg Brandes, *Creative Spirits of the Nineteenth Century* (New York, 1923); Oscar Seidlin, "Georg Brandes, 1842-1927," *Journal of the History of Ideas* (1942) pp. 415-42.

IBSEN'S SOCIAL AND PSYCHOLOGICAL PLAYS. The best critical analysis of Ibsen's social and psychological plays is still Herman Weigand, *The Modern Ibsen* (New York, 1925). For his dramatic technique see John Northam, *Ibsen's Dramatic Method* (London, 1953). For *Doll's House, Wild Duck,* and *Master Builder* see now Brian Downs, *A Study of Six Plays by Ibsen* (Cambridge, Eng., 1950).For critical opinion on Ibsen see Eric Bentley, *The Playwright as Thinker* (New York, 1946); George Bernard Shaw, *The Quintessence of Ibsenism* (New York, 1913); P. J. Eikeland, *Ibsen Studies* (Northfield, Minn., 1934); Theodore Jorgenson, *Henrik Ibsen, A Study in Art and Personality* (Northfield, Minn., 1945). For studies of Ibsen's influence see William H. Eller, *Ibsen in Germany 1870-1900* (Boston, 1918), Ina ten Eyck Firkins, *Henrik Ibsen, A Bibliography of Criticism and Biography* (New York, 1921), Miriam A. Franc, *Ibsen in England* (Boston, 1919), Halfdan Gregersen, *Ibsen and Spain* (Cambridge, Mass., 1936).

BJØRNSON AND THE PROBLEMS OF REALISM. See references in previous chapter on Bjørnson. Georg Brandes, *Henrik Ibsen, Bjørnstjerne Bjørnson* (London, 1899). Article in *Columbia Dictionary of Modern European Literature* (New York, 1947) by H. Koht.

NOVELISTS OF REALISM. On Jonas Lie see Alrik Gustafson, *Six Scandinavian Novelists* (Princeton, N. J., 1940) and in *Columbia Dictionary;* also H. A. Larsen, in *The American-Scandinavian Review* (1933), pp. 461-71, and J. E. Olson, "Introduction to Lie," *Family at Gilje* (New York, 1920). On Arne Garborg see Ingebrigt Lillehei, *A Study in the*

Language and Main Ideas of Arne Garborg's Works (Urbana, Ill., 1916); H. A. Larsen in *Columbia Dictionary*. On Kielland and Elster see *Columbia Dictionary* (E. Haugen).

THE NEOROMANTIC REACTION. See articles in *Columbia Dictionary* on Sigbjørn Obstfelder (E. Haugen), Vilhelm Krag (S. Skard), Gunnar Heiberg (E. Haugen), Nils Collett Vogt (E. Haugen).

CRITICS AND STORYTELLERS. On Andersen see S. Undset in *The American-Scandinavian Review* (1945), 19-31, and article in *Columbia Dictionary* (H.Koht). On Thomas Krag see article in *Columbia Dictionary* (H. A. Larsen).

HAMSUN AND KINCK. On Hamsun see Joseph Wiehr, *Knut Hamsun, His Personality and Outlook Upon Life* (Northampton, Mass., 1922); Hanna A. Larsen, *Knut Hamsun* (New York, 1922); Alrik Gustafson, in *Six Scandinavian Novelists* (New York, 1940).

On Kinck see article (E. Haugen) in *Columbia Dictionary;* J. Bukdahl in *The American-Scandinavian Review* (1927), pp. 589-94.

REGIONAL WRITING. See articles in *Columbia Dictionary* on Aanrud (S. Skard), Tvedt (S. Skard).

THE NEW REALISM. See Carl Gad, *Johan Bojer* (New York, 1920). See also articles in *Columbia Dictionary* on Egge (H. A. Larsen), Bojer (E. Haugen), Undset (A. Gustafson), Falkberget (H. A. Larsen), Uppdal (H. Koht), Wildenvey (E. Haugen), Bull (E. Haugen), Ørjasæter (S. Skard). See also Richard Beck, "Johan Falkberget," in *The American-Scandinavian Review* (1950), pp. 248-51. Additional references will be found in these articles.

SIGRID UNDSET. The latest on Undset is A. H. Winsnes, *Sigrid Undset, A Study in Christian Realism* (New York, 1953); see Alrik Gustafson, *Six Scandinavian Novelists* (Princeton, N. J., 1940), Victor Vinde, *Sigrid Undset, A Nordic Moralist* (Seattle, Wash., 1930), W. Gore Allen, *Renaissance in the North* (New York, 1946). See also article by Richard Beck on Sigrid Undset in *The American-Scandinavian Review* (1952), pp. 34-8.

OLAV DUUN. There is an unfortunate lack of material in English about Duun. An article, "Olav Duun, Spokesman of Peasants," by Phillips Dean Carleton appeared in *The American-Scandinavian Review* (1928), pp. 741-42.

NEW TRENDS BETWEEN THE WARS. See articles in *Columbia Dictionary* on Øverland (E. Haugen), Hoel (E. Haugen), Aukrust (S. Skard), Grieg (E. Haugen), with references. On Grieg see also article by H. Koht in *The American-Scandinavian Review* (1942), pp. 32-40. On Hoel see also article by O. P. Grunt in *The American-Scandinavian Review* (1953), pp. 31-8; and the article by Martin Joos in *Festskrift til Sigurd Hoel på 60-årsdagen* (Oslo, 1950); on Øverland by O. P. Grunt in *The American-Scandinavian Review* (1945), pp. 233-43.

THE OCCUPATION AND AFTER. See articles by Eugenia Kielland, "Norwegian War Fiction," *The American-Scandinavian Review* (1946), pp. 51-5, and "The Literary Scene in Norway," *ibid.* (1951), pp. 38-43. Also Hedin Bronner, "A Comment on the Wartime Function of Norwegian Poetry," *Scandinavian Studies,* XIX (1946), pp. 123-35; and H. Bronner, "War Poems, A Norwegian Secret Weapon," *The American-Scandinavian Review* (1948), pp. 225-33.

On Pronouncing Norwegian Names

The following rules are intended as a guide to an acceptable anglicized pronunciation of Norwegian names. They are not intended to produce a Norwegian pronunciation, which could only be achieved by training in Norwegian phonetics and would in any case be inappropriate in an English context.

(1) The Vowels. These may be given the following values whenever they occur in names of one syllable or in the accented syllables of other names: A as in *father;* E as in *bed;* I as in *machine;* O as in *obey;* U as in *rude;* Y as in *city;* Æ like *a* in *bad;* Ø like *u* in *bum;* Å or AA like *o* in *ford.* These are sometimes doubled (Friis) or followed by *h* (Krohn) or *e* (Lie, Hoel), but this does not change their pronunciation. In the following diphthongs, however, there is some difference: AU (sometimes OU) is like *ou* in *house;* EI (sometimes EJ) is like *ei* in *eight;* OI, OJ, ØI, ØJ are like *oy* in *boy.* In unaccented syllables the vowels have similar values, except that E approaches the English *a* in *senate.*

(2) The Consonants. Most of them may be pronounced as in English. J, however, has the value of English *y* in *yes* by itself and in combination with some consonants: BJ is like the beginning of *beauty.* But preceded by K, SK, and G it is softened, so that KJ (and KI) are like *ch,* SKJ (and SKI, SJ, SCH) are like *sh,* and GJ (and GI, HJ, LJ) are like *y* in *yes.* Even without J, the consonants K, SK, and G are soft before the vowels I and Y. Some consonants are silent in certain positions: T in the final syllable -ET (Falkberget); D after L, N, or R (Wergeland); H before J or V. K is pronounced before N; in a name like Munch the CH is pronounced like *k.* W and V are pronounced like *v;* S and Z are like *s* (never like the sound of English *s* in *easy*). The Old Norwegian symbols þ and ð are like *th* in *thin* and *this* respectively.

(3) The Accent. The general rule is: always accent on the *first* syllable. The only exceptions are a few names with a foreign cast like Caspari, Collin, Torfæus, Tullin, where the *second* syllable is accented. Names of more than one syllable are sometimes compounds and get a secondary accent on the second or third syllable: Falkberget with a pattern like *coal shovel;* Havrevold like *basket ball.*

Index of Names

[348]

[349]

Index of Titles

[368]